THE

PUB
QUIZ BOOK

THE

PUB
QUIZ BOOK

THOUSANDS OF BRAIN-TEASING QUESTIONS TO TEST YOUR KNOWLEDGE TO THE LIMIT

COMPILED BY
DEBBIE KNELL

SIENA

This edition published and distributed by Siena

This edition published 1999
Siena is an imprint of Parragon

Parragon
Queen Street House
4-5 Queen Street
Bath BA1 1HE

Printed and bound in the UK

ISBN 0-75252-975-7

Welcome

to the Pub Quiz Book. Over 6,000 questions have been collected together in what is one of the biggest compendiums of quizzes ever assembled.

It should provide the ultimate challenge for every quiz addict and will test your knowledge to the limit across a whole range of subjects.

Also, if you use the book for a quiz competition that ends in a tie, don't worry. On page 471 we have included 100 tie-break questions. The answers to these questions are all numbers, the winner being the person who gets closest to the actual answer.

As an added bonus, we have included a 'Things you didn't know...' fact box on every page. Just a little snippet of information to help take your mind off the more important matter of getting the questions right! These fact boxes go from the utterly ridiculous to the absolutely fantastic, and will prove to be a continuing source of discussion and amusement.

Good Luck!

QUIZ 1

Answers on page 5

1 Who was the question-master of *Round Britain Quiz* and the *Brains Trust* and a panellist on *What's My Line*?

2 What is the first name of crime writer PD James?

3 What is the legal term for deliberately giving false evidence while under oath?

4 Of which metal is cassiterite an ore?

5 Which film starred Peter Sellers as shop steward Fred Kite?

6 Which of Disney's seven dwarfs wears glasses?

7 In Greek mythology, who was the twin sister of Apollo?

8 Who wrote *Pennies From Heaven, Brimstone and Treacle* and *Lipstick on your Collar*?

9 Which is the largest city of Australia in population?

10 Of which European country is Lazio a region?

11 Who played confused teenager Charlotte in the 1990 film *Mermaids*?

12 How many petals does the common poppy normally have?

13 What is the name of Fred and Wilma's daughter in *The Flintstones*?

14 Kaolin is better known as what?

15 Which family of trees do junipers belong?

Things you didn't know...

The first high-altitude ascent was made in 1804 by Gay-Lussac and Biot in a hot-air balloon. They reached a height of 4.3 miles.

Answers to page 5

1 Anthony Armstrong-Jones, 2 Christopher Gable, 3 Chamberlain, 4 Wales, 5 Satchmo, 6 *Come Dancing*, 7 *Scandal*, 8 Luzon, 9 Eric Idle and Robbie Coltrane, 10 Snakes, 11 William Oughtred, 12 East Sussex, 13 Lusaka, 14 Howard Keel, 15 Adolf Hitler.

QUIZ 2

Answers on page 6

1 Who played Sarah Connor in the *Terminator* films?

2 Of which country is Fiordland the largest National Park?

3 By what name is the infamous leader Saloth Sar known to the world?

4 Who, in 1985, became the second European golfer to win the US Masters?

5 Which actor, who appeared in the film *Titanic*, made his first venture into producing with *Traveller*, in which he also starred?

6 Who said: "Am I dying beyond my means?"?

7 Who is the lead singer with Guns N' Roses?

8 In which year was Queen Elizabeth II born?

9 Name the famous actor brother of Shirley Maclaine?

10 Which musician/composer wrote *The Long March* and *I'll Find My Way Home*?

11 Which Spanish artist had a Blue Period and a Rose Period?

12 Who was the Greek goddess of retribution?

13 Who had a Number One hit in 1979 with *Video Killed the Radio Star*?

14 Cheyenne is the capital of which state in the USA?

15 Which *Coronation Street* family had a cat called Rommel?

Things you didn't know...

The red kangaroo can produce two different types of milk from adjacent teats at the same time.

Answers to page 6

1 Johannesburg, **2** Rowan Atkinson (*Thin Blue Line*), **3** The Times, **4** Enfield, **5** Kenny Rogers, **6** The Beach Boys, **7** 1968, **8** Winston Churchill, **9** Dartmoor, **10** Nine, **11** Deuteronomy, **12** H E Bates, **13** M55, **14** Universities Central Council on Admissions, **15** Tabasco.

QUIZ 3

Answers on page 3

1 Who was created Lord Snowdon after marrying Princess Margaret?

2 Who played opposite Twiggy as *The Boy Friend*?

3 Which Richard played Tchaikovsky in *The Music Lovers*?

4 In which country was the explorer HM Stanley born?

5 What was Louis Armstrong's nickname?

6 Which programme has been compered by Michael Aspel, David Jacobs, Judith Chalmers, Terry Wogan and Angela Rippon?

7 Which 1989 film told the story of the Profumo affair that rocked the British government?

8 What is the largest and most important island of the Phillipines?

9 Who were the *Nuns on the Run* in the 1990 film?

10 What is the primary diet of the king cobra?

11 Which Englishman invented the slide rule?

12 In which English county can Beachy Head be found?

13 What is the capital of Zambia?

14 Who sang on a *Showboat* before moving to *Dallas*?

15 Who had a mistress called Eva Braun?

Things you didn't know...

The female nine-banded armadillo regularly bears litters of identical quads.

Answers to page 3

1 Gilbert Harding, **2** Phyllis, **3** Perjury, **4** Tin, **5** *I'm All Right Jack*, **6** Doc, **7** Artemis, **8** Dennis Potter, **9** Sydney, **10** Italy, **11** Winona Ryder, **12** Four, **13** Pebbles, **14** China Clay, **15** Cypress.

QUIZ 4

Answers on page 4

1 Which city is served by Jan Smuts airport?

2 Who plays Inspector Raymond Fowler in a BBC TV series?

3 Which daily newspaper was closed for a lengthy period due to a union/management conflict in 1978/79?

4 Which borough of Greater London is famous for its arms factory?

5 Who had a Number One UK hit in 1977 with *Lucille*?

6 Who felt *Good Vibrations* in 1966?

7 In what year was Martin Luther King assassinated?

8 Which statesman married Miss Clementine Hozier in 1908?

9 At 2,038 feet, High Willhays is the highest point on which English moor?

10 How many players are there is a baseball team?

11 In which book of the Bible does the death of Moses occur?

12 Who wrote the novel *Fair Stood the Wind For France*?

13 Which motorway runs from Blackpool due east to the M6 motorway?

14 What does UCCA stand for?

15 What 'T' is a very hot sauce from Mexico

Things you didn't know...

Jericho is the oldest walled city on earth at 9,000 years old.

Answers to page 4

1 Linda Hamilton, **2** New Zealand, **3** Pol Pot, **4** Bernhard Langer, **5** Bill Paxton, **6** Oscar Wilde, **7** Axl Rose, **8** 1926, **9** Warren Beatty, **10** Vangelis, **11** Picasso, **12** Nemesis, **13** Buggles, **14** Wyoming, **15** The Ogdens.

QUIZ 5

Answers on page 9

1 What are Birmans and Maine Coons?

2 What product did Mary Holland spend 18 years advertising on TV?

3 Which German football club did Kevin Keegan play for after he left Liverpool?

4 Of which Irish county is Naas the county town?

5 In which English county is Stansted Airport?

6 Which musical term means a composition to be played at a slow tempo, literally 'at ease'?

7 Which element is last alphabetically?

8 How many sides has a 20-pence piece?

9 Which chess piece can only move either one or two squares forward on its first move?

10 To whom did Bob Dylan sing *It ain't me babe*?

11 Which sport would you be watching if you saw Warriors take on All Stars?

12 Who co-hosts *Children In Need* with Terry Wogan and Gabby Roslin?

13 What was the title of Arthur Ransome's famous children's book, published in 1931?

14 Which group had a best selling album called *The Joshua Tree*?

15 What is the alternative title of the Gilbert and Sullivan operetta *The Pirates of Penzance*?

Things you didn't know...

Australia's Great Barrier Reef is 1,250 miles long.

Answers to page 9

1 1904, **2** Flute, **3** *Chariots of Fire,* **4** Lima, **5** Cardiff, **6** Oliver Stone, **7** Jennifer Jason Leigh, **8** Gwynedd, **9** The Samaritans, **10** Gateshead, **11** QVC, **12** Ohm, **13** Windy City, **14** Eureka, **15** Anne Boleyn,

QUIZ 6

Answers on page 10

1 What is the motto of The Girl Guides?

2 Who began his broadcasts: 'Jairmany calling, Jairmany calling'?

3 Who wrote *Jude the Obscure*?

4 The invention of which card game is attributed to Sir John Suckling?

5 The remains of which ship were discovered by archaeologists on the Turkish-Iranian border in January 1994?

6 Where is the Portugese motor racing grand prix held?

7 Which Kenny introduced us to Sid Snot and Gizzard Puke?

8 To which island group does Islay belong?

9 Which *Alice In Wonderland* character disappeared leaving only his smile?

10 What is the title of the American remake of the drama series *Cracker*?

11 Who was the dizzy blonde who couldn't add up in the TV show *The Golden Shot*?

12 What was PJ Proby's most successful record in the UK charts?

13 In which county is Hemel Hempstead?

14 Who became known as the Forces Sweetheart during the Second World War?

15 Who played Maggie in the romantic comedy film *Addicted to*

Things you didn't know...

The first petrol-driven car took to the road in 1885.

Answers to page 10

1 Speedy Gonzales, 2 Enniskillen, 3 Koruna, 4 Heidelberg, 5 Calcium, 6 Hague Whisky, 7 Street car, 8 Electric ray, 9 Doe, 10 Jack London, 11 Whoopi Goldberg, 12 *Rock of Ages*, 13 Tim Rice and Andrew Lloyd Webber, 14 German, 15 John Hancock.

QUIZ 7

Answers on page 7

1 To be eligible for the London to Brighton veteran car run, before which year must a car have been built?

2 With which musical instrument is Irish musician James Galway associated?

3 Which film opens with a scene of men running along a beach?

4 What is the capital of Peru?

5 In which city was the drama series *Tiger Bay* set?

6 Who directed the rock Biopic *The Doors*?

7 Who was Bridget Fonda's flatmate in *Single, White Female*?

8 In which Welsh county is Bala?

9 Which organisation was founded by the Rev Chad Varah in 1953?

10 In which port in NE England did the Metro Centre open in 1986?

11 What is the name of the Sky satellite home shopping service?

12 What is the SI unit of electrical resistance?

13 By what nickname is Chicago known?

14 Which ancient Greek word meant "I have found it!"?

15 Who was the second wife of Henry VIII?

Things you didn't know...

The custom of carrying a flaming torch from Athens to the site of the Olympic Games was started by Adolf Hitler in 1936.

Answers to page 7

1 Breeds of cat, 2 Oxo, 3 SV Hamburg, 4 County Kildare, 5 Essex, 6 Adagio, 7 Zirconium, 8 Seven, 9 Pawn, 10 Joan Baez, 11 Basketball, 12 Sue Cook, 13 *Swallows and Amazons*, 14 U2, 15 *The Slave of Duty*.

QUIZ 8

Answers on page 8

1 Which cartoon character was 'the fastest mouse in all Mexico'?

2 In which town in Northern Ireland did the IRA bomb a Remembrance Day service in 1987

3 What was the unit of currency of Czechoslovakia?

4 Which university did the prince attend in *The Student Prince*?

5 Which element is found in bones, teeth and shells?

6 Which drink has the slogan 'Don't be vague'?

7 What is the usual American name for a tram?

8 Which shocking fish is also known as a torpedo?

9 What is a female deer called?

10 Who wrote *The Sea Wolf* and *White Fang*?

11 Who starred as financial analyst Laurel Hill in the film *The Associate*?

12 After sheltering from a storm near Cheddar Gorge, Augustus Toplady wrote which hymn?

13 Which partnership wrote the musicals *Jesus Christ Superstar* and *Evita*?

14 What nationality was Anne of Cleves?

15 Who was the first signatory of the American Declaration of Independence?

Things you didn't know...

American inventor Thomas Edison patented almost 1,300 inventions in his lifetime.

Answers to page 8

1 Be Prepared, **2** Lord Haw Haw, **3** Thomas Hardy, **4** Cribbage, **5** Noah's Ark, **6** Estoril, **7** Everett, **8** The Inner Hebrides, **9** Cheshire cat, **10** *Fitz*, **11** Anne Aston, **12** Hold Me, **13** Hertfordshire, **14** Vera Lynn, **15** Meg Ryan.

QUIZ 9

Answers on page 13

1 Who partnered Mick Jagger on *Dancing in the Street*?

2 Which Politician said: "I'm sure I was wrong on a number of occasions, but I can't think of anything immediately."?

3 Who wrote *Greenmantle*?

4 IS are the international registration letters for cars from which country?

5 In which Dickens novel is Betsy Trotwood an important character?

6 What type of creature is a Red Eft?

7 What was the capital of England before London?

8 In the art medium tempera, what is mixed with powdered paint?

9 Which character's chief opponent was Carl Peterson?

10 What was the name of John Lennon's biography?

11 Who was detective Sexton Blake's assistant?

12 Which controversial writer wrote *Time For a Tiger* and *The Kingdom of the Wicked*?

13 Who directed the classic film *On The Waterfront*?

14 What word describes completing a hole in golf three strokes below par?

15 Which South African massacre occurred on 21st March 1960?

Things you didn't know...

Mexico City is built on top of an underground reservoir.

Answers to page 13

1 *Knock 3 Times,* 2 On the Moon, 3 Nigel Bruce, 4 The USA, 5 Mother Teresa, 6 Doris Day, 7 Caviare, 8 Stonehenge, 9 Henry Ford, 10 The King of Spain's daughter, 11 A lug, 12 The Old Bailey, 13 Ben Arentoft, 14 Hangman, 15 Victoria Wood.

QUIZ 10

Answers on page 14

1 In what field did Norman Parkinson make his name?

2 With which country do you associate Test cricketer Heath Streak?

3 When was the first photocopier marketed?

4 In which Irish county is Connemara?

5 Of which 1980s pop group was Morrissey lead singer?

6 In which Middle Eastern country is the port of Acre?

7 To which family of birds do house martins belong?

8 Which European capital has the largest population out of the following, Madrid, Ankara or Paris?

9 Which European capital has the largest population out of the following: Vienna, Budapest or Warsaw?

10 What is the name of the cat who left Number 10 Downing Street in 1997?

11 Who had a Number One hit in 1995 with *You Are Not Alone*?

12 Which river flows through Chester?

13 Which Italian town, at the foot of a hill containing a Benedictine monastery, was destroyed during heavy fighting in 1944?

14 Who was appointed cricket captain of England in April, 1989?

15 On which river does Canterbury stand?

Things you didn't know...

More than 8,000 varieties of rose have been developed for garden cultivation.

Answers to page 14

1 Jukebox, **2** Jupiter, **3** Kestrel, **4** Jingles, **5** Karachi, **6** Sea pink, **7** January, **8** Jackdaw, **9** Jamaica, **10** Robert the Bruce, **11** Isle of Man, **12** Jackie Rae, **13** Blue, **14** Herbivores, **15** Italian.

QUIZ 11

Answers on page 11

1 What was Dawn's first 1971 Number One?

2 Where is the Ocean of Storms?

3 Who played Dr Watson to Basil Rathbone's Sherlock Holmes?

4 Which country has won the Davis Cup in tennis more times than any other?

5 Which Catholic missionary and Nobel laureate died in 1997?

6 Who had a Number One hit with *Whatever Will Be Will Be*?

7 Which delicacy consists of salted roe from a sturgeon?

8 Where in Britian did the Battle of the Beanfield occur in 1985?

9 Which industrialist said: 'Any colour as long a it's black!'?

10 In the nursery rhyme, who visited the person with a little nut tree?

11 What word describes a large marine worm, to drag with effort and a projection on a casting by which it may be fixed in place?

12 By what name is the Central Criminal Court in London usually called?

13 Which Danish player played for Newcastle United when they won the Fairs Cup?

14 In which game do you draw part of a gallows for every wrong guess?

15 Which comedienne is married to magician Geoffrey Durham (The Great Soprendo)?

Things you didn't know...

On average, men and women have about 5 million hairs on their bodies.

Answers to page 11

1 David Bowie, **2** Margaret Thatcher, **3** John Buchan, **4** Iceland, **5** *David Copperfield*, **6** Newt, **7** Winchester, **8** Egg yolk, **9** Bulldog Drummond's, **10** *Imagine*, **11** Tinker, **12** Anthony Burgess, **13** Elia Kazan, **14** Albatross, **15** Sharpville.

QUIZ 12

Answers on page 12

1 Which record machine appeared in coffee bars in the 1950s?

2 Which is the largest planet?

3 Which bird has the scientific name 'Falco tinnunculus'?

4 What are the metal discs in the rim of a tambourine called?

5 What was the capital of Pakistan before Islamabad?

6 What is another name for the perennial herb Armeria or Thrift?

7 In which month is Twelfth Night?

8 Which bird has the scientific name 'Corvus monedula'?

9 Where was England footballer John Barnes born?

10 Who led the Scottish forces at Bannockburn?

11 Where were the Gibb brothers, better known as the Bee Gees, born?

12 Who was the first presenter of *The Golden Shot*?

13 What colour is a sapphire?

14 What name is given to animals that only feed on plants?

15 What was the nationality of the artist Titian?

Things you didn't know...

The Taj Mahal took nearly 20 years and twenty thousand men to finish.

Answers to page 12

1 Photography, 2 Zimbabwe, 3 1907, 4 County Galway, 5 The Smiths, 6 Israel, 7 Swallows, 8 Madrid, 9 Budapest, 10 Humphrey, 11 Michael Jackson, 12 Dee, 13 Cassino, 14 David Gower, 15 Stour.

QUIZ 13

Answers on page 17

1 What is the capital of Indonesia?

2 Which christian name derives from the Gaelic for 'handsome'?

3 Within which country are the Zagros mountains?

4 Of which US city is Beverly Hills a suburb?

5 Which architect designed the rebuilt St Paul's Cathedral?

6 Which character in *Star Trek: The Next Generation* had a cat called Spot?

7 Which Chinese leader was famed for his Little Red Book?

8 Which TV show begins with the words - "Ladies and Gentleman, the story you are about to see is true.

9 What is Paddy Ashdown's real first name?

10 After a gap of many years a new *Carry On* film was made in 1992. What was it called?

11 What is the brightest star in Ursa Minor?

12 Who is the central character in John Braine's book *Room At the Top*?

13 In which year did the Munich Olympics take place?

14 What do entomologists study?

15 With which sport would you associate the names of Alison Fisher and Stacey Hillyard?

Things you didn't know...

Mayflies live, on average, for only four to five hours.

Answers to page 17

1 Paul Newman, 2 Gibraltar, 3 A flag, 4 A furry toy, 5 Flying Officer, 6 India, 7 Joe Jackson, 8 Great Dane, 9 New Orleans, 10 Lincolnshire, 11 George, 12 Boston, 13 Swimming, 14 Lassiters, 15 Fingal.

QUIZ 14

Answers on page 18

1 Which US rock star released the album *Destination Anywhere*?

2 Which religious movement was founded by John Thomas in 1848?

3 Which sport is played with an oval ball on a field marked out as a gridiron?

4 Which was England's smallest county before the 1974 changes?

5 Who, in 1941, designed and made the first viable helicopter?

6 Who painted *Snow Storm - Steamboat off a Harbour's Mouth*?

7 Who painted the *Mona Lisa*?

8 What was the name of Bill Haley's backing group?

9 What is the administrative centre for Dyfed?

10 Who succeeded U Thant as Secretary General of the UN?

11 The Bahamas lie off the coast of which US state?

12 Which famous greyhound, first to win the Greyhound Derby twice, won 46 of his 61 races?

13 What name is given to a pillar or supporting column in the shape of a woman?

14 What name did pirates give to the black flags showing skull and crossbones, which they used to fly?

15 Which TV racing commentator retired in 1997 after a career in broadcasting spanning over fifty years?

Things you didn't know...

War-time spy Mata Hari was not beautiful at all. She was really a plump, middle-aged Dutch woman called Margaretha MacLeod.

Answers to page 18

1 Sid Vicious, 2 Ben Kingsley, 3 Oystercatcher, 4 Quincy Watts, 5 Barry Goldwater, 6 5th January, 7 Mick Hucknall, 8 Guatemala, 9 Hugo Horton, 10 Unicorn, 11 Simon Nye, 12 Hyrax, 13 Memphis, 14 Ginger Rogers, 15 Glass.

QUIZ 15

Answers on page 15

1 Who starred in the classic film *The Hustler*?

2 Where did *EastEnders* characters Grant and Tiffany get married?

3 What item has a hoist, a fly and a canton?

4 What is a gonk?

5 What rank is directly below a Flight Lieutenant in the Royal Air Force?

6 Where are cows regarded as sacred animals?

7 Who had a Top Twenty hit single in 1979 with *Is She Really Going Out With Him*?

8 The mastiff and the greyhound were crossed to produce which breed of dog?

9 Where is the House of the Rising Sun?

10 Which English county's emblem is an imp?

11 Which Christian name is applied to a plane's automatic pilot?

12 Which city is served by Logan airport?

13 In 1994 the Chinese sporting World Champions Lu Bin and Yang Aihua tested positive for drugs. In what sport were they world champions?

14 What is the name of the hotel complex featured in *Neighbours*?

15 In Gaelic legend, who had a dog called Bran?

Things you didn't know...

An iceberg bigger than Belgium was seen in the southern Pacific Ocean in 1956.

Answers to page 15

1 Jakarta, 2 Kenneth, 3 Iran, 4 Los Angeles, 5 Sir Christopher Wren, 6 Data, 7 Chairman Mao, 8 *Dragnet,* 9 Jeremy, 10 *Carry On Columbus,* 11 Polaris, 12 Joe Lampton, 13 1972, 14 Insects, 15 Snooker.

QUIZ 16

Answers on page 16

1 Which punk musicians's real name was Simon Ritchie?

2 Who played the title role in *Gandhi* in 1982?

3 The diet of which black and white wading bird consists mainly of shellfish?

4 Who was Olympic Men's 400 Metres champion in 1992?

5 Who did Lyndon Johnson beat in the 1964 US Presidential elections?

6 When is Twelfth Night?

7 Who is the lead singer with Simply Red?

8 Which country is the most heavily populated in Central America?

9 Which character was played by James Fleet in BBC1's *The Vicar of Dibley*?

10 Which mythical creature was the symbol of virginity?

11 Who was the writer of the sitcoms *Men Behaving Badly* and *My Wonderful Life*?

12 Which of these is NOT a member of the antelope family: impala, eland, hyrax, dik-dik?

13 Where is 'Gracelands', Elvis Presley's mansion?

14 Who was Fred Astaire's most frequent dancing partner?

15 Lime-glint, Lead-flint, Bohemian and Jena are all kinds of what?

Things you didn't know...

Avocado pears are so easily digestible that even babies can eat them.

Answers to page 16

1 Jon Bon Jovi, 2 The Christadelphians, 3 American football, 4 Rutland, 5 Sikorsky, 6 Turner, 7 Leonardo Da Vinci, 8 The Comets, 9 Carmarthen, 10 Kurt Waldheim, 11 Florida, 12 Mick the Miller, 13 Carytid, 14 Jolly Roger, 15 Peter O'Sullevan.

QUIZ 17

Answers on page 21

1 To which animals does the adjective feline relate?

2 Which shop in Regent Street is the largest toy shop in the world?

3 In *Treasure Island*, who, apart from Jim Hawkins, narrates part of the story?

4 Who had a Top Ten hit single in 1970 with *Ride A White Swan*?

5 What was the original name of Drake's ship *The Golden Hind*?

6 What Russian word, meaning openness, was given to the policy of more consultative government in the USSR?

7 Which royal figure is credited with popularising the Christmas tree in Britain?

8 In which film did Harrison Ford play a futurist cop assigned to seek and destroy four rogue replicants?

9 What is the name of the offence of marrying a person while being married to another?

10 John Grey Gorton was Prime Minister of which country?

11 Which animal has the scientific name 'Muscardinus avellenarius'?

12 Which fluid remains after blood has been allowed to clot?

13 Which part of the body is affected by otitis?

14 Which revelatory TV show was presented by Simon Mayo?

15 Which country singer and yodeller had a 1955 Number One hit with *Rose Marie*?

Things you didn't know...

The Romans were the first to invent the mile. For them it meant a thousand paces.

Answers to page 21

1 Aldaniti, 2 Idaho, 3 Edward, 4 Jack Klugman, 5 Digger, 6 Level 42, 7 Jesus, 8 Three Degrees, 9 La Paz, 10 Wellesley, 11 Old Bailey, 12 *Dad's Army*, 13 Epiglottis, 14 Toronto, 15 Means test.

QUIZ 18

Answers on page 22

1 Who played Dr Owen in the TV series *Owen MD*?

2 Which cartoonist created *St Trinian's*?

3 Who played the title role in the film *Forrest Gump*?

4 In pickles, what are gherkins?

5 Which team were losing finalists three times in the 1980s in the FA Cup?

6 Which city has football teams called Wednesday and United?

7 Which school film had the theme music *Rock Around the Clock*?

8 Who is the only male athlete to have successfully defended his Olympic 100 metres title?

9 Who had a Number One hit with *Doctorin' the Tardis*?

10 Which day follows Shrove Tuesday?

11 What was supposed to flow in the veins of the Greek gods?

12 What is the second lowest adult male singing voice?

13 Which city is known as the 'Venice of the North'?

14 Which country did Pele play football for?

15 In which county are Romford and Ilford?

Things you didn't know...

The abacus was invented more than 5,000 years ago.

Answers to page 22

1 Athens, **2** Simon and Garfunkel, **3** Metamorphosis, **4** Amazon, **5** Cary Grant, **6** Dead Man's Handle, **7** Gabrielle, **8** Vitamin C, **9** Mini, **10** Black, **11** Ouzo, **12** Gallium, **13** Jersey Lily, **14** In the skull, **15** Lord Lieutenant.

QUIZ 19

Answers on page 19

1 On which horse did Bob Champion win the 1981 English Grand National?

2 In which American state are the towns of Anaconda and Moscow and the Salmon River?

3 Who is Queen Elizabeth II's youngest son?

4 Who played the other half of *The Odd Couple* when Tony Randall played Felix?

5 What nickname was given to Cliff Barnes' father in *Dallas*?

6 Who had Top Ten hits in the 1980s with *Something About You, Lessons in Love* and *Running in the Family*?

7 Who originally travelled the Via Dolorosa?

8 Who had Top Ten hits with *Woman in love, My Simple Heart* and *Take Good Care of Yourself*?

9 What is the capital of Bolivia?

10 What is the family name of the Dukes of Wellington?

11 According to the nursery rhyme *Oranges and Lemons*, which bells asked 'when will you pay me'?

12 What was the popular name for the Home Guard?

13 What name is given to the flap of cartilage which prevents food from entering your windpipe?

14 Which city is served by Lester B Pearson airport?

15 What name is given to an enquiry into a person's resources to establish entitlement to a welfare benefit?

Things you didn't know...

The Bootlace worm, a type of ribbon worm which lives around British coasts, commonly grows to 5m (16.5ft)

Answers to page 19

1 Cats, **2** Hamley's, **3** Dr Livesey, **4** T. Rex, **5** *The Pelican,* **6** Glasnost, **7** Prince Albert, **8** *Blade Runner,* **9** Bigamy, **10** Australia, **11** Dormouse, **12** Serum, **13** The ear, **14** *Confessions,* **15** Slim Whitman.

QUIZ 20

Answers on page 20

1 In which city were the 1896 Olympic Games held?

2 Who had hits with *Homeward Bound, I am a Rock* and *The Boxer*?

3 What is the name of the process in animals by which a larva changes into an adult?

4 Which river is known as the King of Waters?

5 Who starred in the films *Monkey Business, Houseboat, Indiscreet* and *Walk, Don't Run*?

6 What was the original ominous name for the Driver's Safety Device on electric and diesel trains?

7 What was Coco Channel's Christian name?

8 Scurvy is caused by a deficiency of which vitamin?

9 Which car did Austin and Morris launch in 1959?

10 What colour was Alexandre Dumas' tulip?

11 What is the strong aniseed-flavoured alcholic drink of Greece?

12 Which metallic element is represented by the symbol Ga?

13 What was the nickname of actress Emily Charlotte Langtry?

14 Where in the body would you find a fontanelle?

15 Who is the Queen's representative in each country?

Things you didn't know...

Flying fish do not actually fly. They glide, propelled along by their tails at speeds of up to 20 mph.

Answers to page 20

1 Nigel Stock, 2 Ronald Searle, 3 Tom Hanks, 4 Cucumbers, 5 Everton, 6 Sheffield, 7 *Blackboard Jungle*, 8 Carl Lewis, 9 Timelords, 10 Ash Wednesday, 11 Ichor, 12 Baritone, 13 Stockholm, 14 Brazil, 15 Essex.

QUIZ 21

Answers on page 25

1 Which American duo had a Top Ten hit single in 1982 with *I Can't Go For That (No Can Do)*?

2 Which acid builds up in the muslces during strenuous exercise?

3 From what is the setting agent agar-agar obtained?

4 By what name is the medicine consisting of a suspension of magnesium hydroxide in water called?

5 Which fictional hero was born on Krypton?

6 Who directed the classic film *Casablanca*?

7 Which London railway station is named after a battle with Napoleon?

8 Who founded the National Viewers and Listeners Association?

9 Which British actor starred as Detective Moony in the 1990 film *Heart Condition*?

10 What was the title of the spoof version of *The Maltese Falcon*, starring George Segal as Sam Spade Jr?

11 With what does Grove's Dictionary deal?

12 Which German town is famous for the legend of the Pied Piper?

13 Which Archbishop of Canterbury, later canonised, was said to have seized the devil's nose in a pair of red-hot tongs?

14 What is the administrative centre of the Orkney Islands?

15 Which Queen was married to Prince Albert?

Things you didn't know...

The dachshund dog was originally bred for hunting badgers.

Answers to page 25

1 Anthony Trollope, **2** Milos Forman, **3** Romulus, **4** Beestings, **5** Nose, **6** Abacus, **7** Balaclava, **8** Portugal, **9** Creutzfeldt-Jakob Disease, **10** Origami, **11** Gottlieb Daimler, **12** Bedrock, **13** Squash, **14** Photography, **15** Steely Dan.

QUIZ 22

Answers on page 26

1 From which planet does *Dr Who* come?

2 Which European country was visited by the Pope early in September 1996?

3 Who is the Patron Saint of motorists?

4 In 1926 Gertrude Ederle was the first woman to do what?

5 What does quiescent mean?

6 Who paid £3000 for a turkey in December 1995?

7 Which American spinster was accused of killing her parents in 1892?

8 The Cod Wars of the 1970s were between Britian and which country?

9 Which is the loudest insect?

10 Which British order of chivalry is represented by the initials OM?

11 Fort de France is the capital of which Caribbean island?

12 Who had a Top Ten hit in 1996 with *Un-Break My Heart*?

13 Which video-cassette system couldn't compete with VHS and disappeared?

14 What is the capital of the Philippines?

15 To which dramatist was the actress Anne Bracegirdle mistress?

Things you didn't know...

All the pet hamsters in the world are descended from a single female wild golden hamster found in Syria in 1930.

Answers to page 26

1 Canada, 2 *The Merchant of Venice,* 3 Swinton, 4 Pericardium, 5 Lake District, 6 Ice skating, 7 G B Shaw, 8 Newton Abbot, 9 Bangladesh, 10 Brabinger, 11 Eight, 12 Acetic, 13 Andrew Johnson, 14 George Harrison, 15 Ladybird.

QUIZ 23

Answers on page 23

1 Who set stories in the imaginary county of Barsetshire?

2 Who directed *The People Vs Larry Flynt*?

3 In Roman mythology, who killed Remus?

4 What name is given to a cow's first milk after calving?

5 What part of your body would interest a rhinologist?

6 Which calculating device was invented by ancient Babylonians?

7 The 'charge of the Light Brigade' took place in which battle?

8 In which European country is the resort of Estoril?

9 What does CJD stand for?

10 What is the name for the oriental art of paper folding?

11 Who is generally credited as being the inventor of the motorcycle?

12 In which town did Fred and Wilma Flintstone live?

13 With which sport do you associate Jahangir Khan?

14 In what field did Norman Parkinson make his name?

15 Which American group recorded the album *Pretzel Logic* in 1974?

Things you didn't know...

Only 29 per cent of the Earth's surface is dry land.

Answers to page 23

1 Daryl Hall and John Oates, 2 Lactic Acid, 3 Seaweed, 4 Milk of magnesia, 5 Superman, 6 Michael Curtiz, 7 Waterloo, 8 Mary Whitehouse, 9 Bob Hoskins, 10 *The Black Bird*, 11 Music, 12 Hamelin, 13 Dunstan, 14 Kirkwall, 15 Victoria.

QUIZ 24

Answers on page 24

1 To which country did Sergeant Nick Rowan and his family emigrate in TV's *Heartbeat*?

2 In which Shakespeare play do suitors have to choose from three caskets for the hand of the heroine?

3 Who invented the military tank in 1914?

4 What is the membranous sac enclosing the heart called?

5 Which is the largest English national park?

6 In which sport did Irina Rodnina win 23 World Olympic and European gold medals?

7 Who wrote the plays *Arms and the Man* and *The Devil's Disciple*?

8 At which Devon market town was William of Orange first proclaimed king?

9 In which Asian country can the city of Chittagong be found?

10 What was the name of the butler in the TV series *To the Manor Born*?

11 How many incisor teeth should a human adult have?

12 Vinegar is a dilute solution of which acid?

13 Who succeeded Abraham Lincoln as US President?

14 Which former pop star owned the company that made *The Life of Brian* and had a one line part in a crowd scene?

15 Which publishers introduced us to *Peter & Jane*, in 1964?

Things you didn't know...

The total amount of gold mined is estimated to be about 100,000 tonnes, half of this since 1850.

Answers to page 24

1 Gallifrey, 2 Hungary, 3 St Christopher, 4 Swim the English Channel, 5 Motionless, Silent or Inert, 6 Linda McCartney, 7 Lizzie Borden, 8 Iceland, 9 Cicada, 10 Order of Merit, 11 Martinique, 12 Toni Braxton, 13 Betamax, 14 Manila, 15 William Congreve.

QUIZ 25

Answers on page 29

1 In which Scottish city is the football club Queens Park based?

2 Annapolis is the capital of which American state?

3 Who starred as PC Rowan in the television series *Heartbeat*?

4 In legend, who slew the gorgon Medusa?

5 What is the capital of Malta?

6 Who starred as Fletcher Reede in the film *Liar, Liar*?

7 What do the initials APR represent?

8 Which actor is credited with the line 'You Dirty Rat'?

9 In which city would you find the Golden Gate Bridge?

10 In 1960 who became the world's first woman Prime Minister?

11 What can be upside down, ginger or Dundee?

12 What sort of creature is a drill?

13 Who partnered Elaine Paige to reach Number One with *I Know Him So Well*?

14 Which hard grey metallic element is also called wolfram?

15 Which city hosted the summer Olympics in 1932?

Things you didn't know...

Most of the world's silver goes to make photographic films.

Answers to page 29

1 Belgium, 2 *Dr Dolittle*, 3 Northwich, 4 North Korea, 5 Tea, 6 Duck, 7 Nashwan, 8 A Study in Scarlet, 9 PDSA (People's Dispensary for Sick Animals), 10 Cruise Control, 11 Cook, 12 Eleanor, 13 Boris Spassky, 14 Intelligence, 15 Rossini.

QUIZ 26

Answers on page 30

1 What is the oldest and largest city in Australia?

2 Who chalked up his first ever hat trick when his team put seven goals past Southampton in a November 1996?

3 What is the millionth of a metre called?

4 Of which African country is Addis Ababa the capital?

5 What sort of bedcover gets its name from the soft feathers of a sea duck?

6 Under what other name does the authoress Catherine Marchant also write?

7 Which vegetable is known as rutabaga in the USA and a neep in Scotland?

8 Which European city is know as The Bride of the Sea?

9 What organs does silicosis affect?

10 What is the largest natural harbour in the world?

11 On which river are the Victoria Falls?

12 Brights disease affects which organs of the body?

13 On which river does Amsterdam stand?

14 Which child star went on to become a US ambassador?

15 What would your occupation be if your work involved you with stretchers and headers?

Things you didn't know...

Tycho's Star exploded in 1572 and became so bright for a few weeks that is was visible to the naked eye in broad daylight.

Answers to page 30

1 1991, **2** Peanuts, **3** Virginia McKenna, **4** Bing Crosby, **5** Red Squirrel, **6** *Kes* (by Barry Hines), **7** Dover, **8** Dermot, **9** Yellow, **10** 'Amen' - last sentence in the whole book, **11** Chelsea, **12** Harold, **13** Knight Of The Garter, **14** Michael Bond, **15** Carly Simon.

QUIZ 27

Answers on page 27

1 Which country's football team ended the Republic of Ireland's hopes of qualifying for the 1998 World Cup?

2 Who had a pet chimp called Chee Chee?

3 Which Cheshire town is renowned for salt?

4 Of which country was Kim Il Sung Prime Minister and President for 46 years?

5 What sort of drink is pekoe?

6 If you saw canard on a French menu, what type of meat would be on offer?

7 On which horse did Willie Carson win the 1989 Derby?

8 What was the title of the first *Sherlock Holmes* tale?

9 Which institution for animal welfare did Maria Elizabeth Dickens found in 1917?

10 What was the subtitle of the film *Speed 2*?

11 Who sailed around the world on *The Endeavour*?

12 What was the name of Miss Rigby in the song by the Beatles?

13 Which Russian chess player lost the world championship to Bobby Fischer in 1972?

14 In the USA what does the letter I stand for in CIA?

15 Which Italian composed *The William Tell Overture*?

Things you didn't know...

Man has probably been able to make fire for himself since about 12,000 years ago.

Answers to page 27

1 Glasgow, 2 Maryland, 3 Nick Berry, 4 Perseus, 5 Valletta, 6 Jim Carrey, 7 Annual Percentage Rate, 8 James Cagney, 9 San Francisco, 10 Mrs Bandaranaike, 11 Cake, 12 A monkey, 13 Barbara Dickson, 14 Tungsten, 15 Los Angeles.

QUIZ 28

Answers on page 28

1 In which year did Monica Seles win her first US Open singles title?

2 Which comic strip features Charlie Brown?

3 Which actress played Jean Paget in the 1956 film *A Town Like Alice* and then played the same role in a serialised radio programme?

4 Who co-starred with Bob Hope in the *Road* films and died playing golf?

5 Which animal has the scientific name 'Sciurus vulgaris'?

6 In which book is Billy Casper the anti-hero?

7 At which of the Cinque ports did Charles II land on his return from exile in May 1660?

8 Who did Harry Enfield play in *Men Behaving Badly*?

9 What colour is the dust jacket of the Wisden Cricketers' Almanack?

10 What is the shortest sentence in the Bible?

11 Which English football team won the 1998 Coca Cola Cup?

12 Which English king was killed at the Battle of Hastings?

13 In April 1995 what honour was bestowed by the Queen on Baroness Thatcher?

14 Who created *Paddington Bear*?

15 Who sung the theme song in *The Spy Who Loved Me*, starring Roger Moore?

Things you didn't know...

Jupiter is 89,400 miles in diameter, Earth is only 7,926 miles.

Answers to page 28

1 Sydney, 2 Gary Speed (Everton), 3 Micron, 4 Ethiopia, 5 Eiderdown, 6 Catherine Cookson, 7 Swede, 8 Venice, 9 The lungs, 10 Pearl Harbour, 11 Zambezi, 12 Kidneys, 13 Amstel, 14 Shirley Temple, 15 Bricklayer.

QUIZ 29

Answers on page 33

1 If ursine is bearlike and equine horselike, what is vulpine?

2 Which is the longest river in the UK?

3 Which sports programme started in 1958, and can still be seen on Saturday afternoons?

4 What is the name of the Bishop of Argyll who went missing in September 1996?

5 Which television series of the Sixties and Seventies developed from *Police Surgeon* starring Ian Hendry?

6 What is Radar an acronym for?

7 Who plays Hamish Macbeth and was awarded an OBE in 1998?

8 Which *Coronation Street* character married Samir Rachid?

9 What is the nickname of the golfer Greg Norman?

10 What is the name for the firm cushion used for kneeling on in church?

11 Which historic building was damaged by fire on 31st March 1986?

12 Who sang *Nothing Compares 2U* in 1990?

13 Soling, Star and Finn are categories in which sport?

14 Islamic life is based on a set of rules which are called what?

15 Who wrote the book *Mussolini, His Part in My Downfall*?

Things you didn't know...

Man has probably been able to make fire for himself since about 12,000 years ago.

Answers to page 33

1 Cultivation, 2 Walter Swinburn, 3 Inheritance tax, 4 R-101, 5 Graham Hill, 6 Spain's, 7 *Cinderella*, 8 John Smith, 9 D.H. Lawrence, 10 Queen Alexandra, Edward VII's consort, 11 Arthur Lowe, 12 Jacques Chirac, 13 Donna Summer, 14 Drums (distant), 15 Dracula.

QUIZ 30

Answers on page 34

1 For which county did Godfrey Evans play cricket?

2 What travels the 'mean free path'?

3 Where did methyl isocyanate cause 2,600 deaths in 1984?

4 New Brunswick is a province in which country?

5 Off which South American port was the Graf Spee scuttled in 1939?

6 Who played a youth club leader whose humble clubhouse is about to be demolished by property tycoons in the 1962 film The Young Ones?

7 Which animal has the scientific name 'Lepus Europaeus'?

8 Which flower was nicknamed 'kiss-behind-the-garden-gate'?

9 Aquamarine is the birthstone for which month?

10 What is Europe's second longest river?

11 In what capacity did the writer Ernest Hemingway serve in the First World War?

12 In which modern country would you locate the source of the River Rhine?

13 What was the name of Freddy Laker's cheap transatlantic air service of 1977?

14 What was the subtitle of the film Bean?

15 In which 1993 film did Clint Eastwood play a presidential bodyguard, who had feelings of guilt over the assassination of JF Kennedy?

Things you didn't know...

Silbury Hill, Wiltshire, is the largest man-made mound in Europe, although nobody knows why it was ever built 4,500 years ago!

Answers to page 34

1 Mascagni, 2 Tyrannosaurus, 3 Head, 4 Hoagy Carmichael, 5 Spiders, scorpions and mites, 6 Lady's smock, 7 Cliff Richard, 8 *I'm Still Waiting*, 9 Braised in white wine, 10 Roberts, 11 *Wheel of Fortune*, 12 Benfica, 13 White, 14 Omicron, 15 Peter Davison.

QUIZ 31

Answers on page 31

1 What is tilth?

2 Which jockey shared a table with the Queen at a banquet to celebrate her 50th wedding anniversary?

3 Which tax was introduced to the UK in the 1986 Budget to replace capital-transfer tax?

4 Which British airship crashed in France on a flight from Britain to Egypt?

5 Who won the World Driver's championship in 1962?

6 Which European country's civil war lasted from 1936 to 1939?

7 Which fairy tale inspired an opera by Rossini and a much-loved ballet by Prokofiev?

8 Who was Labour leader before Tony Blair?

9 Which British novelist wrote *Lady Chatterley's Lover*?

10 Who or what is Alexandra in Crewe Alexandra?

11 Which actor played Captain Mainwaring in *Dad's Army*?

12 Which continental head of state learned his English when he worked in America as a motel dish washer and chauffer?

13 Which female disco singer once performed with the Vienna Folk Opera?

14 Which musical instrument appears in the title of a Jim Reeves Number One hit in 1966?

15 Which character has been played in films by, among others, Jack Palance, Gary Oldman and Francis Lederer?

Things you didn't know...

Paper tissues have been used by the Japanese for more than 300 years.

Answers to page 31

1 Foxlike, **2** Severn, **3** *Grandstand*, **4** Roderick Wright, **5** *The Avengers,* **6** Radio Detection and Ranging, **7** Robert Carlyle, **8** Deirdre, **9** The Great White Shark, **10** A hassock, **11** Hampton Court, **12** Sinead O'Connor, **13** Yachting, **14** The Five Pillars of Islam, **15** Spike Milligan.

QUIZ 32

Answers on page 32

1 Who composed the opera *Cavalleria Rusticana*?

2 Which was the largest of the meat eating dinosaurs?

3 Which part of the body appears in an Iris Murdoch novel?

4 Who played the singer/pianist in *To Have and Have Not*?

5 Which are the principal animals in the class named 'arachnida'?

6 By what name is cuckoo flower also known?

7 Who is the only singer to have had Number One hits in each of the last five decades?

8 With which song did Diana Ross have a UK hit in 1971, and again in 1990?

9 If you were eating fish 'a la Normande' how would the fish be cooked?

10 What was Margaret Thatcher's maiden name?

11 John Leslie replaced Nicky Campbell as host of which television game show?

12 Which European football team put seven goals past Coventry in an August 1996 friendly?

13 What colour is a kingfisher's egg?

14 Which letter of the Greek alphabet is the equivalent to 'O'?

15 Which actor was the fifth to play TV's *Dr Who*?

Things you didn't know...

When George I, married Caroline of Brunswick he had already been secretly wed for ten years to Maria Fitzherbert.

Answers to page 32

1 Kent, 2 A molecule, 3 Bhopal in India, 4 Canada, 5 Montevideo, 6 Cliff Richard, 7 Hare, 8 Pansy, 9 March, 10 Danube, 11 Ambulance Driver, 12 Switzerland, 13 Skytrain, 14 The Ultimate Disaster Movie, 15 *In The Line Of Fire*.

QUIZ 33

Answers on page 37

1 From which club did Manchester United sign Lee Sharpe?

2 Which creature represents the star sign Taurus?

3 Which actor played the title role in *Lovejoy*?

4 What is the minimum number of points required to win a game of badminton?

5 In which year did Kerry Packer instigate his breakaway world cricket series?

6 What is the capital of Colombia?

7 What sort of plant is fly agaric?

8 What sort of creature is a mamba?

9 At which number in Downing Street does the Government Chief Whip live?

10 Who wrote the novel *Fair Stood the Wind for France*?

11 Who wrote the Booker prize winner *Possession*?

12 What would you use if you practised ikebana?

13 Which member of the Spice Girls is known as 'Baby Spice'?

14 Which American film star married supermodel Cindy Crawford?

15 What is the only bird that can hover in the air and also fly backwards?

Things you didn't know...

King George I could not speak English.

Answers to page 37

1 Cub, **2** From head to foot, **3** Kingsley Amis, **4** Pansy, **5** Mandrake, **6** Tower Bridge, **7** Coco (the clown), **8** Riboflavin, **9** River Severn, **10** Majorca, **11** Ena Sharples, **12** India, **13** The Victoria Line, **14** Geoffery Chaucer, **15** Capybara.

QUIZ 34

Answers on page 38

1 According to Lonnie Donegan, what might lose its flavour on the bedpost overnight?

2 At which sporting venue did Erika Roe streak?

3 Who wrote the novel *The History of Pendennis*?

4 Originals of what can be found only in Lincoln and Salisbury Cathedrals and the British Museum?

5 Which group of people believed that the world would end unless they sacrificed people to their sun god, Huitzilopochtli?

6 In which 1960 epic film did Peter Ustinov win an Oscar for Best Supporting Actor?

7 Who had Top Ten hits with *Goodbye To Love, Top of the World* and *Only Yesterday*?

8 What are John, Paul, George and Ringo better known as?

9 Who released an album entitled *Bizarre Fruit*?

10 Which public school did Sir Winston Churchill go to?

11 In which film did Richard Burton star with Elizabeth Taylor and Alec Guiness in a Graham Greene drama set in Haiti?

12 David Mellor was the Conservative MP for which London constituency until 1997?

13 In which film did Martin Sheen seek Marlon Brando?

14 Which brand of soup featured in an Andy Warhol painting?

15 What was the name of the woman for whom Edward VIII abdicated?

Things you didn't know...

During the 1930s farmers in Canada hitched horses to their cars because they could not afford to buy petrol.

Answers to page 38

1 The Gloster IVB seaplane of 1927, 2 Perfumes, 3 Paula Abdul, 4 Nairobi, 5 Charity, 6 Lapwing, 7 The dish, 8 Yukon Territory, 9 Magpie, 10 Devon Malcolm, 11 Washington, 12 10 inches, 13 Battenburg, 14 106, 15 I'm free.

QUIZ 35

Answers on page 35

1 What is a young fox called?

2 What does 'cap-a-pie' mean?

3 Who wrote the novels *Lucky Jim* and *The Old Devils*?

4 Which type of flower is sometimes known as heartsease?

5 Which plant was believed to shriek when pulled up?

6 Which bridge on the River Thames has a central portion that can be raised to allow ships into London?

7 By what name was Nikolai Poliakov better known for his entertainment in the 'ring'?

8 By what name is vitamin B2 also known?

9 What is the longest river in the United Kingdom?

10 Which is the largest Balearic island?

11 Which *Coronation Street* character was played by Violet Carson?

12 In which country can the Malabar Coast be found?

13 On a London Underground map which line is coloured light blue?

14 Who wrote *The Canterbury Tales*?

15 Which is the world's largest species of rodent?

Things you didn't know...

The Mazateco Indians of Mexico can hold a complete conversation just by whistling.

Answers to page 35

1 Torquay United, 2 Bull, 3 Ian McShane, 4 Fifteen, 5 1977, 6 Bogota, 7 A mushroom, 8 Snake, 9 12, 10 H.E. Bates, 11 A S Byatt (Antonia Susan), 12 Flowers, 13 Emma Bunton, 14 Richard Gere, 15 Hummingbird.

QUIZ 36

Answers on page 36

1 What was the fastest-ever biplane?

2 What is the town of Grasse in France famous for?

3 Who did Emilio Estevez marry in April 1992?

4 Which city is served by Jomo Kenyatta airport?

5 According to the proverb, what begins at home?

6 Which bird has the scientific name 'Vanellus vanellus'?

7 In the nursery rhyme, who ran away with the spoon?

8 Whitehorse is the capital of which Canadian Province?

9 Which black and white bird of the crow family has the Latin name Pica Pica?

10 Which cricketer took 9 South African wickets in an innings in 1994?

11 Olympia is the capital of which US state?

12 What is the maximum amount of rainfall per year for an area to be designated desert?

13 What is the name of the two-coloured oblong cake usually covered in almond paste?

14 How long, in miles, is Scotland's River Clyde?

15 In *Are You Being Served* what was John Inman's catchphrase?

Things you didn't know...

Queen Elizabeth was the first English Queen to see herself in a mirror. She banned them from court as she aged.

Answers to page 36

1 Chewing gum, 2 Twickenham, 3 William M Thackeray, 4 Magna Carta, 5 The Aztecs, 6 Sparticus, 7 The Carpenters, 8 The Beatles, 9 M People, 10 Harrow, 11 The Comedians, 12 Putney, 13 *Apocalypse Now,* 14 Campbells, 15 Wallis Simpson.

QUIZ 37

Answers on page 41

1 In which country do the Ashanti live?

2 What is the name of the scheme that allows people to have part or all of their legal costs paid from public funds?

3 What was the name of the spiv played by James Beck in *Dad's Army*?

4 Which one word means a unit of weight, an enclosure for animals and to beat?

5 Which actress was stabbed in the shower in *Psycho*?

6 Who was known as the 'King of Swing'?

7 To which country do the Canary Islands belong?

8 Which sea is connected to the Baltic Sea by the Kiel Canal?

9 In which Welsh county is Montgomery?

10 Which composer wrote the *Scottish Symphony* and the *Italian Symphony*?

11 Which evil *Dr Who* character's voice was provided by the Peter Hawkins, the man behind the voices of *Bill and Ben, the Flowerpot Men*?

12 By what name did Rose Louise Hovick achieve fame?

13 Which daughter of King Priam prophesied the fall of Troy, but was not believed?

14 Who met the Little People in Lilliput?

15 What is the main ingredient in a brick?

Things you didn't know...

The only state in the world with a nil birthrate is the Vatican City.

Answers to page 41

1 *The Crystal Maze* (Ed Tudor Pole), **2** Fanny Hill, **3** Danish, **4** Hitler, **5** Oedipus, **6** Carrantuohill, **7** The Mekon, **8** Gary Mallett, **9** 1978, **10** *3 Coins In a Fountain*, **11** Green, **12** International Monetary Fund (IMF), **13** George 1, **14** Aniseed, **15** 6 Day War.

QUIZ 38

Answers on page 42

1 What is the name for food permissible under Moslem dietary laws?

2 Who owns Selfridges?

3 Which prison was demolished after the death of its last inmate, Rudolf Hess?

4 Which group topped the singles chart in 1997 with *The Drugs Don't Work*?

5 Who created *Winnie the Pooh*?

6 Quaker, William Penn, founded which American city?

7 In which county is the Parliamentary constituency of South Hams?

8 Which lanthanide element is represented by the symbol Ce?

9 Who played Wolfie in the TV series *Citizen Smith*?

10 What musical instrument did Jimmy Dorsey play?

11 Who won the race in *Those Magnificent Men in their Flying Machines*?

12 How many players are there in an American Football team?

13 Which country joined the European Community on the same day as Britain and Ireland?

14 Who asked the questions in the sci-fi comedy quiz show *Space Cadets*?

15 Which type of car do you most associate with T.Vs Jim Bergerac?

Things you didn't know...

The American state of Texas has an agreement that it can divide itself into as many as five states whenever it chooses.

Answers to page 42

1 27, 2 Poetry, 3 USSR, 4 Mercury, 5 Gloria Gaynor, 6 Heart, 7 Six, 8 Canterbury and York, 9 Croatia, 10 Pasteurisation, 11 The Final Test, 12 Antonio, 13 Shanghai, 14 Joan Sanderson, 15 Swansea.

QUIZ 39

Answers on page 39

1 Which Channel 4 programme was hosted by a former member of the punk band The Sex Pistols?

2 What is the alternative name for John Cleland's novel *Memoirs of a Woman of Pleasure*?

3 What nationality was Canute, King of England?

4 Who said: "The great masses of the people will more easily fall victim to a big lie than to a small one."?

5 Who first answered the riddle of the Sphinx?

6 Which is the highest mountain in Ireland?

7 Who was *Dan Dare*'s arch rival?

8 Which *Coronation Street* character is played by Ian Mercer?

9 In which year did New Zealand first beat England in a test?

10 Which of Frank Sinatra's number one hits contains number 3 in the title?

11 What colour light do ships display at night on the starboard side?

12 Which UN agency was established in 1944 to stabalize exchange rates and facilitate internatonal trade?

13 For which English king did Handel compose his *Water Music*?

14 Of what do fennel leaves taste?

15 What name is given to Israel's invasion of Egypt in June 1967?

Things you didn't know...

Cape Town has a higher murder rate than Chicago, Detroit or any other North American city.

Answers to page 39

1 Ghana, 2 Legal Aid, 3 Walker, 4 Pound, 5 Janet Leigh, 6 Benny Goodman, 7 Spain, 8 North Sea, 9 Powys, 10 Mendelssohn, 11 The Daleks, 12 Gypsy Rose Lee, 13 Cassandra, 14 Gulliver, 15 Clay.

QUIZ 40

Answers on page 40

1 What is the square root of 729?

2 With which branch of the arts would you associate Robert Southey?

3 Where did spies Burgess, Maclean and Philby defect to?

4 An alloy referred to as an 'amalgam' must always contain which metal?

5 Which American singer had a British hit in both 1979 and 1993 with *I Will Survive*?

6 In the human body, what has four chambers?

7 How many counties are there in Northern ireland?

8 Which two cities have the only archbishops in the Church of England?

9 Zagreb is the capital of which country?

10 Which type of heat treatment used to destroy microorganisms in milk is named after a French chemist?

11 In which film did Jack Warner captain England?

12 In Shakespeare's *Merchant of Venice*, what is the name of the merchant?

13 Which city, in terms of population, is the largest in China?

14 Name the late actress who played parts in *Please Sir, Fawlty Towers* and *After Henry*?

15 What is the second-largest city in Wales?

Things you didn't know...

No woman or female animal is allowed to set foot on Mt Athos on a rocky peninsula in Macedonian Greece.

Answers to page 40

1 Halal, 2 Sears, 3 Spandau, 4 The Verve, 5 AA Milne, 6 Philadelphia, 7 Devon, 8 Cerium, 9 Robert Lindsay, 10 Clarinet, 11 James Fox, 12 11, 13 Denmark, 14 Greg Proops, 15 Triumph 2000 Roadster.

QUIZ 41

Answers on page 45

1 Who won the Oscar for Best Actress in 1978 for her role in *Coming Home*?

2 When was decimal currency introduced in Britain?

3 Which West Indian islands were split between Britain & Denmark until 1917 when the latter sold its part to the U.S.A.?

4 What is the French for 'bottom of the bag'?

5 Of which American state is Tallahassee the capital?

6 What is the name for a morbid fear of public places?

7 By what name was John Gutteridge better known for his entertainment in the 'ring'?

8 Whose only No 1 hit in the UK was called *If You Leave Me Now*?

9 Gerald Campion played which pupil of Greyfriars school?

10 What did Edmund Hillary climb in 1953?

11 For which strongly addictive narcotic drug is diamorphine the technical name?

12 Who wrote *Moll Flanders*?

13 Who had hits with *When I Fall In Love* and *Stardust*?

14 *It ain't what you do it's the way that you do it* was the first hit for which 1980's group?

15 Which city was 'so good they named it twice'?

Things you didn't know...

In a 1632 edition of the Bible, the seventh commandment reads "Thou shalt commit adultery."

Answers to page 45

1 Hamster, 2 Glasgow, 3 Beirut, 4 Charlie Drake, 5 Lundy, 6 Gold Coast, 7 Mountain Ash, 8 Croquet, 9 July 15th, 10 Life Peers, 11 Bramall, 12 1965, 13 The Treasury, 14 Sheffield, 15 John Braine.

QUIZ 42

Answers on page 46

1 What was the maiden name of the tennis player Billie Jean King?

2 In which country is the Golden Horn?

3 Who was the male star of the film *Grease*?

4 Who wrote *The Forsyte Saga*?

5 Which canadian city was originally called Bytown?

6 What was Leo Sayer's only No 1 hit in the UK?

7 Which British writer wrote his plays in shorthand?

8 Which cabinet post did Nigel Lawson first hold in 1983?

9 Who is the patron saint of Ireland?

10 Who was Henry VIII's third wife

11 How is the date of Easter Sunday determined?

12 Mn is the symbol for Mananese. True of False?

13 What was the nickname of athlete Florence Griffith-Joyner?

14 In which country would you come from if your native tongue was Flemish?

15 What sort of precious stone is the koh-i-noor?

Things you didn't know...

The rain forest Amazonia in S America covers 2.5 million square miles – an area larger than Western Europe.

Answers to page 46

1 Methuselah, 2 Aubergines, 3 Su Pollard, 4 Richard III, 5 Hindi, 6 Henry Mancini, 7 Hedgehog, 8 Zirconium, 9 Cabbage, 10 Margarine, 11 France, 12 Cuckoo, 13 January, 14 Guadalajara, 15 Lotus Elan.

QUIZ 43

Answers on page 43

1 What type of animal was Freddie Starr reported to have eaten?

2 What is the administrative centre of Scotland's Strathclyde Region?

3 What is the capital of Beirut?

4 With which comedian would you have associated with the catch-phrase "Hello My Darlings"?

5 Which island off the coast of Devon is a National Trust bird sanctuary?

6 What was the former name of the country now called Ghana?

7 What is another name for the rowan tree?

8 In which game are the balls of one side black and blue and the balls of the other side red and yellow?

9 Tradition has it that if it rains on St Swithin's day it will rain for a further 40 days. On which date is St Swithin's day?

10 What is the collective name of politicians who have been made Lords?

11 Which Lane do Sheffield United play at?

12 In which year was Stanley Matthews knighted?

13 Which UK government department is responsible, with the Bank of England, for the management of the economy?

14 Copper plated with silver, which was superseded by electroplate, was named after which city?

15 Which British novelist wrote *Room at the Top*?

Things you didn't know...

In winter, temperatures in the Sahara can plummet to -4°C (24°F) after dark because there are no clouds to retain the day's heat.

Answers to page 43

1 Jane Fonda, 2 1971, 3 Virgin Islands, 4 Cul de Sac, 5 Florida, 6 Agoraphobia, 7 Jackie Pallo (The wrestler), 8 Chicago, 9 Billy Bunter, 10 Everest, 11 Heroin, 12 Daniel Defoe, 13 Nat King Cole, 14 Fun Boy 3, 15 New York.

QUIZ 44

Answers on page 44

1 What bottle size is equivalent to eight standard bottles?

2 Which vegetable do Americans call eggplants?

3 Who played Peggy in the comedy series *Hi-de-Hi!*?

4 Which British monarch's dying words were 'Treason, Treason'?

5 From which language does the word 'shampoo' originate?

6 Who wrote *Moon River*?

7 Which animal has the scientific name 'Erinaceus Europaeus'?

8 Which metal is represented by the symbol Zr?

9 What sort of vegetable is kohlrabi?

10 What was the world's first substitute food?

11 Which European country produces Champagne?

12 Which bird has the scientific name 'Cuculus canorus'?

13 In which month of 1996 did President Francois Mitterand die?

14 What is the second largest city in Mexico?

15 Which type of car do you most associate with Emma Peel of *The Avengers*?

Things you didn't know...

The average person in the West eats 50 tonnes of food and drinks 50,000 litres of liquid during their lifetime.

Answers to page 44

1 Moffitt, 2 Turkey, 3 John Travolta, 4 John Galsworthy, 5 Ottawa, 6 *When I Need You,* 7 George Bernard Shaw, 8 Chancellor of the Exchequer, 9 St Patrick, 10 Jane Seymour, 11 It is the first Sunday after the first full moon following the vernal equinox, 12 True, 13 Flo Jo, 14 Belgium, 15 Diamond.

QUIZ 45

Answers on page 49

1 Which Welsh composer wrote *Keep the Home Fires Burning*?

2 Southern Comfort is a drink comprising of Bourbon whiskey flavoured with which fruit?

3 Which country do Renault cars come from?

4 Which actress plays the title role in *The Vicar of Dibley*?

5 What nickname was given to young men in the 1950s who wore mock Edwardian fashions?

6 Which British dance outfit released an album called *Shelter* in 1997?

7 What is the motto of The Scouting Association?

8 In which country did the Boxer Rising of 1900 take place?

9 Who was the 1991 World Snooker Champion?

10 The Russian Wolfhound is more commonly known by what name?

11 What is the largest Canadian province?

12 Which song title has given Fontella Bass and Madonna hit singles?

13 Who was head of the German SS?

14 What name is given to the condition of being resitant to infection?

15 What colour is puce?

Things you didn't know...

Gunpowder was used to fuel the first working internal combustion engine.

Answers to page 49

1 Stephen Foster, 2 Basketball, 3 Ten pence, 4 Scapa Flow, 5 *Swan Lake*, 6 *Countdown*, 7 A crossbow, 8 Americas Cup (yachting), 9 Andrew Ridgeley, 10 Argentina, 11 k d lang, 12 Supreme Headquarters Allied Powers Europe, 13 America, 14 New Orleans, 15 A bird.

QUIZ 46

Answers on page 50

1 Which rock is on the south coast of Spain?

2 What sort of creature is a ruff?

3 Which three young brothers had a number one hit single in 1997 with *Mmm Bop*?

4 Who starred as New York Daily News columnist Jack Taylor in the film One Fine Day?

5 Who won Best Actor Oscar in 1989 for *My Left Foot*?

6 In which US town is the Rose Bowl, venue for the post season football game between college champions?

7 In which country is the city of Timisoara?

8 In the drink 'Gin and It' what is 'It'?

9 In the Bible which king's doom was foretold by the writing on the wall?

10 In which country are Europe's only wild bison?

11 Who was Hitler's mistress?

12 In which African country do the Hausa people live?

13 Which city is served by Leonardo Da Vinci airport?

14 Who was Foreign Secretary when Ted Heath was PM between 1970-74?

15 Which bone, with the tibia, is the main bone of the lower leg?

Things you didn't know...

Until 1930 riders of bicycles had to ring their bells non-stop whilst the machine was in motion.

Answers to page 50

1 Christopher Wren, 2 Lhasa, 3 Snapdragon, 4 Mentor, 5 The Kinks, 6 Nose, 7 Vera Lynn, 8 Andy Warhol, 9 Echo and the Bunnymen, 10 Gerald Durrell, 11 Antelope, 12 Cricket, 13 Fencing, 14 Nick Faldo, 15 Mellors.

QUIZ 47

Answers on page 47

1 Which American composer wrote the songs *Beautiful Dreamer* and *The Old Folks at Home*?

2 In which sport did Wilt Chamberlain and Alton Byrd achieve fame?

3 How much in new money was the old coin known as the florin worth?

4 Where was the German fleet scuttled in 1919?

5 Which ballet did Tchaikovsky write in 1875?

6 What was the first programme shown when Channel 4 began transmission on 2nd November 1982?

7 What sort of weapon was an arbalest?

8 Which sporting trophy was held by the United States for 132 years until a team from Australia won it in 1983?

9 Who made up the other half of the pop duo Wham! Alongside George Michael?

10 Who beat Holland in the 1978 World Cup Final?

11 Which female vocalist released an album called *Drag*?

12 What does the acronym S.H.A.P.E. stand for?

13 In which country was Lady Astor, first woman MP to enter the Commons, born?

14 Which Louisiana port is regarded at the traditional birthplace of jazz?

15 What sort of creature is a quetzal?

Things you didn't know...

Mushrooms are bigger than they look. The fruiting body - the part that is picked - represents only 10 per cent of the fungus.

Answers to page 47

1 Ivor Novello, **2** Peach, **3** France, **4** Dawn French, **5** Teddy Boys, **6** The Brand New Heavies, **7** Be Prepared, **8** China, **9** John Parrot, **10** The Borzoi, **11** Quebec, **12** Rescue Me, **13** Himmler, **14** Immunity, **15** Purple Brown.

QUIZ 48

Answers on page 48

1 Which architect rebuilt 51 London churches after the Great Fire of 1666?

2 What is the capital of Tibet?

3 What is the popular name for the antirrhinum?

4 Who was adviser to Odysseus whose name is now synonymous with a trusted counsellor?

5 Who had a top ten hit single in 1970 with *Lola*?

6 In which part of the body would a rhinologist specialise?

7 Who was know as The Forces Sweetheart?

8 Which American artist is famous for a picture of a can of beans?

9 Who had Top Ten hits with *The Cutter* and *The Killing Moon*?

10 Which British naturalist and novelist wrote *My Family and Other Animals*?

11 Gazelle, Springbok and Impala are all types of what?

12 In which sport might you see a long leg and a third man?

13 In which sport would you use the term 'flanconnade'?

14 Which golfer beat Greg Norman by five strokes to win the US Masters title in 1996?

15 What was the name of Lady Chatterley's lover?

Things you didn't know...

The South American milk tree produces a sap which looks, tastes and is used just like cow's milk by Venezuelans.

Answers to page 48

1 Gibraltar, 2 A bird, 3 Hanson, 4 George Clooney, 5 Daniel Day-Lewis, 6 Pasadena, 7 Romania, 8 Italian Vermouth, 9 Belshazzar, 10 Poland, 11 Eva Braun, 12 Nigeria, 13 Rome, 14 Alec Douglas-Home, 15 Fibula.

QUIZ 49

Answers on page 53

1 What nationality was the painter Rembrandt?

2 In which city was Mussolini hung by a meat hook in 1945?

3 Which Roman palace is one mile west of Chichester?

4 What colour is a giraffe's tongue?

5 Which country does Roquefort cheese come from?

6 Who wrote *The Scorpio Illusion* and *The Road To Omaha*?

7 Which US novelist wrote *Uncle Remus, His Songs and His Sayings*?

8 According to the musical, what was Jesus Christ?

9 Which naturalist and writer owned the Jersey Zoo?

10 Who directed and starred in the film *Absolute Power*?

11 Which land-locked republic lies between Russia and China?

12 Who was the leading National Hunt jockey in the 1995/96 season?

13 What was the title of Gary Barlow's solo debut album?

14 Who played the title role in the film *The Millionairess*?

15 Who wrote *Tropic of Cancer* and *Tropic of Capricorn*?

Things you didn't know...

Scorpions are not immune to their own poison.

Answers to page 53

1 The Boston Strangler, 2 Killed by a dragon, 3 Wiltshire, 4 Four, 5 Lancashire, 6 Grape, 7 Guilder, 8 Michelle Pfeiffer, 9 Burma, Thailand, Laos, Vietnam and China, 10 Eddie Waring, 11 Singing The Blues, 12 John Francome, 13 John Entwhistle, 14 Joan Collins, 15 Tommy Trinder.

QUIZ 50

Answers on page 54

1 Who invented the radio?

2 What instrument was played by jazz musician John Coltrane?

3 Who was the last of the Kings of Wessex who died in 1016?

4 What is the more common name for grape-sugar?

5 In which novel did Catherine Earnshaw marry Edgar Linton?

6 What does anti emetic drug do?

7 What was the final battle that Napoleon fought in?

8 *Oh you Beautiful Doll* is from which musical?

9 Who is the patron saint of singers?

10 Which TV talent show did Jim Davidson win?

11 Who composed the *Blue Danube Waltz*?

12 Hydrophobia is the fear of what?

13 Which was Britain's first 'garden city'?

14 The first and last wives of Henry VIII both had the same first name, what was it?

15 What was the setting for the 1987 film *Gardens of Stone*?

Things you didn't know...

A bumblebee can fly at speeds up to 11 km per hour.

Answers to page 54

1 George Cross, 2 *Oliver!*, 3 The Mantee, 4 Dire Straits, 5 Greece's, 6 Scorpio, 7 Olney, 8 Flora, 9 Maureen Lipman, 10 Trafalgar, 11 Emilio Estevez, 12 Nessun Dorma, 13 Subbuteo, 14 Salem, 15 Colorado.

QUIZ 51

Answers on page 51

1 Under what nickname did Albert de Salvo become infamous?

2 In the poem *Beowulf*, how does Beowulf die?

3 Of which English county is Trowbridge the administrative centre?

4 In music, how many quavers equal a minim?

5 J.E.R. Gallien was an opening batsman for which Cricket county in the 1996 season?

6 What is the fruit of a plant of the genus Vitis called?

7 What is the currency unit of Holland?

8 Who played Catwoman in *Batman Returns*?

9 On a flight from Sri Lanka to Hong Kong, over which countries would one pass?

10 Which sports commentator talked of an 'up and under' and an 'early bath'?

11 What was Tommy Steele's only No 1 hit in the UK charts?

12 Which former jockey and now racing commentator rode Sea Pigeon to victory in the 1981 Champion Hurdle at Cheltenham?

13 Name the bass guitarist in the legendary rock band The Who.

14 Which British actress played Alexis in *Dynasty*?

15 Who was the original host of *Sunday Night at the London Palladium*?

Things you didn't know...

The eggs of the Darwin's frog of South America are kept in the father's croaking sac until the young are hatched.

Answers to page 51

1 Dutch, **2** Milan, **3** Fishbourne, **4** Blue, **5** France, **6** Robert Ludlam, **7** Joel Chandler Harris, **8** A superstar, **9** Gerald Durrell, **10** Clint Eastwood, **11** Mongolia, **12** Tony McCoy, **13** *Open Road*, **14** Sophia Loren, **15** Henry Miller.

QUIZ 52

Answers on page 52

1 What is the highest British decoration for civilian bravery?

2 From which musical does the song *Food, Glorious Food* come?

3 Which animal is said to be the origin of the legends of mermaids?

4 Who had a hit with *Sultans of Swing*?

5 Which country's soldiers might wear a stiff skirt called a fustanella?

6 What is the eigth sign of the zodiac?

7 In which Buckinghamshire town is there an annual Pancake Race?

8 Who was the Roman goddess of flowers?

9 Who played Trisha in the film version of *Educating Rita*?

10 The signal 'England expects that every man shall do his duty' was supposedly sent before which battle?

11 Who did Paula Abdul marry in April 1992?

12 What was the title of the 1990 World Cup anthem, sung by Pavarotti?

13 Which game takes it name from the Latin name from the falcon whose head adorns its pack?

14 What is the state capital of Oregon?

15 The Hoover Dam supplies electricity for the states of California, Arizona and Nevada. Which river does it span?

Things you didn't know...

Joseph Haydn was dismissed from the choir at St Stephen's Cathedral for cutting off the pigtail of the boy in front of him.

Answers to page 52

1 Marconi, 2 Saxophone, 3 Ethelred the Unready, 4 Glucose, 5 *Wuthering Heights,* 6 Reduces or stops nausea/ vomiting, 7 Waterloo, 8 *Me And My Gal,* 9 St Gregory, 10 *New Faces,* 11 Strauss, 12 Water, 13 Letchworth, 14 Catharine, 15 Arlington National Cemetery.

QUIZ 53

Answers on page 57

1 In which county are all ten of England's highest peaks?

2 In which city was the TV comedy *Cheers* set?

3 To which TV personality is Debbie McGee married?

4 Who played the part of Benny Hill's straight man?

5 How many standard bottles are there in a magnum?

6 Who was George Michael's partner in the pop-duo Wham?

7 Nemesis was the Greek goddess of what?

8 Which European city is served by Marco Polo airport?

9 Which Brian appeared in *Z Cars* and *Cats* and is an authority on Mount Everest?

10 What is another name for a leopard, particularly one with a lot of black pigmentation?

11 Who directed and starred in the 1955 Second World War movie *The Cockleshell Heroes*?

12 Which bird has the scientific name 'Tyto alba'?

13 What term for a turncoat was especially applied to a Christian who turned to Islam?

14 For which film did Clint Eastwood win an Oscar as Best Director?

15 What is a male honeybee called?

Things you didn't know...

After a quarrel with his wife, Robert Louis Stevenson threw the first draft of Dr Jekyll and Mr Hyde on the fire and burnt it.

Answers to page 57

1 Saint Tropez, 2 Ernest Hemingway, 3 Trombone, 4 Mountains of Donegal, 5 Winston Churchill, 6 Hip, 7 Sirius, 8 The dog family, 9 Brazil, 10 Baron Frankenstein, 11 Cheepers, 12 Alma, 13 The Mayor of Casterbridge, 14 USA, 15 Transpiration.

QUIZ 54

Answers on page 58

1 Which Sinead O'Connor single topped the charts in 1990?

2 What is the world's fastest mammal?

3 In a game of snooker, which colour ball is worth 5 points?

4 How did Saturday get its name?

5 Sloes are the fruit of which shrub?

6 Which chemical element has the symbol Ca?

7 Who said 'Television is something you appear on:you don't watch it'?

8 In what year was *The Wind in the Willows* first published?

9 By what name is singer Harry Webb better known?

10 Which war was fought between 1853 and 1856

11 By what name is 1st November known as?

12 Which Kenneth played the title role in *Shine on Harvey Moon*?

13 What is the name of the pilgrim in John Bunyan's famous book?

14 What was the surname of the character portrayed by Clint Eastwood in the series of *Dirty Harry* films?

15 Which furnishing chain was founded in 1950 in Sweden by Ingvar Kamprad?

Things you didn't know...

Two army teams once competed in a Tug of War battle for 2 hours and 41 minutes.

Answers to page 58

1 The Candelabrum, 2 Tchaikovsky, 3 Measles, 4 Owls, 5 Istanbul, 6 Hedge sparrow, 7 Mickey Walker, 8 Halifax, 9 Dioptre, 10 Larry Grayson, 11 Cambridgeshire, 12 Fulham, 13 Lettuce, 14 Richard Nixon, 15 The Establishment.

QUIZ 55

Answers on page 55

1 Which Riviera fishing village was an independent republic from the 15th to the 17th century?

2 Who wrote the novels *The Sun Also Rises. For Whom The Bell Tolls* and *A Farewell To Arms*?

3 Of which modern insturment was the sackbut a forerunner?

4 Which mountains are in the north west corner of Ireland?

5 Who said 'When you have to kill a man it costs nothing to be polite'?

6 What did the Queen Mother have replaced in December 1995?

7 Which is the brightest star in the sky?

8 To which family of animals does the hyena belong?

9 Who were the first country to win football's World Cup four times?

10 Which screen role connects Peter Cushing, Boris karloff, Sting and Kenneth Branagh?

11 What are young grouse or partridge called.

12 In *Coronation Street*, what is the name of Mike Baldwins's wife?

13 In which novel did Michael Henchard sell his wife for 5 guineas?

14 In which country is Cape Cod?

15 What is the loss of water from the leaves of plants called?

Things you didn't know...

Russian astronaut Yuri Gagarin died when a jet he was flying crashed during a training flight..

Answers to page 55

1 Cumbria, 2 Boston, 3 Paul Daniels, 4 Bob Todd, 5 Two, 6 Andrew Ridgeley, 7 Vengeance, 8 Venice, 9 Blessed, 10 Panther, 11 Jose Ferrer 12, Barn owl, 13 Renegade, 14 Unforgiven, 15 A Drone.

QUIZ 56

Answers on page 56

1 What is the national emblem of Israel?

2 Who wrote the ballets *Swan Lake* and *The Nutcracker*?

3 Which childhood disease is also known as Rubella?

4 What is the nickname of Sheffield Wednesday AFC?

5 In which city is the Blue Mosque?

6 Which common bird is also called the dunnock?

7 Who captained the European side in the 1996 Solheim Golf Cup?

8 Which town in West Yorkshire shares its name with a major city and port in E Canada?

9 Which unit used to measure the power of a lens is equal to the reciprocal of its focal length in metres?

10 Whose catchphrase was 'Shut that door'?

11 In which county was John Major's constituency in the 1992 General Election?

12 Before he was manager of Ipswich, which club did Bobby Robson manage?

13 How is the salad plant Lactuca sativa commonly known?

14 Who was the first American president to resign from office?

15 What was the name of the night club opened by Peter Cook in 1961?

Things you didn't know...

Howard Carter unearthed the tomb of Tutankhamun in November 1922.

Answers to page 56

1 *Nothing Compares 2 U,* 2 Cheetah, 3 Blue, 4 It was named after the Roman god Saturnus, 5 The blackthorn, 6 Calcium, 7 Noel Coward, 8 1908, 9 Cliff Richard, 10 Crimean War, 11 All Saint's Day, 12 Cranham, 13 Christian, 14 Callaghan, 15 Ikea.

QUIZ 57

Answers on page 61

1 In what year did Margaret Thatcher first become prime minister?

2 In which year did Essex first win cricket's County Championship?

3 What is the popular name of the pyracantha?

4 What is Switzerland divided into?

5 KLF reached no.1 in 1991 with which single?

6 What was the favourite food of Paddington Bear?

7 Which leading British sports personality has a book out called *From Zero to Hero*?

8 At which sport did Geoffrey Boycott represent England?

9 Who starred in *Darby's Rangers, Mister Buddwing* and *Marlowe*?

10 Which well known Latin phrase means 'in good faith'?

11 In which English county is Welwyn Garden City?

12 Proverbially, when is the darkest hour?

13 In which Middle East city is the famous Mosque of Omar dating from 643AD?

14 For what is bhp the abbreviation?

15 What name is given to an isolated mountain peak protruding through an ice sheet?

Things you didn't know...

Ninkasi was the Sumerian goddess of intoxicating drink.

Answers to page 61

1 Russia, 2 Every 500 years, 3 Cytology, 4 A kepi, 5 Iain Cuthbertson, 6 Daniel, 7 Henry Fielding, 8 Ice Skating, 9 Italy, 10 Entomology, 11 Dog, 12 Nirvana, 13 Beirut, 14 K, 15 A poult.

QUIZ 58

Answers on page 62

1 Who was the first black actor to win an Oscar?

2 What is the national airline of Portugal?

3 Which English king was nicknamed The Merry Monarch?

4 Which football team plays at Old Trafford?

5 Who was the first US President to have been born in the twentieth century?

6 Which Olympic sport takes place in a velodrome?

7 What was to be suppressed by 'comstockery'?

8 Which actress played the eponymous heroine in the BBC 1 series *Hetty Wainthropp Investigates*?

9 What sort of creature is a chafer?

10 Who played Gaz in *The Full Monty*?

11 According to the nursery rhyme, on which day of the week was Solomon Grundy married?

12 What is the name of brown sauce with redcurrants served with venison?

13 With which sport is Clare Francis associated?

14 Which mountain in the Lake District is the highest mountain in England?

15 Who painted *Dedham Vale* and *The Haywain*?

Things you didn't know...

Elephant fighting was popular amongst Indian emperors. The elephants were not hurt but the riders were often killed.

Answers to page 62

1 Deer, 2 Rudyard Kipling, 3 112, 4 Chairman Mao, 5 Shrewsbury, 6 Mut, 7 Mistletoe, 8 Leopold, 9 Ice Skating, 10 Le Mans, 11 Cricket, 12 1415, 13 Ringo Starr, 14 Zloty, 15 Nirvana.

QUIZ 59

Answers on page 59

1 In what country is the port of Archangel?

2 How often does the phoenix rise from the ashes?

3 What name is given to the study of the structure and function of cells?

4 What is the name of the distinctive hat worn by French gendarmes?

5 Who played Charlie Endell in *Budgie*?

6 Who interpreted the writing on the wall?

7 Which British author wrote the novels *Joseph Andrews* and *Tom Jones*?

8 Brian Orser was a world champion in which sport?

9 Which country produces the wine Lambrusco?

10 What is the branch of zoology that deals with insects known as?

11 What type of animal is a Lhasa Apso?

12 Which pop group had albums called *Nevermind* and *Bleach*?

13 What is the capital of Lebanon?

14 Which is the only letter worth five points in a game of Scrabble?

15 What is a young turkey called?

Things you didn't know...

To become a US president, candidates must have lived in the United States for at least 14 years and be at least 35 years old.

Answers to page 59

1 1979, **2** 1979, **3** Firethorn, **4** Cantons, **5** 3 A.M. Eternal, **6** Marmalade sandwiches, **7** Frank Bruno, **8** Cricket, **9** James Garner, **10** Bona fide, **11** Hertfordshire, **12** Before the dawn, **13** Cairo, **14** Brake horse power, **15** Nunatak.

QUIZ 60

Answers on page 60

1 Which animal is sometimes said to be 'in velvet'?

2 Who wrote the *Just So* Stories?

3 In Britain how many pounds are there in a hundred weight?

4 Which leader wrote his thoughts in a little red book?

5 What is the administrative HQ of Shropshire?

6 Who appeared in an American comic strip with Jeff?

7 Which parasitic plant was sacred to the Druids?

8 Which uncle of Queen Victoria was the first King of the Belgians?

9 In which sport did Rodnina and Zaitev compete?

10 Jacky Ickz holds the record for 6 wins in which road race?

11 With which sport do you associate Michael Atherton?

12 In what year was the Battle of Agincourt?

13 Who starred on TV as *Edna, The Inebriate Woman*?

14 What is the currency in Poland?

15 Which US rock band had a top twenty hit single in 1992 with *Lithium*?

Things you didn't know...

Prime minister Harold Macmillan was given the nickname Supermac for his political skill.

Answers to page 60

1 Sidney Poitier, 2 TAP, 3 Charles II, 4 Manchester United, 5 John F. Kennedy, 6 Cycling, 7 Corrupting literature, 8 Patricia Routledge, 9 Beetle, 10 Robert Carlyle, 11 Wednesday, 12 Alboni sauce, 13 Sailing, 14 Scafell Pike, 15 John Constable.

QUIZ 61

Answers on page 65

1 Which Englishmen took all ten Australian wickets in a test match innings in 1956 for just 53 runs?

2 Name the English landcape artist that painted *The Haywain*.

3 Where was Bob Marley born?

4 What is the more common name for the clavicle?

5 With which sport do you associate Michael Jordan?

6 What is the largest island in the Caribbean Sea?

7 Who won Best Actress Oscar for her role in *Coming Home*?

8 Which animal has the scientific name 'Capra hircus'?

9 Which French phrase means a mortal blow especially delivered to someone as an act of mercy?

10 Which empire builder's last words were: "So little done; so much to do."?

11 In which European city does the Red Cross have its' headquarters?

12 What is a dirndl?

13 Which American people were the first to drink cocoa?

14 Which Commonwealth president began divorce proceedings to end his 37 year marriage in August 1995?

15 What kind of clothing is a dolly varden?

Things you didn't know...

Napoleon tried to kill himself but because the poison he took was old it had lost its potency and gave him hiccups instead.

Answers to page 65

1 Jane Seymour, **2** Greece, **3** Guitar, **4** Robbie Williams, **5** Spare, **6** Brazil, **7** Little Big Man, **8** Princess Anne, **9** Red, **10** Flush, **11** Lawn Tennis, **12** Tuberculosis, **13** Wren, **14** Joan Hickson, **15** 70 years.

QUIZ 62

Answers on page 66

1 Who performed the theme song in the Bond movie *Thunderball*?

2 Which puppet on TV was operated by Ivan Owen?

3 What are caught in a kheda?

4 In which religion is the mystic formula Om Mani Padme Hum chanted?

5 What is the capital of the Dominican republic?

6 Which of the Welsh counties is largest in area?

7 Which mountain, the second highest in the world, is also called Mount Godwin Austen?

8 Who played the male lead in Hitchcock's *Marnie*?

9 The original Charing Cross was erected to commemorate Edward I's queen. What was her name?

10 Which Bishop signs himself Roffen?

11 What is the name for a person who will eat no food of animal origin?

12 What is an odalisque?

13 In which U.S.city would you find the Pentagon?

14 In the TV series *Edward and Mrs Simpson*, who played Edward?

15 Who had top ten hits in 1989 with *Can't Stay Away From You* and *Don't Want To Lose You*?

Things you didn't know...

William Pitt introduced Income Tax in Great Britain in 1799, with a top rate of just 10 per cent.

Answers to page 66

1 ACES, 2 Mosquitoes, 3 Jimmy Edwards, 4 Boston, 5 Lion, 6 1983, 7 Scotland, 8 Eric Coates, 9 Boulder Dam, 10 Half inch (rhyming with 'pinch'), 11 A loose sweater, 12 A fish, 13 Ennio Morricone, 14 Anthony Eden, 15 T S Eliot.

QUIZ 63

Answers on page 63

1 Which of Henry VIII's wives is buried alongside him at Windsor?

2 'Hellas' appears on stamps produced by which country?

3 What instrument can be bass, electric or Spanish?

4 Which former member of Take That was looking at *Life Thru a Lens* in 1997?

5 In ten-pin bowling, what term is used for the knocking down of all ten pins with the first two balls in a frame?

6 In which country does the Amazon reach the sea?

7 In which film was Dustin Hoffman 121 years old?

8 Which royal survived a kidnap attempt in 1974?

9 What colour eggs are in the Chinese symbol of luck and new life?

10 In poker, which is the best hand of flush, run (straight) and three of a kind?

11 Which sport was played by Peanut Louie?

12 Which once common disease was also known as The White Death?

13 Which bird has the scientific name 'Troglodytes troglodytes'?

14 Which actress first played *Miss Marple* on TV in 1984?

15 How long would you have been married if you were celebrating a Platinum Anniversary?

Things you didn't know...

Charles Darwin's Origin of Species was such a bestseller it sold out on publication day in 1859.

Answers to page 63

1 Jim Laker, 2 John Constable, 3 Jamaica, 4 Collarbone, 5 Basketball, 6 Cuba, 7 Jane Fonda, 8 Goat, 9 Coup De Grace, 10 Cecil Rhodes, 11 Geneva, 12 Dress, 13 The Aztecs, 14 Nelson Mandela, 15 A large hat.

QUIZ 64

Answers on page 64

1 What is the national airline of Colombia?

2 What sort of creatures transmit the disease malaria?

3 Who played the headmaster in the TV series *Whack-O*?

4 Which city hosts the world's oldest marathon?

5 Which creature represents the star sign Leo?

6 In which year were £1 coins introduced in Britain?

7 In which country did the King of Alba rule?

8 Who composed the orchestral suites *London, London Again* and *From Meadow to Mayfair*?

9 What was the name of the Hoover Dam on the Colorado River from 1933 to 1947?

10 In Cockney slang, which distance means 'to steal'?

11 What sort of garment was a Sloppy Joe?

12 What is a tench?

13 Who composed the music for *A Fistful of Dollars, For a Few Dollars More* and *The Good, the Bad and the Ugly*?

14 Which Prime Minister resigned as a result of the Suez crisis?

15 Who wrote the plays *The Cocktail Party* and *The Family Reunion*?

Things you didn't know...

Thailand's capital has been Krung Thep for over 130 years, but foreigners persist in calling it Bangkok.

Answers to page 64

1 Tom Jones, 2 Basil Brush, 3 Elephants, 4 Buddism, 5 Santo Domingo, 6 Dyfed, 7 K2, 8 Sean Connery, 9 Eleanor, 10 Bishop of Rochester, 11 Vegan, 12 Female slave, 13 Washington D.C., 14 Edward Fox, 15 Gloria Estefan.

QUIZ 65

Answers on page 69

1 Who would have practised his skill on a quintain?

2 What does a colporteur sell?

3 In 1926 Gertrude Ederle was the first woman to do what?

4 Who produced an album called *An Innocent Man*?

5 Which expression for a devoted couple originates in a 1735 poem?

6 In the 1990s TV sitcom *Keeping Up Appearances*, what is the first name of the character played by Patricia Routledge?

7 What is the name of the American football team from New England?

8 What is the name of the dinosaur monster which has appeared in many Japanese films?

9 Where is the Ideal Home Exhibition held?

10 Who bought the Castle of Mey in 1952?

11 Apart from a dance, what is a bolero?

12 Who became British Prime Minister at the age of 24?

13 Who had Top Ten hits in the 1970s with *Come On Over To My Place, There Goes My First Love,* and *Kissin' In the Back Row of the Movies*?

14 Who is the mother of James Ogilby?

15 How many cards are there in a tarot pack?

Things you didn't know...

More than 75 per cent of the world's fresh water is locked up in permanent ice fields.

Answers to page 69

1 Mexico, 2 National Heritage, 3 Kite, 4 Wessex, 5 Southend United, 6 Winston Churchill, 7 Lord Nicholas Ridley, 8 Doctor Hook, 9 Paul Newman, 10 Roy Orbison, 11 Croesus, 12 A Christmas Carol, 13 Thames, 14 Her daughter, 15 Mike.

QUIZ 66

Answers on page 70

1 Who wrote the *Mister Men* series of books?

2 Which African president was assassinated at a military review in 1981?

3 Who produced the multi Oscar-winning *Gone With the Wind*?

4 Why was General Claus von Stauffenberg executed in 1944?

5 In which film did POWs use a vaulting horse to disguise the digging of an escape tunnel?

6 What is the capital of Qatar?

7 Who was the first man to drive at more than 400 mph?

8 Which unit amalgamated with the Royal Flying Corps in 1918 to form the RAF?

9 By what name was tap dancer Luther Robinson known?

10 Which sport was founded in Britain on 28th August 1895?

11 Which duo's theatrical performances were called *At the Drop of a Hat*?

12 In which country is the Vosges mountain range?

13 What is the capital of Pakistan?

14 True or false: Glyndebourne Opera House is in East Sussex?

15 Which city hosted the 1982 Commonwealth Games?

Things you didn't know...

The world's first traffic lights were installed near the House of Commons in London in December 1868.

Answers to page 70

1 A bison, 2 Frank Swift, 3 Australia, 4 St Martins, 5 Sears Tower, 6 Chalky, 7 Mexico, 8 Pergamon Press, 9 St James's Palace, 10 Cormorants, 11, Egon Krenz, 12 Oval Room, 13 Duke of Beaufort, 14 Deep Throat, 15 Platinum.

QUIZ 67

Answers on page 67

1 From which country does the dish enchilada come?

2 Which Government Department is responsible for broadcasting and the media?

3 Which toy, long popular in China, has now acquired more popularity in the west, especially in the 'stunt' version?

4 In which area did Thomas Hardy set his novels?

5 Which English football club play at Roots Hall?

6 Which Briton won the Nobel Prize for Literature in 1953?

7 Which British politician and Lord died in March. 1993?

8 Who had a hit in 1972 with *Sylvia's Mother*?

9 Who married actress Joanne Woodward?

10 Who was known as 'The Big O'?

11 Which King of Lydia is renowned for his great fortune?

12 In which story does Bob Cratchit have a crippled son called Tiny Tim?

13 Which river runs through London?

14 Who won the Nobel Prize for chemistry the year after Marie Curie died?

15 If A is Alpha and T is Tango what is M?

Things you didn't know...

Joshua Slocum, the first man to sail around the world, could not swim.

Answers to page 67

1 A (Mounted) knight, 2 Religious books and tracts, 3 Swim the English Channel, 4 Billy Joel, 5 Darby and Joan, 6 Hyacinth, 7 Patriots, 8 Godzilla, 9 Earl's Court, 10 The Queen Mother, 11 Short jacket, 12 William Pitt, 13 The Drifters, 14 Princess Alexandra, 15 78.

QUIZ 68

Answers on page 68

1 What sort of creature is a wisent?

2 Which ex-England goalkeeper was killed in the Munich air crash?

3 In which country would you find Lake Disappointment?

4 Which bell said 'You owe me five farthings'?

5 Which Chicago building was the tallest in the world when it was built in the 1970s?

6 What is the traditional nickname of people with the surname White?

7 In which country is the city of Tijuana?

8 What was the name of the first publishing company owned by the late Robert Maxwell?

9 What was the official residence of British sovereigns from 1698 until 1837?

10 Which birds are traditionally used by Japanese fishermen?

11 Who was the last Communist leader of East Germany?

12 Which White House room is the President's office?

13 Which Duke's seat is Badminton?

14 Which character in *The X-Files* was played by Jerry Hardin?

15 Which precious metal has the symbol Pt?

Things you didn't know...

Lighthouses have been used as an aid to navigation for more than 2,000 years.

Answers to page 68

1 Roger Hargreaves, 2 President Sadat of Egypt, 3 David O Selznick, 4 He tried to assassinate Hitler, 5 The Wooden Horse, 6 Doha, 7 John Cobb, 8 Royal Naval Air Service, 9 Bojangles, 10 Rugby League, 11 Flanders and Swann, 12 France, 13 Islamabad, 14 True, 15 Brisbane.

QUIZ 69

Answers on page 73

1 Of which country is Zagreb the capital?

2 Into which bay does the River Ganges flow?

3 Who was Liverpool's manager for the 1984 European Cup triumph?

4 Who was the male star of the film *Lolita*?

5 In cricket, 111 is believed to be an unlucky score. What is it called?

6 Which *Darling Buds of May* star played district nurse Peggy in ITV's *Where the Heart is*?

7 Of which country is Cali the third largest city?

8 What is the largest cemetery in the United States?

9 What was Charlie Chaplin's middle name?

10 Which word connects crab, mite , monkey, plant and wasp?

11 Which golfer won the 1997 US Open?

12 In *The Screwtape Letters*, who was Screwtape?

13 Who directed *On the Waterfront*?

14 What was Hank's 12-year-old son called in TV's *King of the Hill*?

15 Who had a No 1 hit with *When You're In Love With A Beautiful Woman*?

Things you didn't know...

The foxglove is the main source of the drug digitalis, which is used to treat heart disease.

Answers to page 73

1 Back Home, 2 Fifteen, 3 Alcatraz, 4 Detroit, 5 Ming the Merciless, 6 Liverpool, 7 Rangers, 8 Kiawah Island, 9 Nicholas Lyndhurst, 10 Luxembourg, 11 Beefeaters, 12 Los Angeles, 13 Sid Owen, 14 Larry Grayson, 15 Sarah Lancashire.

QUIZ 70

Answers on page 74

1 Which town is known as the capital of the Cotswolds?

2 What is the family name of the Dukes of Northumberland?

3 How many years are there in a millennium?

4 Which stadium hosted its first FA Cup semi-final in 1991?

5 In which city did American Bobby Fischer defeat Boris Spassky to win the world chess championship in 1972?

6 What was called the jewel in Queen Victoria's crown?

7 What was the number of the Dambuster squadron?

8 What is the name of the Radio Four programme that runs from 6.30 a.m. to 9a.m. every day except Sunday?

9 How many chambers has the human heart?

10 What nationality was World Motor Racing Champion Juan Fangio?

11 Who had a no 1 hit in 1981 with *Don't You Want Me*?

12 What does a hippophobe fear?

13 Which 20th century novelist wrote *Rabbit Run* and *Couples*?

14 What first ran from Paddington to Farringdon Street in 1863?

15 Who sang *Deeply Dippy* in 1992?

Things you didn't know...

Loofahs are a tropical relative of the marrow and can be eaten when they are young.

Answers to page 74

1 Ingrid Bergman, 2 Duke of Windsor, 3 Woolbearing, 4 Black, 5 The River Amazon, 6 Lesley Gore, 7 Stephen Byers, 8 *The King and I*, 9 Yorkshire, 10 Johnny Carson, 11 Mink, 12 Daniel Day Lewis, 13 Eucalyptus, 14 Nostradamus, 15 Hungary.

QUIZ 71

Answers on page 71

1 What was the England World Cup Squad's No 1 hit in 1970?

2 How many notes are there in two octaves?

3 Which infamous former American federal prison was sited on an island in San Francisco Bay?

4 Which American city is the home of Motown records?

5 Who was Flash Gordon's arch rival?

6 Which team first won an FA Cup semi-final on a penalty shoot-out?

7 Who plays against Celtic in an Auld Firm derby match?

8 At which venue in 1991 did The USA golfers regain the Ryder Cup?

9 Who played Peter Chapman, the quiet college lecturer recruited by M15, in the TV sitcom *The Piglet Files*?

10 Which country is served by Findel airport?

11 How are the Yeoman of the Guard commonly known?

12 Which city hosted the 1994 football World Cup Final?

13 Who plays Ricky Butcher in *EastEnders*?

14 Who presented the TV show *Sweethearts* in 1987?

15 Who played the role of Raquel in *Coronation Street*?

Things you didn't know...

North American beavers have been known to build dams up to 660m (2,000ft) long. Average dams are 20m (65ft) long.

Answers to page 71

1 Croatia, 2 Bay of Bengal, 3 Joe Fagan, 4 James Mason, 5 Nelson, 6 Pam Ferris, 7 Colombia, 8 The Arlington National Cemetery, 9 Spencer, 10 Spider, 11 Ernie Els, 12 A devil, 13 Elia Kazan, 14 Bobby, 15 Dr Hook.

QUIZ 72

Answers on page 72

1 Who was shunned by Hollywood when she left her husband and children for director Roberto Rossellini?

2 Which title did Edward VIII take after he abdicated?

3 Sheep, goats & llamas are laniferous animals; what does laniferous mean?

4 At the start of a game of chess, does the white king stand on a black or a white square?

5 What is the largest river of South America?

6 Who said in a song that 'she would cry if she wanted, it was her party'?

7 Which Labour politician said too much to journalists at the Seafood Restaurant in Blackpool in September 1996?

8 In which film did Yul Brynner win his only Oscar?

9 For which county did England cricketer Herbert Sutcliffe open the batting?

10 Who hosted the *Tonight* show in the USA during 1970 and 1980's?

11 What is the name for an irresistible tendency to steal things?

12 Who won best actor award in 1989 for '*My Left Foot*'?

13 Gum-trees are common in Australia. What is their proper name?

14 Which 16th century astrologer became famous for his obscure prophecies?

15 A Magyar originates from which country?

Things you didn't know...

A visitor to the Empire State Building in New York can see up to 130km (80m) away on a clear day.

Answers to page 72

1 Cirencester, 2 Percy, 3 1000, 4 Wembley, 5 Reykjavik, 6 India, 7 617 squadron, 8 Today, 9 4, 10 Argentinian, 11 Human League, 12 Horses, 13 John Osborne, 14 London Underground, 15 Right Said Fred.

QUIZ 73

Answers on page 77

1 Who wrote the song *White Christmas*?

2 Who duetted with Paul McCartney on the 1982 UK Number One hit single *Ebony and Ivory*?

3 In which American city was Abraham Lincoln assassinated?

4 In which US state is the city of Reno, famous for gambling and divorces?

5 Which Rugby League team play at The Watersheddings?

6 Who invented the steam turbine in 1884?

7 Who played the title role in the film *The Prime of Miss Jean Brodie*?

8 In which city is Schiphol airport?

9 What are Ashvine Challenger, Old Hooky, White Boar and Hard Tackle?

10 Which programme was presented on radio by Roy Plomley from 1942 to 1985?

11 What kind of animal is a Wessex Saddleback?

12 What is your philtrum?

13 What does the musical expression 'con fuoco' mean?

14 Of what country was Catherine the Great empress?

15 Which Briton won his fourth gold medal in consecutive Olympics at Atlanta in 1996?

Things you didn't know...

Dutch artist Vincent van Gogh painted a picture a day for the last seventy days of his life.

Answers to page 77

1 Calf Of Man, 2 Amanda Barrie, 3 Dirk Bogarde, 4 Everglades, 5 Burma (Myanmar), 6 Brazil, 7 Liberia's, 8 On coins, 9 *Fawlty Towers*, 10 Baseball, 11 Fosse Way, 12 Peach Melba, 13 Haydn, 14 Iceland, 15 Plymouth.

QUIZ 74

Answers on page 78

1 What does the Trachtenberg System involve?

2 Which player had to be restrained from confronting Peter Schmeichel after Arsenal were beaten at home by Manchester United in February 1997?

3 What is a chaise?

4 In which African country do the Hausa people live?

5 What does a pedologist study?

6 What was a ducat?

7 Which infectious disease was once treated with quinine?

8 During the 1998 World Cup Finals in France, who was the only player to have a shirt number higher than his age ?

9 What was Newcastle University called when it was a college of Durham University?

10 Which vegetable is in the dish Egg Florentine?

11 Marcus Samuel developed Shell Oil, but what was the original family business?

12 What was once the traditional name for the holiday period in northern industrial towns?

13 Which radioactive metallic element used in nuclear reactors has the symbol U?

14 What name is given to foolishly extravagant or useless structures built for amusement or pride?

15 Which cricket team won their first county championship title for 21 years in 1996?

Things you didn't know...

Spanish novelist Miguel de Cervantes began writing Don Quixote in Seville prison after he was jailed for debt in 1597.

Answers to page 78

1 El Alamein, 2 London, 3 Legate, 4 Lawson, 5 Kronor, 6 1969, 7 Elvis Presley, 8 Karate, 9 Duke Orsino, 10 Joseph, 11 Jordan, 12 Jesus, 13 Joiner (or carpenter), 14 Tommy Steele, 15 Havana.

QUIZ 75

Answers on page 75

1 What is the name of the small island off the southern tip of the Isle of Man?

2 How is Shirley Ann Broadbent better known?

3 Who starred in *Death in Venice, The Damned* and *The Servant*?

4 What is the name of the swampy region of southern Florida?

5 Which country is the major exporter of teak?

6 Which country's national anthem is called *The Peaceful Banks of the River Ipiranga*?

7 Which African country's capital is named after an American President?

8 Where can the letters DG REG FD be seen every day?

9 In which comedy TV series did Ballard Berkeley play Major Gowen?

10 In which sport might you score a 'home run'?

11 Which Roman road ran from Exeter to Lincoln?

12 Which dessert was named after the Australian soprano Helen Porter Mitchell?

13 Who composed the *Clock* symphony?

14 Of which country is Reykjavik the capital?

15 Which American car manufacturer produces the 'Barracuda'?

Things you didn't know...

In Japanese chess, captured pieces change sides and are replaced on the board in any position the player chooses.

Answers to page 75

1 Irving Berlin, 2 Stevie Wonder, 3 Washington, 4 Nevada, 5 Oldham, 6 Sir Charles Parsons, 7 Maggie Smith, 8 Amsterdam, 9 Real ales, 10 *Desert Island Discs*, 11 Pig, 12 The groove between nose and top lip, 13 With fire, 14 Russia, 15 Steve Redgrave.

QUIZ 76

Answers on page 76

1 Where in the Sahara did Montgomery have his most notable victory over Rommel?

2 In which city is The Oval cricket ground?

3 What name is given to a cardinal who represents the Pope?

4 Which Nigel is a former Chancellor of the Exchequer?

5 What is the unit of currency in Sweden?

6 In what year was the first decimal coin circulated in Britian?

7 Which performer was shown on the *Ed Sullivan Show* only from the waist up?

8 Which Japanese word means 'empty hand'?

9 Whom does Viola love in *Twelfth Night*?

10 Who in the Bible had a coat of many colours?

11 In which country is the town of Bethlehem?

12 Who originally travelled the Via Dolorosa?

13 What would your occupation be if your work involved you with mortices and tenons?

14 Who played Tommy Steele in the film *The Tommy Steele Story*?

15 Which city is known as La Habana in Spanish?

Things you didn't know...

At any given moment there are about 1,800 thunderstorms raging around the world.

Answers to page 76

1 Mathematical calculations, **2** Ian Wright, **3** A horse-drawn carriage, **4** Nigeria, **5** Soils, **6** A coin, **7** Malaria, **8** Michael Owen, **9** King's College, **10** Spinach, **11** Importing sea shells, **12** Wakes Week, **13** Uranium, **14** Follies, **15** Leicestershire.

QUIZ 77

Answers on page 81

1 Which drink's advertising slogan was "It's the real thing."?

2 Which British author wrote *The Jungle Book*?

3 Which disease is a virus infection and swelling of the parotid salivary glands?

4 Who went down to Hades to rescue his wife Eurydice?

5 Which palace was the main London residence of British monarch from 1697 until it was superseded by Buckingham Palace?

6 Where would you be if you ate al fresco?

7 Under which name was Luke McMasters a professional wrestler?

8 What is produced by placing a fodder crop in an airtight structure and letting it ferment?

9 With which sport do you associate Will Carling?

10 In *Last of the Summer Wine* who is married to Wally?

11 Which great bird carried of *Sinbad the Sailor*?

12 What is the name of the dog in *Peter Pan*?

13 In which two rowing events did Great Britain win gold medals at Barcelona?

14 Which is the largest of these islands: Zanzibar, Sri Lanka or Madagascar?

15 Which spirit forms the base of the liqueur Benedictine?

Things you didn't know...

Each day is longer than the previous one by 0.00000002 seconds, which works out to be 13 seconds each century.

Answers to page 81

1 Troy, 2 Lincoln, 3 Costner, 4 Pompeii, 5 John Lennon, 6 Yasser Arafat, 7 South Africa, 8 Spice Girls, 9 Richard Chamberlain, 10 Carbon, 11 Arnold Schwarzenegger, 12 Sweden, 13 Eldorado, 14 Frog, 15 Susan Hampshire.

QUIZ 78

Answers on page 82

1 Which singer was born Marie McLaughlin?

2 Which car manufacturer designed Chris Boardman's gold medal-winning bike?I

3 Who played The Forger in the film *The Great Escape*?

4 Who played the title role in the film *The Elephant Man*?

5 Which *EastEnders* character was played by Paul Bradley?

6 Devil's Apron and Purple Laver are types of what?

7 Of the various religions practised in Indonesia, which is the largest?

8 What type of music is produced by French speaking settlers of Louisiana?

9 In which continent are the Altai Mountains situated?

10 Who formed his own pop group called Wizzard?

11 If you were at Goodison Park, who would be playing at home?

12 In which town is the National Library of Wales?

13 Which city is capital of Estonia?

14 On the flag of which Asian country is there an Asoka wheel in navy blue?

15 In which U.S. state is the city of Tacoma?

Things you didn't know...

Written examinations were being used to select Chinese civil servants as far back as the 2nd century BC.

Answers to page 82

1 Triangular, 2 *Upstairs, Downstairs,* 3 *Platoon,* 4 Vivien Leigh, 5 Neptune, 6 Shot, 7 Glucose, 8 Granada, 9 Holland, 10 A Gill, 11 Inner Hebrides, 12 St. John's, 13 1990, 14 Glynis Barber, 15 1910-1919 (1911).

QUIZ 79

Answers on page 79

1 Which ancient city gave its name to a system of weights?

2 Who was the first US president to be assassinated?

3 Which Kevin starred in *The Bodyguard*?

4 Which town was destroyed by Vesuvius?

5 Who had a biography called *Imagine*?

6 Who became leader of the Palestine Liberation Organisation in 1968?

7 Which country is divided into four provinces?

8 Simon Fuller was sacked as manager of which pop group in 1997?

9 Who played *Dr Kildare*?

10 What is the principal chemical element found in diamonds?

11 Who played *Mr Freeze* in the film *Batman And Robin*?

12 Which of these countries does NOT drive on lthe left: New Zealand, Cyprus, Sweden or South Africa?

13 Which short-lived BBC soap opera was set in Spain?

14 What name is given to the indentation on a brick which holds the mortar?

15 Who was the leading female star of the TV series The Pallisers?

Things you didn't know...

The Roman empire was founded in 27 BC by Octavian, the grand-nephew and adopted son of Julius Caesar.

Answers to page 79

1 Coca Cola's, 2 Rudyard Kipling, 3 Mumps, 4 Orpheus, 5 St James's Palace, 6 Outside, in the open air, 7 Giant Haystacks, 8 Silage, 9 Rugby Union, 10 Nora, 11 Roc, 12 Nana, 13 Coxless pairs and Coxed pairs, 14 Madagascar, 15 Brandy.

QUIZ 80

Answers on page 80

1 What shape is the body of a balalaika?

2 In which TV series did Gordon Jackson appear as Hudson and Jean Marsh as Rose?

3 Which Oliver Stone war film won Best Picture Oscar in 1986?

4 Who starred with Clark Gable in *Gone With the Wind*?

5 Which planet in our solar system was discovered by JG Galle in 1846?

6 In which athletics event are competitors described as spinners or shifters?

7 What is the more common name for grape-sugar?

8 Which British TV company makes *Coronation Street*?

9 Which country does Edam cheese come from?

10 What is a female ferret called?

11 In which group of islands is Iona situated?

12 What is the capital of the Canadian province of Newfoundland?

13 In which year did *Dances With Wolves* win the Oscar for Best Film?

14 On television, who played the female half of *Dempsey and Makepeace*?

15 In which decade did MP's receive a salary for the first time?

Things you didn't know...

John F Kennedy was the first Roman Catholic President of the USA.

Answers to page 80

1 Lulu, 2 Lotus, 3 Donald Pleasance, 4 John Hurt, 5 Nigel Bates, 6 Seaweed, 7 Muslim, 8 Cajun, 9 Asia, 10 Roy Wood, 11 Everton, 12 Aberystwyth, 13 Tallinn, 14 India, 15 Washington.

QUIZ 81

Answers on page 85

1 What does a palaeontologist study to determine the structure and evolution of ancient organisms?

2 According to The Animals, where was the *House of the Rising Sun*?

3 Which actor and playwright was born in London in 1921, the son of white Russian parents?

4 In which county is the coastal resort of Worthing?

5 What term is used to describe the disintegration of a nuclear reactor?

6 Kurt Waldheim was president of which European country?

7 What was *Rambo*'s first name?

8 On which date is Armistice Day?

9 With which sport do you associate Eddy Merckx?

10 For which sign was Churchill particularly famous during World War II?

11 *The Colbys* was a spin-off from which other soap?

12 In 1975, whose album entitled *Still Crazy After All These Years* won a Grammy award?

13 Which group had a top ten hit in 1995 with *Waterfalls*?

14 Which group had UK hit singles with *One Step Beyond*, *Baggy Trousers* and *House of Fun*?

15 Which European country has an area called Flanders?

Things you didn't know...

The name Tory - now used for members of the Conservative Party - was once an insult!

Answers to page 85

1 Cavalier, 2 Jim Bolger, 3 Epidermis, 4 Dynamite, 5 Gondola, 6 Gloria Estefan, 7 Henry Fielding, 8 The Senate, 9 55 Days at Peking, 10 South Africa, 11 Hydrogen, 12 Prunella Scales, 13 Tadpoles, 14 A hurricane, 15 A musical instrument.

QUIZ 82

Answers on page 86

1 What name is given to a plane straight-sided figure with three or more sides?

2 In which American city was Martin Luther King assassinated in?

3 In the film *The King and I*, which actress danced with Yul Brynnner to the song *Shall We Dance*?

4 William the Conqueror ordered the compilation of which historical log?

5 Who was the first president of Chile?

6 What is the medieval latin name for Wales?

7 Which Pierce starred in *Tomorrow Never Dies*?

8 Who succeeded Barbara Castle as Labour MP for Blackburn?

9 Which is the longest river in Africa?

10 Russian, Fleury, Tau and Papal are all types of what?

11 On which river does Washington DC stand?

12 What is British Honduras now called?

13 What is the name given to a young horse?

14 What is the county town of Tipperary?

15 Of what did Prince Albert die?

Things you didn't know...

Nelson's body was brought back to England for burial pickled in a barrel of brandy to stop it decomposing on the journey home.

Answers to page 86

1 Biscuit, 2 Chicago, 3 George Burns, 4 Somerset, 5 Avon, 6 Gladiators, 7 Hydrogen, 8 Diana Dors, 9 Puck, 10 Merlin, 11 Paraffin, 12 Tower of London, 13 Winston Churchill, 14 Dr Richard Beeching, 15 *Quadrophenia*.

QUIZ 83

Answers on page 83

1 Which model replaced the Vauxhall Victor in 1975?

2 Who became Prime Minister of New Zealand in 1990?

3 In mammals, which is the outer layer of the skin called?

4 Which explosive did Alfred Nobel invent?

5 What boat is traditionally manoeuvred around the canals of Venice?

6 Who recorded the album *Hold Me, Thrill Me, Kiss Me*?

7 Who wrote *Joseph Andrews, Jonathon Wild* and *Tom Jones*?

8 What was the supreme council of ancient Rome called?

9 Which film ends with Charlton Heston saying to a little girl "Here, take my hand"?

10 Which country's languages include English, Zulu and Afrikaans?

11 Which element makes up over 90% of the atoms in our galaxy?

12 Which actress played Basil Fawlty's wife in *Fawlty Towers*?

13 What are the aquatic larvae of frogs and toads called?

14 What is a wind of force 12 or more on the Beaufort scale called?

15 What is a Zither?

Things you didn't know...

Devout Jews obey no fewer than 613 commandments, including the ten of the Christian faith.

Answers to page 83

1 Fossils, 2 New Orleans, 3 Peter Ustinov, 4 West Sussex, 5 Meltdown, 6 Austria, 7 John, 8 November 11, 9 Cycling, 10 'V' for Victory, 11 *Dynasty*, 12 Paul Simon, 13 TLC, 14 Madness, 15 Belgium.

QUIZ 84

Answers on page 84

1 Garibaldi, Nice and Ginger Nut are all types of what?

2 Which American city is known as the Windy City?

3 Who co-starred with Walter Matthau in *The Sunshine Boys*?

4 In which English county is Watchet?

5 On which river does Salisbury stand?

6 What were the people who fought in ancient Roman amphitheatres called?

7 Which element has the Atomic Number 1?

8 Born with the surname Fluck, which popular blonde British actress died in 1984?

9 Which Shakespearean character said: I'll put a girdle round about the earth in forty minutes."?

10 Who was the famous wizard who assisted Arthur in the Arthurian legends?

11 What is the usual British name for the domestic heating fuel also called kerosene?

12 Prior to 1810, where in London was all British coinage minted?

13 Who said: "The maxim of the British people is 'Business as usual'."?

14 In 1962 a rail strike was called in protest against planned cuts, by which Transport Commission Chief?

15 Which film about Mods and Rockers was based upon an album of Pete Townshend's?

Things you didn't know...

Hercules, a Greek demigod and son of Zeus, began his life of heroic violence by strangling two serpents whilst still in his cot.

Answers to page 84

1 Polygon, **2** Memphis, **3** Deborah Kerr, **4** Domesday Book, **5** Carrera, **6** Cambria, **7** Brosnan, **8** Jack Straw, **9** The Nile, **10** Crosses, **11** Potomac, **12** Belize, **13** A foal, **14** Clonmel, **15** Typhoid fever.

Answers on page 89

1 Who was chancellor of the Exchequer from 1979 to 1983?

2 With which business activity would you associate the company MSL?

3 What name is given to a reusable spacecraft such as Columbia or Challenger?

4 In which Dutch city can the Rijksmuseum be found?

5 What was the name of the cook in TV's *Upstairs Downstairs*?

6 When was Sigmund Freud born?

7 When was Nat King Cole born?

8 Which US general was granted an honorary knighthood by the Queen in 1991?

9 Who sang with Sarah Brightman on the 1986 hit single *The Phantom of the Opera*?

10 By what name was M.A. Buonarotti better known?

11 Which fruit's other name is the Chinese Gooseberry?

12 Chaka, Dingaan and Cetewayo were leaders of which people?

13 Which bandleader's catchphrase was 'Wakey Wakey'?

14 Who painted *The Rake's Progress*?

15 In what year was Princess Margaret married?

Things you didn't know...

Queen Victoria chose Ottawa as the capital of Canada.

Answers to page 89

1 Morris Oxford, 2 Mr Spock, 3 Trust House, 4 Salt Lake City, 5 A gosling, 6 Clint Eastwood, 7 Greenland & Iceland, 8 Lillie Langtry, 9 The Stone Age, 10 Pantomime, 11 Sundries, 12 He was a horse, 13 Kate Ritchie, 14 Lebanon, 15 Derbyshire.

QUIZ 86

Answers on page 90

1 What name is given to words such as deed, minim, madam and rotavator?

2 From which film did Stevie Wonder's *I Just Called To Say I Love You* come?

3 Which QC does John Thaw play on television?

4 If you carry out bel canto, what are you doing?

5 Which company launched Strand cigarettes?

6 From which animal did Jenner develop his smallpox vaccine?

7 Who had the Christmas 1998 Number One *Goodbye*?

8 Which Sunday newspaper first hit the streets of London in 1843?

9 With what sort of music is Ronnie Scott primarily associated?

10 What is the capital of Cyprus?

11 Which David presented *Juke Box Jury*?

12 Which Philistine giant was killed by David with a stone from his sling?

13 What was the third stage of man?

14 In which modern country woud you locate the birthplace of Adolf Hitler?

15 Which actress played the part of Hot Lips Houlihan in the TV series, *M.A.S.H.*?

Things you didn't know...

The Great Wall of China, the world's largest man-made structure, is 2,240km (1,400 miles) long.

Answers to page 90

1 Avocado, 2 Hiller, 3 Martin Peters, 4 Grandson, 5 Irish Potato Famine (1847), 6 Julie Covington, 7 Sweden, 8 Dos, 9 The Rank Organisation, 10 Dumdum, 11 King Baudouin (Belgium), 12 Eel, 13 Kevin Costner, 14 Auld Reekie, 15 Flipper.

QUIZ 87

Answers on page 87

1 What car was produced in 1913 in Britain, for the first time?

2 Which *Star Trek* character was played by Leonard Nimoy?

3 Which British hotel group merged with the Forte group in 1970, to form a nationwide chain?

4 Which city is the headquarters of the Mormon Church?

5 What name is given to a young goose?

6 Which film star was born in San Francisco on 31st May, 1930?

7 Demark Strait separates which two countries?

8 What was the name of Edward VII's mistress, when he was Prince of Wales?

9 If something is described as "eolithic" from what age is it?

10 The name of what form of theatre or acting is derived from the two Greek words for "all mimic"?

11 In cricket, what do the Australians call extras?

12 What was unusual about the Roman consul incitatus?

13 Who plays Sally in ITV's *Home and Away*?

14 Cedar is the national tree of which country?

15 In which English county can Creswell Crags be found?

Things you didn't know...

The Incas of South America carried out blood transfusions 400-500 years before the technique was mastered in Europe.

Answers to page 87

1 Geoffrey Howe, 2 Recruitment, 3 Space shuttle, 4 Amsterdam, 5 Mrs Bridges, 6 1856, 7 1919, 8 Norman Schwarzkopf, 9 Steve Harley, 10 Michelangelo, 11 Kiwi fruit, 12 Zulus, 13 Billy Cotton, 14 Hogarth, 15 1960.

QUIZ 88

Answers on page 88

1 What do people usually call an alligator pear?

2 Who was the presiding judge in the 1997 trial of Louise Woodward?

3 Which footballer did Alf Ramsey describe as being ten years ahead of his time?

4 What relation was Kublai Khan to Genghis Khan?

5 What in history was referred to as Black Forty Seven?

6 Which member of the *Rock Follies* cast went on to sing on the original recording of *Evita*?

7 Which Scandinavian country's traffic changed from the left to right in 1967?

8 What is the Spanish for 'two'?

9 Who owns Haven the holiday centre and camping group?

10 What is the name of the soft nosed bullet that expands and inflicts lacerations?

11 Which European king died in 1993?

12 Which fish has the scientific name 'Anguilla anguilla'?

13 Which actor directed and starred in the 1998 film *The Postman*?

14 What nickname is given to Edinburgh?

15 Which 1960s TV show featured a dolphin and brothers Sandy and Bud Ricks?

Things you didn't know...

The first underground railway opened in London in 1863.

Answers to page 88

1 Palindrome, 2 *The Woman in Red,* 3 *Kavanagh,* 4 Singing, 5 Wills, 6 Cow, 7 Spice Girls, 8 News Of The World, 9 Jazz, 10 Nicosia, 11 Jacobs, 12 Goliath, 13 Iron Age, 14 Austria, 15 Loretta Swit.

QUIZ 89

Answers on page 93

1 What is the name of the villain of the *A Nightmare on Elm Street* series of horror films?

2 Who was the last astronaut to walk on the moon in 1972 from Apollo 17?

3 Who is known as the Great White Shark?

4 Which novel begins, "An easterly is the most disagreeable wind in Lyme Bay"?

5 Which metal is a liquid at ordinary temperatures?

6 With which fruit is Southern Comfort flavoured?

7 What is the first name of Nat King Cole's singing daughter?

8 Which naturalist established the theory of evolution by natural selection?

9 Who wrote *Great Expectations*?

10 How many unions merged to form UNISON in 1993?

11 What character was played by Peter Sellers in the film *I'm Alright Jack*?

12 In *Macbeth*, who was Banquo's son?

13 Who was the first Brirish woman to win the U.S. Golf Masters?

14 What makes stainless steel stainless?

15 Who played the title role in the film *Shirley Valentine*?

Things you didn't know...

Oats originated as a weed growing with other cereal such as wheat or barley.

Answers to page 93

1 Crystal Palace, 2 Fingerprints, 3 Abba, 4 Afghans, 5 Mr Spock, 6 Maplins, 7 Tarzan's son, 8 *Coronatioin Street* creator Tony Warren, 9 Yen, 10 J B Priestley, 11 Bragi, 12 Manila, 13 Louis XVl, 14 Ice skating, 15 *Duty Free.*

QUIZ 90

Answers on page 94

1 Opium, Californian and Yellow Horned are all varieties of which flower?

2 From which language does the word 'ketchup' come?

3 Of which country was Pakistan a part until 1947?

4 Which Canadian province is named after one of Queen Victoria's daughters?

5 Which high-jumper used his flop technique to win the high jump at the 1968 Olympics

6 Which plucked stringed instrument has a body in the shape of a half pear?

7 Who wrote *The Wonderful Wizard of Oz*?

8 What 'remedy', of no medicinal value, is given to humour a patient?

9 Kelts, alevins and grilse are all forms of what?

10 Which English girls name means strange or foreign in Greek?

11 Which novel by Michael Crichton was No 1 bestseller paperback in 1993?

12 Who led the British expedition which conquered Everest in 1953?

13 What nationality was the first ever UN Secretary General?

14 Who said: "There are only two kinds of music; good and bad."?

15 Which British conductor was in charge of the Halle Orchestra from 1949 until his death in 1970?

Things you didn't know...

Spiders large enough to eat birds live in holes and under fallen trees in South America, Asia and Africa.

Answers to page 94

1 *Happy Talk,* 2 Elaine, 3 Cyprus, 4 Fingal, 5 Tribune, 6 Falstaff, 7 Bits and pieces, 8 Durban, 9 Stephen Fry, 10 They were vampires, 11 Tonga, 12 Goldfinger, 13 Spinach, 14 Hot Metal, 15 Temples.

QUIZ 91

Answers on page 91

1 Which famous building was erected for the Great Exhibition of 1851?

2 Arch, whorl and loops are all parts of what?

3 Who had a No 1 hit with *Dancing Queen*?

4 What name was given to the long, embroidered sheepskin coats, trimmed with natural wool and worn by hippies?

5 With which fictional character do you associate the line 'Live long and prosper'?

6 On TV, which holiday camp is featured in the series *Hi De Hi!*?

7 In the *Tarzan* novels, who was known as Korak?

8 Whose autobiography was called *I Was Ena Sharples' Father*?

9 Which Japanese currency unit is equal to 100 sen?

10 Who wrote *The Good Companions*?

11 Who was the Norse god of poetry?

12 What is the capital of the Philippines?

13 Who was King of France at the time of the French Revolution?

14 In which sport is there something named after Ulrich Salchow?

15 Which TV sitcom featured Linda and Robert Cochrane?

Things you didn't know...

The mudskipper, a small fish that inhabits mangroves and mud-flats in tropical Africa, spends much of its time out of water.

Answers to page 91

1 Freddy Krueger, **2** Ed Cernan, **3** Greg Norman, **4** *The French Lieutenant's Woman,* **5** Mercury, **6** Oranges, **7** Natalie, **8** Charles Darwin, **9** Charles Dickens, **10** 3, **11** Fred Kite, **12** Fleance, **13** Laura Davies, **14** Chromium, **15** Pauline Collins.

– 93 –

QUIZ 92

Answers on page 92

1 Which song from a Rodgers and Hammerstein musical was a U.K. number one hit for Captain Sensible in 1982?

2 In Arthurian legend, who was the mother of Sir Galahad?

3 Which island country has two official languages, Greek and Turkish?

4 In Gaelic legend, who had a dog called Bran?

5 Which Labour weekly did Michael Foot edit for nine years?

6 Which character appears in the most Shakespeare plays?

7 What does 'Chop Suey' literally mean?

8 Which city is served by Louis Botha airport?

9 Who said about sex: "The whole thing is like finding a frog in a coffee jar."?

10 What was odd about the teenage gang in the film *The Lost Boys*?

11 Which islands did Captain Cook name the Friendly Islands?

12 In which film does the character Oddjob appear?

13 What makes green pasta green?

14 Which TV series featured the Daily Crucible newspaper?

15 What did the Mayan people build pyramids to use as?

Things you didn't know...

The bones of a bird are honeycombed for strength and lightness.

Answers to page 92

1 Poppy, 2 Chinese, 3 India, 4 Alberta, 5 Dick Fosbury, 6 Lute, 7 Frank Baum, 8 Placebo, 9 Salmon, 10 Barbara, 11 *Jurassic Park*, 12 John Hunt, 13 Norwegian, 14 Duke Ellington, 15 Sir John Barbirolli.

Answers on page 97

1 Which group was at No 1 at Christmas 1974 with *Lonely This Christmas*?

2 Which one word fits all these definitions: rubbish, drugs and a boat?

3 What originally gave foolscap paper its name?

4 Which strong fibrous tissue joins one bone to another at a joint?

5 Who played the role of Grace Van Owen in the TV drama series *L.A. Law*?

6 What is the name of the big cannon in Edinburgh Castle?

7 Would you find an escapement below a rampart, in a castle or in a clock?

8 Of which African country is Banjul the capital?

9 Which people of Kenya and Tanzania are particularly noted for their warriors?

10 In a famous children's book what was Cedric Errol's title?

11 What sort of music did Ira D Sankey compose?

12 With which art form is Rodin primarily associated?

13 Which word means to turn a ship on one side for cleaning and caulking?

14 Which is the largest island in England?

15 In which European country is the resort of Antibes?

Things you didn't know...

In the Tokelau Islands in the South Pacific, pigs wade and swim in the shallow reef waters in search of food.

Answers to page 97

1 Joe Orton, 2 Uncle Mac, 3 The Lions in Trafalgar Square, 4 Irene Handl, 5 Cubit, 6 *Good Food Guide*, 7 Calling All Stations, 8 Jim Henson, 9 Grasshopper, 10 Mosque, 11 666, 12 Mandrill, 13 Jerboa, 14 A prison, 15 The Tote.

QUIZ 94

Answers on page 98

1 Which comedian was the star of the television series *It's a Square World*?

2 What is pop star Gary Glitter's real name?

3 In which TV series did Googie Withers play prison governess Faye Boswell?

4 Steve Hislop won which trophy several times on a Honda?

5 Elvis Presley had three successive No 1 hits in the UK charts in 1961. Name one.

6 What is the capital of the state of Tennessee?

7 Easter Island is a dependency of which country?

8 In the sci-film *Them*, what were 'them'?

9 Who is generally credited as being the inventor of the Gramophone?

10 Which star of *The Full Monty* played a gangleader in the British thriller *Face*?

11 Where did 'experts' replace 'confides' to save the number of flags?

12 Who was the first unseeded tennis player to win the men's singles title at Wimbledon?

13 Which country hosted a motor racing Grand prix in East London in 1962, 1963 and 1965?

14 Which palace was given to the Duke of Marlborough as a reward for military services?

15 Which European airport is nearest to a city centre?

Things you didn't know...

Doberman dogs get their name from the German tax-collector Ludwig Dobermann who bred the fierce dog to help him on his rounds.

Answers to page 98

1 *Anastasia,* 2 Martina Hingis, 3 The Harp, 4 Midwife, 5 Fine Young Cannibals, 6 Retail Prices Index, 7 Spanish, 8 Tony McCoy, 9 Anne of Cleves, 10 Nectar, 11 Plum cake, 12 Woodstock, 13 Skin separating nostrils, 14 Trampolining, 15 Agatha Christie.

QUIZ 95

Answers on page 95

1 Which English playwright was murdered by his lover, Kenneth Halliwell, in 1967?

2 By what name was broadcaster Derek McCulloch better known?

3 Which London monument was cast from the guns recovered from the wreck of the Royal George?

4 Who played Ada in *For the Love of Ada*?

5 Which unit of measurement was based on the distance from the elbow to the tip of the middle finger?

6 Which restaurant guide was launched by Raymond Postgate in 1949?

7 What was the 1997 Genesis album release?

8 Who created the Muppets?

9 Which insect belongs to the order Acrididae of which there are 5,000 species?

10 What is a Muslim place of worship called?

11 According to Revelations, what is the numer of the Beast?

12 Which is the world's largest species of monkey?

13 Which hopping rodent is known as the 'desert rat'?

14 What was a bridewell?

15 What was originally known as the Pari Mutuel?

Things you didn't know...

*The female praying mantis eats her partner after mating.
Sometimes she starts eating him while they are still copulating.*

Answers to page 95

1 Mud, **2** Junk, **3** The watermark, **4** Ligament, **5** Susan Dey, **6** Mons Meg, **7** In a clock, **8** The Gambia, **9** Masai, **10** Lord Fauntleroy, **11** Hymns, **12** Sculpture, **13** Careening, **14** Jesse, **15** France.

QUIZ 96

Answers on page 96

1 Whom did Anna Anderson claim to be?

2 Who won the 1997 women's singles title at Wimbledon aged 16?

3 What cried out to warn the giant when it was stolen by Jack before he escaped down the beanstalk?

4 In fairy folklore, what was the job of Mab?

5 Who had Top Ten hits with *Johnny Come Home* and *Suspicious Minds*?

6 What is used to measure inflation in the UK?

7 What nationality was Fermin Cacho who won the 1992 Olympic 1500 metres?

8 Which jockey rode Mr Mulligan to victory in the 1997 Cheltenham Gold Cup?

9 Other than Catherine Parr, his last wife, which one of Henry VIII's wives outlived him?

10 In Greek mythology what was the drink of the Gods?

11 According to the nursery rhyme, what kind of cake were the fighting lion and unicorn given?

12 What was the only No 1 record for Matthews Southern Comfort?

13 What is your columella?

14 In which sport are there moves called Triffus, Miller and Rudolf?

15 By what name was writer Mary Westmacott better known?

Things you didn't know...

There have been 300 film productions of Shakespeare plays, with over 40 versions of Hamlet alone.

Answers to page 96

1 Michael Bentine, 2 Paul Gadd, 3 *Within These Walls,* 4 Isle of Man TT Trophy, 5*Are You Lonesome Tonight, Wooden Heart,* or *Surrender,* 6 Nashville, 7 Chile, 8 Giant ants, 9 Thomas Alva Edison, 10 Robert Carlyle, 11 Trafalgar, 12 Boris Becker, 13 South Africa, 14 Blenheim, 15 Gibraltar.

QUIZ 97

Answers on page 101

1 Which wading bird was sacred to ancient Egyptians?

2 Who wrote the ballet *Giselle*?

3 Which US national holiday is celebrated annually on the fourth Thursday in November?

4 Which Saint's Feast Day is July 15th?

5 Which oscar winning film of the 1980s was directed by Hugh Hudson?

6 In which year did Breakfast TV start in the UK?

7 Which Hebrew name is An the English form of?

8 Which band had a 1963 top ten hit with *You Were Made For Me*?

9 Which 1997 biopic starred Stephen Fry in the title role?

10 Which Welsh bay lies between St Govan's Head and Worms Head?

11 Who was heard to *Shout* in 1964?

12 What breed of dog was originally used to rescue travellers in the Alps?

13 To what does the adjective 'Pontic' apply?

14 Which people worshipped the rain god Apu Ilapu?

15 Which musical is set in Vietnam?

Things you didn't know...

Chinese people were so frightened of the evil power of 'moving spirits' that the first cinema audiences in Hong Kong had to be paid.

Answers to page 101

1 Shula, Kenton, David and Elizabeth, 2 Baseball, 3 Humphrey Davy, 4 Kato, 5 Carrington, 6 Greyfriars, 7 Herbert Asquith, 8 Clark Kent, 9 *Baby Love,* 10 1930's (1931), 11 Uruguay, 12 Keke Rosberg, 13 The Taj Mahal, 14 Eel, 15 Pontoon.

QUIZ 98

Answers on page 102

1 Which monarch wrote the *Casket Letters*?

2 Which sport is enjoyed by the Leander Club

3 Which animal has the scientific name 'Talpa Europaea'?

4 Which drink was advertised by Leonard Rossiter and Joan Collins?

5 Which city is capital of the Ukraine?

6 What does a mycologist study?

7 Which team scored a hat trick of wins in the Football League Championship between 1982 and 1984?

8 Which British city is served by Aldegrove airport?

9 Who composed *The Barber of Seville*?

10 What is the name of the fictional district of Manchester which is the setting for *Coronation Street*?

11 Which Peter was the voice of *Bluebottle* on radio?

12 Which fruity sauce is the traditional accompaniment to turkey?

13 Which was the last film in which Michael Caine played the spy 'Harry Palmer'?

14 Who played the title role in the 1991 film *Bugsy*?

15 Which Geordie managed the Republic of Ireland's national football team?

Things you didn't know...

The ancient Olympic Games, which had lasted for 1,100 years, were outlawed by Theodosius I because he deemed them pagan.

Answers to page 102

1 Yorkshire Post, 2 Litre, 3 35, 4 Jaguar mark II, 5 Flat racing, 6 Villandry, 7 911, 8 An anchorl, 9 Crossbencher, 10 Turkey, 11 Brunel, 12 Ian Hislop   (Private Eye editor), 13 Jim Hacker, 14 Harrow, 15 21.

QUIZ 99

Answers on page 99

1 Who are Phil and Jill Archer's four children?

2 In which sport might you encounter pitchers, catchers and shortstops?

3 Who invented the miner's safety lamp?

4 What was the name of Inspector Clousseau's valet?

5 What was Blake and Krystle's surname in *Dynasty*?

6 Which school did Billy Bunter go to?

7 Who was British PM from 1908 to 1916?

8 What is *Superman*'s secret identity?

9 What was Little Richard's most successful record in the UK charts?

10 In which decade was the first woman elected to the U.S. Senate?

11 Noted for its meat-processing, in which country is Fray Bentos?

12 Who was world motor racing champion in 1982, for the first and only time?

13 What reminds people of Shah Jehan's wife?

14 What is an adult elver called?

15 Which card game is also known as Blackjack?

Things you didn't know...

Toby jugs immortalise Yorkshire drinker Harry 'Toby' Elwes, said to have downed 16,000 pints of beer without eating in between.

Answers to page 99

1 Ibis, 2 Adolphe Adam, 3 Thanksgiving, 4 Swithin, 5 *Chariots of Fire*, 6 1983, 7 Hannah, 8 Freddie and the Dreamers, 9 Wilde, 10 Camarthen Bay, 11 Lulu, 12 St Bernard, 13 The Black Sea, 14 The Incas, 15 *Miss Saigon*.

QUIZ 100

Answers on page 100

1. Which newspaper is descended from the Leeds Intelligencer?

2. Which metric unit of volume is equal to one cubic decimetre?

3. What is the minimum age a US President has to be?

4. Which type of car is associated with T.Vs Inspector Morse?

5. In what form of horse racing are horses not required to jump obstacles?

6. Which famous chateau, renowned for its famous gardens, is situated a few miles south west of Tours?

7. What telephone number is dialled in an emergency in the USA?

8. What is the shape of the tattoo on Popeye's arm?

9. Which term is used to describe a member of the House of Lords who does not take a party whip?

10. In which country would you be if you landed a Dalaman airport?

11. After which famous engineer is the university at Uxbridge named?

12. Who said. 'If this is justice, I'm a banana!' after losing a libel case in May 1989 ?

13. What character did Paul Eddington play in *Yes Minister*?

14. Which Public School's school song begins:"Forty years on, when far and asunder"?

15. What is the minimum number of points required to win a game of table tennis?

Things you didn't know...

Cow dung can be used to produce a substitute for fuel oil. The dung from 1,000 cows is equivalent to 2,000 litres of fuel oil.

Answers to page 100

1 Mary Queen of Scots, **2** Rowing, **3** Mole, **4** Cinzano, **5** Kiev, **6** Fungi, **7** Liverpool, **8** Belfast, **9** Rossini, **10** Weatherfield, **11** Sellers, **12** Cranberry sauce, **13** The Million Dollar brain, **14** Warren Beatty, **15** Jack Charlton.

QUIZ 101

Answers on page 105

1 What is the family name of the Dukes of Wellington?

2 Which cartoon character has a cat called Jess?

3 What was the 'Boston Strangler's real name?

4 What was the name of Brian Poole's backing group in the 1960s?

5 On which Apollo mission did Armstrong and Aldrin land on the moon?

6 What type of creature is a Blue Point?

7 Which country produces the most wine?

8 Which actor played the title role in *Blott on the Landscape*?

9 Who published a novel called *The Black Book*, during the 1996 Tory Party conference?

10 What is the most northerly point in mainland Great Britain?

11 Who had a No 2 chart hit in 1966 with *Nineteenth Nervous Breakdown*?

12 What was the title of the solo album released by Paul McCartney in 1997?

13 In which of Shakespeare's plays is the tune *Greensleeves* referred to twice?

14 Yellowknife is the capital city of which Canadian Province?

15 What was the name of Perry Mason's secretary?

Things you didn't know...

Tidal waves race through the sea at speeds up to 790km (490 miles) per hour, and can be 85m (278ft) high.

Answers to page 105

1 Wimbledon, 2 Egypt, 3 The United States and Canada, 4 *Play Misty For Me,* 5 Somerset, 6 Jane Asher, 7 Marti Caine, 8 66 feet, 9 Sarah Brightman, 10 Jessica, 11 Bald Eagle, 12 Australia, 13 1901, 14 Percy Sugden, 15 Virginia.

QUIZ 102

Answers on page 106

1 Which novel was made into a film twice - the first starred Michael Redgrave and Donald Pleasance and the second John Hurt and Richard Burton?

2 What was Christopher Dean's job before he became a professional ice-skater?

3 Who designed the Glasgow School of Art?

4 Which vocal group comprised Cass, Michelle, John and Denny?

5 Who was *Worzel*'s girlfriend?

6 Which creature's Latin name is bufo bufo?

7 Which sign of the zodiac was Elvis Presley born under?

8 In which year was Grace Kelly born?

9 Who played the title role in *The Duchess of Duke Street*?

10 Between which two cities did the first international air service take place in 1919?

11 In what year did Martin Luther King make his famous "I have a dream.." speech?

12 During which process in the Roman Catholic church is use made of a bell, book and candle?

13 In which sport would you find a shotgun, a bomb, a blitz and a tight end?

14 Who co-wrote the *Blackadder* TV series and penned the 1994 hit film *4 Weddings And A Funeral*?

15 What is the collective word for a group of foxes?

Things you didn't know...

In November 1960 an American rocket, launched from Cape Canaveral, went off course and crashed in Cuba, killing a cow.

Answers to page 106

1 Sri Lanka, **2** Stoned to death, **3** A faucet, **4** Massachusetts, **5** Pinchbeck, **6** Worcester, **7** Susan St James, **8** Pigs, **9** *The Mary Tyler Moore Show*, **10** King Arthur, **11** Daily Mirror, **12** Sixteen, **13** Both had sons who were kidnapped, **14** Mount Kilimanjaro, 19,340 feet, in Tanzania, **15** Hummingbird.

QUIZ 103

Answers on page 103

1 On which Common would you find the *Wombles*?

2 Cleopatra was Queen of which country?

3 The Niagara Falls are situated on the border between which two countries?

4 Which film was the first to be directed by Clint Eastwood?

5 In which English county are the Mendip Hills?

6 Which actress has had a number of books on cakes published?

7 Which British comedienne was born Lynne Shepherd?

8 How long is a Gunter's chain?

9 With whom did Cliff Richard have a UK top ten hit called *All I Ask of You* in 1986?

10 In the film *Who Framed Roger Rabbit*?, starring Bob Hoskins, what was Roger's wife called?

11 What is the national bird of the USA?

12 Where are budgerigars found in their natural habitat?

13 When were Nobel Prizes first awarded?

14 Which character played by Bill Waddington left *Coronation Street* in 1997?

15 In which US state is Charleston?

Things you didn't know...

Saturn is not the only planet to have rings. Smaller, but similar, belts have been discovered around both Uranus and Jupiter.

Answers to page 103

1 Wellesley, 2 *Postman Pat,* 3 Albert De Salvo, 4 Tremeloes, 5 Apollo 11, 6 Cat, 7 Italy, 8 David Suchet, 9 Sara Keays, 10 John O'Groats, 11 Rolling Stones, 12 *Flaming Pie,* 13 *The Merry Wives of Windsor,* 14 North West Territories, 15 Della Street.

QUIZ 104

Answers on page 104

1 Which island to the south of India used to be called Ceylon?

2 If you were lapidated, what would happen to you?

3 What is the American word for a tap?

4 Of which state of the USA is Boston the capital?

5 What word of 9 letters describes an alloy of copper and zinc, used as imitation gold?

6 In which cathedral is the tomb of King John?

7 On television, who played the female half of *Macmillan and Wife*?

8 Welsh, Berkshire, Hampshire and Gloucester Old Spot are all breeds of which kind of animal?

9 The TV sitcoms *Rhoda* and *Lou Grant* were spin-offs from which other series?

10 Whose legendary horse was called 'Lamri'?

11 What first tabloid newspaper was founded in 1903 by Alfred Harmsworth?

12 How old was Dana when she won the *Eurovision Song Contest*?

13 What do Marlon Brando and Frank Sinatra have in common?

14 Which is Africa's highest mountain and in which country is it?

15 Which is the only bird that can fly backwards?

Things you didn't know...

Ancient Egyptians mummified the bodies of sacred animals such as cats as well as those of humans.

Answers to page 104

1 *1984* by George Orwell, 2 Policeman, 3 Charles Rennie Mackintosh, 4 The Mamas and The Papas, 5 Aunt Sally, 6 Toad, 7 Capricorn, 8 1928, 9 Gemma Jones, 10 London and Paris, 11 1963, 12 Excommunication, 13 American football, 14 Richard Curtis, 15 Skulk.

QUIZ 105

Answers on page 109

1 In which city will the Summer Olympics be held in the year 2,000?

2 Who is the patron saint of Scotland?

3 Which Wendy starred in *Butterflies*?

4 What was invented by Lewis Waterman in the 1880s?

5 How many standard bottles are there in a nebuchadnezzar?

6 Who discovered the circulation of blood?

7 What is the world's most southern capital?

8 What do the initials C.G. stand for on an Ordnance Survey Map

9 Which undefeated boxing champion died in an aircrash the day before his 46th birthday?

10 Which cartoon character did Charles M. Schulz create?

11 Who is the goddess of destruction in Hindu mythology?

12 What is the deepest adult male singing voice?

13 What animal did ancient Egyptians regard as sacred?

14 What is celebrated on July 15th?

15 What was the first name of the character played by Felicity Kendal in the 1970s television series *The Good Life*?

Things you didn't know...

Roman women are known to have worn two-piece bathing costumes made of leather.

Answers to page 109

1 Major General Menendez, 2 Truncheon, 3 Dublin, 4 Dock Green, 5 China, 6 Shells, 7 Shot put, 8 Black Forest, 9 Twelve, 10 Fennel, 11 Turkey, 12 Perry, 13 Nerys Hughes, 14 A fish, 15 Greyhound Derby.

QUIZ 106

Answers on page 110

1 Which pop star starred in the title role of the film *Merry Christmas, Mr Lawrence*?

2 What is the capital of Malaysia?

3 Which meteorological instrument was invented by Evangelista Torricelli?

4 Which bestselling author wrote the book *Wheels*?

5 Which extremely common object derives its name from the Latin for 'a little tail'?

6 Which British novelist wrote *The Horse's Mouth*?

7 What sort of creature is a cockatiel?

8 Who played the lead in the 1957 Second World War film *Paths of Glory*?

9 Which film, written and directed by Oliver Stone, won four Oscars in 1986?

10 Who was world heavyweight boxing champion following the retirement of Joe Louis in 1949?

11 Who invented the pendulum?

12 What was the stage name of Roy Scherer?

13 VE Day commemorated victory on which continent?

14 What occupation did Jean Alexander, Mao TseTung and Philip Larkin have in common?

15 Of which U.S. state is Helena the capital?

Things you didn't know...

The oldest man to become president of the USA was Ronald Reagan, who was 69 when he took office in 1981.

Answers to page 110

1 Valentino, 2 East Sussex, 3 *The Muppet Show,* 4 18th Century, 5 *Paint Your Wagon,* 6 Guinea-pig, 7 George Burns, 8 Australia, 9 Pierre Choderlos de Laclos, 10 *King Kong,* 11 Bucks Fizz, 12 English, 13 Cuba, 14 Roger Moore, 15 1900's (1905).

QUIZ 107

Answers on page 107

1 Who led the Argentinian Forces during the Falklands War?

2 The Americans call it a nightstick - what do we call it?

3 Where is the Chester Beatty Library?

4 Where was PC George Dixon's 'patch'?

5 Of which country is the Yangtze the longest river?

6 What do you use if you foretell the future by conchomancy?

7 In which athletics event is a metal sphere thrown as far as possible?

8 The Germans call it Schwarzwald, what do we call it?

9 In the Bible how many Tribes of Israel were there?

10 Which strong smelling herb, which tastes of aniseed, is most often used in fish dishes?

11 In which European country is the port of Gallipoli situated?

12 What drink does pear juice make?

13 Which actress played the title role in *The District Nurse*?

14 What sort of creature is a saithe?

15 Tartan Khan, I'm Slippy and Tico have all won what famous race?

Things you didn't know...

Sir Robert Walpole held office continuously for almost 21 years – longer than any other British prime minister.

Answers to page 107

1 Sydney, 2 Andrew, 3 Craig, 4 Fountain pen, 5 Twenty, 6 William Harvey, 7 Wellington, 8 Coast Guard Station, 9 Rocky Marciano, 10 *Charlie Brown*, 11 Kali, 12 Bass, 13 Cat, 14 St Swithin's Day, 15 Barbara.

QUIZ 108

Answers on page 108

1 Which silent movie star Rudolph died at an early age?

2 In which English county are seaside towns Brighton and Eastbourne?

3 Which puppet series sprang out of *Sesame Street*?

4 In which century was platinum discovered?

5 In which Clint Eastwood film did Lee Marvin sing the million selling record *Wanderin' Star*?

6 Which domestic pet is descended from the cavy?

7 Under what name did Nathan Birnbaum become famous?

8 Which country originated the term 'plonk' for wine?

9 Which French novelist wrote *Les Liaisons Dangereuses*?

10 Who, in a classic film, did film producer Carl Denham bring to New York and bill as "The Eighth Wonder of the World"?

11 Who had a No 1 hit with *Making Your Mind Up*?

12 What is the official language of Dominica?

13 Which country has the International Vehicle Registration Letter C?

14 Who played Simon Templar in the TV series *The Saint*?

15 In which decade was the Royal Naval College founded in Dartmouth?

Things you didn't know...

The Roman emperor Julius Caesar knew how to do a form of shorthand writing invented in 63 BC.

Answers to page 108

1 David Bowie, 2 Kuala Lumpur, 3 Mercury barometer, 4 Authur Hailey, 5 Pencil, 6 Joyce Cary, 7 A bird, 8 Kirk Douglas, 9 *Platoon*, 10 Ezzard Charles, 11 Galileo, 12 Rock Hudson, 13 Europe, 14 Librarian, 15 Montana.

QUIZ 109

Answers on page 113

1 What is the name of the magical kingdom in *The lion, the Witch and the Wardrobe*?

2 What is the largest city in Switzerland?

3 Which fruit did Columbus discover on Guadeloupe in 1493?

4 Which Orson Welles film was inspired by the career of the US newspaper proprietor William Randolph Hearst?

5 Which great painter and sculptor died in the Chateau Cloux, Amboise in France in 1519?

6 Which character did Dawn French play in BBC's *The Vicar of Dibley*?

7 What is a fedora?

8 What name is given to the pouch worn on the front of a kilt?

9 Which continent was home to the Incas?

10 Of which Caribbean country is Nassau the capital?

11 Which spice is made from the outer covering of the nutmeg?

12 What nationality was the composer Rachmaninov?

13 Honshu, Kyushu, Hakkaido and Shikoku are the main islands of which country?

14 Which Asian country's currency is called 'taka'?

15 Which Irish comedian presented four series of *And There's More* for Central TV?

Things you didn't know...

Eighty per cent of Russian embassy staff around the world are thought to be KGB agents.

Answers to page 113

1 Juliette Gruber, 2 Anti-freeze, 3 Svetlana Savitskaya, 4 Mick Jagger, 5 Arsenal, 6 33-1, 7 *Be Here Now,* 8 Birthmark or Mole, 9 John Buchan, 10 Grey Squirrel, 11 Chewing gum, 12 Red, 13 Normans, 14 Rockall, 15 Ilie Nastase.

QUIZ 110

Answers on page 114

1 What are auctioned at Tattersalls?

2 C is the symbol of which chemical element?

3 In which Italian city can the Ponte Vecchio be found?

4 Of which state of the USA is Topeka the capital?

5 Which is the largest land carnivore in Britain?

6 Who are in charge of theoracy?

7 Which of the Seven Wonders of the World was constructed by the sculptor Phidias about 430BC?

8 In which sport would you compete for the America's Cup?

9 Which sea route between the Atlantic and Pacific Oceans was first traversed by Roald Amundsen from 1903 to 1906?

10 What is the name of the dog in *Oliver Twist*?

11 Which planet, first discovered in 1930, takes 248 years to orbit the Sun?

12 Which former organist of Westminster Abbey wrote the opera *Dido and Aeneas*?

13 Which household appliance was patented by Cecil Booth in 1901?

14 What is the capital of New York state?

15 Who played Dian Fossey in the 1988 film *Gorillas in the Mist*?

Things you didn't know...

Canada has the longest coastline of any country in the world.

Answers to page 114

1 Victor Hugo, 2 Mannekin Pis, 3 Calf, 4 *Edward VIII and Mrs Simpson,* 5 Blackpool, 6 Gainsborough, 7 James, 8 Topaz, 9 France, 10 Echo, 11 Geiger Counter, 12 *Paint Your Wagon,* 13 Epsilon, 14 Leeds, 15 Backstroke.

QUIZ 111

Answers on page 111

1 Who played Jo in the TV series *Heartbeat*?

2 How is the chemical Ethylene Glycol better known?

3 Which cosmonaut became the first woman to walk in space, make two space trips and hold world records for parachuting?

4 Who is the lead singer of the Rolling Stones?

5 For which team did Alan Sunderland score the winning goal in the 1979 F.A. Cup Final?

6 In bookmakers' slang, what odds are denoted by the term 'double carpet'?

7 What was the 1997 Oasis album called?

8 What on the body is a naevus?

9 Who wrote The Three Hostages?

10 Which animal has the scientific name 'Sciurus carolinensis'?

11 What did goalkeeper Gordon Banks reputedly put on his hands to improve his grip?

12 What colour is the spot in the middle of the Japanese flag?

13 Who conquered England in 1066?

14 Which British island is 230 miles west of the Hebrides?

15 Who did Bjorn Borg defeat in 1976 to win his first Wimbledon singles title?

Things you didn't know...

Russia and the USA are only 4km (2.5 miles) apart at their closest point. (Two separately owned islands in the Bering Strait)

Answers to page 111

1 Narnia, 2 Zurich, 3 Pineapple, 4 Citizen Kane, 5 Leonardo Da Vinci, 6 Geraldine Granger, 7 A hat, 8 Sporran, 9 South America, 10 The Bahamas, 11 Mace, 12 Russian, 13 Japan, 14 Bangladesh, 15 Jimmy Cricket.

QUIZ 112

Answers on page 112

1 Who was considered the greatest French poet of the 19th century?

2 What statue is known as Brussels' oldest citizen?

3 What is the young of a rhino called?

4 Which famous couple were portrayed by Edward Fox and Cynthia Harris?

5 With which football club did Alan Ball begin his playing career?

6 Who painted *The Morning Walk*?

7 What is the first christian name of Paul McCartney?

8 What is the birthstone for November?

9 In which country did the D-Day landings take place?

10 Who became so heart-broken when Narcissus rejected her that she pined away to nothing until only her voice remained?

11 Which instrument is used to measure levels of radioactivity?

12 In which 1969 film musical did Clint Eastwood have a singing role?

13 Which letter of the Greek alphabet is the equivalent to 'E'?

14 Marks and Spencer started as a penny bazaar in which city?

15 Which swimming stroke is used first in a medley relay race?

Things you didn't know...

The biggest bell in the world, the Tsar Kolokol, stands 5.87m (19ft 3in) high and weighs 196 tonnes. It has never been rung.

Answers to page 112

1 Racehorses, 2 Carbon, 3 Florence, 4 Kansas, 5 Badger, 6 Priests, 7 Statue of Zeus, 8 Yachting, 9 Northwest Passage, 10 Bullseye, 11 Pluto, 12 Henry Purcell, 13 Vacuum cleaner, 14 Albany, 15 Sigourney Weaver.

QUIZ 113

Answers on page 117

1 Which word is used to describe a cross-breed between two animals or two plants?

2 Which football club is nicknamed The Canaries?

3 What is the largest French island?

4 Which medieval defensive fortification stretches nearly 1500 miles inland from the Yellow Sea north of Peking?

5 In which sound on the coast of Alaska did the massive oil spillage from the Exxon Valdez take place?

6 Which animal forms the one word title of a D.H. Lawrence novel?

7 Corazon Aquino became President of which country in 1986?

8 Which tea is known as 'the champagne of teas'?

9 Where would you find cerumen in the human body?

10 Which horse won the Irish Hennessey Gold Cup in February 1997?

11 Which group's only No 1 hit in 1964 was called *Go Now*?

12 Whom did Achilles kill and drag round Troy behind his chariot?

13 Which is the largest instrument in the string section of an orchestra?

14 With which British public school would you associate the wall game?

15 Who was the first British woman to take her seat in the House of Commons?

Things you didn't know...

The Niagara Falls moves upstream at an average rate of about 90m (295ft) a century.

Answers to page 117

1 Femur (thigh bone), 2 *Life Of Brian*, 3 Kent, 4 Henry, 5 Dressage, 6 Washington, 7 Mowgli, 8 Silver, 9 James Hazell, 10 Four, 11 Scope, 12 Hamelin, 13 Harry S. Truman, 14 *Seven Years in Tibet*, 15 Bill Haley and his Comets.

QUIZ 114

Answers on page 118

1 Which poet wrote about the charms of *Miss Joan Hunter Dunn*?

2 Where are cows regarded as sacred animals?

3 What shape is a lateen sail?

4 On which river does the city of Leeds stand?

5 What word describes how fabric lies?

6 Richard Widmark starred in the TV series *Madigan*. What was his christian name?

7 What was the name of the general knowledge game in the 1994 film *Quiz Show* based upon a 1950's real life television scandal?

8 Of which country is Malabo the capital?

9 What is the name for a fear of enclosed places?

10 Which ghost ship associated with the Cape of Good Hope inspired a Wagner opera?

11 Which dessert is made of cream mixed with wine into a soft curd then whipped or solidified with gelatine?

12 In which Bond film did Pussy Galore appear?

13 What is the administrative centre for Powys?

14 What word completes the phrase: 'Liberty, Equality and ---?

15 With what is the Birkenhead Drill Concerned?

Things you didn't know...

In a small area of S American tropical rain forest, covering just 2.6km² (1 square mile), 117 different species of plants were found.

Answers to page 118

1 Amelia Earhart, 2 Neptune, 3 Right Said Fred, 4 Lords Cricket Ground, 5 Amsterdam, 6 Stoat, 7 William Wyler, 8 John Nettles, 9 Ted Willis, 10 Adam Faith, 11 Bear market, 12 Humber, 13 Belgium, 14 *Roy of the Rovers,* 15 Zog (Albania).

QUIZ 115

Answers on page 115

1 Which is the longest bone in the human body?

2 Which film featured the song *Always Look on the Bright Side of Life*?

3 In which county is Romney Marsh?

4 What is Prince Harry's proper name?

5 In equestrianism, which event tests the horse's obedience?

6 On which city are the US football team The Redskins based?

7 What name did the Mother Wolf give to the "Man Child" in the *Jungle Book*?

8 Which metal is the best conductor of both heat and electricity?

9 What detective did Nicholas Ball play?

10 How many times was Franklin D. Roosevelt elected U.S. President?

11 To what did the Spastics Society change its name in the 1990s?

12 In which town did Robert Browning set his poem about a *Pied Piper*?

13 Who was U.S. President when Germany surrendered after World War II?

14 In which film did Brad Pitt play Heinrich Harrer, an egotistical Austrian climber and real-life Nazi?

15 Who had a hit single in 1955 with *Rock Around the Clock*?

Things you didn't know...

About 30 million people - more than a quarter of the population - died in Europe when the bubonic plague struck in 1347.

Answers to page 115

1 Hybrid, 2 Norwich City, 3 Corsica, 4 The Great Wall of China, 5 Prince William Sound, 6 Kangaroo, 7 Phillipines, 8 Darjeeling, 9 In the ear, 10 Danoli, 11 Moody Blues, 12 Hector, 13 Double Bass, 14 Eton, 15 Nancy Astor.

QUIZ 116

Answers on page 116

1 Who was the first woman to fly solo across the Atlantic?

2 Triton and Nereid are satellites of which planet?

3 Which 1990's pop group are named after a hit record by Bernard Cribbins?

4 Which sports venue is at St. John's Wood Road, NW8?

5 Where did the 1928 Summer Olympics take place?

6 Which animal produces fur called ermine?

7 Who directed the epic film *Ben Hur*?

8 Which actor played the title role in *Bergerac*?

9 Who wrote the play *Hot Summer Night* in 1959?

10 Which actor played the title role in *Budgie*?

11 Which term describes a stock market in which there is a continuing downward movement in prices?

12 Which English estuary flows from the Rivers Ouse and Trent to the North Sea?

13 In which country was Toc H founded in 1915?

14 How is the fictional hero Roy Race better known?

15 Which 'King' did Mussolini defeat in 1939?

Things you didn't know...

More than 123,000 million Aspirins are consumed each year, an average of 2 pills a month for every man, woman and child.

Answers to page 116

1 Betjeman, **2** India, **3** Triangular, **4** Aire, **5** Nap, **6** Dan, **7** Twenty one, **8** Equatorial Guinea, **9** Claustrophobia, **10** Flying Dutchman, **11** Syllabub, **12** *Goldfinger,* **13** Llandrindod Wells, **14** Fraternity, **15** Women and children first in lifeboats.

QUIZ 117

Answers on page 121

1 Who wrote *The Aspern Papers*, *The Ambassadors* and *The Golden Bowl*?

2 Which city on the River Wear has a Norman cathedral and an 11th century castle which are part of its university?

3 Who played the rich rock star in the TV series *Roll Over, Beethoven*?

4 What character does Tom Oliver play in *Neighbours*?

5 Who was the Queen's first grandchild?

6 In which decade the the 19th century did Beethoven die?

7 What are the water buses called that ply their trade on the canals of Venice?

8 Which footballer became the then record signing for a transfer deal between two English clubs on January 10th. 1995?

9 What is the second book of the Bible?

10 Which sci-fi series starred Gary Conway and Don Marshall?

11 Which former *Auf Wiedersehen, Pet* actor played Jacob Collins in ITV's *The Grand*?

12 Who were in the British top ten in 1973 with *Stuck in the Middle of You*?

13 Who defected to Russia with Guy Burgess in 1951?

14 Which 20th century playwright wrote *Luther* and *Inadmissible Evidence*?

15 Who created *The Kiss*?

Things you didn't know...

The Volkswagen Beetle was designed in the 1930s to meet Adolf Hitler's demand for a 'people's car'.

Answers to page 121

1 Jarvis Cocker, 2 Wiltshire, 3 Wensum, 4 Rollerskates, 5 Sugar Kane, 6 Gabon, 7 Bing Crosby, 8 Himself, 9 *The Final Days*, 10 No smoking, 11 85 feet, 12 Virginia Woolf, 13 Sloe, 14 An antelope, 15 Anthony Burgess.

QUIZ 118

Answers on page 122

1 Ceylon and which other type of tea are blended to make traditional breakfast tea?

2 Who starred as Jim Hacker in TV's *Yes Minister*?

3 Who wrote *Blue Suede Shoes*?

4 In the nursery rhyme, what did Tom, Tom the piper's son steal?

5 In which city did the diarist Anne Frank live?

6 Which actress played the title role in *Bionic Woman*?

7 What is the oldest university in the USA?

8 What appears in the top left hand corner of the National Flag of Malta?

9 What name is given to an animal who eats both plants and animals?

10 What nickname was given in World War 2 to scientists or backroom boys?

11 Which Britpop band had a hit with *MOR*?

12 In which country does the Danube reach the sea?

13 By what name is Hydera commonly known?

14 What was introduced in Britain in 1936 by the GPO?

15 Which county is Sandringham in?

Things you didn't know...

The world's first airship flight took place in Versailles, France in September 1852.

Answers to page 122

1 Forty, 2 Germany, 3 Shinai, 4 Crewe Alexandra, 5 Switzerland, 6 Tortoise (upper shell), 7 Vijay Singh, 8 Loch Ness, 9 Lincolnshire, 10 240, 11 Liverpool, 12 Alton Towers, 13 Nehru's, 14 Davy Crockett, 15 Afghanistan.

QUIZ 119

Answers on page 119

1 Who was invited to present an award at the 1997 Brit Awards, despite upsetting Michael Jackson at the 1996 ceremony?

2 In which English county is Longleat?

3 On which river does Norwich stand?

4 In the musical, *Starlight Express*, what do the performers wear on their feet?

5 Which role did Marilyn Monroe play in the film *Some Like It Hot*?

6 Of which African country is Libreville the capital?

7 Who has had three U.K. top ten hits duetting with Ronald Reagan's first wife, Princess Grace of Monaco and David Bowie?

8 At the end of *The Prisoner*, Patrick McGoohan unmasks Number One and finds what?

9 What was the name of the 1976 book by Bob Woodward & Carl Bernstein?

10 What does 'Rauchen verboten' mean?

11 What is the length of a basketball court in feet?

12 Who wrote *The Waves*?

13 What name is given to the fruit of the blackthorn tree?

14 What sort of creature is a dik-dik?

15 Whose novel was the 1971 film, *A Clockwork Orange*, based upon?

Things you didn't know...

In the First World War, no Allied pilot was ever equipped with a parachute, though by 1918 some Germans were.

Answers to page 119

1 Henry James, 2 Durham, 3 Nigel Planer, 4 Lou Carpenter, 5 Peter Philips, 6 1820's, 7 Vaporetti, 8 Andy Cole, 9 Exodus, 10 *Land of the Giants,* 11 Tim Healy, 12 Stealers Wheel, 13 Donald MacLean, 14 John Osborne, 15 Rodin.

QUIZ 120

Answers on page 120

1 How many years are celebrated by a ruby anniversary?

2 In which modern country would you locate the birthplace of John McEnroe?

3 What are the bamboo swords called that are used in Kendo?

4 Which soccer side has Alexandra in its name?

5 Which European country contains the ski resorts of Davos and Klosters?

6 Which animal has a carapace?

7 Who was runner up in the 1996 Golf Toyota Matchplay Championship?

8 What Scottish lake is the home of a monster?

9 The coastal resort of Skegness is in which English county?

10 How many pennies made an old pound?

11 In which city was W.E. Gladstone born?

12 The grounds of which mansion, formerly the home of the Earls of Shrewsbury, were developed during the 1980's into a successful leisure park?

13 Which Indian Prime Minster's daughter became Prime Minister herself in 1966?

14 Who had a rifle called 'Old Betsy'?

15 Kabul is the capital of which Asian country?

Things you didn't know...

The wood popular with model makers, Balsa, is actually classified as a hard wood.

Answers to page 120

1 Assam, 2 Paul Eddington, 3 Carl Perkins, 4 A pig, 5 Amsterdam, 6 Lindsay Wagner, 7 Harvard University, 8 The George Cross, 9 Omnivore, 10 Boffins, 11 Blur, 12 Romania, 13 Ivy, 14 Tim, the Speaking Clock, 15 Norfolk.

QUIZ 121

Answers on page 125

1 Whose silent film star career was finished when he was charged with rape and murder?

2 What flavour are Pontefract cakes?

3 What sort of creature is an eland?

4 Which big cat is also known as an ounce?

5 What type of animal is a booby?

6 Which Greater London Borough was created in 1965 from the former boroughs of East and West Ham & parts of Woolwich?

7 'Helvetia' appears on stamps produced by which country?

8 Which vocalist released an album entitled *Am I The Kinda Girl*? in 1997?

9 Who was the Israelite's leader when the walls of Jericho fell?

10 Which lager was advertised on TV by a bear?

11 In which country is Lake Como?

12 The Gold Cup is run at which racecource every March?

13 In which body of water is the Isle of Man?

14 What do we call a small personal ornament of no great value?

15 What did Mark Twain describe as "a cabbage with a college education"?

Things you didn't know...

Sea urchins, the spiky, ball-shaped creatures, are eaten as an delicacy in many parts of the world.

Answers to page 125

1 Rolls Royce, 2 Artificial Intelligence, 3 Bird, 4 Red, 5 Metastasis, 6 Founder, 7 Boyzone, 8 Prunella Scales, 9 Celine Dion, 10 Sardine, 11 James Hewitt, 12 Marion, 13 Foinavon, 14 Skelmsdale, 15 32.

QUIZ 122

Answers on page 126

1 Which Scottish village was famous for clandestine marriages?

2 Which writers real name was Josef Korzeniowski?

3 The current Duke of St Albans is a direct descendant of Charles 11's mistress. Who was she?

4 In which TV series did Ralph Waite play the father of a big family?

5 In sport, which game has the largest playing pitch?

6 Which part of the mint plant is used to make mint sauce?

7 What is the indicator that casts the shadow on a sundial called?

8 Whom did Californian model Kelly Fisher claim to have been jilted by?

9 Which tourist attraction can be found at Anaheim, just south of Los Angeles?

10 In Greek mythology, what hung from an oak tree in the grove of Ares in Colchis guarded by a dragon?

11 Who said: "I'll bet your father spent the first year of your life throwing rocks at the stork."?

12 How many English kings have been called George?

13 In which decade of the 1900's did Howard Carter discover the tomb of Tutankhamun?

14 Which all-woman Cambridge college recorded the lowest ever score in the history of University Challenge?

15 What is the stage name of Harry Webb?

Things you didn't know...

The mulberry silkworm can spin a single thread up to 1.2km (3,900ft) long.

Answers to page 126

1 D;Ream, 2 Greenpeace, 3 Ernest Bevin, 4 Madrid, 5 Postcards, 6 Gustav Klimt, 7 Trevi, 8 Apple tree, 9 Simply Red, 10 Thomas Harris, 11 White, 12 John Lloyd, 13 Cork, 14 *Godspell,* 15 North Dakota.

– 124 –

QUIZ 123

Answers on page 123

1 Who produced the Silver Ghost?

2 In computer glossary what does AI stand for?

3 What type of creature is a Yellow Hammer?

4 What colour are Manchester United's home shirts?

5 What is the spreading of a disease from one part of the body to another called?

6 Which one word means fill with water and sink, an originator and a person who casts metal?

7 Whose has an album called *Said and Done*?

8 Who played the Queen in the 1991 TV play *A Question of Attribution*?

9 Who had a No 1 hit in 1994 with *Think Twice*?

10 What is a small pilchard called?

11 Who did Lady Diana know as 'Squidgy'?

12 Which maid married legendary outlaw Robin Hood?

13 Which 100-1 outstander won the 1967 Grand National?

14 Which Lancashire new town is 18 miles West of Wigan?

15 How many points does a compass have?

Things you didn't know...

Only female honeybees have stings. The male drones are completely harmless.

Answers to page 123

1 Fatty Arbuckle, 2 Liquorice, 3 An antelope, 4 Snow leopard, 5 Tropical bird, 6 Newham, 7 Switzerland, 8 Cathy Dennis, 9 Joshua, 10 Hofmeister, 11 Italy, 12 Cheltenham, 13 Irish Sea, 14 Trinket, 15 Cauliflower.

QUIZ 124

Answers on page 124

1 Who had a No 1 hit with *Things Can Only get Better*?

2 Which international environmental pressure group was founded in 1971?

3 Which British politician was Foreign Secretary from 1945 to 1951?

4 Which city is served by Barajas airport?

5 What do Deltiologists collect?

6 Which artist, whose paintings include *The Kiss*, was a founder member of the Vienna Sezession?

7 In which fountain in Rome must visitors throw a coin if they wish to return?

8 What type of tree is a Pirus Malus?

9 Mick Hucknall is lead singer with which group?

10 Who wrote the bestseller *Silence of the Lambs*?

11 What colour is a moonstone?

12 Who was the last British tennis player before Greg Rusedski to reach a men's grand slam tournament final?

13 Which Irish County is Blarney in?

14 From which musical does *Day by Day* come?

15 Of which state of the USA is Bismarck the capital?

Things you didn't know...

In 1877 a wealthy widow promised Russian composer Tchaikovsky a generous annual allowance – on condition that they never met.

Answers to page 124

1 Gretna Green, 2 Joseph Conrad, 3 Nell Gwynn, 4 *The Waltons,* 5 Polo, 6 Leaves, 7 A gnomon, 8 Dodi Fayed, 9 Disneyland, 10 The Golden Fleece, 11 Groucho Marx, 12 Six, 13 1920's (1922), 14 New Hall, 15 Cliff Richard.

QUIZ 125

Answers on page 129

1 Which Scottish burgh is the administrative centre for the Central region?

2 In which country was Anthony Hopkins born?

3 Who composed *An American in Paris*?

4 Who was the first American to orbit the earth?

5 What was Rick Astley's 1987 Number One hit?

6 The Bummalo fish, salted and dried, is eaten as a relish called what?

7 In what year were dog licences abolished?

8 Which William was hanged in 1829 for grave robbing after his partner gave evidence against him?

9 Which federation of seven sheikdoms in the Middle East has Abu Dhabi as its capital?

10 Who played Isadora Duncan in the film *Isadora*?

11 Who was the 'fastest mouse in all Mexico'?

12 Which Reverend founded The Samaritans in 1953?

13 Which American novelist wrote *Big Sur*?

14 Of which branch of medicine is Mesmer associated?

15 Who was the first American president to resign from office?

Things you didn't know...

English novelist Arnold Bennet drank a glass of water in a Paris hotel to prove it was safe. He died two months later of typhoid.

Answers to page 129

1 Art Gunfunkel, 2 Cleveland, 3 Dinar, 4 Bette Midler, 5 Swan river, 6 Wiltshire, 7 Collapsible top hat, 8 Nutwood, 9 Sheffield, 10 Rain, 11 The 1960s, 12 Pancakes, 13 Len Deighton, 14 Spinks, 15 1450.

QUIZ 126

Answers on page 130

1 What would a cooper make you?

2 In which Hitchcock film did James Stewart play John 'Scottie' Ferguson?

3 What is the religious language of all Muslims?

4 Which musical includes the songs *Gee, Officer Krupke* and *America*?

5 Which British monarch's dying words were 'All my possessions for a moment of time'?

6 At which Thames crossing is there a tunnel and the Queen Elizabeth bridge?

7 What is the chief product of Zanzibar?

8 Who is the most famous child of Prince Andrew of Greece and Princess Alice of Battenburg?

9 What is the name of Clint Eastwood's son who starred along side him in the 1982 movie *Honkytonk Man*?

10 What sort of creature is a mudskipper?

11 Who won the Monaco Grand Prix in 1996?

12 In which sport woud you use a trudgen?

13 In which situation comedy did John Alderton and Pauline Collins play 'CD and Clara'?

14 Who played the title role in the 1966 film *Alfie*?

15 Which relief organisation has twice won the Nobel Peace Prize?

Things you didn't know...

Reuter's, now one of the world's biggest news agencies, began in 1850 – using pigeons!

Answers to page 130

1 Camden, 2 The Automobile Association's, 3 Simon Ward, 4 Shropshire (aka Salop), 5 The Crazy Gang, 6 Australia, 7 17, 8 Matthew, 9 Supergrass, 10 *David Copperfield,* 11 Alto, 12 Monday, 13 Robert Wise, 14 Four and a half feet, 15 Blue.

QUIZ 127

Answers on page 127

1 Which singer co-starred in the 1971 film *Carnal Knowledge*?

2 Which city is served by Hopkins airport?

3 What is the currency in Iraq?

4 With which actress would you associate the films *Outrageous Fortune, Down And Out In Beverley Hills* and *Ruthless People*?

5 Fremantle is a major port at the mouth of which Australian river?

6 In which English county is Stonehenge?

7 What is a gibus?

8 Where is *Rupert Bear*'s home town?

9 In which city is the Embassy World Snooker Championship held?

10 What would you expect in a pluvial region?

11 In which decade was Alec Douglas-home prime minister?

12 Which food item is used in an annual race at Olney?

13 Which author created the character Harry Palmer, twice portrayed by Michael Caine in films?

14 What is the surname of boxing brothers Leon and Michael?

15 Is the Great wall of China 1250, 1450 or 1650 miles long?

Things you didn't know...

England and Arsenal goalkeeper, David Seaman, wears a new pair of gloves each game.

Answers to page 127

1 Stirling, 2 Wales, 3 George Gershwin, 4 John Glenn, 5 *Never Gonna Give You Up,* 6 Bombay Duck, 7 1988, 8 Burke, 9 United Arab Emirates, 10 Vanessa Redgrave, 11 *Speedy Gonzales,* 12 Chad Varah, 13 Jack Kerouac, 14 Hypnotism, 15 Richard Nixon.

QUIZ 128

Answers on page 128

1 Hampstead Heath is in which Greater London borough?

2 Which organisation's motto is "Courtesy and Care"?

3 Who played James Herriot in the 1974 film *All Creatures Great and Small*?

4 In which English county is Much Wenlock?

5 What nickname have Wimbledon football club earned?

6 For which country did David Campese play rugby union?

7 How many syllables are there in a haiku?

8 Who is the patron saint of tax collectors?

9 Which Oxford group released an album called *In It For The Money* in 1997?

10 In which novel by Charles Dickens does Mr Micawber appear?

11 Which singing voice is between tenor and soprano?

12 Which day of the week is named after the moon?

13 Who directed *The Sound of Music*?

14 How wide apart are the 'tramlines' in lawn tennis?

15 What colour is a giraffe's tongue?

Things you didn't know...

Public telephone boxes have been in use since June 1880.
Payment was made to an attendant.

Answers to page 128

1 A barrel, 2 *Vertigo,* 3 Arabic, 4 *West Side Story,* 5 Elizabeth I, 6 Dartford, 7 Cloves, 8 Prince Philip, 9 Kyle, 10 A fish, 11 Olivier Panis, 12 Swimming, 13 *No honestly,* 14 Michael Caine, 15 Red Cross.

QUIZ 129

Answers on page 133

1 John Rivers and Lord Napier are types of what?

2 True or false: there is actually a country named Cape Verde?

3 Which star sign has the bull as its symbol?

4 Who had a No 1 hit with *Belfast Child*?

5 Which perennial herb is also called a Paris daisy?

6 Which town is 10 miles west of Brighton?

7 Covallaria Majalis is the national flower of Sweden. By what name is it better known?

8 Which is the fifth book of the New Testament?

9 Charles Rolls founded Rolls Royce in 1906, but what aviation record did he set in 1910?

10 What is the capital of Portugal?

11 In a game of tenpin bowling, if a person starts by throwing twelve consecutive strikes, what would be their score?

12 Under what name did Nathan Birnbaum become famous?

13 What is the longest river in Ireland?

14 Which was the first 3rd division side to reach an FA Cup semi-final?

15 How many dice are used in the game of craps?

Things you didn't know...

When television licences were first introduced in Britain in June 1946 the combined fee for radio and TV was £2.

Answers to page 133

1 Longleat, 2 *The Perishers,* 3 Eight, 4 The Shadows, 5 Liam Neeson, 6 Max, 7 The Alamo, 8 Eyes, 9 Lincoln, 10 Charlene, 11 El Greco, 12 Falklands War, 13 Gabon, 14 Australian, 15 Kings School, Canterbury.

QUIZ 130

Answers on page 134

1 Who played Agent Dale Cooper in TV's *Twin Peaks*?

2 What is Fred Flintstone's daughter called?

3 Who wrote the play *Equus* in 1973?

4 Who designed the Volkswagen car?

5 Who wrote *The Firm, The Pelican Brief* and *The Rainmaker*?

6 Which football club folded in 1992 after 66 years in the League?

7 In which book of the Bible are the Ten Commandments set out for the first time?

8 Who was the first prime minister of Australia?

9 In which year was Lord Mountbatten killed by the IRA?

10 What is a young male zebra called?

11 What does a mycologist study?

12 What name is given to the study of the structure and form of the human body?

13 If you were described as an ectomorph, what woud you be?

14 Which New York street is famous for its theatres?

15 Where did America's unsuccesful invasion of Cuba take place?

Things you didn't know...

Pipe tobacco was the first product to be made available by vending machine.

Answers to page 134

1 Panorama, 2 Tugela, 3 Archery, 4 The Pyrenees, 5 Judy Garland, 6 Prunella Scales, 7 Erasure, 8 Blood and Fire, 9 Brighton and Hove Albion, 10 The Woolpack, 11 Spoonerism, 12 Catherine of Aragon, 13 Michael Douglas, 14 Cary Grant, 15 SDP.

QUIZ 131

Answers on page 131

1 What is the country home of the Marquess of Bath?

2 Which daily newspaper strip cartoon is drawn by Maurice Dodd?

3 How many furlongs in a mile?

4 Who was Cliff Richard's backing group?

5 Who was nominated for Best Actor Oscar for his role in *Schindler's List*?

6 What was the chauffeur's name in *Hart to Hart*?

7 What is the major tourist attraction in the Texan town of San Antonio?

8 Which parts of the body are affected by conjunctivitis?

9 Which US president was assassinated in a Washington theatre?

10 Which *Neighbours* character was played by Kylie Minogue?

11 Which painters real name was Domenikos Theotokopoulos?

12 In which conflict did Prince Andrew fly a helicopter?

13 Libreville is the capital of which African country?

14 What nationality was Wimbledon champion Rod Laver?

15 Which is the oldest school in the UK dating from 600 AD.?

Things you didn't know...

Zip fasteners have been around since 1893.

Answers to page 131

1 Nectarine, 2 True, 3 Taurus, 4 Simple Minds, 5 Marguerite, 6 Worthing, 7 Lily of the Valley, 8 Acts of the Apostles, 9 First to fly non stop across the channel and back, 10 Lisbon, 11 300, 12 George Burns, 13 Shannon, 14 Millwall, 15 2.

QUIZ 132

Answers on page 132

1 On which programme did the Princess of Wales give her first solo TV interview?

2 Which is the highest waterfall in Africa?

3 In which sport could you have a York Round and a Hereford Round

4 Which mountain range stretches from the Bay of Biscay to the Mediterranean Sea?

5 Who was Liza Minelli's famous mother?

6 Who played the character Mrs Fawlty?

7 Which group sang Abba - esque in 1992?

8 What is the motto of The Salvation Army?

9 Which football league club used to play at the Goldstone Ground?

10 What is the name of the pub in *Emmerdale*?

11 What name is given to expressions like 'catch the town drain' and 'tasted two worms'?

12 Who was the first wife of Henry VIII?

13 Who played the part of Gordon Gecko in the 1987 film *Wall Street*?

14 Who played Cole Porter in the 1946 biopic *Night and Day*?

15 Roy Jenkins was a founder of which political party?

Things you didn't know...

Early air hostesses were required to type letters dictated by passengers.

Answers to page 132

1 Kyle MacLachlan, 2 Pebbles, 3 Peter Shaffer, 4 Porsche, 5 John Grisham, 6 Aldershot, 7 Exodus. Chapter 20, 8 Sir Edmund Barton, 9 1979, 10 A colt, 11 Fungi, 12 Anatomy, 13 Thin, 14 Broadway, 15 Bay Of Pigs.

QUIZ 133

Answers on page 137

1 What is the capital of Honduras

2 At which racecourse is the Grand National run?

3 Which is the smallest breed of bat in Britain?

4 Which animal has the scientific name 'Mustela erminea'?

5 Over what distance is the Classic horse race 'The Oaks' run?

6 Who was the original lead singer with heavy rock band Black Sabbath?

7 Blenheim Palace and Versailles Palace are examples of which style of architecture?

8 Which American actor was married to Madonna?

9 Who was the original lead singer with heavy rock band Deep Purple?

10 What sort of creature is a flying phalanger?

11 Who wrote three symphonies in the space of 42 days?

12 Which drink is known as 'the right one'?

13 How many eggs does a peacock lay in a year?

14 Which of the *Road To* films was set in the klondike Gold Rush?

15 In what year did Queen Victoria die?

Things you didn't know...

British people consume twice as many baked beans as American people.

Answers to page 137

1 Henry Segrave, 2 Cilla Black, 3 Kenya, 4 Full of Woe, 5 Queen, 6 Fred Astaire & Ginger Rogers, 7 1848, 8 Great Ormond Street, 9 Battle of the Nile, 10 Beta, 11 Reduces fever and high temperature, 12 Tchaikovsky, 13 The Potteries, 14 Crescent and Star, 15 Barnes Wallis.

QUIZ 134

Answers on page 138

1 Which British mountaineer climbed the Eiger in 1962 and Everest in 1985?

2 What language was devised by LL Zamenhof?

3 Which bird has the scientific name 'Garrulus glandarius'?

4 In which event did Mary Peters win an Olympic gold medal?

5 Which ocean lies between Europe and America?

6 What name is given to small flakes of scurf shed from the scalp?

7 Which football club won the FA Cup just 11 years after being elected to the Football League?

8 Which is the most easterly town in England?

9 In which country was President Allende overthrown by General Pinochet?

10 What does the K stand for in Jerome K Jerome's name?

11 Who wrote the poem *Dover Beach*?

12 What are the names of the Princess Royal's two children?

13 What is the capital of Latvia?

14 Who coined the phrase "a land fit for heroes to live in"?

15 Which reactive metal is represented by the symbol Ba?

Things you didn't know...

Boy's Own Magazine began publcation in January 1855, priced 2d.

Answers to page 138

1 The Torre Canyon, **2** Yew, **3** Spike Lee, **4** Blair Hospital, **5** Red, **6** Eastwood, **7** Tintoretto, **8** Frankie Laine, **9** Birmingham, **10** Rho, **11** Los Angeles, **12** Mr Hudson, **13** The Searchers, **14** Base of spine, **15** Agatha Christie.

QUIZ 135

Answers on page 135

1 Which Briton broke the world land speed record at Daytona in 1927 and 1929?

2 Which Liverpool lady took *Anyone Who Had A Heart* to No 1?

3 In which African country was the series *The Flame Trees of Thika* set?

4 If Mondays's child is fair of face, what is Wednesdays's child?

5 Who had a No 2 chart hit in 1976 with *Somebody to Love*?

6 Which double act made their debut in the film *Flying down to Rio?*

7 When was cricketer W G Grace Born?

8 To which children's hospital do royalties from productions of *Peter Pan* go?

9 Brueys was defeated by Nelson in 1798, in which battle?

10 Which letter of the Greek alphabet is the equivalent to 'B'?

11 What does an antipyretic drug do?

12 Who wrote *The Sleeping Beauty*?

13 What is the area around Stoke-on-Trent known as?

14 What is the national emblem of Turkey?

15 Who invented the Bouncing Bomb?

Things you didn't know...

The deepest lake in the world is Lake Baykal in Russia, which at some points is a mile deep.

Answers to page 135

1 Tegucigalpa, 2 Aintree, 3 Pipistrelle, 4 Stoat, 5 1.5 miles, 6 Ozzy Osborne, 7 Baroque, 8 Sean Penn, 9 Ian Gillan, 10 A marsupial, 11 Mozart, 12 Martini, 13 None (Peahens do), 14 *Road To Utopia*, 15 1901.

QUIZ 136

Answers on page 136

1 What struck the Pollard Rock on March 18th 1967?

2 The wood of which tree used to be used to make bows for archery?

3 Who directed the 1989 film *Do The Right Thing*?

4 In which hospital did Dr Kildare and Dr Gillespie practise medicine?

5 What colour eggs are the Chinese symbol of luck?

6 Which Clint was the mayor of Carmel?

7 Which 16th century Venetian painter's name means "Little dyer" in Italian?

8 Which singer enjoyed 27 weeks at number one in the singles chart in 1953?

9 In which British city can Spaghetti Junction and Aston University be found?

10 Which letter of the Greek alphabet is the equivalent to 'R'?

11 In which US city was the comedy film *Swingers* set?

12 What was the butler's name in *Upstairs, Downstairs*?

13 Who had a number one single with *Needles and Pins* in 1964?

14 Where is your coccyx?

15 Who created *Miss Marple*?

Things you didn't know...

6,000 new chemicals are added to the lists of American Chemical Society every week.

Answers to page 136

1 Chris Bonington, 2 Esperanto, 3 Jay, 4 Pentathlon, 5 Atlantic, 6 Dandruff, 7 Wimbledon in 1988, 8 Lowestoft in Suffolk, 9 Chile, 10 Klapka, 11 Matthew Arnold, 12 Peter and Zara, 13 Riga, 14 Lloyd George, 15 Barium.

QUIZ 137

Answers on page 141

1 In which Swiss city was the Bank for International Settlements established in 1929?

2 What are ossicles and osselets?

3 What is the name of Michael Barrymore's television talk show?

4 Which boxer used to ask 'Know what I mean 'Arry'?

5 What name was given collectively to the twelve sons of Ge and Uranus?

6 What is the name of the stone that medieval alchemists sought in the belief that it could turn base metals into gold?

7 Which ranges of chalk hills in SE England are separated by the Weald?

8 Which bay housed the island prison Alcatraz?

9 Who had top ten hits in 1989 with *This Time I Know It's For Real* and *I Don't Want To get Hurt*?

10 Who scored the only goal in Newcastle United's 1998 FA Cup semi-final victory over Sheffield United?

11 What was the name of the *Lone Ranger*'s horse?

12 Which city hosted the summer Olympics in 1904?

13 Which Ray won the world snooker championship in 1978?

14 Thetford is in which English county?

15 What is the collective noun for jellyfish?

Things you didn't know...

Leonardo da Vinci drew designs for a flushing toilet and a helicopter hundreds of years before they were produced.

Answers to page 141

1 Blucher, **2** Judi Dench, **3** Daley Thompson, **4** Hello, **5** Chair, **6** Birds, **7** Rooster, **8** Sydney, **9** KLM, **10** Harold Wilson, **11** 29, **12** Imagination, **13** Stamps, **14** Sydney, **15** Amarillo.

Answers on page 142

1 For which film did Jane Fonda win an Oscar for Best Actress in 1978?

2 Which drug is used as a substitute for morphine and heroin?

3 What sort of creature is a weever?

4 What is the technical name for German measles?

5 Do peanuts grow above or under the ground?

6 If you sailed west from Land's End and followed the same line of latitude, which country would you reach first?

7 Which British monarch began the tradition of a Royal Christmas broadcast?

8 What is the capital of Yemen?

9 How long is a dog watch at sea?

10 Who in 1992 broke Pat Eddery's run of four consecutive Flat Jockey Championships?

11 What is the common name for a myocardial infarction?

12 Which actress Shirley became a US ambassador?

13 What nationality was the Protestant reformer Martin Luther?

14 Which US president died just 16 months after taking office?

15 In which decade was Calcutta still the capital of India?

Things you didn't know...

Charlie Chaplin once entered a Charlie Chaplin look-a-like competition in Monte Carlo – and came third!

Answers to page 142

1 Hindi, **2** Stoat, **3** Gamma, **4** Pole vault, **5** T'Pau, **6** Arkwright, **7** Speedway, **8** Lizard, **9** A Mullion, **10** Vermont, **11** Jodie Foster, **12** The Who, **13** Dalmatian, **14** Seahorse, **15** Jealousy.

QUIZ 139

Answers on page 139

1 What was the name of George Stephenson's first locomotive?

2 Who played M in the James Bond film *Goldeneye*?

3 Which British athlete was the first to be Commonwealth, European, Olympic, World Champion and world record holder simultaneously?

4 What do you say to *Dolly* in the title of the show?

5 Sedan, arm and high are all types of what?

6 What does an ornithologist study?

7 Which is the only bird in the Chinese calendar?

8 What is Australia's oldest city?

9 What is the national airline of the Netherlands?

10 Which British PM once said 'A week is a long time in politics'?

11 At what age did Mrs Beeton, Anne Boleyn, Carole Landis and Percy Shelley die?

12 Who had Top Ten hits with *Body Talk, Just an Illusion* and *Music and Lights*?

13 What do philatelists collect?

14 What is the capital of New South Wales?

15 In pop music, where did Tony Christie go to meet *Sweet Marie*?

Things you didn't know...

David Niven, the debonair British actor, played nothing but Mexicans in his first 27 films.

Answers to page 139

1 Basle, 2 Bones, 3 *My Kind Of People*, 4 Frank Bruno, 5 Titans, 6 The Philosophers Stone, 7 North and South Downs, 8 San Francisco, 9 Donna Summer, 10 Alan Shearer, 11 Silver, 12 St Louis, 13 Reardon, 14 Norfolk, 15 Smuck.

QUIZ 140

Answers on page 140

1 From which language does the word 'shampoo' originate?

2 Which small carnivore has a winter coat known as ermine?

3 Which letter of the Greek alphabet is the equivalent to 'G'?

4 With which sport do you associate Sergey Bubka?

5 Who had a No 1 hit with *China In Your Hand*?

6 What is the name of the grocer played by Ronnie Barker in *Open All Hours*?

7 Which sport would you be watching if you saw Diamonds take on Bandits?

8 What is a chuckwalla?

9 What is the name of the vertical bar dividing lights in a window, called?

10 Montpelier is the capital of which American state?

11 Who won a Best Actress Oscar for the 1988 film *The Accused*?

12 Which successful rock group were called The Detours and The High Numbers prior to 1964?

13 Which romantic language and also a breed of dog, is now extinct in Southern Europe?

14 What name is commonly given to the Hippocampus?

15 What did Shakespeare describe as the 'Green-eyed monster'?

Things you didn't know...

The world's largest hotel was knocked down to build the Empire State Building.

Answers to page 140

1 *Coming Home*, 2 Methadone, 3 A fish, 4 Rubella, 5 Under, 6 Canada, 7 George V (in 1932), 8 Sana, 9 Two hours, 10 Michael Roberts, 11 Heart attack, 12 Temple, 13 German, 14 Taylor, 15 1910-19 (1912).

QUIZ 141

Answers on page 145

1 Which June starred in the sitcom Happy Ever After?

2 Which specialised agency of the United Nations is represented by the initials WHO?

3 In what year did the IRA bomb a hotel in Brighton during the Conservative Party Conference?

4 Which scientist, who produced the Laws of Motion, was born on Christmas Day in 1642?

5 Who had Top Twenty hits with *I Feel Free, Strange Brew* and *Badge*?

6 The shortest war on record occurred in 1896 and lasted for just 38 minutes. Who were the countries involved?

7 What is the ninth month of the Muslim year?

8 What is Britain's most remote inhabited island?

9 Which home secretary founded the Metropolitan Police in 1829?

10 Bilbo Baggins appears in which book?

11 Which traveller took the recipe for ice cream to Italy from China?

12 What sort of creature is a kittiwake?

13 In which part of the body can the retina be found?

14 What is the capital of France?

15 Which hero was the subject of a Rossini opera?

Things you didn't know...

Every continent in the world contains a city called Rome.

Answers to page 145

1 Los Angeles, 2 Australia, 3 Jellyfish, 4 French, 5 Mel Brookes, 6 Steve McQueen, 7 *The Mask of Dimitrios,* 8 George Orwell, 9 Conspiracy Theory, 10 Bob Holness, 11 Lisbon, 12 Denver, 13 Laboheme, 14 Caustic soda, 15 Robert E. Lee.

– 143 –

QUIZ 142

Answers on page 146

1 Which was Puccini's last opera?

2 Which series of UK satellites were launched by the USA from 1962 to 1979?

3 Who had a Top Ten hit with *Hooray Hooray It's A Holi-Holiday* in 1979?

4 Which actress played the lead in the 1938 film *Jezebel*?

5 Egon Muller was a world champion in which sport?

6 What was the surname of TV's rag-and-bone men Harold and Albert?

7 With which sport do you associate Ryan Giggs?

8 What are a flower's female sex organs called?

9 Which cartoon character has Bluto as his arch rival?

10 In which soap was there a plane crash in December 1993?

11 On which day of the week does Pancake Day fall?

12 Which system of writing for the blind to read by touch is named after the French teacher who devised it?

13 Who played the lead in the films *The Joker is Wild. A Hole in the Head* and *Never So Few*?

14 Who played Test cricket for England in 1930 when he was 52 years old?

15 Which Finnish runner died in 1973 having won nine gold Olympic medals?

Things you didn't know...

The only two words in the English language with the vowels in their correct order are abstemious and facetious.

Answers to page 146

1 Shogun, 2 1901-1909 (1905), 3 Richard Nixon, 4 Chlorine, 5 Berlin, 6 Falconet, 7 80 per cent, 8 Harold II, 9 A drosometer, 10 Brisbane, 11 Reliant, 12 Sweden, 13 The number thirteen, 14 Zloty, 15 Dorchester.

QUIZ 143

Answers on page 143

1 Where were the 1984 Olympics held?

2 In which country can Barkly Tableland be found?

3 What type of creature is a Pacific sea wasp?

4 What nationality was John Calvin?

5 Who directed *Blazing Saddles* in 1974?

6 Who starred in the title role of the 1972 film *Junior Bonner*?

7 Which Eric Ambler story was filmed in 1944 with Peter Lorre and Sidney Greenstreet?

8 Under which name did Eric Blair write?

9 Which 1997 film starred Mel Gibson and Julia Roberts?

10 Who hosted *Call My Bluff* when it returned to the screens in 1996?

11 Which European city was almost totally destroyed by an earthquake in 1755?

12 Which American city is served by Stapleton airport?

13 In which Puccini opera does Mimi appear?

14 By what name is sodium hydroxide better known?

15 Which General lost at Gettysburg?

Things you didn't know...

Meat-flavoured toothpaste for dogs is available in America.

Answers to page 143

1 Whitfield, 2 World Health Organisation, 3 1984, 4 Isaac Newton, 5 Cream, 6 England and Zanzibar, 7 Ramadan, 8 Fair Isle, 9 Sir Robert Peel, 10 *The Hobbit,* 11 Marco Polo, 12 A bird, 13 The eye, 14 Paris, 15 *William Tell.*

QUIZ 144

Answers on page 144

1 Which Japanese word translates as 'Leader of the Army'?

2 In which decade was the Simplon Tunnel officially opened?

3 Which U.S. President had the middle name Milhous?

4 Which element, symbol Cl, is used as a disinfectant in swimming pools?

5 In which European city, would you find the famous Tiergarten Park?

6 Which is the smallest bird of prey?

7 What proportion of the human brain is water?

8 Who was the last Saxon king of England?

9 What instrument is used to measure dew?

10 What is the capital of Queensland?

11 Which car manufacturer had the Kitten, Rebel and Sabre models?

12 Which country was the first to use paper banknotes?

13 What is terdekaphobia the fear of?

14 What is the unit of currency in Poland?

15 Which Dorset town did Thomas Hardy often refer to in his novels as 'Casterbridge'?

Things you didn't know...

The uniforms worn by Swiss guards at the Vatican were designed by Michelangelo.

Answers to page 144

1 Turandot, 2 Ariel, 3 Boney M, 4 Bette Davis, 5 Speedway, 6 Steptoe, 7 Football, 8 Carpels, 9 Popeye, 10 *Emmerdale,* 11 Tuesday, 12 Braille, 13 Frank Sinatra, 14 Wilfred Rhodes, 15 Paavo Nurmi.

QUIZ 145

Answers on page 149

1 Which British queen had the longest reign?

2 Which film legend was so unhappy with his nose that he wore a false one whenever he acted on stage?

3 LOT is the national airline of which country?

4 Which vegetable has varieties called Ailsa Craig, Brunswick and Lancastrian?

5 Who said: "This is the greatest week in the history of the world since the creation."?

6 Adam Bell, Clym of the Clough and William of Cloudesley were all famous what?

7 Which frigate was launched secretly in 1986 in Wallsend to replace a ship lost in the Falklands?

8 What is the longest river in France?

9 Which island, situated in the Arctic Ocean, is the largest in the world?

10 Who was Desmon Lynam's co-presenter on the first series of *How Do They Do That*?

11 Who fronted and devised the TV show *It's A Square World*?

12 Whose only No 1 hit in the UK in 1975 was called *Tears on my Pillow*?

13 Fullerenes, discovered in 1985, were a new form of which element?

14 Who played Miss Jones in the sitcom *Rising Damp*?

15 What type of creatures are "Whitstable natives"?

Things you didn't know...

A fifteenth-century law banning all Jews from Spain was only repealed in 1968.

Answers to page 149

1 Julie Walters, **2** Glamis, **3** Mumps, **4** Six, **5** John Moores, **6** Ronnie Corbett, **7** Saturn, **8** Liqueurs, **9** Ash, **10** Iran, **11** Deserts, **12** Leeds, Bradford and Wakefield, **13** Romeo and Juliet, **14** Sacha Distel, **15** Mayfair.

QUIZ 146

Answers on page 150

1 Which Egyptian queen was killed by an asp?

2 In which English county is the picturesque village of Clovelly situated?

3 Where were the tulips from, which Max Bygraves sang about?

4 Who starred in and driected the 1965 Second World War drama *None But the Brave*?

5 Who wrote the novels *Mansfield Park* and *Northanger Abbey*?

6 Who was the first Conservative prime minister?

7 Which idol did the Israelites make when they believed Moses would not return from Mount Sinai?

8 To which group of dogs does the Dalmatian belong?

9 Which European country produces Chianti?

10 Which TV series is set in Holby City Hospital?

11 Which Australian state is Hobart the capital of?

12 Which Swiss mountain features in the title of a film starring Clint Eastwood and George Kennedy?

13 Which city is served by Schipol airport?

14 Which is the first animal listed in the dictionary?

15 What is the difference between French and American roulette?

Things you didn't know...

Violet is the colour of mourning in Turkey, not black.

Answers to page 150

1 Bran, 2 Atlantic Ocean, 3 Rosa Mota, 4 Necessity, 5 The Beach Boys, 6 Fleetwood Mac, 7 Arcturus, 8 Frets, 9 Frank Sinatra, 10 Lincoln City, 11 Jonathon, 12 The speed of sound at sea-level, 13 West Bengal, 14 De Havilland Comet, 15 Oliver Tambo.

QUIZ 147

Answers on page 147

1 Who played Madame Cyn in the film *Personal Services*?

2 In which Scottish castle was Princess Margaret born?

3 By what name is the infectious disease Epidermic Parotitis better known?

4 How many dots are used in each letter in the Braille system?

5 Who created the football pools in 1923 with a top dividend of £150?

6 Which comedian had a trial as a schoolboy for Heart of Midlothian FC, but was not tall enough?

7 Saturday is named after which Roman god?

8 What name is given to sweetened alcoholic drinks such as Benedictine, Cointreau and Drambuie?

9 What tree can be white, black, green and blue?

10 In which modern day country was Parthia?

11 'Thar' and 'Mojave' are both examples of which kind of geographical feature?

12 Name the three largest cities in West Yorkshire in order of population.

13 From which of Shakespeare's plays does the line ' A plague o'both your houses', come from?

14 Who had a 1970 Top Ten hit with *Raindrops Keep Falling On My Head*?

15 What is the most expensive property on a British Monopoly board?

Things you didn't know...

The English language has more words than any other.

Answers to page 147

1 Victoria, 2 Orson Welles, 3 Poland, 4 Onions, 5 Richard Nixon, 6 Archers, 7 HMS Coventry, 8 Loire, 9 Greenland, 10 Jennie Hull, 11 Michael Bentine, 12 Johnny Nash, 13 Carbon, 14 Frances De la Tour, 15 Oysters.

QUIZ 148

Answers on page 148

1 In Gaelic legend, what was Fingal's dog called?

2 Into which sea or ocean does the Orinoco flow?

3 Which Portuguese runner won the Womens Olympic Marathon in 1988?

4 What is said to be the mother of invention?

5 By what famous name were the pop group Carl and the Passions later known?

6 Whose Top Ten hits included *Oh Well, Man of the World* and *Tusk*?

7 What is the brightest star in the northern hemisphere?

8 What name is given to the metal ribs on the fingerboard of a guitar?

9 Whose female fans were once knows as Bobby Soxers?

10 Which was Graham Taylor's first club as a manager?

11 Which Dimbleby brother hosted ITV's *Election '97* coverage?

12 What is MACH 1?

13 Calcutta is the capital of which Indian state?

14 Which commercial aircraft made its maiden flight in 1949?

15 Who was leader of the ANC during Nelson Mandela's long imprisonment?

Things you didn't know...

Vincenzo Peruggia stole the Mona Lisa from the Louvre in 1911 and kept it in a suitcase under his bed for two years.

Answers to page 148

1 Cleopatra, 2 Devon, 3 Amsterdam, 4 Frank Sinatra, 5 Jane Austen, 6 Robert Peel, 7 The Golden Calf, 8 Utility, 9 Italy, 10 *Casualty*, 11 Tasmania, 12 *The Eiger Sanction,* 13 Amsterdam, 14 Aardvark, 15 The 00 box exists in American roulette.

QUIZ 149

Answers on page 153

1 Which country in the world has the greatest mileage of roads?

2 What tragedy did baker John Faynor's carelessness cause?

3 What do aardvarks normally eat?

4 In which American state is Fort Knox?

5 What is Margaret Thatcher's middle name?

6 On which island is the holiday resort of Palma?

7 Which perennial plant, whose stalks are cooked and used in desserts, has poisonous leaves?

8 Who designed the fighter bomber the Mosquito?

9 Which unit of weight shares its name with the alternative name for a snow leopard?

10 What was Wendy Richard's character in *Are You Being Served* called?

11 Which murderer lived at No10 Rillington Place?

12 Which country does Ryan Giggs play for?

13 Which British football team was originally called Newton Heath?

14 In which year was the execution of King Charles 1?

15 Red, yellow and blue are what type of colour?

Things you didn't know...

An electric eel can produce 550 volts.

Answers to page 153

1 Earthquakes, 2 Mickey Rooney, 3 Elephants, 4 *Howards End,* 5 A butterfly, 6 Froze to death, 7 An otter, 8 Berlin, 9 Liz Hurley, 10 *Thank Your Lucky Stars,* 11 He required an emergency appendectomy, 12 Hawthorn, 13 Pastern, 14 Cowslip, 15 Reading.

QUIZ 150

Answers on page 154

1 Under what name does David Cornwell write?

2 What do arctophiles collect?

3 Which New Zealand born physicist was knighted in 1914 and made a baron in 1931?

4 Which star of *Casablanca* married Lauren Bacall?

5 Which Shakespeare character killed his wife, Desdemona?

6 Which 19th century French novelist spent 20 years exiled in Guernsey, writing?

7 Which Scottish group released an album in 1997 called *It Doesn't Matter Anymore*?

8 Who married Richard Burton twice?

9 When Ronald Reagan was US President who was his vice president?

10 If equine is horselike and canine doglike, what is vulpine?

11 What was the Latin name for England?

12 Which British soap was set in a motel?

13 If you had the letters FRCVS after your name, what would be your profession?

14 What is the capital of Costa Rica?

15 Who was the first Scottish footballer to make 100 appearances for his country?

Things you didn't know...

The Foreign Legion march at 88 steps a minute.

Answers to page 154

1 Sydney, 2 Tchaikovsky, 3 Frankenstein, 4 Fruit, 5 Luxor, 6 Kalahari, 7 Scotland, 8 Ken Dodd, 9 Crete, 10 *The Chicken Song,* 11 Germaine Greer, 12 Frankie Laine, 13 Nigeria, 14 Elton John, 15 Zimbabwe.

QUIZ 151

Answers on page 151

1 Which natural phenomena are measured on the richter scale?

2 Which much-married actor said "I'm the only man in the world who has a marriage licence made out To Whom It May Concern"?

3 Which animals took Hannibal over the Alps?

4 For which film did EmmaThompson win her 1993 Oscar?

5 What sort of creature is a painted lady?

6 How did Gerald Crich die in *Women in Love*?

7 What type of animal lives in a holt?

8 Where were the 1916 Olympic Games originally due to take place?

9 Which British actress/model played Vanessa Kensington in *Austin Powers: International Man of Mystery*?

10 On which programme did the Rolling Stones make their first TV appearance?

11 Why was the Coronation of Edward VII delayed for six weeks?

12 The flower of which tree is called May blossom?

13 What part of a horse's foot lies between the fetlock and foot bone?

14 Which flower of the primula family has the latin name primula veris?

15 What is the county town of Berkshire?

Things you didn't know...

Donald Duck is referred to in the Vatican newspaper as Donald Anus.

Answers to page 151

1 The USA, **2** The Fire of London, **3** Ants, **4** Kentucky, **5** Hilda, **6** Majorca, **7** Rhubarb, **8** De Havilland, **9** Ounce, **10** Miss Brahms, **11** John Christie, **12** Wales, **13** Manchester United, **14** 1649, **15** Primary.

QUIZ 152

Answers on page 152

1 Which city, in terms of population, is the largest in Australia?

2 Who wrote *Swan Lake*?

3 Which book, written by a 19-year-old, has been filmed many times including a 1994 version starring Robert de Niro and Kenneth Branagh ?

4 What kind of food is a tomato?

5 Near which city would you find the Colossi of Memnon?

6 Which large desert is situated in Botswana?

7 In which country is Hampden Park Stadium?

8 Which British comedian had a No 1 hit with *Tears* in 1965?

9 On which island was the maze containing the Minotaur?

10 What was the name of *Spitting Image*'s one and only No 1 UK chart hit?

11 Which Australian feminist wrote *The Female Eunuch*?

12 Who sang the theme song to *Rawhide*?

13 Which West African country is a federation of 19 states, including Abia, Delta and Plateau?

14 Who is Reg Dwight better known as?

15 Of which country did the Rev. Canaan Banana become President in 1980?

Things you didn't know...

The game of ice hockey was invented by the English when Kingston Harbour, Ontario, froze over in 1860.

Answers to page 152

1 John Le Carre, 2 Teddy bears, 3 Ernest Rutherford, 4 Humphrey Bogart, 5 Othello, 6 Victor Hugo, 7 *The Supernaturals,* 8 Elizabeth Taylor, 9 George Bush, 10 Foxlike, 11 Anglia, 12 *Crossroads,* 13 Veterinary Surgeon, 14 San Jose, 15 Kenny Dalglish.

QUIZ 153

Answers on page 157

1 If something is 'caseous' what is it like?

2 Name the most northerly and the most southerly points of the Australian mainland.

3 Which animal has the scientific name 'Vulpes vulpes'?

4 What sort of creature is a flying fox?

5 How long does it take to pour a pint of Guinness properly according to the advertising campaign in 1998?

6 What word is used to refer to the chess opening where a pawn or other piece is sacrificed for a later advantage?

7 In which film did Bing Crosby win his only Oscar?

8 Who played Private Walker in *Dads Army*?

9 Which German motor company bought Rolls Royce motor cars in 1998?

10 In which American city was there a famous 'Tea Party' in 1773?

11 In which city was the first public performance of Handel's *Messiah*?

12 Which sitcom was set on Craggy Island?

13 What sort of creature is a red admiral?

14 Who directed *The Quiet Man, Rio Grande* and *Stagecoach*?

15 Which pop group had a hit with *My Generation*?

Things you didn't know...

The giraffe was first known to English-speaking discoverers as the camelopard.

Answers to page 157

1 Pacific, 2 New Zealand, 3 Roe, 4 Cornish pasty, 5 Inverness, 6 Lada, 7 John Lydon, 8 Carl Perkins, 9 Sam Cooke, 10 Peace, 11 Crimean War, 12 Lambeth, 13 Peru, 14 *Dennis The Menace,* 15 Grover Cleveland.

QUIZ 154

Answers on page 158

1 Who was the mother of Queen Elizabeth 1?

2 Which guitarist is nicknamed 'Slow-hand'?

3 For which pint would Jack Dee sacrifice his professional integrity?

4 In the show *The Music Man*, how many cornets followed the trombones in the 'big parade'?

5 In general terms, what kind of food is bisque?

6 Which English cathedral is also a College chapel?

7 Which TV show surprises it's 'victims' with a big red book?

8 Which 19th century French novelist who wrote 300 short stories died aged 43, insane?

9 Who directed the 1989 film *The War Of The Roses*?

10 Who did Maddy Prior sing with?

11 What is James Bond's favourite tipple

12 Which prime minister made Queen Victoria Empress of India?

13 Which soccer club chairman once called his fans 'scum' and offered to forfeit a match?

14 How many legs does a queen bee have?

15 What was the title of the first U.K. number one hit for the pop group Queen?

Things you didn't know...

Golfballs were originally made of leather stuffed with feathers.

Answers to page 158

1 James Stewart, 2 The Bay City Rollers, 3 The eye, 4 Cain, 5 Charles Dickens, 6 Goat Island, 7 *Who Framed Roger Rabbit,* 8 Lanolin, 9 French, 10 Aberdeen, 11 Tom Keating's, 12 Tsunami, 13 Moscow, 14 A marsupial, 15 A long spoon.

QUIZ 155

Answers on page 155

1 Of which ocean is the sea of Japan a part?

2 The Kowhai is the national flower of which country?

3 What is caviar made from?

4 What is a Tiddy-oggie?

5 Which Scottish town is the administrative centre of the Highland Region?

6 Which car manufacturer produced the Samara?

7 What is punk star Johnny Rotten's real name?

8 Who wrote the song *Blue Suede Shoes*?

9 Who wrote *Twisting the Night Away*?

10 What are you seeking if you hold out an olive branch?

11 In which war did the Battle of Inkerman take place?

12 In which London borough is the Royal Festival Hall?

13 From which country did Paddington Bear come?

14 Hank Ketcham created which cartoon strip character in 1951?

15 Which US President born in 1837, was the only president to serve two separate terms?

Things you didn't know...

It took 5,000 calf skins to bind the 30 copies of the Gutenberg Bible printed in 1456.

Answers to page 155

1 Cheese, 2 Cape York and Wilson's Promontory, 3 Fox, 4 A bat, 5 119.5 seconds, 6 Gambit, 7 *Going My Way,* 8 James Beck, 9 VW, 10 Boston, 11 Dublin, 12 *Father Ted,* 13 Butterfly, 14 John Ford, 15 The Who.

QUIZ 156

Answers on page 156

1. Which actor thought he was the man who shot Liberty Valance?

2. Which Scottish band had a Number One hit single with *Give A Little Love* in 1975?

3. In which organ of the body is aqueous humour found?

4. In the Bible, who was the father of Enoch?

5. Who wrote *A Christmas Carol* and *The Cricket on the Hearth*?

6. Which island separates the two principal parts of Niagara Falls?

7. In which film did Bob Hoskins play Eddie Valiant?

8. What grease is extracted from sheep's wool?

9. What is the official language of the Ivory Coast?

10. Which club won the Scottish FA Cup three years running from 1982?

11. Which artist's biography was entitled *The Fake's Progress*?

12. What name is given to the wave caused by an earthquake on the sea bed?

13. In which city is the Kremlin?

14. What sort of creature is a honey mouse?

15. What do you need to sup with the devil?

Things you didn't know...

The total cost of building the Eiffel Tower was recouped in visitors' entrance fees a year after it had been finished.

Answers to page 156

1 Anne Boleyn, **2** Eric Clapton, **3** John Smiths, **4** 110, **5** Soup, **6** Christ Church, Oxford, **7** *This is Your Life,* **8** Guy de Maupassant, **9** Danny De Vito, **10** Steeleye Span, **11** Vodka Martini, **12** Benjamin Disraeli, **13** Ken Bates (Chelsea), **14** Six, **15** *Bohemian Rhapsody.*

QUIZ 157

Answers on page 161

1 Which country won the 1997 football tournament Le Tournoi?

2 Which 1997 British film starred Toby Stephens, Frances Barber and Ben Kingsley?

3 What does the place name suffix 'Kirk' signify?

4 Which pianist and sister of a famous actor accompanied Muffin the Mule?

5 What is champaign?

6 What are the grades of proficiency in judo called?

7 Which Prince is Duke of Edinburgh?

8 What is the term which means unsing a gentler expression to soften a blunt one?

9 According to The Platters, what gets in your eyes?

10 Who hosts the TV game show Family Fortunes?

11 Who was the first Habsburg Holy Roman Emperor?

12 Who first said: "A week is a long time in politics."?

13 Which word, Italian for air is used to describe a solo song with instrumental accompaniment in opera?

14 What is the artist Picasso's first name?

15 Who played the murderer in Kind Hearts and Coronets?

Things you didn't know...

The Statue of Liberty's nose is 4ft 6in long.

Answers to page 161

1 *Bedazzled*, 2 Badminton, 3 Dan Akroyd, 4 There was no winner!, 5 Sir Stanley Matthews, 6 James Ramsay MacDonald, 7 India, 8 Pfizer, 9 Faust, 10 Gigot, 11 Manilow, 12 A dog, 13 Wilson Kipketer, 14 George Boole, 15 Peter Mandelson.

QUIZ 158

Answers on page 162

1 Which car manufacturer has an Omega model in its range?

2 Which fish is the traditional ingredient of the Scandinavian dish Gravad Lax?

3 Which French philosopher refused the Nobel Prize for Literature in 1964?

4 Which TV detective was played by Raymond Burr?

5 Who demanded the head of John the Baptist?

6 Which of the five senses develops first?

7 Who had Top Ten hits in the 1960s with *Calendar Girl, I Go Ape* and *Little Devil*?

8 In which film did Meg Ryan's character battle alcoholism?

9 From which fruit is Slivovitz made?

10 Which artist painted 62 self portraits?

11 Which country had the world's first woman prime minister?

12 Which singer had a Top Ten hit single *Hotlegs* in 1978?

13 Where would you wear espadrilles?

14 What type of animal is a skink?

15 Which American rock-and-roll pianist had a hit with the song *Blueberry Hill*?

Things you didn't know...

Novelist Edgar Allan Poe used to write with a black cat sitting on his shoulder.

Answers to page 162

1 Eight, 2 Sebastian, 3 Ireland, 4 Julie Walters, 5 Howard Stern, 6 Cherry (wild) tree, 7 Phil Taylor, 8 Brazil, 9 Omdurman, 10 *Willie Wonka*, 11 Telescope, 12 USA, 13 Ernest Borgnine, 14 President John F. Kennedy, 15 Daddy-longlegs.

QUIZ 159

Answers on page 159

1 In which film did Peter Cook play the devilish George Spigott?

2 Which indoor court game is played with rackets and a shuttlecock?

3 Who traded places with Eddie Murphy in *Trading Places*?

4 Which horse won the 1993 Grand National?

5 Who was the first professional footballer to be knighted?

6 Who was the first Labour prime minister?

7 In which country was Salman Rushdie born?

8 Which company is responsible for producing the male impotency drug Viagra?

9 Which German scholar sold his soul to the devil in return for power and knowledge?

10 Which French word describes a leg of lamb or mutton prepared for the table?

11 Which Barry had a hit with a song called *Mandy*?

12 What sort of creature is a kelpie?

13 Which Kenyan-born runner broke Sebastian Coe's 16 year-old world 800m record in 1997?

14 Which British mathematician gave his name to a sort of algebra used in computing?

15 Which Labour minister did deputy prime minister John Prescott liken to a crab in 1997?

Things you didn't know...

The Old Testament contains 592,439 words.

Answers to page 159

1 England, **2** Photographing Fairies, **3** Church, **4** Annette Mills, **5** Flat, open country, **6** Dans, **7** Philip, **8** Euphemism, **9** Smoke, **10** Les Dennis, **11** Rudolph, **12** Harold Wilson, **13** Aria, **14** Pablo, **15** Dennis Price.

QUIZ 160

Answers on page 160

1 How many English kings have been called Henry?

2 Which saint was shot to death by arrows in 288 AD?

3 Against which team did Will Carling captain England for the last time?

4 Who starred as a middle-aged landlady in the film *Intimate Relations*?

5 Which US disc jockey was the inspiration for the film *Private Parts*?

6 What type of tree is a Prunus Avium?

7 Who was the world professional darts champion in 1990 and 1992?

8 Which is the only country through which both the equator and the Tropic of Capricorn pass?

9 Where did Lord Kitchener defeat the Mahdi in 1898?

10 Who owned the chocolate factory visited by Charlie Bucket in a Roald Dahl story?

11 What astronomy aid was built by Sir Isaac Newton in 1672?

12 Which country has the motto "E Pluribus Unum" on its Great Seal?

13 Who won Best actor award in 1956 in the film *Marty*?

14 A memorial to whom was unveiled by the Queen at Runnymede in May 1965?

15 How is a cranefly commonly known?

Things you didn't know...

Ice cream sodas were banned on Sundays, so somebody came up with a new invention – ice cream sundaes.

Answers to page 160

1 Vauxhall, 2 Salmon, 3 Jean Paul Sartre, 4 *Ironside,* 5 Salome, 6 Smell, 7 Neil Sedaka, 8 *When A Man Love A Woman,* 9 Plums, 10 Rembrandt, 11 Sri Lanka, 12 Rod Stewart, 13 On your feet, 14 A lizard, 15 Fats Domino.

QUIZ 161

Answers on page 165

1 What have you been doing if you finish by casting off?

2 According to legend, which city was founded by Romulus and Remus?

3 What is an army worm?

4 Who wrote the play *All's Well That Ends Well*?

5 Which airport was the subject of the TV 'docusoap' *Airport*?

6 What is singer Sade's surname?

7 Bargeman's Cabbage is also known as?

8 Which event featured the first live UK performance of the Spice Girls?

9 Who is the President of South Africa?

10 Which chain of stores was founded by Selim Zilkha in 1961?

11 Which horse won the 1998 Derby?

12 What is the architectural term for a bell tower?

13 What is a belvedere?

14 What is a saxhorn?

15 What was revealed by a letter to Lord Monteagle?

Things you didn't know...

Arnold Palmer became the world's first golf millionaire.

Answers to page 165

1 *Rawhide,* 2 A bird, 3 British thermal unit, 4 Macduff, 5 Mark Phillips, 6 Chartwell, 7 David, 8 Polio, 9 Jules Verne, 10 Robert Carlyle, 11 John Curry, 12 Disraeli, 13 Empire Day, 14 Geometry, 15 Aegean Sea.

QUIZ 162

Answers on page 166

1 Which car manufacturer produced the Corolla?

2 Which of Verdi's operas is set in Egypt?

3 What did Sir James Chadwick discover in 1932 while working at Cambridge?

4 On a monopoly board, which property clockwise is situated after the Water Works?

5 In which building are the Promenade Concerts now held?

6 In which country did Guy Gibson die?

7 Which country was Stalin leader of?

8 Who devised the radio programme *Desert Island Discs*?

9 Who starred in the title role of the TV series *Lou Grant*?

10 In what year was Lord Mountbatten murdered?

11 In which U.S. state is Palm Springs?

12 Which type of anaesthetic was first used in 1842?

13 Which *EastEnders'* character was played by Peter Dean?

14 Which Surrey golf course hosts the World MatchPlay Championships?

15 Who was the first to be buried in Poets' Corner, at Westminster Abbey?

Things you didn't know...

The aubergine is technically a fruit – it is a member of the tomato family.

Answers to page 166

1 Graham Hill, 2 Bradley Walsh, 3 Blondie, 4 Fern Britton, 5 Colin Firth, 6 Mexico, 7 Eastern Seaboard Standar Oil, 8 Nigeria, 9 Channel Isles, 10 Rotterdam, 11 Milton Keynes, 12 Legs, 13 US Civil War, 14 Walker Brothers, 15 Dexy's Midnight Runners.

QUIZ 163

Answers on page 163

1 In which 1950's and 60's TV western drama series did Clint Eastwood play a scout?

2 What sort of creature is a kite?

3 Which unit of energy is represented by the initials btu?

4 Who killed *Macbeth* in Shakespeare's play?

5 What was Princess Anne's first husband called?

6 What was Winston Churchill's home in Kent called?

7 Which saint's day is celebrated on 1 March?

8 Against which disease was the Salk vaccine developed?

9 Who wrote *Journey To the Centre of the Earth*?

10 Who starred as TV's *Hamish Macbeth*?

11 Which British skater won Olympic, European and World titles in 1976?

12 Which British prime minister wrote *Vivian Grey*?

13 What was Commonwealth Day called before 1958?

14 In which field of science would you encounter the Pons Asinorum?

15 Which section of the Mediterranean Sea contains the Clyclades and Dodecanese islands?

Things you didn't know...

When Masai tribesmen meet they spit at each other,
it's considered polite!

Answers to page 163

1 Knitting, 2 Rome, 3 Caterpillar, 4 William Shakespeare, 5 Heathrow, 6 Adu, 7 Wild Turnip, 8 A Royal Gala, 9 Nelson Mandela, 10 Mothercare, 11 High Rise, 12 Campanile, 13 Viewing turret, 14 Musical instrument, 15 The Gunpowder Plot.

QUIZ 164

Answers on page 164

1 Which Briton was World Motor Racing Champion in 1962 and 1968?

2 Who presented the TV gameshow *Midas Touch*?

3 Which American band had a Number One hit with *Heart of Glass*?

4 Who presented TV's *Celebrity Ready Steady Cook*?

5 Who played Mr.Darcy in the BBC production of *Pride and Prejudice*?

6 In 1986 which became the first country to host football's World Cup for a second time?

7 What does ESSO stand for?

8 Which was the only football team from a Commonwealth country to play in the 1994 World Cup Final tournament in the U.S.A.?

9 In which part of the British Isles would you find bailiwicks?

10 What is the world's biggest port?

11 Which city was allocated an extra M.P. at the 1992 general election?

12 On what part of the body would you wear a pair of puttees?

13 In which war was the Battle of Gettysburg?

14 Who had a 1960's hit with *Make it Easy On Yourself*?

15 Who had a Number One hit single with *Geno* in 1980?

Things you didn't know...

Bagpipes were played in Persia, Egypt and Greece long before the Scots adopted them from the Romans.

Answers to page 164

1 Toyota, **2** *Aida,* **3** The Neutron, **4** Piccadily, **5** Royal Albert Hall, **6** Holland, **7** USSR, **8** Roy Plomley, **9** Ed Asner, **10** 1979, **11** California, **12** Ether, **13** Pete Beale, **14** Wentworth, **15** Geoffrey Chaucer.

QUIZ 165

Answers on page 169

1 Who co-starred with Clint Eastwood and won an Oscar nomination for his performance in the1974 film *Thunderbolt And Lightfoot*?

2 Which was the world's first antibiotic?

3 Who wrote *Mrs Dalloway*?

4 Which club knocked Liverpool out of the UEFA Cup in October 1995?

5 Which John Lennon song was said to have been inspired by a police two-tone siren?

6 What sort of animal is a Lippizaner?

7 By what name is the plant Lonicera better known?

8 Which ocean was at the heart of Michael Palin's *Full Circle*?

9 Which TV comedy drama about the Territorial Army was set in *Roker Bridge*?

10 What was the title of the famous folklore study by Sir J G Frazer?

11 Which *Goodfellas* star played a serial killer in the film *Turbulence*?

12 To what does the adjective 'Pontic' apply?

13 What is the capital of Scotland?

14 Who wrote *The Rector's Wife*?

15 What is the national airline of the Czech Republic?

Things you didn't know...

The first advert on Radio Luxembourg was for a laxative.

Answers to page 169

1 Paul Scott, 2 An Eyrie, 3 In Mali, West Africa, 4 Turkish, 5 The Yangtse-Kiang, 6 Severn, 7 Ernest Marples, 8 Mercury, 9 Camelot, 10 Kim Campbell (First lady PM), 11 Queen's Park, 12 Naseem Hamed, 13 Perihelion, 14 Laos, 15 Cooper.

QUIZ 168

Answers on page 170

1 How many points win a game of cribbage?

2 What is Bill Clinton's middle name?

3 Which actor played the part of Hercule Poirot in the 1974 film *Murder on the Orient Express*?

4 Who is the quiz-master on Radio Four's *The News Quiz*?

5 Who starred in the title role in the 1970s television sitcom *Queenie's Castle*?

6 Which American building can be found at 1600 Pennsylvania Avenue?

7 How did Georgi Markov make the headlines in 1978?

8 At which battle did the Campbells kill 38 members of the rival MacDonald clan?

9 What are Jerseys, Guernseys and Dexters?

10 In which film did Dustin Hoffman play Tom Cruise's autistic brother?

11 Which US state is Little Rock the capital of?

12 What were the first names of the England cricketer W.G. Grace?

13 Which group had their first Number One single in 1995 with *Fairground*?

14 Which number is at twelve o'clock on a dart board?

15 In the *Avenger's* TV series, what name was given to the wheelchair ridden boss?

Things you didn't know...

Frederick the Great used Champagne instead of water in his coffee.

Answers to page 170

1 Bristol, **2** Milan, **3** *Cat On A Hot Tin Roof,* **4** Oasis, **5** Devon Malcolm, **6** Dundee, **7** Judy Loe, **8** Muff, **9** Geoffrey Robinson, **10** CATS, **11** Sudan, **12** Gene Hackman, **13** Debbie Reynolds, **14** Judy Garland, **15** *Apocalypse Now.*

QUIZ 167

Answers on page 167

1 Which British novelist wrote *The Jewel in the Crown*?

2 What name is given to an eagle's home?

3 Where is Timbuktu?

4 From what language do the words kiosk, tulip and coffee come?

5 What is the name of China's greatest river?

6 Which river flows through Shrewsbury?

7 Who opened the first motorway in England in 1959?

8 Hg is the chemical symbol for which element?

9 What is the name of the consortium that runs the National Lottery?

10 Who became PM of Canada in 1993 and set a 'first' record?

11 What is Scotland's oldest football club?

12 Which British boxer is commonly called Prince?

13 What is the point in the orbit of a body around the sun at which it is closest to the sun called?

14 Of which country is the Kip the basic unit of currency?

15 Which Henry was British heavyweight champion in 1963?

Things you didn't know...

Bear grease was used as a hair restorer in the 18th century.

Answers to page 167

1 Jeff Bridges, 2 Penicillin, 3 Virginia Woolf, 4 Brondby, 5 *I Am The Walrus*, 6 A horse, 7 Honeysuckle or Woodbine, 8 The Pacific, 9 *Preston Front,* 10 *The Golden Bough,* 11 Ray Liotta, 12 The Black Sea, 13 Edinburgh, 14 Joanna Trollope, 15 CSA.

QUIZ 168

Answers on page 168

1 Which city had the dialling code was 0272 prior to April 1995?

2 In which city would you find the streets Via Morte, Via Napoleone and Via Spiga?

3 In which 1958 film did Burl Ives, Paul Newman and Elizabeth Taylor star in?

4 Which rock band had a hit with the single *D' You know What I Mean*?

5 Which English bowler took 9 wickets in an innings against South Africa in 1994?

6 Which Scottish city stands on the River Tay?

7 Which actress was the wife of the late actor Richard Beckinsale?

8 On what part of your body would you wear a muff?

9 Which paymaster-general resigned from office in December 1998?

10 Which West End and Broadway musical was adapted from T.S. Elliott's *Old Possum Poems*?

11 Which country lies immediately to the south of Egypt?

12 Who played Lex Luthor in the *Superman* films of the 1970s and 1980s?

13 Who is Carrie Fisher's mother?

14 Who is Liza Minelli's mother?

15 In which film, based on Conrad's *Heart of Darkness*, did Martin Sheen seek Marlon Brando?

Things you didn't know...

The liver of the polar bear is so rich in Vitamin A that it's poisonous to humans.

Answers to page 168

1 121, 2 Jefferson, 3 Albert Finney, 4 Barry Took, 5 Diana Dors, 6 The White House, 7 Died from poisoned tip of umbrella stab, 8 Glencoe, 9 Breeds of cattle, 10 *Rain Man,* 11 Arkansas, 12 William Gilbert, 13 Simply Red, 14 20, 15 Mother.

QUIZ 169

1 In which town is the brewing company of Hook Norton based?

2 Which former Radio One DJ was appointed to the Tory's new 'creative forum'?

3 To which common English surname would the Italian surname 'Sartori' translate?

4 Who did Richard Branson sell 49% of Virgin Rail to?

5 Which national newspaper editor was named as an MI6 agent in 1998?

6 Who won the FA Premiership in 1998?

7 What does the symbol HB stand for on a pencil?

8 Which aircraft has become the best selling airliner in history?

9 What is the motto of the BBC?

10 Which ventriloquist partners Lord Charles?

11 Who is the lead singer with Simple Minds?

12 Which Englishman invented the calculating machine?

13 What is the longest river in the British Isles?

14 Who is the lead singer of the "Britpop" group Pulp?

15 England's best win at soccer was 13-0 in 1982. Who were they playing?

Things you didn't know...

Japanese women wear padded underwear to make their bottoms appear more rounded.

Answers to page 173

1 Virginia Woolf, 2 Peter Gabriel, 3 Peru, 4 Austria, 5 Graffiti, 6 Germany, 7 Drums, 8 Germany, 9 Nectarine, 10 C S Forester, 11 1903, 12 Doha, 13 *Treasure Island,* 14 Barbarossa, 15 The Mantle.

QUIZ 172

Answers on page 174

1 How many years are celebrated by a platinum anniversary?

2 With which swimming stroke do races begin in the water?

3 What is the administrative centre Derbyshire?

4 In which cult TV series will you find FBI agents Mulder and Scully?

5 Which European country has 482 islands?

6 Where was Jesus born?

7 What colour is a motorway destination sign?

8 What is the name of the park where *Yogi Bear* lives?

9 In what year did Salman Rushdie go into hiding?

10 What was Mariah Carey's 1997 album release?

11 What is the capital of Nicaragua?

12 Which highly salted body of water lies between the borders of Israel and Jordan?

13 What is the world's tallest mammal?

14 Which German band that had a 1991 hit with *Wind Of Change*?

15 What is Scotland's largest city?

Things you didn't know...

The tuna fish has to keep swimming, otherwise it suffocates.

Answers to page 174

1 Bill Bailey, 2 Cabbage, 3 Yemen, 4 Suzi Quatro, 5 June Allyson, 6 Geometry, 7 Wall Street, 8 90 feet, 9 Johnson Matthey Bankers, 10 Neville Chamberlain, 11 Gerald Ford, 12 Argentina, 13 Butcher, 14 Sandringham, 15 Buddhism.

QUIZ 171

Answers on page 171

1 Who wrote *To the Lighthouse*?

2 Who had a Top Twenty hit with *Solsbury Hill* in April 1977?

3 What was *Paddington Bear*'s country of origin?

4 The Spanish Riding School is in which country?

5 Which Italian word is used for scribblings found on the walls of public buildings?

6 From which country does the wine Johannisberger come from?

7 Gene Krupa is rated the greatest jazz musician on what instrument?

8 Which European country produces Hock?

9 What is the name given to the fruit which is a cross between a plum and a peach?

10 Who created the naval character *Hornblower*?

11 In which year were cars first required to be registered?

12 What is the capital of Qatar?

13 Which famous adventure story was originally titled *The Sea Cook*?

14 What was the Second World War German invasion of Russia codenamed what by Hitler?

15 What is the layer of rock immediately under the crust of the Earth called?

Things you didn't know...

Ducks only lay eggs in the morning.

Answers to page 171

1 Banbury, 2 Bruno Brooks, 3 Taylor, 4 Stagecoach, 5 Dominic Lawson (The Sunday Telegraph), 6 Arsenal, 7 Hard-black, 8 Boeing 737, 9 Nation shall speak peace unto nation, 10 Ray Alan, 11 Jim Kerr, 12 Charles Babbage, 13 Shannon, 14 Jarvis Cocker, 15 Ireland.

QUIZ 172

Answers on page 172

1 Who, in a song, was thrown out 'with nothing but a fine tooth comb'?

2 'Brassica oleracea' is better known as what?

3 Which country is Sana the capital of?

4 Who had Number One hits with *Can the Can* and *Devil Gate Drive*?

5 Who played Glenn Miller's wife in *The Glenn Miller Story*?

6 Euclid is associated with which branch of mathematics?

7 In which street is the New York Stock Exchange situated?

8 What is the distance in feet between bases in baseball?

9 Which British bank was baled out in September 1984?

10 Who did Churchill replace as prime minister in May 1940?

11 In September 1975, two assassination attempts were made in the space of 17 days on which American president?

12 Which South American country were runners-up in the first football World Cup?

13 What was the trade of Thomas Wolsey's father?

14 What is the name of the Queen's residence in Norfolk?

15 Of the various religions practised in Singapore, which is the largest?

Things you didn't know...

Although Walt Disney had a moustach, nobody who worked for him was allowed to grow one.

Answers to page 172

1 Seventy, 2 Backstroke, 3 Matlock, 4 *The X Files*, 5 Denmark, 6 Bethlehem, 7 Blue, 8 Jellystone Park, 9 1989, 10 Butterfly, 11 Managua, 12 Dead Sea, 13 Giraffe, 14 Scorpion, 15 Glasgow.

QUIZ 173

Answers on page 177

1 What is the popular name of the garden flower Tropaeolum?

2 What surname are you most likely to have if your nickname was Spud?

3 Who was the star of *Zorba The Greek*?

4 By what name is 24th June known as?

5 With which sport does one associate Sugar Ray Robinson?

6 Which animal lives in a citadel?

7 What is the worlds largest city in population?

8 How many sides does a heptagon have?

9 What was Chris de Burgh's 1986 Number One hit?

10 Which revolutionary was the first leader of communist Russia?

11 Which fungal disease of trees was first described in the Netherlands?

12 Which veteran actor won an Oscar in 1981 for his role as Dudley Moore's valet in *Arthur*?

13 Which Archbishop of Canterbury seized the devil's nose in a pair of red-hot tongs?

14 The Ancient Olympics were held in honour of which Greek god?

15 Which infectious disease of rabbits and hares was introduced to the UK during the 1950s as a pest-control measure?

Things you didn't know...

Richard I spent only six months of his ten-year reign in England.

Answers to page 177

1 Sir Herbert Beerbohm Tree, 2 Apple, 3 George Peppard, 4 Primo Carnera, 5 Dams, 6 Odysseus, 7 A fish, 8 Anna Karenina, 9 Jack Johnson, 10 Barley, 11 Dooley Wilson, 12 *Last of the Summer Wine*, 13 John Landy, 14 King Arthur, 15 Aneurin Bevan.

QUIZ 174

Answers on page 178

1. In which Simon and Garfunkel song do the words 'Jesus loves you more than you can say' appear?

2. Which film from *Muriel's Wedding* director P.J. Hogan starred Julia Roberts in a comic role?

3. Which British novelist wrote *The Forsyte Saga*?

4. How many points are scored for a try and conversion in Rugby Union?

5. Which tennis player once said 'People go to Laver to talk about tennis, they come to me to talk about abortions'?

6. What wouldn't come back for Charlie Drake in 1961?

7. Who directed Whitney Houston in the film *The Bodyguard*?

8. In which city is the Fitzwilliam Museum?

9. Which U.S. state has shores on four of the five Great Lakes?

10. In which decade was 30mph speed limit introduced in Britain in built-up areas?

11. Cheddar Gorge runs through which hills?

12. Who is the host of TV's *The South Bank Show*?

13. Which national newspaper was launched on 15 February 1998?

14. What sort of creature is a goby?

15. Who was the faithful wife of Ulysses?

Things you didn't know...

Mark Twain was the first author to send his publisher a typewritten manuscript.

Answers to page 178

1 Bananarama's, **2** The Coburg, **3** *Wee Willie Winkle,* **4** Hawkeye, **5** Gemini, **6** *So You Win Again,* **7** It is the only feature film to have been made in Esperanto, **8** Royal Society for the Prevention of Accidents, **9** Neil Armstrong, **10** Napoleon, **11** Seaweed, **12** Supermarket, **13** Cambridge, **14** Luxembourg, **15** A snake.

QUIZ 175

Answers on page 175

1 Which actor and theatre manager founded the Royal Academy of Dramatic Art?

2 What sort of fruit is a Laxton Superb?

3 Who played the TV detective *Banacek*?

4 Which Italian former heavyweight boxing champion acted in the film *On the Waterfront*?

5 Inguri, Nurek and Guavio are among the world's highest what?

6 Which Greek first thought of the idea of the Trojan Horse?

7 What sort of creature is a dace?

8 Which Tolstoy heroine threw herself under a train?

9 Who was the first coloured boxer to be World Heavyweight Champion?

10 Which is the main cereal used to make both Irish and Scotch whisky?

11 In *Casablanca* who played Sam, the piano player?

12 In which popular TV series did a character called Seymour Atterthwaite appear for one series?

13 Who broke Roger Bannister's mile record?

14 Who was *The Once and Future King* written about by T H White?

15 Which British Labour politician was the architect of the National Health Service as minister of health from 1945 to 1951?

Things you didn't know...

Popcorn was invented by the American Indians.

Answers to page 175

1 Nasturtium, 2 Murphy, 3 Anthony Quinn, 4 Midsummer Day, 5 Boxing, 6 Mole, 7 Tokyo, Japan, 8 Seven, 9 *The Lady in Red,* 10 Lenin, 11 Dutch elm disease, 12 John Gielgud, 13 Dunstan, 14 Zeus, 15 Myxomatosis.

QUIZ 176

Answers on page 176

1 Which pop group's road manager was shot dead in Northern Ireland in 1986?

2 What was the original name of the building now known as The Old Vic?

3 Who ran through the town, upstairs and downstairs, in his nightgown?

4 What nickname was given to *M*A*S*H* character Benjamin Pearce?

5 Which sign of the zodiac covers part of both May and June?

6 What was the name of Hot Chocolate's only Number One hit in the UK?

7 What is unqique about the 1965 film *Incubus*, starring *Star Trek* actor William Shatner?

8 Which society is abbreviated RoSPA?

9 Who was the commander of Apollo 11?

10 Who sailed away to die on HMS Bellerophon?

11 Devil's Apron and Purple Laver are types of what?

12 What was the setting for the 1984 TV series *Tripper's Day*?

13 In which city is Harvard University?

14 What is the capital of the Grand Dutchy of Luxembourg?

15 What is a taipan?

Things you didn't know...

A vast area of Japan's shallow inland sea is taken up with the nets, fences and buoys used to cultivate seaweed.

Answers to page 176

1 Mrs Robinson, 2 My Best Friend's Wedding, 3 John Galsworthy, 4 Seven, 5 Billy Jean King, 6 Boomerang, 7 Mike Jackson, 8 Cambridge, 9 Michigan, 10 1930's (1935), 11 The Mendips, 12 Melvyn Bragg, 13 Sunday Business, 14 A fish, 15 Penelope.

QUIZ 177

Answers on page 181

1 Which Noel said 'Television is something you appear on:you don't watch it'?

2 Where in London is the American Embassy?

3 Where does a Manx person come from?

4 What appears on the flag of Cyprus beneath the outline of the island?

5 Who plays against Rangers in an Auld Firm derby match?

6 Babylon was situated south of which modern day capital city?

7 Which of the big cats have tear stain facial markings?

8 What is kohlrabi?

9 Which actor co-starred with Katherine Hepburn in nine films, including *Guess Who's Coming to Dinner*?

10 What is the most popular cheese in America?

11 Which vegetables, popular in Chinese dishes, are the bulb-like stems of the bulrush?

12 Which Chris hosted *Win a Million* on TV?

13 Who had a 1962 hit with *Right Said Fred*?

14 Which country did the first Miss World come from?

15 Who is the youngest of the three Bronte sisters?

Things you didn't know...

The kiwi has its nostrils at the end of its beak.

Answers to page 181

1 Doric, 2 Sir Gary Sobers, 3 Sea of Marmara, 4 Geoffrey Palmer, 5 Equestrianism - 3 day event, 6 You'd vomit, 7 John Kenneth Galbraith, 8 The Brontes, 9 Crown Jewels, 10 (Jean) Martinet, 11 The midnight oil, 12 Nitrogen, 13 Rockall, 14 They are cousins, 15 Billy Joel.

QUIZ 178

Answers on page 182

1 What type of dance involves moving under a low horizontal pole?

2 Which singer did former Welsh secretary Ron Davies mistakenly believe had sent him a letter of support following his resignation?

3 Which nineteenth century Russian composed *Pictures At An Exhibition*?

4 In which country does the Nile reach the sea?

5 In which US city did the summer Olympic Games of 1984 take place?

6 In which TV hospital does Charlie Fairhead work?

7 Who created the *Peanuts* cartoon?

8 What is the capital of South Australia?

9 In which famous adventure story is Harry Faversham the central character?

10 Which former pupil of Plato founded the Peripatetic school at Athens?

11 From which country did the Bashi Bazouks come?

12 *God Bless Africa* is the national anthem of which country?

13 What was the only religion in Japan prior to the sixth century A.D.?

14 Who recorded the albums *After the Goldrush* and *Harvest*?

15 Who is married to Brabantio's daughter?

Things you didn't know...

International athletics races are always run in an anti-clockwise direction.

Answers to page 182

1 Dumfries, 2 Belgium, 3 Cilla Black, 4 Holland, 5 An opera, 6 Bedrock, 7 Fungi, 8 Louise Brown, 9 Simon Ward, 10 Kevin Keegan, 11 Shelagh Delaney, 12 Balmoral, 13 White, 14 Patsy Kensitt, 15 Morris Motors Ltd.

QUIZ 179

Answers on page 179

1 Which style of architecture is the Parthenon in Athens?

2 Which cricketer was the first to hit six sixes in an over?

3 Which sea lies between the Bosporus and the Dardanelles?

4 Who played Major Harry Truscott in the TV series *Fairly Secret Army*?

5 In which sport did Richard Meade win Olympic gold?

6 What would happen if you took an emetic medicine?

7 Which American economist and diplomat wrote *The Affluent Society*?

8 Which literary family lived at Haworth in Yorkshire?

9 What did Colonel Thomas Blood attempt to steal in 1671?

10 Which French soldier's name became the word for a strict disciplinarian?

11 Proverbially, what do late workers burn?

12 Which chemical element is found in all proteins?

13 Which British island, about 80 feet across, is in the Atlantic, 230 miles west of the Hebrides?

14 What is the relationship between Prince Andrew and Lord Lindley?

15 In 1979, whose album called *52nd Street* won a Grammy award?

Things you didn't know...

For a horse to win racings 'Triple Crown' he must win the Derby, St Leger and Two Thousand Guineas.

Answers to page 179

1 Coward, 2 Grosvenor Square, 3 Isle of Man, 4 Two olive branches, 5 Celtic, 6 Baghdad, 7 Cheetahs, 8 A vegetable (cabbage), 9 Spencer Tracy, 10 Cheddar, 11 Water chestnuts, 12 Tarrant, 13 Bernard Cribbins, 14 Sweden, 15 Anne.

QUIZ 180

Answers on page 180

1 If you travelled directly north from Workington by air over which city would you fly first?

2 Sabena is the national airline of which country?

3 How is Priscilla White better known?

4 Which country is also known as The Netherlands?

5 In musical terms who, or what is a Boris Godunov?

6 In which town do the *Flintstones* live?

7 Mycology is the study of what?

8 What is the name of the world's first test tube baby?

9 Who played the title role in *Young Winston*?

10 Which soccer player advertised Brut in the 1980s?

11 Who wrote *A Taste of Honey*?

12 What is the Queen's residence in Scotland called?

13 To which common English surname would the German surname Weiss translate?

14 Who played fashion designer Suzette in the 1986 film *Absolute Beginners*?

15 Which car manufacturing firm was founded by the late Lord Nuffield?

Things you didn't know...

Liverpool's FA Cup winning side of 1986 did not contain a single Englishman.

Answers to page 180

1 Limbo, 2 Diana Ross, 3 Mussorgsky, 4 Egypt, 5 Los Angeles, 6 Holby General (*Casualty*), 7 Schulz, 8 Adelaide, 9 *The Four Feathers*, 10 Aristotle, 11 Turkey, 12 Zimbabwe, 13 Shintoism, 14 Neil Young, 15 Othello.

QUIZ 181

Answers on page 185

1 The Norwegian Spruce is better known by what name?

2 What name is given to a complete set of print characters of the same typeface, size and style?

3 With which instrument is Max Roach associated?

4 What is a labret?

5 What name was given to the race of one-eyed giants in Greek mythology?

6 Who played Leslie Grantham's brother in *The Paradise Club*?

7 Which model replaced the Ford Anglia in 1967?

8 A jumbuck is an Australian slang word for which type of animal?

9 Which city is served by O'Hare airport?

10 What sort of creature is a lynx?

11 A pearl wedding celebrates how many years of marriage?

12 Which US rap duo had 1988 hits with *Push it and Twist* and *Shout*?

13 Which TV detective is played by Peter Falk?

14 Lindos, Ixia and Trianda are towns on which Greek holiday island?

15 In which constituency did Shirley Williams win a by-election for the SDP in 1981?

Things you didn't know...

Tennis sensation Martina Hingis was the youngest-ever person to reach No 1 in the World rankings.

Answers to page 185

1 U2, **2** Aldwich, **3** Harold Wilson, **4** Don Cockell, **5** Managua, **6** TWA, **7** El Cid, **8** Nairobi, **9** Spanish, **10** Scampi, **11** George Best, **12** Mario Soares, **13** Copenhagen, **14** Captain Matthew Webb, **15** Munih.

QUIZ 182

Answers on page 186

1 Which TV series made Jonathan Routh famous?

2 What name is given to a Church in Scotland?

3 How much did the first Jaguar car cost when it rolled off the production line in 1935?

4 Who was King of England, Scotland, and Ireland from 1625 to 1649?

5 Which island was called Mona by Caesar in the first century BC?

6 Which soft yellow precious metal has the chemical symbol Au?

7 Who was the mother-in-law of Angus Ogilvy?

8 Who swam the Hellespont every night to see his lover, Hero?

9 On television, who played the female half of *Sapphire and Steel*?

10 Who is the patron saint of carpenters?

11 Which bird has the scientific name 'Aluad arvensis'?

12 In which English county is Glastonbury?

13 What is the capital of Byelorussia?

14 Which battle of 1645 is said to have cost Charles I his throne?

15 Which *Brookside* character was played by Bill Dean?

Things you didn't know...

Lea and Perrins Worcestershire sauce is aged for
two years before it is bottled.

Answers to page 186

1 Peter Brook, 2 Eden, 3 Dana, 4 Bolivia, 5 Austria, 6 Sir Alec Guinness, 7 Petticoat Lane, 8 Hockenheim, 9 6, 10 Hammerfest, 11 Ten, 12 Elvis Costello, 13 Marseilles, 14 Freddie, 15 Maria Callas.

QUIZ 183

Answers on page 183

1 Who had a Number One hit single with *The Fly in 1991*?

2 Where in London did an IRA bus bomb occur in February 1996?

3 Who said 'That doesn't mean of course, that the pound here in Britain - in your pocket, purse or bank - has been devalued'?

4 Which British boxer went 9 rounds with Rocky Marciano in 1955 before being knocked out?

5 What is the capital of Nicaragua?

6 Which American airline did Howard Hughes once own?

7 How is Spanish Soldier Rodrigo Diaz de Vivar better known?

8 What is the capital of Kenya?

9 What is the official language of Uruguay?

10 By what other name is a Norway Lobster called?

11 In the 1960s which footballer was called 'The Fifth Beatle'?

12 Who was elected president of Portugal in 1986?

13 Where would you see the statue of *The Little Mermaid*?

14 Who was the first man to swim the English Channel?

15 Which German city has a chiming clock with two tiers of dancing figures which emerge twice daily?

Things you didn't know...

Bulls chase clothed people but tend to ignore naked intruders.

Answers to page 183

1 Christmas tree, **2** Font, **3** Drums, **4** A lip ornament, **5** Cyclops, **6** Don Henderson, **7** Escort, **8** Sheep, **9** Chicago, **10** A wildcat, **11** 30, **12** Salt 'N' Pepa, **13** Columbo, **14** Rhodes, **15** Crosby.

QUIZ 184

Answers on page 184

1 Who directed the film version of William Golding's *Lord of the Flies*?

2 Which British PM resigned over the Suez crisis?

3 Who had a Number One hit with *All kinds of Everything*?

4 Which country is the leading producer of tin in the world?

5 In which country was Adolf Hitler born?

6 Which leading British actor has a book out called *My Name Escapes Me*?

7 Middlesex Street has another more famous, though unofficial name. What is it?

8 Where is the German motor racing grand prix held?

9 How many geese were a laying in the Christmas song?

10 Which is Europe's most northerly town?

11 How many arms bearing suckers does a squid possess?

12 Who had a Top Ten hit in 1979 with *Oliver's Army*?

13 What is France's biggest sea port?

14 Who sang with The Dreamers?

15 Which great soprano earned the name of La Divina?

Things you didn't know...

Benjamin Disraeli's false teeth once fell out whilst he was making a speech in the House of Commons.

Answers to page 184

1 Candid Camera, 2 Kirk, 3 £385, 4 Charles 1, 5 Isle of Man, 6 Gold, 7 Princess Marina, 8 Leander, 9 Joanna Lumley, 10 Joseph, 11 Skylark, 12 Somerset, 13 Minsk, 14 Naseby, 15 Harry Cross.

QUIZ 185

Answers on page 189

1 In which year of the 1980's was President Zia of Pakistan killed in an air crash?

2 What medical word is used for white blood cells?

3 Which letter is at the bottom right of a standard typewriter keyboard?

4 Which rap outfit released an album entitled *No Way Out*?

5 What would your occupation be if your work involved you with MIG and TIG?

6 Born in Canada in 1858, which Prime Minister died in office after only 7 months?

7 William Shakespeare was a part owner of the Globe and which other theatre?

8 Which spirit forms the base of a 'Horse's Neck'?

9 Who is the ruling prince of Monaco?

10 Who composed the Pathetique symphony?

11 Which player came on as substitute and scored two goals to win the F.A. Cup in 1989?

12 In the Bible whose wife was turned into a pillar of salt?

13 What did Persia change its name to in 1935?

14 Which sportsman is nicknamed 'Guy the Gorilla'?

15 What is the capital of Grenada?

Things you didn't know...

The 1908 Olympics should have been held in Rome, but the Italians withdrew because of financial problems.

Answers to page 189

1 Henry Rider Haggard, 2 Haemoglobin, 3 Stethoscope, 4 Capercaillie, 5 Old Kent Road, 6 The capybara, 7 Warren Beatty, 8 The Pyramids at Giza, 9 Airtours PLC, 10 Duke of Windsor, 11 Andrew, 12 Belinda Carlisle, 13 Grand National, 14 Jimmy McGovern, 15 The Vatican City.

QUIZ 186

Answers on page 190

1 Who was Prime minister when the First World War started?

2 Who co-starred with Charles Grodin in the film *Midnight Run*?

3 There are two Cleopatra's needles. One on the London embankment, where's the other?

4 Sb is the symbol for antimony. True or False?

5 Who starred with Vivien Leigh in *Gone With the Wind*?

6 What record was a chart topping hit for Showaddywaddy in 1975?

7 Who discovered the basic laws of genetics whilst analysing peas in a monastery garden?

8 Who sang the theme song to the Bond film *The Spy Who Loved Me*?

9 Who wrote *Pygmalion*?

10 With which wood did Thomas Chippendale principally work in the 18th century?

11 In what field was the Bauhaus movement?

12 What do we call the constellation that Americans call The Big Dipper?

13 Which former President of the Board of trade was nicknamed Mandy?

14 Which 1985 film starred Mickey Rourke, Kim Basinger and a fridge?

15 What type of aircraft crashed over Lockerbie?

Things you didn't know...

During his spell in charge of England, Terry Venables lost only one match, excluding penalty shoot-outs.

Answers to page 190

1 River Tay, 2 Tunisia, 3 Peter Lilley, 4 *Big Spender,* 5 Eleven, 6 Basil Spence, 7 *Countdown,* 8 Private Eye, 9 R D Blackmore, 10 Nijinsky, 11 Bees, 12 Fort Knox, 13 Uncle Remus, 14 Little John, 15 Hedges and shrubs.

QUIZ 187

Answers on page 187

1 Who wrote *King Solomon's Mines* in 1885?

2 What is the most important component of Red Blood cells?

3 Which medical device was invented by Dr Rene Laennec to preserve his female patients' modesty?

4 Which game bird's group name is a tok?

5 On a British Monopoly board which is the first property you reach after passing 'GO'?

6 What is the world's largest rodent?

7 Who was the male star of the film *Shampoo*?

8 What are the only survivors of the ancient Seven Wonders of the World?

9 Who owns the travel agency network Going Places?

10 Who was Governor of the Bahamas during the Second World War?

11 Which Prince was a helicopter pilot in the Falklands War?

12 Who had a Number One hit in 1988 with *Heaven Is a Place On Earth*?

13 In which steeplechase did Devon Loch fall when victory was in sight?

14 Who created *Cracker* the TV series?

15 What is the smallest independent state in the World?

Things you didn't know...

The first film to be shown on television was The Bride featuring George Robey.

Answers to page 187

1 1988, 2 Leucocytes, 3 M, 4 *Puff Daddy & The Family*, 5 Welder, 6 Andrew Bonar Law, 7 Blackfriars, 8 Brandy, 9 Rainier, 10 Tchaikovsky, 11 Ian Rush, 12 Lot, 13 Iran, 14 Ian Botham, 15 St. George's.

QUIZ 188

Answers on page 188

1 What is the longest river in Scotland?

2 Of which country is Sfax the second largest city?

3 Who was deputy leader of the Conservative party in December 1998?

4 Which song from *Sweet Charity* has since become strongly associated with Shirley Bassey?

5 How many Academy Awards did *Titanic* win?

6 Who designed Coventry Cathedral and Sussex University?

7 Which long-running game shown was the first programme to be shown on Channel Four?

8 Which magazine has been edited by Richard Ingrams and Ian Hislop?

9 Who wrote the historical romance *Lorna Doone*?

10 Which horse won racing's 'Triple Crown', the Derby, St Leger and Two Thousand Guineas in 1970?

11 Which insects live in apiaries?

12 Which Kentucky army post is the location of the U.S. gold bullion depository?

13 In the stories by Joel Chandler Harris about the exploits of Brer Rabbit and Brer Fox, who is the narrator?

14 Who was the tallest of Robin Hood's men?

15 On what material does a topiarist work?

Things you didn't know...

Newscaster Reginald Bosanquet's cricketer father, BJT Bosanquet, invented the googly.

Answers to page 188

1 Herbert Asquith, 2 Robert De Niro, 3 Central Park, New York, 4 True, 5 Clark Gable, 6 *3 Steps To Heaven,* 7 Gregor Mendel, 8 Carly Simon, 9 George Bernard Shaw, 10 Mahogany, 11 Architecture, 12 The Plough, 13 Soil, 14 *91/2 Weeks,* 15 Boeing 747.

QUIZ 189

Answers on page 193

1 Which former Japanese capital happens to be an anagram of the current capital?

2 From which Walt Disney cartoon film does the Oscar winning song *When You Wish Upon a Star* come?

3 What name is given to the roof of the mouth?

4 Built in the 12th century where is Wales's largest cathedral?

5 Who in literature was haunted by the ghost of Banquo?

6 Who wrote the 1981 Roxy Music hit *Jealous Guy*?

7 What name links a *Magic Roundabout* character with the father of the disciples James and John?

8 Which is the brightest star in the constellation Gemini?

9 What does a haematologist study?

10 Which Christopher stars as DI Burnside in *The Bill*?

11 What name is given to a mixture of sodium hydrogencarbonate and tartaric acid when used in cooking?

12 Who starred as the university drop-out in the eighties sitcom *Shelley*?

13 Who presented the 1990s television series *Animal Hospital*?

14 Which South African tennis player put an end to Steffi Graf's 45 match winning run by defeating her at the Australian Open in 1997?

15 What is the medical name for rabies?

Things you didn't know...

King Zog of Albania smoked more than 100 cigarettes a day.

Answers to page 193

1 Kent, 2 Jimmy Carter, 3 New South Wales, 4 Rugby Union, 5 Penzance, 6 Billy Cotton, 7 Dorset, 8 Scotland, 9 US President (1850-52), 10 *Something in the Air,* 11 *Dr Dolittle,* 12 South China Sea, 13 Indian and Pacific, 14 Loganberry, 15 July.

QUIZ 190

Answers on page 194

1 What is the second largest planet in the solar system?

2 With which art form is Antonio Canova associated?

3 Which country in 1958 introduced an economic policy called the Great Leap Forward?

4 When was the OBE introduced?

5 Which female vocalist had a Top Ten hit single in 1988 with *Je Ne Sais Pas Pourquoi*?

6 Who joined Liverpool from Nottingham Forest in 1995 for over £8 million?

7 Who was the incurable optimist in *David Copperfield*?

8 Which range of hills stands on the border between England and Scotland?

9 What is the date of St. Patrick's Day?

10 Which singer-songwriter released an album called *Hourglass* in 1997?

11 If B is bravo and N is November what is S?

12 What name is given to a group of ravens?

13 What is the national airline of Paraguay?

14 Which animal derived its name from two Greek words meaning terrible lizard?

15 Which crimefighter was played by Peter Weller in a 1987 film?

Things you didn't know...

The word 'bride' comes from an ancient German word meaning 'the one who cooks'.

Answers to page 194

1 39, 2 Iraq, 3 Charles 1 (abdicated in 1918), 4 Reg Varney, 5 Somalia, 6 Vincent Price, 7 Jerusalem, 8 11, 9 Lichfield cathedral, 10 Queen Elizabeth II, 11 12 noon, 12 Diogenes, 13 Manila, 14 Massachusetts, 15 Israel.

QUIZ 191

Answers on page 191

1 In which English county is Knole House?

2 Who came second when Ronald Reagan was first elected US president?

3 Which Australian state lies on most of the southern border of Queensland?

4 In which sport did the Russian, Prince Oblensky, represent England?

5 Which is the most southerly railway station on the British mainland?

6 Whose catchphrase was 'Wakey Wakey'?

7 In which English county is the seaside resort of Bournemouth?

8 Which country was ruled by William the Lion?

9 Who was Millard Fillmore?

10 What was the only U.K. Number One hit for Thunderclap Newman?

11 Which literary doctor travelled to the South Seas in search of the Great Pink Sea Snail?

12 Into which sea or ocean does the Mekong flow?

13 Which two oceans are linked by the Strait of Malacca?

14 What is the name given to the fruit which is a cross between a raspberry and a blackberry?

15 What is the date of St Swithin's Day?

Things you didn't know...

More than 72 million Penny Black stamps were sold within six months of introduction.

Answers to page 191

1 Kyoto, **2** *Pinocchio,* **3** The palate, **4** St David's (Exeter), **5** *Macbeth,* **6** John Lennon, **7** Zebedee, **8** Pollux, **9** The blood, **10** Ellison, **11** Baking powder, **12** Hywel Bennett, **13** Rolf Harris, **14** Amanda Coetzer, **15** Hydrophobia.

QUIZ 192

Answers on page 192

1 How many days after Ash Wednesday is Palm Sunday?

2 Which country is ruled by Saddam Hussein?

3 Who was the last emperor of Austria?

4 Who played Stan Butler in *On the Buses* on TV?

5 Of which African country is Mogadishu the capital?

6 Which actor starred in the films *House of Wax, House on Haunted Hill* and *House of Usher*?

7 In which city would you find the Wailing Wall?

8 How old was Benedict IX when he became Pope?

9 Which Staffordshire cathedral is famous for its three spires?

10 Who was born on 21st April 1926 at 17 Bruton Street, London?

11 When it's 12 noon (GMT) in London, what time is it in Casablanca?

12 Which Greek philosopher was said to have lived in a tub?

13 What is the capital of the Philippines?

14 In which US state is Cape Cod?

15 In which country is the port of Haifa situated?

Things you didn't know...

Prince Charles was the first royal to give blood when he donated some in 1985.

Answers to page 192

1 Saturn, **2** Sculpture, **3** China, **4** 1917, **5** Kylie Minogue, **6** Stan Collymore, **7** Mr Micawber, **8** Cheviot Hills, **9** 17th March, **10** James Taylor, **11** Sierra, **12** Unkindness, **13** LAP, **14** Dinosaur, **15** *Robocop*.

QUIZ 193

Answers on page 197

1 Who wrote the novels on which the TV series *Cadfael* was based?

2 Who had a Number One hit single in 1956 with *Just Walkin' In The Rain*?

3 How many symphonies did Haydn compose?

4 Who sang the theme song for *Dad's Army*?

5 Which capital city's name means 'meeting of the muddy waters'?

6 In which country is the Encyclopaedia Britannica published?

7 Who won the 1997 USPGA championship at Winged Foot?

8 Which Russian novelist wrote the trilogy *Childhood, In the World,* and *My Universities*?

9 What is a brumby?

10 Who created *Noggin the Nog, Bagpuss* and *The Clangers*?

11 Which record producer created the *Wall of Sound* for the Crystals and Ronettes?

12 Who wrote the music *The Four Seasons*?

13 From which Italian island does Marsala wine come?

14 Who wrote the novel *Under the Volcano*?

15 In which country can koalas be found in the wild?

Things you didn't know...

Russian maps used to show Moscow a few miles away from its actual position to confuse guided missile programmers.

Answers to page 197

1 Hugh Gaitskell, 2 An egg (poached), 3 Linlithgow, 4 Bay of Biscay, 5 Jose Ferrer, 6 Beaulieu, 7 R-34, 8 Grasmere, 9 Atlas, 10 Honeysuckle, 11 Caracas, 12 Hanoi, 13 *Girls On Top*, 14 Netherlands, 15 Phil Hill and Mario Andretti.

QUIZ 194

Answers on page 198

1 Which Russian author refused the Nobel Prize in 1958?

2 In what year did Olga Korbut win three Olympic gold medals?

3 In the nursery rhyme *Cock A Doodle Doo*, what has my master lost?

4 In what country is the Algarve?

5 Which flavouring is added to brandy and egg yolks to make advocaat?

6 What is a turnstone?

7 Which postal item was copyrighted by J P Charlton in 1861?

8 Which Italian expression meaning 'in the church style' denotes unaccompanied singing?

9 Who wrote the novel *Sense and Sensibility*?

10 Which Arctic marine mammal has webbed flippers, a bristly moustache and large tusks?

11 Which drink was advertised by a toucan?

12 Which *EastEnders* character was played by Anita Dobson?

13 Which common object has an inertia reel?

14 The metal copper derives its name from which country?

15 Who was the men's figure skating gold medallist at the 1976 Winter Olympics?

Things you didn't know...

The onion is the most widely-used vegetable in the world.

Answers to page 198

1 A Stinger, 2 Earth Summit, 3 Noel Edmonds, 4 Austrian, 5 Malaysia, 6 Graphite, 7 Biggles, 8 Thomas Jefferson/Theodore Roosevelt, 9 *Dick Turpin,* 10 Lord Kitchener, 11 William Caxton, 12 Spiny anteater, 13 Fools, 14 Sunshine Desserts, 15 New South Wales.

QUIZ 195

Answers on page 195

1 Which political leader in 1962, called for a referendum on Britain's entry into the Common Market?

2 What does a Buck Rarebit have that a Welsh Rarebit does not?

3 In which Scottish palace was Mary, Queen of Scots born?

4 Which large bay lies off the coasts of France and Spain?

5 Who played Toulouse Lautrec in the film Moulin Rouge?

6 In which Hampshire village is Lord Montagu's Motor Museum?

7 Which was the first airship to make a successful transatlantic crossing?

8 In which Lake District village did Wordsworth live at Dove Cottage?

9 Who was made to carry the sky as punishment for his part in the war between Olympian gods and the Titans?

10 By what name is the flower Woodbine better known?

11 Which city is served by Simon Bolivar airport?

12 Which Asian capital city lies on the Red River?

13 What was the name of the 1980's comedy series in which Dawn French, Jennifer Saunders, Tracy Ullman & Ruby Wax lived together?

14 In which modern country would you locate The International Court of Justice?

15 Only two Americans have won the Formula 1 Motor Racing Championship. Who are they?

Things you didn't know...

Flamingos can only eat with their heads held upside down.

Answers to page 195

1 Ellis Peters, 2 Johnnie Ray, 3 104, 4 Bud Flannagan, 5 Kuala Lumpur, 6 USA, 7 Davis Love, 8 Maxim Gorki, 9 A wild horse, 10 Oliver Postgate, 11 Phil Spector, 12 Vivaldi, 13 Sicily, 14 Malcolm Lowry, 15 Australia.

QUIZ 196

Answers on page 196

1 Brandy and Créme de Menthe make which cocktail?

2 Which horse won the 1998 Grand National?

3 Who presents the TV quiz show *Telly Addicts*?

4 What nationality was the psychiatrist Sigmund Freud?

5 Which Commonwealth country has the Ringgit as its unit of currency?

6 Which substance is most used for pencil lead?

7 Which hero was accompanied by Algy and Ginger?

8 Apart from Washington and Lincoln, which other two US presidents are depicted on Mount Rushmore?

9 Which criminal was made into a romantic figure by the novel *Rookwood*?

10 Which famous soldier drowned when HMS Hampshire struck a mine off the Orkneys in 1916?

11 Who established the first English printing press in 1476?

12 By what name is the Australian echidna also known?

13 Who rush in where angels fear to tread?

14 For which company did Reggie Perrin originally work?

15 Of which state of Australia is Sydney the capital?

Things you didn't know...

20,000 men lost their lives during construction of the Panama Canal.

Answers to page 196

1 Boris Pasternak, 2 1972, 3 His fiddling stick, 4 Portugal, 5 Vanilla, 6 A bird, 7 Postcard, 8 A cappella, 9 Jane Austen, 10 Walrus, 11 Guinness, 12 Angie Watts, 13 Car seat belt, 14 Cyprus, 15 John Curry.

QUIZ 197

Answers on page 201

1 What is the capital of Tasmania?

2 Who commanded the British Land Forces in the Falklands?

3 Which Japanese word translates as 'Empty Orchestra'?

4 Which British group's third album was called *Be Here Now*?

5 Who could only play one tune - *Over The Hills And Far Away*?

6 In what year was poison gas used in war for the first time?

7 In which city is the world's largest store of uncut diamonds kept?

8 Off which group of islands would you find Bishop Rock lighthouse?

9 In which English county is Kings Lynn?

10 Which English Monarch's horse was called 'White Surrey'?

11 Who played *Wonder Woman* in the US TV series?

12 When was Sir Walter Scott born?

13 Who missed the last penalty of the 1994 football World Cup?

14 Who had a Number One hit with *Space Oddity*?

15 What are the three ingredients of the cocktail Harvey Wallbanger?

Things you didn't know...

Bing Crosby hated his big ears so much that he stuck them to the side of his head with glue.

Answers to page 201

1 Lancaster and York, 2 Montreal, 3 Robbie Williams, 4 Christmas rose, 5 Elvis Costello, 6 Beaver, 7 Timmy, 8 David Suchet, 9 Kamikaze, 10 Benjamin, 11 Ursine, 12 Corniche, 13 1952, 14 Bushbaby, 15 County Cork.

QUIZ 198

Answers on page 202

1 On what date does Hallowe'en fall?

2 Who are thespians?

3 What, in the building trade, is called 'harling' in Scotland?

4 In which 1984 film did Sean Connery return as James Bond after a thirteen year gap?

5 Who was the first woman to participate in the University Boat Race?

6 In which street is *Neighbours* set?

7 In which country was Salman Rushdie born?

8 With which sport do you associate Babe Ruth?

9 Which colourless liquid, once used as an anaesthetic, is also called trichloromethane?

10 What sort of creature is a pipistrelle?

11 Which TV series starred Jan Francis and Dennis Waterman?

12 In which Scottish town was James Watt born?

13 Which composer married Cclara Wieck?

14 Which Labour MP resigned in 1912 to fight for votes for women?

15 What is the smallest British pony breed?

Things you didn't know...

The Venus Flytrap feeds mainly on ants, not flies.

Answers to page 202

1 No Ball, 2 Oscar Wilde, 3 1826, 4 Tom Weiskopf, 5 Westerns, 6 Tennis, 7 Juneau, 8 Eton, 9 Norwegian, 10 Tower of London, 11 Pine cone, 12 Alan Ladd's, 13 Vienna, 14 1955, 15 Robert Peary.

QUIZ 199

Answers on page 199

1 Which two Houses contested the Wars of the Roses?

2 Which major North American city is served by Dorval International airport?

3 Who left Take That in July 1995?

4 Helleborus niger is better known as which perennial plant?

5 Who had a Top Ten hit single in 1981 with *A Good Year For The Roses*?

6 Which animal is Canada's official emblem?

7 What was the name of the dog in Enid Blyton's *Famous Five* books?

8 Who played Blott in the TV serial *Blott On The Landscape*?

9 Which word meaning "divine wind" describes suicide missions of Japanese aircraft?

10 Who, in the Bible, was the youngest son of Jacob?

11 If dogs are canine and horses are equine, what are bears?

12 What is the name of the two tierred roads which run from Nice along the coast to Menton?

13 In which year were identity cards abolished?

14 Which small nocturnal primate is also called a galago?

15 In which Irish county is the castle that contains the famous Blarney Stone?

Things you didn't know...

Spain, or Spania, as it was originally called, means 'land of rabbits'.

Answers to page 199

1 Hobart, 2 Major General Jeremy Moore, 3 Karaoke, 4 Oasis, 5 Tom, the piper's son, 6 1915, 7 London (Holborn), 8 Scilly Isles, 9 Norfolk, 10 Richard III, 11 Lynda Carter, 12 1771, 13 Roberto Baggio, 14 David Bowie, 15 Vodka, Orange Juice & Galiano.

QUIZ 200

Answers on page 200

1 What does a cricket umpire signal by raising one arm horizontally?

2 Which writer was imprisoned as a result of his relationship with Lord Alfred Douglas?

3 In what year was London Zoo established?

4 Which American golfer won the 1973 British Open for the first and only time?

5 What type of novels were written by Zane Grey?

6 With which sport do you associate Steffi Graf?

7 What is the state capital of Alaska?

8 In which school did Fives originate?

9 What nationality was the composer Edvard Grieg?

10 Where in London would you see the White Tower?

11 A strobilus is another name for what?

12 Which tough guy actor's last film was *The Carpetbaggers*?

13 Which city is served by Schwechat airport?

14 In which year was Bill Haley's *Rock Around the Clock* Number One in the UK charts?

15 Who is recognised to have been the first man to reach the North Pole?

Things you didn't know...

The first European car to sell more than a million was the VW Beetle.

Answers to page 200

1 October 31st, 2 Actors, 3 Pebble dash or rough cast, 4 *Never Say Never Again*, 5 Susan Brown, 6 Ramsay, 7 India, 8 Baseball, 9 Chloroform, 10 A bat, 11 *Stay Lucky*, 12 Greenock, 13 Robert Schumann, 14 George Lansbury, 15 Shetland pony.

QUIZ 201

Answers on page 205

1 Of which country was Georges Pompidou president from 1969 to 1974?

2 What was the occupation during the French revolution of a tricoteuse?

3 When referring to radio waves, what do the initials AM stand for?

4 Which US organisation is represented by the initials FBI?

5 What is the capital of the Australian state Victoria?

6 Which sport featured in the film *The Stratton Story*?

7 In which classic novel did Inspector Javert hunt down Jean Valjean?

8 Which sorceress turned Odysseus' men into swine?

9 Karachi is in which country?

10 In which TV time travel series does Scott Bakula play the lead?

11 What sort of animal is an aardvark?

12 Who launched the Zike (electric bike) in 1992?

13 What is the state capital of New Mexico?

14 With what form of transport was Otto Lilienthal associated?

15 What is the Celtic name for river?

Things you didn't know...

Only two men know the secret list of ingredients of Coco-Cola and they never fly in the same plane.

Answers to page 205

1 Frederick Forsyth, 2 Imran Khan, 3 Coypu, 4 Orangutan, 5 Undercover Customs, 6 Cheam, 7 Ice Hockey, 8 Five, 9 Ted Ray, 10 *Why Do Fools Fall In Love*, 11 The libretto, 12 Iraq, 13 Steven Spielberg, 14 *Spender*, 15 Fats Domino.

QUIZ 202

Answers on page 206

1 What was the name for the ancient trade route between China and the Mediterranean?

2 Which creature gets its name from the Spanish for lizard?

3 What is the unit of currency of Algeria?

4 Which singer starred in a film called *Purple Rain*?

5 The Tsar Kolokol is the biggest what in the world?

6 In which sport has Ard Schenk been a world champion and record holder?

7 In what does an Oncologist specialise?

8 The Pindus Mountains run north to south through which country?

9 Which TV series featured the character Boss Hogg?

10 What was the name of Harry Llewellyn's gold-medal-wining horse in the 1952 Olympics?

11 Which Motor Racing team is named after India's sacred flower?

12 Which large object was discovered by Clyde Tombaugh in 1930?

13 Who played the title role in the 1995 film *Cobb*?

14 In the 1960s, which London street was the fashion centre for the young?

15 Who said 'We live over the shop'?

Things you didn't know...

Al Capone's business card gave his profession as a 'secondhand furniture dealer'.

Answers to page 206

1 Tunisia, 2 White, 3 Uranus, 4 Honduras, 5 New Zealand, 6 Debussy, 7 Irene, 8 Scrumps, 9 Hummingbirds, 10 Links, 11 Woburn Abbey, 12 Victoria, 13 Isle of Wight, 14 Harold Macmillan, 15 St Stephen's.

QUIZ 203

Answers on page 203

1 Who wrote *The Fourth Protocol*?

2 Which cricketer was known as 'The Lion of Pakistan'?

3 Which animal gives us nutria fur?

4 Which animals' name translated into English means 'Man of the Woods'?

5 Which documentary series about smuggling was presented by Trevor McDonald?

6 Which Berkshire school did Prince Charles attend?

7 Which sport would you be watching if you saw Flyers take on Racers?

8 How many circles appear on the Olympic flag?

9 Who played the headmaster in *Carry on Teacher*?

10 Which song gave Frankie Lymon and the Teenagers a Number One hit in 1956?

11 What is the text of an opera or operatta called?

12 Which country is Baghdad the capital of?

13 Who directed the 1987 film *Empire of the Sun*?

14 In which TV series did Jimmy Nail play a Geordie detective?

15 Who sang *Blueberry Hill*?

Things you didn't know...

Redheads have fewer hairs on their heads than brunettes or blondes.

Answers to page 203

1 France, 2 Knitting, 3 Amplitude modulation, 4 Federal Bureau of Investigation, 5 Melbourne, 6 Baseball, 7 *Les Misérables,* 8 Circe, 9 Pakistan, 10 *Quantum Leap,* 11 Anteater, 12 Clive Sinclair, 13 Sante Fé, 14 Gliders, 15 Avon.

QUIZ 204

Answers on page 204

1 Which country lies between Algeria and Libya?

2 What colour is the cue ball in a game of pool?

3 Titania, Oberon, Miranda and Ariel are all moons of which planet?

4 Of which Central American country is Tegucigalpa the capital?

5 The Sutherland Falls, among the highest in the world, are in which country?

6 Who composed *Clair De Lune*?

7 What is the Greek equivalent of the Roman deity Pax?

8 What name is given to stunted and withered apples used to make rough cider?

9 Which birds are famous for the sound made by their wings and being able to fly backwards?

10 What name is often given to a golf course next to the sea?

11 What is the Duke of Bedford's stateley home?

12 What was the name of Kaiser Bill's mother?

13 Which part of Britain was called Vectis by the Romans?

14 Who succeeded Anthony Eden as prime minister?

15 On whose feast did Good King Wenceslas look out?

Things you didn't know...

The Statue of Liberty's index finger is eight feet long.

Answers to page 204

1 Silk Road, **2** Alligator, **3** Dinar, **4** Prince, **5** Bell, **6** Speed skating, **7** Cancers, **8** Greece, **9** *The Dukes of Hazzard,* **10** Foxhunter, **11** Lotus, **12** Pluto, **13** Tommy Lee Jones, **14** Carnaby Street, **15** Prince Philip.

QUIZ 205

Answers on page 209

1 Which instrument measures pressure of atmosphere?

2 The Star of Africa is what type of gem?

3 Which country was once called Gold Coast?

4 If you travelled directly north from Weston Super Mare by air, over which city would you fly first?

5 Which British architect designed the Cenotaph?

6 Bakewell is in which English county?

7 What was the name of Beatrix Potter's hedgehog laundress?

8 Who wrote the book *The Prime of Miss Jean Brodie*?

9 How did Mrs Janet Walton make the headlines in 1983?

10 What breed of dog is Scooby Doo?

11 What is the other name of the sword sometimes called Caliburn?

12 Who played Robert Wagner's wife in the American television series *Hart to Hart*?

13 What would a 'cruciverbalist' like doing?

14 Which planet is fourth from the sun?

15 Which impressionist played Spock in TV's *Preston Front*?

Things you didn't know...

The CIA once employed a magician to teach agents how to use sleight of hand in their work.

Answers to page 209

1 Flubber, 2 March 15th, 3 Radioactivity, 4 Pheasant, 5 Scafell Pike, 6 Archery, 7 Elk, 8 Drambuie, 9 Rafiki, 10 Switzerland, 11 Honda, 12 Indonesia, 13 Preston North End, 14 Ground-hog-Day, 15 Australian.

QUIZ 206

Answers on page 210

1 Which beverage was advertised on TV by Sharon Maughan and Anthony Head?

2 What instrument is played by the leader of an orchestra?

3 Which part of the body is affected by Crohn's Disease?

4 In which country are Maoris the indigenous population?

5 From which country do Moselle wines come?

6 In which sport is there a bonspiel?

7 Which television series was based on the *Constable* books by Nicholas Rhea?

8 On TV, who played the aristrocratic Audrey Forbes-Hamilton?

9 On what sort of tree do coconuts and dates grow?

10 How many cubic centimetres are there in a cubic metre?

11 From which island did Bonnie Prince Charlie row a boat to the Isle of Skye?

12 Which sport would you be watching if you saw Robins take on Swans?

13 What was the real name of the 'Singing Nun'?

14 Name the authors of the four Gospels.

15 Who starred as English teacher John Keating in the 1989 film *Dead Poets Society*?

Things you didn't know...

The man who invented cornflakes, Dr Kellogg, also invented peanut butter.

Answers to page 210

1 Pte. Godfrey, 2 Acton Bell, 3 Mayo, 4 Jack Benny, 5 Arnold Schwarzenegger, 6 Bomber jacket, 7 65-70, 8 *Dallas,* 9 Princess Beatrice, 10 Stretchers, 11 Krypton, 12 Secretary of State for Education and Science, 13 Turkey, 14 Sunderland, 15 Toasted oatmeal.

QUIZ 207

Answers on page 207

1 Which 1998 Disney movie, starring Robin Williams, was a remake of the 1961 film *The Absent-Minded Professor*?

2 Julius Caesar was murdered on the Ides of March. What date was this?

3 What does a Geiger counter detect?

4 Which game bird season runs from 1st October to 1st February each year?

5 What is the highest mountain in England?

6 In which sport did Simon Terry win a bronze medal at the Barcelona Olympics and the Mens team win a bronze also?

7 By what other name is a moose called?

8 According to tradition, Bonnie Prince Charlie gave Captain McKinnon the recipe for which liqueur?

9 What is the name of the wise baboon in *The Lion King*?

10 In which country does the River Rhine rise?

11 Which motor manufacturer produces the Civic and the Accord?

12 Djakarta is the capital of which country?

13 Which English football team play at Deepdale?

14 What is the 2nd of February called in the USA?

15 What nationality was Herb Elliott, 1500m gold medallist at the 1960 Olympics?

Things you didn't know...

George VI, Mozart and Casanova were all Freemasons.

Answers to page 207

1 Barometer, **2** Diamond, **3** Ghana, **4** Newport, **5** Sir Edwin Landseer Lutyens, **6** Derbyshire, **7** Mrs Tiggy Winkle, **8** Muriel Spark, **9** She gave birth to sextuplets, **10** Great Dane, **11** Excalibur, **12** Stefanie Powers, **13** Crossword puzzles, **14** Mars, **15** Alistair McGowan.

QUIZ 208

Answers on page 208

1 In *Dad's Army* which character carried the first aid kit?

2 What was the pen name of Anne Brönte?

3 Of which Irish county is Castlebar the county town?

4 Which American comedian, known for his meanness, used *Love in Bloom* as his signature tune?

5 Who played Conan in the films *Conan the Barbarian* and *Conan the Destroyer*?

6 Which type of short, padded jacket got its name because it was worn by air crews during the Second World war?

7 How many decibels is the noise of busy traffic?

8 Which city provided the title for a TV series starring Larry Hagman, Linda Gray, Patrick Duffy, Victoria Principal?

9 Which member of the Royal Family was born in August 1988?

10 In bricklaying, what term is applied to courses of bricks laid end-to-end?

11 Which noble gas is represented by the symbol Kr?

12 What was Margaret Thatcher's only Cabinet post prior to becoming prime minister?

13 Which animal performed the wedding ceremony for the *Owl and the Pussycat*?

14 Which team did Leeds United play in their 1973 appearance in the FA Cup Final?

15 What is the rich double cream Scottish cheese Caboc, rolled in?

Things you didn't know...

Vampire bats rarely bite the necks of their human victims – they normally go for the ears, nose or toes!

Answers to page 208

1 Gold Blend Coffee, 2 Violin, 3 Intestines, 4 New Zealand, 5 Germany, 6 Curling, 7 *Heartbeat,* 8 Penelope Keith, 9 Palm, 10 One million, 11 Benbecula, 12 Football, 13 Jeanine Deckers, 14 Matthew, Mark, Luke and John, 15 Robin Williams.

QUIZ 209

Answers on page 213

1 Which actor had a hit in 1992 with *Aint no Doubt*?

2 Who co-starred with Tom Hanks in the 1993 film *Sleepless in Seattle*?

3 What name is given to a French abbot?

4 Which country is the main producer of Feta cheese?

5 Apart from Newcastle which other team are nicknamed The Magpies?

6 Who does Viola love in *Twelfth Night*?

7 What character did Leonardo DiCaprio play in *Titanic*?

8 Maximilian was installed as emperor of which country by Napoleon III?

9 Who connects the archaeological programme *Time Team* with the comedy series *Blackadder*?

10 Who played Donna in the sitcom *My Wonderful Life*?

11 What is the capital of Finland?

12 What did you do if you took the King's shilling?

13 What is the official language of Ecuador?

14 What sort of creature is a hairstreak?

15 What character did Gene Hackman play in *The French Connection*?

Things you didn't know...

The Russian composer, Tchaikovsky, tried to commit suicide by standing in a freezing river all night.

Answers to page 213

1 Hungary, **2** 1961, **3** Germany, **4** Haddock, **5** A dog, **6** Herman Melville, **7** Baz Luhrmann, **8** Shoulder blade, **9** Ireland, **10** Exchange money, **11** Nod, **12** Lead, **13** Pacific, **14** Six, **15** Cher.

QUIZ 210

Answers on page 214

1 Which carbohydrate makes jam gel?

2 Which of Mr Pickwick's friends married Arabella Allen?

3 By what name is the U.S. Military Academy in New York State usually known?

4 What is the capital of Switzerland?

5 Who had a Number One hit in 1956 with *I'll Be Home*?

6 In which Shakespeare play do Beatrice and Benedick appear?

7 Who was Frank Sinatra's second wife?

8 Which country has the Leone as its unit of currency?

9 Of which Asian country is New Delhi the capital?

10 Who on TV appears as Alan Partridge and Paul Calf?

11 Who engaged in the old American custom of bundling?

12 Who played Commissioner Dreyfus in the *Pink Panther* films?

13 Which disease is carried by bark beetles?

14 Bayern is the German name for which region of Germany?

15 Which Persian word for gratuity has come to mean a bribe?

Things you didn't know...

After Blackbeard the pirate was killed, his murderers cut off his beard and flew it from their mast.

Answers to page 214

1 Cornwall, 2 The Drifters, 3 John Milton, 4 Iceland, 5 Esau, 6 Reykjavik, 7 Horst Jankowski, 8 James Stewart, 9 *The Defiant Ones,* 10 Elvis Presley, 11 Henry Winkler, 12 Pocahontas, 13 Gorilla, 14 Georgia, 15 Lisa Dingle.

QUIZ 211

Answers on page 211

1 Which European country produces Tokay?

2 In which year did *Coronation Street* begin?

3 Which country does a car come from if it has the international registration letter D?

4 Which fish is smoked and cured and called 'finnan'?

5 What sort of creature is a Beagle?

6 Who wrote the novel *Billy Budd*, published in 1924?

7 Who directed the 1997 film version of Shakespeare's *Romeo and Juliet* starring Leonardo DiCaprio??

8 How is the scapula commonly known?

9 Which country would you visit to kiss the Blarney Stone?

10 What would you do in a Cambio?

11 In Genesis, which land was said to lie to the east of Eden?

12 The ore galena is the chief source of which metal?

13 In which ocean is Fiji?

14 How many programmes were made for the spoof police series *Police Squad*?

15 Which Oscar-winning actress had a UK Number One in 1998 with *I Believe*?

Things you didn't know...

Oliver Cromwell passed a law forbidding anyone to eat mince pies or Christmas pudding.

Answers to page 211

1 Jimmy Nail, 2 Meg Ryan, 3 Abbe, 4 Greece, 5 Notts County, 6 Duke Orsino, 7 Jack, 8 Mexico, 9 Tony Robinson, 10 Emma Wray, 11 Helsinki, 12 Joined the army, 13 Spanish, 14 A butterfly, 15 Popeye Doyle.

QUIZ 212

Answers on page 212

1 Kernow is the Celtic name for what?

2 Who had a Top Ten hit single in 1974 with *Kissin' in The Back Row Of The Movies*?

3 Which poet wrote *Paradise Lost*?

4 Which country in Europe has the oldest Parliament?

5 Which Biblical character had a Hebrew name meaning 'hairy'?

6 In which city did Boris Spassky lose his world chess title to Bobby Fischer in 1972?

7 Who took a walk in the Black Forest?

8 Who was the male star of the film *Vertigo*?

9 In which 1958 film did Sidney Poitier make his name starring with Tony Curtis as two escaping convicts, chained together?

10 Who starred in *Blue Hawaii*?

11 Who played The Fonz in TV's *Happy Days*?

12 By what name is Rebbeca Rolfe better known?

13 What is the largest breed of ape?

14 Of which state of the USA is Atlanta the capital?

15 Who gave birth to a baby girl in *Emmerdale* on Christams Day 1998?

Things you didn't know...

Noel Coward once poured boiling water down the ear-trumpet of a deaf hall porter.

Answers to page 212

1 Pectin, 2 Nathaniel Winkle, 3 West Point, 4 Bern, 5 Pat Boone, 6 *Much Ado About Nothing,* 7 Ava Gardner, 8 Sierra Leone, 9 India, 10 Steve Coogan, 11 Engaged couples, 12 Herbert Lom, 13 Dutch Elm Disease, 14 Bavaria, 15 Baksheesh.

QUIZ 213

Answers on page 217

1 Which British actor played 8 parts in the 1949 film *Kind Hearts And Coronets*?

2 Which new soft cheese was launched by the Milk Marketing Board in 1982?

3 Which metal is represented by the symbol Hf?

4 Who released *Blue Monday* and *I'm Walkin'* in 1957?

5 Who was the first prime minister of Israel?

6 Which gemstone is a black variety of lignite?

7 If you were born on 31 July, what would your star sign be?

8 Where was Joan of Arc burnt at the stake?

9 What is the name of the working horse named after a district in Northern France?

10 In which programme do a panel of celebrities try to guess someone's occupation?

11 By what name is 15th July known as?

12 From which country do The Gurkhas come from?

13 Who was the original presenter of *The Old Grey Whistle Test*?

14 By what name is the vegetable Brassica oleracea gemmifera, better known?

15 What was Richard Griffiths's charcter in BBC1's *Pie in the Sky* called?

Things you didn't know...

Judy Garland's role in The Wizard of Oz was originally intended for Shirley Temple.

Answers to page 217

1 Bill Wyman, 2 Hungary (Lazio Biro), 3 Donna Summer, 4 Indonesia, 5 Rock Hudson, 6 Olaf Palme, 7 Russell Harty, 8 Cardiff, 9 Iron Horse, 10 Samson, 11 Charles Lindbergh's, 12 It has no tail, 13 Michael Gambon, 14 Hummus, 15 Bethlehem.

QUIZ 214

Answers on page 218

1 On which ship did Sir Francis Drake sail around the world?

2 Which female vocalist joined The Pogues on the hit single *Fairytale of New York*?

3 Which US state is situated on the Northern border of Iowa?

4 What aircraft first crossed the Atlantic non-stop in 1919 and who were the pilots?

5 What type of dog was Ren in *The Ren and Stimpy Show*?

6 Which television series has been presented by Terry Wogan, David Jacobs and Rosemarie Ford?

7 Who was Henry VIII's fourth wife?

8 Which *Beverly Hills Cop* star appeared in the film *Metro*?

9 In which county is Jodrell Bank?

10 What is the capital of Niger?

11 What was the name of Don Lang's backing group?

12 Who became known as 'Hanoi Jane' because of her anti-Vietnam war activities?

13 On which horse did Walter Swinburn win the 1981 English Derby?

14 Which Shakespeare play includes the characters Petruchio, Katharina and Bianca?

15 Which cereal grass is used to make American whiskey?

Things you didn't know...

1,627,968 people turned out to vote in the 1982 Albanian election – only one person voted against the ruling Communist Party

Answers to page 218

1 Shakespeare's, 2 Mendips, 3 1959, 4 Leslie Charteris, 5 *The Night Of The Iguana,* 6 Stormont, 7 Borodin, 8 Tyne, 9 Billy Connelly, 10 Snooker, 11 Kid Galahad, 12 Soot, 13 Mae West, 14 *Macbeth,* 15 Le Mans.

QUIZ 215

Answers on page 215

1 Who owns the London restaurant Sticky Fingers?

2 In which country was the ballpoint pen invented?

3 Who wanted to have *Dinner with Gershwin* in 1987?

4 Which country was formerly called Dutch East Indies?

5 Which Hollywood star was born Roy Scherer?

6 Which European prime minister was assassinated in February 1986?

7 Which television presenter often used the phrase, 'you are, are you not ...'?

8 Which was the first Welsh side to win the FA Cup?

9 What name was given to railway engines by Red Indians?

10 Who made a Biblical riddle out of bees nesting in a dead lion?

11 Which famous American's two year old son was kidnapped and murdered in 1932?

12 What distinguishes a Manx cat from other cats?

13 On TV, who played *The Singing Detective*?

14 What is the Greek starter made from chick peas known as?

15 Which town is the presumed birthplace of Jesus Christ?

Things you didn't know...

The firefly is the official insect of Pennsylvania.

Answers to page 215

1 Alec Guinness, **2** Lymeswold, **3** Hafnium, **4** Fats Domino, **5** David Ben-Gurion, **6** Jet, **7** Leo, **8** Rouen, **9** Percheron, **10** *What's My Line?*, **11** St Swithin's Day, **12** Nepal, **13** Ian Whitcomb, **14** Brussels sprout, **15** Henry Crabbe.

QUIZ 216

Answers on page 216

1 Whose collected plays were published in *The First Folio*?

2 In which hills is Cheddar Gorge?

3 In which year was Adam Faith's first Number One hit?

4 Which writer created *The Saint*?

5 In which 1964 film did Richard Burton star with Ava Gardner and Deborah Kerr in a Tennesse Williams drama set in Mexico?

6 Which Belfast castle houses the parliament of Northern Ireland?

7 Who composed the opera *Prince Igor*?

8 Which major river flows through Newcastle?

9 Which comedian presented the *World Tour of Scotland*?

10 Which game was invented in India in 1875 and reached England ten years later?

11 In which 1962 film did Elvis Presley play an up and coming boxer?

12 From what is the brown pigment bistre prepared?

13 Who said "I used to be Snow White....but I drifted"?

14 From which of Shakespeare's plays does the line 'When shall we three meet again', come from?

15 On which circuit is motor racing's Grand Prix d'Endurance run?

Things you didn't know...

Marlon Brando made his stage debut in I Remember Broadway.

Answers to page 216

1 Golden Hind, 2 Kirsty MacColl, 3 Minnesota, 4 Vickers Vimy piloted by Arthur Whitten-Brown and John Alcock, 5 A chihuahua, 6 *Come Dancing*, 7 Anne of Cleves, 8 Eddie Murphy, 9 Cheshire, 10 Niamey, 11 *The Frantic Five*, 12 Jane Fonda, 13 Shergar, 14 *The Taming of the Shrew*, 15 Rye.

QUIZ 217

Answers on page 221

1 What safety device protects electrical circuits from the effects of excessive currents?

2 Who is the Duke of Edinburgh?

3 Which former king is said to haunt Windsor Castle?

4 In which modern country would you locate the Home of SABENA Airlines?

5 In how many of the films he appeared in did John Wayne play the leading role?

6 Whose wife turned into a pillar of salt?

7 Bombay is the capital of which state?

8 In which modern country is the site of the ancient city of Troy?

9 By what name is a leopard, especially the black variety, also known?

10 What is the minimum number of points required to win a game of squash?

11 What is the occupation of a leprechaun?

12 Which *Brookside* character was played by Louis Emerick?

13 Who won the Eurovision Song Conest in bare feet?

14 Which country's prime minister was apparently drowned in 1967?

15 In which decade was cable TV first developed?

Things you didn't know...

George Michael was sacked from his Saturday job at BHS for not wearing a shirt and tie in the stockroom.

Answers to page 221

1 Paris (on the metro), 2 Glue, 3 Blackburn Rovers, 4 Paradine, 5 Theodore Roosevelt, 6 Tom Robinson, 7 Warsaw, 8 Prima Donna, 9 DNA, 10 Elaine Paige, 11 Beethoven, 12 Calamity Jane, 13 Iron, 14 Somerset, 15 Lace.

QUIZ 218

Answers on page 222

1 Who was the bully in the book Tom Brown's Schooldays?

2 By what name is the femur commonly known?

3 In which country was the military Tet Offensive launched in 1968?

4 Which Carry On star took his own personal toilet with him whenever he moved to a theatre for a play?

5 Which Asian kingdom was formerly known as Siam?

6 In which city was Abraham Lincoln assassinated?

7 Who was world motor racing champion in 1980, for the first and only time?

8 Which football club play at Gresty Road and are nicknamed the Railwaymen?

9 In which Scottish castle was Princess Margaret born?

10 What is the name for a dislike of foreigners?

11 Who directed and starred in the film Yentl?

12 Which PM took Britain into the EEC?

13 What is the name of the globe fish, whose flesh is poisonous, eaten in Japan?

14 Who devised the package tour?

15 What does a galactophagist drink?

Things you didn't know...

Poet Robert Burns had a pet ewe called Poor mallie and even wrote two poems about her.

Answers to page 222

1 Mesopotamia, **2** A snake, **3** Edward Fox, **4** John Bruton, **5** Portishead, **6** Alsatian, **7** Ohio, **8** Geoffrey Howe, **9** Ian Botham, **10** Don Thompson, **11** Aerolineas, **12** Sir Arthur Bliss, **13** Gail Devers, **14** Ainsley Harriott, **15** Suffolk.

QUIZ 219

Answers on page 219

1 In which city would you find stations called George V, Franklin D.Roosevelt, St Paul and Garibaldi?

2 What binding medium is used in gouache painting?

3 Who plays their home games at Ewood Park?

4 What is David Frost's middle name?

5 Who was the first U.S. President to win the Nobel Peace Prize?

6 Who had a 1977 U.K. Top Ten hit with *2-4-6-8 Motorway*?

7 What is the capital of Poland?

8 What is the principal female singer in an opera called?

9 How is deoxyribonucleic acid commonly known?

10 Who partnered Barbara Dickson to reach Number One with the song *I Know Him So Well*?

11 Which composer said on his death bed "I shall hear in heaven"?

12 Cowgirl Martha Jane Canary is better known by what name?

13 Fe is the symbol of which chemical element?

14 With which county did Ian Botham begin his cricketing career?

15 Which product is particularly associated with the Devon town of Honiton?

Things you didn't know...

French king Louis XIV hated washing so much that he only took three baths in his whole life.

Answers to page 219

1 Fuse, 2 Prince Philip, 3 George III, 4 Belgium, 5 142, 6 Lot, 7 Maharastra, 8 Turkey, 9 Panther, 10 Nine, 11 Cobbler, 12 Mick Johnson, 13 Sandie Shaw, 14 Australia's, 15 1940's (1949).

QUIZ 220

Answers on page 220

1 What was the ancient name of Iraq?

2 What is a water moccasin?

3 Who played the Jackal in the film *The Day of the Jackal*?

4 Who succeeded Albert Reynolds as prime minister of the Republic of Ireland?

5 Which Bristol band released an album called *Dummy*?

6 What breed of dog was Rin Tin Tin?

7 Of which American state is Columbus the capital?

8 Of whom did Dennis Healey say that being attacked by him was like being savaged by a dead sheep?

9 Who was banned for two one-day cricket internationals in 1986 after admitting he'd smoked cannabis?

10 Who won a gold medal for Britain in the 1960 Olympics for the 50 kilometre walk?

11 What is the national airline of Argentina?

12 Who was Master of the Queen's Music from 1953 until 1975?

13 Who won the women's Olympic 100 metres in 1992?

14 Which chef presented his *Barbecue Bible* on TV?

15 In which English county are Ipswich and Lowestoft?

Things you didn't know...

Soviet cosmonaut Valentina Tereshkova was the first woman in space.

Answers to page 220

1 Flashman, 2 Thigh bone, 3 South Vietnam, 4 Kenneth Williams, 5 Thailand, 6 Washington D.C., 7 Alan Jones, 8 Crewe Alaexandra, 9 Glamis Castle, 10 Xenophobia, 11 Barbra Streisand, 12 Edward Heath, 13 Fugu, 14 Thomas Cook, 15 Milk.

QUIZ 221

Answers on page 225

1 In which English county is the Isle of Purbeck?

2 Who wrote the book *Mein Kampf*?

3 Which U.S. sociologist wrote *The Structure of Social Action*?

4 Which foreign king married and divorced an Englishwoman named Toni Gardiner?

5 Which was the first *Harry Palmer* film?

6 After which frontier scout was the capital of Nevada named?

7 What is the green-eyed monster?

8 Who starred as the artist in the film *Surviving Picasso*?

9 Who played the radio talk-show host in TV's *Midnight Caller*?

10 Iguanas belong to which reptile family?

11 What was Conservative politician RAB Butler's first name?

12 Who had a *Commercial Breakdown* on BBC1?

13 From which country does Chianti wine come?

14 Which terrier is the largest of the terrier breeds?

15 In mythology, what happened if you drank the water of the River Lethe?

Things you didn't know...

The desert rat can have sex as often as 122 times per hour.

Answers to page 225

1 Krueger, 2 Lace, 3 Theodore Roosevelt, 4 Megalomania, 5 Turin, 6 Stephen, 7 Cher, 8 Japan, 9 Dennis Potter, 10 Sugar Ray Robinson's, 11 Oscar Wilde, 12 Henry Robinson Luce, 13 Photocopying, 14 Bolton Wanderers, 15 Brazil.

QUIZ 222

Answers on page 226

1 What industrial injury does doing the same task repeatedly cause?

2 Who founded the Christian Science movement in the 19th century?

3 Iodine is necessary for the functioning of which gland?

4 In which street did the Fire of London start?

5 What is the chemical symbol for arsenic?

6 Who won the Booker Prize for *The Old Devils*?

7 Who composed the opera *The Bartered Bride*?

8 Who is the patron saint of messengers?

9 Near which North American city are the Plains of Abraham?

10 Lake Balaton is the largest lake in Central Europe. In which country is it?

11 In which city and seaport is Yale University?

12 Which children's author married lawyer William Heelis in 1913?

13 Which letter of the Greek alphabet is the equivalent to 'T'?

14 What is magnesium sulphate called when used as a laxative?

15 The Dome of the Rock was built in 691 by Abd-al-Malik. Where is it?

Things you didn't know...

What's The New Mary Jane was supposed to have been the next Beatles single but they split before the recording was released.

Answers to page 226

1 Keith Moon, 2 Fish Farming, 3 St James, 4 Bournemouth, 5 Blur, 6 Night and Day, 7 Flyweight, 8 Prince Henry, 9 Artificial Insemination, 10 King Charles I, 11 1983, 12 1918, 13 Whooping Cough, 14 Sonny, 15 Marc Rosset.

QUIZ 223

Answers on page 223

1 What is Freddy's surname in the fim series *Nightmare on Elm Street*?

2 What was the town of Mechelen in Belgium once famous for?

3 Who was the first US President to be awarded the Nobel Peace Prize in 1906?

4 What is the name for an all-consuming passion for power?

5 How is the Italian city of Torino known in English?

6 Wenceslas looked out the feast of whom?

7 Which actress was Oscar nominated for *Silkwood* and won an Oscar for *Moonstruck*?

8 Whom did New Zealand beat 145-17 in the 1995 Rugby union World Cup?

9 Who wrote the drama series *The Singing Detective*?

10 Which boxer's real name was Walker Smith?

11 Which dramatist and poet wrote the fairy tale *The Happy Prince*?

12 Who founded the magazine *Time* and the *Pictorial Weekly Life*?

13 If you were doing some xerography in the office, what would you be doing?

14 Who was the first team to win the FA Cup at Wembley?

15 In which country is the plateau known as the Mato Grosso?

Things you didn't know...

The 1969 Eurovision Song Contest ended in a four-way tie between France, Holland, Spain and the UK.

Answers to page 223

1 Dorset, **2** Adolf Hitler, **3** Talcott Parsons, **4** King Hussein of Jordan, **5** *The Ipcress File*, **6** Kit Carson, **7** Jealousy, **8** Sir Anthony Hopkins, **9** Gary Cole, **10** Lizard, **11** Richard, **12** Rory McGrath, **13** Italy, **14** Airedale, **15** You forgot.

QUIZ 224

Answers on page 224

1 Which drummer with The Who was renowned for dumping Rolls Royces in swimming pools?

2 What is aquaculture also known as?

3 Who is the patron saint of Spain?

4 Which football league club plays at Dean Court?

5 Which group's first Top Ten hit came in 1991 with *There's No Other Way*?

6 Which Cole Porter song was inspired by a leaky tap?

7 In boxing what name is given to a class under 8 stone?

8 Which member of the Royal Family was born on 15th September 1984?

9 In animal husbandry, what is AI?

10 Which King was on the English throne during the English Civil War?

11 In which year was the wearing of front seat belts made compulsory in Britain?

12 In what year did the First World War end?

13 Pertussis is the medical name for which infectious disease?

14 Who was Cher's singing partner on her first hit song?

15 Who defeated Tim Henman in the final of the European Community Championship in February 1997?

Things you didn't know...

*Elton John played piano on the Hollies record
He Ain't Heavy, He's My Brother.*

Answers to page 224

1 RSI (Repetitive Strain Injury), 2 Mary Baker Eddy, 3 Thyroid, 4 Pudding Lane, 5 As, 6 Kinglsey Amis, 7 Smetana, 8 St Gabriel, 9 Quebec, 10 Hungary, 11 New Haven, 12 Beatrix Potter, 13 Tau, 14 Epsom salts, 15 Jerusalem.

QUIZ 225

Answers on page 229

1 What is the capital of Australia's Northern Territory?

2 What fires a SLBM?

3 Which footballer was the first player to be sent off playing for England?

4 In which year was the Wall Street Crash?

5 Which actor starred with Sigourney Weaver and Melanie Griffiths in *Working Girl*?

6 Which Spanish singer was a goalkeeper with Real Madrid before a car crash ended his playing career?

7 Frank Sinatra made a guest appearance dressed as a cop in which US show?

8 What sort of guides were published by George Bradshaw?

9 Which US President's presidency was called the Thousand Days?

10 Which British boxer lost to Joe Louis on points in 1937 when fighting for the World Heavywieght Title?

11 What did Sir Lancelot's adultery prevent him from doing?

12 Which day of the week is a child who is said to be 'loving and giving' born?

13 Whose only Number One was *I'm Into Something Good*?

14 Ryeland, Kerry Hill and Roscommon are all breeds of which animal?

15 What is gneiss a type of?

Things you didn't know...

Mia Farrow shot to fame as Allison Mackenzie in the American soap Peyton Place.

Answers to page 229

1 Eskimoes, 2 Kangaroo, 3 Adversary, 4 It's haunted, 5 Bob Dylan, 6 Table Tennis, 7 Oxford, 8 Battle of the Nile, 9 Bill Bixby, 10 James Boswell, 11 Donald Sutherland, 12 Ordinal, 13 Edward 1, 14 *The Partridge Family,* 15 Judy Garland.

QUIZ 226

Answers on page 230

1 Which is the largest island just off the west coast of North America?

2 Which American became World Chess Champion in 1972?

3 Which bird was once known as the halcyon?

4 What would you do with spelding?

5 Who played the title role in the comedy film *The Missionary*?

6 Who said "I've been accused of every death except the casualty list of the World War"?

7 Which is the largest theatre in the West End?

8 What is varicella the correct name for?

9 In which month is Valentine's Day?

10 In which American state is the Garden of the Gods?

11 Which children's writer, Mrs Heelis, spent 30 years breeding Herdwick sheep?

12 What was silent film star Fatty Arbuckle's first name?

13 On TV, who co-starred with Roger Moore in *The Persuaders*?

14 Of which bird did Wordsworth write: "While I am lying on the grass/Thy twofold shout I hear"?

15 Which alcoholic drink's name, when translated literally, means water of life?

Things you didn't know...

Errol Flynn was imprisoned three times for assault, the final time for hitting a New York cop who asked for his autograph.

Answers to page 230

1 Jordan, 2 Marmalade, 3 Joshua Reynolds, 4 The American Civil War, 5 Edith Cavell, 6 Titian, 7 Isis, 8 Michael Foot, 9 Bruce Springsteen's, 10 Bananarama, 11 Elvis Costello, 12 Tunisia, 13 Trombone, 14 Daffodil, 15 Six.

QUIZ 227

Answers on page 227

1 Which people's name means "eaters of raw meat"?

2 Which of D H Lawrence's novels is set in Australia?

3 In Hebrew, what does the name Satan mean?

4 For what is Chinge Hall in Lancashire famous?

5 Who made an album called *Highway 61 Revisited*?

6 At which sport was Fred Perry World Champion in 1929?

7 Which university has a rowing eight called Isis?

8 At which battle of 1798 did the boy stand on the burning deck?

9 Who played the title role in *The Incredible Hulk*?

10 Who wrote the biography of Dr Johnson?

11 Who played the title role in Fellini's *Casanova*?

12 If one, two and three are Cardinal, what are first, second and third?

13 Of which king was Eleanor of Castile queen?

14 In which TV series did Shirley Jones play David Cassidy's mother before becoming his real step mother?

15 By what name did Frances Glumm become better known?

Things you didn't know...

Joan Crawford's contract with MGM went so far as to specify what time she had to be in bed each night.

Answers to page 227

1 Darwin, 2 Submarine, 3 Alan Mullery, 4 1929, 5 Harrison Ford, 6 Julio Inglesias, 7 *Magnum P.I.*, 8 Railway, 9 J F Kennedy's, 10 Tommy Farr, 11 Finding the Holy Grail, 12 Friday, 13 Herman's Hermits, 14 Sheep, 15 Rock.

QUIZ 228

Answers on page 228

1 Which country suffered serious 'bread riots' in August 1996?

2 Who had a Number One hit in 1968 with *Ob-La-Di Ob-La-Da*?

3 Who painted *The Three Graces*?

4 The original carpetbaggers were people trying to profit from the disruption after which war?

5 Which executed British nurse is said to have claimed that patriotism is not enough?

6 Which painter gave his name to a shade of red?

7 Who was the wife of Osiris in Egyptian mythology?

8 Which post-war party leader had the middle name Mackintosh?

9 Whose *Born In the USA* album was a massive bestseller in 1985?

10 Who had a Top Ten hit single in 1984 with *Robert De Niro's Waiting*?

11 *Extreme Honey* is a compilation of songs by which British singer-songwriter?

12 Of which African country is Tunis the capital?

13 Which musical instrument did Tommy Dorsey play?

14 Which flower is sometimes called the Lent Lily?

15 How many standard bottles are there in a Rehoboam?

Things you didn't know...

Justin Henry the Oscar-nominated child star of Kramer vs. Kramer was working as a painter and decorator ten years later.

Answers to page 228

1 Vancouver Island, 2 Bobby Fischer, 3 Kingfisher, 4 Eat it (it's a fish), 5 Michael Palin, 6 Al Capone, 7 Coliseum, 8 Chickenpox, 9 February, 10 Colorado, 11 Beatrix Potter, 12 Roscoe, 13 Tony Curtis, 14 The cuckoo, 15 Whisky.

QUIZ 229

Answers on page 233

1 Which Ricky Valance song was banned by the BBC in 1960?

2 James IV was defeated by the Earl of Surrey in 1513, in which battle?

3 Which mountains form a border between France and Spain?

4 What sort of creature is a greylag?

5 What was the name of the charity collective that had a Number One in 1987 with *Let It Be*?

6 What is the name of the large park in Paris, containing Longchamps racecourse?

7 Who did John Bellingham shoot and kill in the House of Commons in 1812?

8 P.N. Weekes was an opening batsman for which cricket county in the 1996 season?

9 In what year did the first football World Cup take place?

10 Which British athlete competed in her sixth Olympics in 1996?

11 Which county is known as the Garden of England?

12 Who was known by her husband Henry VIII as The Flanders Mare?

13 Which Commonwealth country is divided into three counties - Surrey, Middlesex and Cornwall?

14 What is a twayblade?

15 Who was King Solomon's mother?

Things you didn't know...

Charles Dickens always touched things three times for luck.

Answers to page 233

1 Lear, 2 Three, 3 River Ruhr, 4 Nevada, 5 Lancasters, 6 Diphtheria, 7 Eclipse, 8 John Buchan, 9 A dog, 10 Linconshire, 11 Everton, 12 Southfork, 13 Souwester, 14 Paul Weller, 15 W C Fields.

QUIZ 230

Answers on page 234

1 Which suspension bridge near San Francisco was completed in 1937?

2 What is pedagogy the science of?

3 Which member of the Royal Family took the surname Mountbatten in 1947 when he became a British citizen?

4 Which US city is known as the rubber capital of the world?

5 What sort of creature is a Shih tzu?

6 Who played the police chief in the film *Jaws*?

7 The artist George Stubbs is best known for paintings of which animal?

8 Which many-headed monster's blood killed Hercules?

9 In which African country is the town of Timbuktu?

10 What is the maximum number of clubs that a golfer is allowed?

11 What is a mature horse below the height of fourteen and a half hands called?

12 According to Greek mythology, which god was the father of Apollo, Athena and Dionysus?

13 Which letter of the Greek alphabet is the equivalent to 'I'?

14 Which large town stands on the Orwell estuary?

15 Visual communication between ships by manual use of flags is called what?

Things you didn't know...

British boxer, Henry Cooper, starred as prizefighter John Gully in the 1975 film Royal Flush.

Answers to page 234

1 Coco-cola, 2 Audrey Hepburn, 3 Nucleus, 4 Chalk, 5 California, 6 Zinc, 7 Cliff Richard - following his appearance on *Oh Boy!* where he was apparently 'smouldering on screen'!, 8 John Thaw, 9 Denis Weaver, 10 Bronze, 11 Centaurs, 12 Jack Dempsey, 13 Abraham Lincoln, 14 1997, 15 Antonio.

QUIZ 231

Answers on page 231

1 Which British poet was noted for his illustrated nonsense poems?

2 How many of Henry VIII's children later succeeded to the throne?

3 Which major river flows past Essen to join the River Rhine at Duisburg?

4 In which state of the USA are the cities of Las Vegas and Reno situated?

5 Which planes were used by the Dam Busters?

6 Which disease is tested for by the Schich Test?

7 Which word describes the passage of all or part of an astronomical body into the shadow of another?

8 Who wrote *The Thirty-Nine Steps*?

9 What exactly is a chow-chow?

10 In which county is Skegness?

11 Which football team reached three consecutive FA Cup Finals during the 1980's?

12 What is the name of the ranch in *Dallas*?

13 What is the name of the waterproof hat worn by sailors?

14 Who released an album called *Heavy Soul* in 1997?

15 Who said: "It's a funny old world - a man's lucky if he gets out of it alive."?

Things you didn't know...

Croquet made a solitary appearance as an Olympic sport in the 1900 Games in Paris. All the competitors were French.

Answers to page 231

1 *Tell Laura I Love Her*, 2 Flodden Field, 3 Pyrenees, 4 A goose, 5 Ferry Aid, 6 Bois De Boulogne, 7 Spencer Perceval, 8 Middlesex, 9 1930, 10 Tessa Sanderson, 11 Kent, 12 Anne of Cleves, 13 Jamaica, 14 An orchid, 15 Bathsheba.

QUIZ 232

Answers on page 232

1 What did pharmacist John Styth Pemberton concoct as a headache cure?

2 Who played Eliza Doolittle in the film My Fair Lady?

3 What is the central part of an atom called?

4 Which TV comedy series was set in Galfast high school?

5 In which US State are the Sierra Nevada mountains?

6 Which metal provides an outer protective layer after iron has been galvanised?

7 When a national newspaper warned "Don't let your daughter go out with people like this" who were they talking about?

8 On TV who played Kavanagh QC?

9 Who played McCloud on television?

10 Of which metal is a British penny made?

11 In Greek mythology, what name was applied to creatures who were half-men, half-horse?

12 Which beaten boxer said to his wife in 1926: "Honey, I forgot to duck."?

13 The election of whom in America in 1860 was the main cause of the American Civil War?

14 In which year was Hong Kong handed back to China?

15 From who did Shylock wish to take his pound of flesh?

Things you didn't know...

Churches in Malta have two clocks both showing different times to confuse the Devil about the time of the next service.

Answers to page 232

1 The Golden Gate Bridge, **2** Teaching, **3** The Duke of Edinburgh, **4** Akron, **5** A dog, **6** Roy Scheider, **7** Horse, **8** Hydra, **9** Mali, **10** Fourteen, **11** A pony, **12** Zeus, **13** Iota, **14** Ipswich, **15** Semaphore.

QUIZ 233

Answers on page 237

1 Which All Saints singer was banned from apearing on *The Big Breakfast* for six months after swearing on-air?

2 What was the name of the hurricane that lashed the coast of Carolina in September 1996?

3 What name is given to the flat piece of iron that connects railway rails?

4 Which perennial herb is also known as milfoil?

5 What is the capital of the Bahamas?

6 Where did Rosemary West live?

7 Which is the only poisonous snake in Britain?

8 Which planet in our solar system is nearest the sun?

9 Which popular radio and TV doctor was created by Scottish physician and novelist A J Cronin?

10 From which plant is tapioca derived?

11 Which German artist pioneered the artistic technique of frottage?

12 Which evergreen tree's berries are used to flavour gin?

13 Who played the lead in the TV series *Sorry*?

14 What was the name of Queen Victoria's residence on the Isle of Wight?

15 The Trans-Siberian railway runs from Moscow to which city?

Things you didn't know...

*Lucille Ball was never allowed to say 'pregnant' on
I Love Lucy – It had to be 'expecting'.*

Answers to page 237

1 Euthanasia, 2 Somerset House, 3 New Amsterdam, 4 Nightingale, 5 Ian Gow, 6 Richard Adams, 7 Neil Sedaka, 8 Ian Smith, 9 Gene Anthony Ray, 10 Bird (Oriole), 11 Bismarck, 12 Melbourne, 13 England, 14 Shakespeare, 15 The Farthing.

QUIZ 234

Answers on page 238

1 Which common substance is made by boiling down horns, hides and hoofs?

2 What was Shakespeare's son's name?

3 Who, in 1955, became the youngest player to be capped for England at soccer?

4 What is the highest-pitched woodwind instrument?

5 What is the capital of Kenya?

6 Ashton Cross and Bedford Giant are varieties of which fruit?

7 Bullace and Czar are varieties of which fruit?

8 True or false: Henry Patrick McCarty was Billy the Kid's real name?

9 Who died before work on her last film *Something's Gotta Give* was completed?

10 Which letter of the Greek alphabet is the equivalent to 'E'?

11 By what name was Domenico Theotocupuli better known?

12 In what year did England host and win football's World Cup?

13 Who scored a double century in England's Test Match victory over Australia at Edgbaston in 1997?

14 In which French city can the Folies-Bergere be found?

15 Which band had a Number One hit single in 1978 with *Figaro*?

Things you didn't know...

Liz Taylor made a voice-only guest appearance on The Simpson's by gurgling baby Maggie Simpson's first words.

Answers to page 238

1 Winnipeg, 2 Five, 3 Cow, 4 *The Mikado,* 5 Carol Ann Ford, 6 Rainfall, 7 Mark Walters, 8 Panhandle, 9 Edward Woodward, 10 Michele Dotrice, 11 Astaire, 12 Estonia, 13 Earnest, 14 Ecuador, 15 Humerus.

QUIZ 235

Answers on page 235

1 With what is the society called EXIT concerned?

2 Which government building in the Strand, London, was formerly the home of the General Register Office?

3 What was the original name of New York?

4 In the song, which bird sang in Berkeley Square?

5 Which Treasury Minister was murdered by an IRA bomb outside his home in 1990?

6 Who wrote *Watership Down*?

7 Who had a hit with *Oh Carol*?

8 Who plays Harold Bishop in *Neighbours*?

9 Who played Leroy in the film version of *Fame*?

10 What is a grackle?

11 Who was known as the Iron Chancellor?

12 In which Australian city is *Neighbours* set?

13 In which country was writer Arthur Hailey born?

14 Who had children called Suzanna, Hamnet and Judith?

15 Which British coin ceased to be legal currency in January 1961?

Things you didn't know...

Singer Elaine Page had a small part as Caroline Winthrop in Crossroads in the 1960s.

Answers to page 235

1 Melanie Blatt, **2** Fran, **3** Fishplate, **4** Yarrow, **5** Nassau, **6** 25 Cromwell Street, **7** The adder, **8** Mercury, **9** *Doctor Finlay,* **10** Cassava, **11** Max Ernst, **12** Juniper, **13** Ronnie Corbett, **14** Osborne House, **15** Vladivostok.

QUIZ 236

Answers on page 236

1 What is the capital of Manitoba province in Canada?

2 For every seven white keys on a piano, how many black keys are there?

3 Hathor, the Egyptian goddess of love, had the head of which animal?

4 In which Gilbert and Sullivan operetta does Pooh Bah appear?

5 Which actress was the first one to travel with *Dr Who*?

6 What does a pluviometer gauge?

7 Which former Liverpool player's middle name was Everton?

8 What is Fitz's nickname for Penhaligan in *Cracker*?

9 Which actor played *Callan* in the TV series about a secret service agent?

10 And which actress is he married to?

11 Which Fred danced with Ginger Rogers?

12 Tallinn is the capital of which country?

13 *The Importance of Being* what is the name of an Oscar Wilde play?

14 Quito is the capital of which South American country?

15 What is the proper name for the funny bone?

Things you didn't know...

Anthony Hopkins turned down the part of Gandhi which won Ben Kingsley an Oscar in 1982.

Answers to page 236

1 Glue, 2 Hamnet, 3 Duncan Edwards, 4 Piccolo, 5 Nairobi, 6 Blackberry, 7 Plum, 8 True, 9 Marilyn Monroe, 10 Epsilon, 11 El Greco, 12 1966, 13 Nasser Hussain, 14 Paris, 15 The Brotherhood Of Man.

QUIZ 237

Answers on page 241

1 In *The Likely Lads*, what was Bob's girlfriend called?

2 Who replaced Phil Collins as lead singer of Genesis?

3 What was David Bowie's first British Number One hit?

4 Which football team won the English 1997-98 Premier League and F.A.Cup double?

5 Which disease does the BCG vaccine protect against?

6 Which former Chilean dictator was arrested at a West London clinic in October 1998??

7 Which poet is buried in Grasmere churchyard?

8 Which Greek island was home to the Minoan civilisation?

9 What were The Kinks *Dedicated Followers of* in 1966?

10 What is the name of the box in which a ship's compass is stored?

11 Who had a Number One hit with *Three Steps to Heaven*?

12 The deficiency of which vitamin can cause rickets?

13 By what name is a smoked herring better known?

14 Which actor played the title role in *Lou Grant*?

15 Who wrote *It Shouldn't Happen to a Vet*?

Things you didn't know...

Clark Gable is listed on his birth certificate as a girl.

Answers to page 241

1 Grace Kelly, 2 Mozambique, 3 Led Zeppelin, 4 Ice-cream, 5 David II, 6 Horses, 7 Baseball (Brooklyn Dodgers), 8 Somerset Maughan, 9 Burt Lancaster, 10 Mediterranean, 11 Geri Halliwell (Ginger Spice), 12 Russell Harty, 13 Swansea, 14 World's heaviest bell, 15 Stanley Baldwin.

QUIZ 238

Answers on page 242

1 Which Derby-winning horse was kidnapped by the IRA and never been recovered?

2 Which engine was patented by Frank Whittle in 1930?

3 Which Edinburgh football club takes its name from the Roman name for Ireland?

4 Which member of the Royal family was spotted with her tongue pierced with a metal stud in August 1998?

5 How many cents are there in a nickel?

6 What was the surname of the Everest climber Sherpa Tensing?

7 Where exactly in Japan did Damon Hill become 1996 world motor racing champion?

8 Which British monarch died in the battle of Flodden Field?

9 On a monopoly board, which property clockwise is situated after the Electric Co.?

10 Which British actor, director and dramatist wrote the plays *Romanoff and Juliet* and *Beethoven's Tenth*?

11 Which Benny was known as the 'King of Swing'?

12 Who played *Dr Phibes* in two films?

13 Of which South American republic is Paramaribo the capital?

14 Tehran is the capital of which country?

15 Which is the second largest city in England?

Things you didn't know...

John Pierpont Morgan, the owner of Titanic, missed the maiden voyage due to ill health.

Answers to page 242

1 Crab, 2 A Caribou, 3 George II's, 4 Nightingale, 5 Princess Margaret, 6 Good Friday, 7 Israel, 8 York, 9 Michael Hutchence, 10 John Higgins, 11 C.S. Lewis, 12 Judy, 13 Switzerland, 14 Ian Lavender, 15 Caroline Quentin.

QUIZ 239

Answers on page 239

1 Who was the female star of the film *High Noon*?

2 In which country does the Zambezi reach the sea?

3 Robert Plant was lead singer with which group founded in 1968?

4 What is cassata a type of?

5 Who succeeded Robert the Bruce as King of the Scots?

6 For what kind of paintings was Alfred Munnings famous?

7 Jackie Robinson was the first black man to play which sport at league level?

8 Which writer, who died in 1965, wrote the novel *Of Human Bondage*?

9 Who starred in the title role of the 1960 film *Elmer Gantry*?

10 Which sea separates Europe and Africa?

11 Which member of the Spice Girls quit the band in May 1998?

12 Which TV presenter said: "There was life before *Coronation Street*, but it didn't add up to much."?

13 What is the second largest city in Wales?

14 What is the Tsar Kolokol?

15 Who was British PM from 1924-29?

Things you didn't know...

Gordon Sumner was christened 'Sting' as a teenager because he often wore a wasp-striped T-shirt.

Answers to page 239

1 Thelma, 2 Ray Wilson, 3 *Space Oddity,* 4 Arsenal, 5 Tuberculosis, 6 General Pinochet, 7 Wordsworth, 8 Crete, 9 Fashion, 10 Binnacle, 11 Eddie Cochran, 12 Vitamin D, 13 Kipper, 14 Ed Asner, 15 James Herriot.

QUIZ 240

Answers on page 240

1 Which creature represents the star sign Cancer?

2 What do the Americans call reindeer?

3 Which English king's son was nicknamed Prince Titi?

4 Which Florence was known as the lady with the lamp?

5 Which member of the Royal family suffered a stroke on the holiday isle of Mustique in February 1998?

6 On which day in April 1998 was the peace agreement signed in Northern Ireland?

7 Which country does the trans-sexual Eurovision Song Contest winner Dana International come from?

8 Which Royal house ruled England from 1461 to 1485?

9 Which INXS star hanged himself in an Australian hotel room?

10 Which Englishman won the 1998 Embassy World Snooker Championship?

11 Who wrote *The Lion, the Witch and the Wardrobe*?

12 Who is Punch's puppet wife?

13 What country does Gruyere cheese come from?

14 Who played 'Pike' in BBC's *Dads Army*?

15 Who played crime writer Madelaine Magellan in the TV crime mystery series *Jonathon Creek*?

Things you didn't know...

Mary, Queen of Scots became Queen at the age of one week.

Answers to page 240

1 Shergar, 2 Jet, 3 Hibernian, 4 Princess Anne's daughter Zara, 5 5, 6 Norgay, 7 Suzuku, 8 James IV, 9 Whitehall, 10 Peter Ustinov, 11 Goodman, 12 Vincent Price, 13 Suriname, 14 Iran, 15 Birmingham.

QUIZ 241

Answers on page 245

1 What is the correct medical terminology for inflammation of the brain?

2 In which country did Queen Beatrix succeed her mother Queen Juliana in 1980?

3 What is the administrative centre of East Sussex?

4 Who was the last British writer to win the Nobel prize for literature?

5 What name is given to the study of the relationship between living things and the environment in which they live?

6 Which American state is Atlanta the capital of?

7 Where does a breast buffer work?

8 What is a female trout called?

9 To which genus of plants does the snapdragon belong?

10 What is the tallest living four-legged mammal?

11 Who was the eldest of the Bronte sisters?

12 Which country does Jurgen Klinsmann come from?

13 Who released an album called *The Immaculate Collection*?

14 What is the only flying mammal?

15 Who in Great Britain can never legally be a minor?

Things you didn't know...

Attila the Hun died the night after his wedding.

Answers to page 245

1 Sleep on it, 2 Stanley Kubrick, 3 Hot air balloon, 4 Peter Snow, 5 Sunday, 6 Sicily, 7 Little boys, 8 Moose, 9 A beetle, 10 Punt, 11 Walt Disney, 12 Bluebell Railway, 13 Butchers, 14 Denver, 15 *My Fair Lady*.

QUIZ 242

Answers on page 246

1 Who became World chess champion in 1975?

2 In which country did Chris Eubank make his comeback to boxing in 1996?

3 Who won the Saga World Indoor Singles Bowls title in February 1997?

4 What was the name of the US Spy vessel seized by the North Koreans in 1968?

5 What is the chief food of baby whales?

6 Which famous stones can be found on Salisbury Plain?

7 In which card game would you 'meld'?

8 Who is the heroine of Beethoven's opera *Fidelio*?

9 Of the seven colours of the rainbow, which one is in the middle?

10 Under what name did Lord Tweedsmuir write several novels?

11 Which US national holiday is celebrated with roast turkey and pumpkin pie?

12 What is the first book of the Bible?

13 In which year did the Battle of Bannockburn take place?

14 Who invented the hovercraft?

15 When Argentinians landed on South Georgia in 1982 what had they supposedly come to collect?

Things you didn't know...

The albatross can sleep in mid-air and can glide for six days without beating its wings.

Answers to page 246

1 Kenneth Grahame, 2 Dr Who, 3 David Essex, 4 Jewish bread, 5 Sir Arthur Conan Doyle, 6 Tennis, 7 The USA, 8 Colony, 9 John Wayne, 10 Arsenal, 11 *Father of the House,* 12 Brooklands, 13 Card games, 14 Lady Jane Grey, 15 Mussolin.

QUIZ 243

Answers on page 243

1 What would you do with a futon?

2 Who directed the Vietnam war drama *Full Metal Jacket*?

3 What did the Mongolfier brothers fly in 1783?

4 Which *Newsnight* presenter joined *Tomorrow's World*?

5 On what day of the week must a month start for it to have a Friday the 13th?

6 On which Italian island is the volcano Mount Etna?

7 According to the nursery rhyme, what are made from frogs, snails and puppy-dogs tails?

8 What do the Americans call an elk?

9 Which is the heaviest insect?

10 What name is given to the flat-bottomed boat, steered with a long pole?

11 Who has won more Oscars than any other person in the film industry?

12 Sheffield Park and Horsted Keynes are two stations on which railway line?

13 Who are members of the Q Guild?

14 Which American Football team are called the Broncos?

15 In which film did Rex Harrison win his only Oscar?

Things you didn't know...

The Falkland Islands has a human population of under 2,000 but a sheep population of 700,000 – making 350 sheep for every person.

Answers to page 243

1 Encephalitis, **2** The Netherlands, **3** Lewes, **4** William Golding, **5** Ecology, **6** Georgia, **7** In a shoe factory, **8** Hen, **9** Antirrhinum, **10** Giraffe, **11** Charlotte, **12** Germany, **13** Madonna, **14** Bat, **15** The Sovereign.

QUIZ 244

Answers on page 244

1 Who wrote *The Wind in the Willows*?

2 Who made enemies of the Orgons, the Zygons and the Kroll?

3 Who played the lead role in the TV series *The River*?

4 What is matze?

5 Who wrote *Rodney Stone, The White Company* and *The Lost World*?

6 With which sport are Bob Falkenberg, Dick Savitt and Ted Schroeder associated?

7 Which country won all the track and field events at the 1904 Olympics?

8 What is the collective name for beavers?

9 Who played the male lead in *Blood Alley, The High and Mighty* and *in Harm's Way*?

10 Which football team sold Ian Wright to West Ham United?

11 Which honorary title is given to the MP who has sat in the Commons for the longest uninterrupted period?

12 Where was the first British Grand Prix held in 1926?

13 On which area of leisure was Edmond Hoyle an authority?

14 Which English queen was married to Lord Guildford Dudley?

15 Which Second World War leader was executed and exhibited by his own people?

Things you didn't know...

The Malaysian pitcher plant not only eats innsects but is also capable of devouring rats and frogs.

Answers to page 244

1 Anatoly Karpov, 2 Egypt, 3 High Duff, 4 U.S.S Pueblo, 5 Their mother's milk, 6 Stonehenge, 7 Canasta, 8 Leonore, 9 Green, 10 John Buchan, 11 Thanksgiving Day, 12 Genesis, 13 1314, 14 Sir Christopher Cockerell, 15 Scrap metal.

QUIZ 245

Answers on page 249

1 What is the popular name for the painful spasmodic contraction of a muscle?

2 Which country is divided into twenty-three cantons?

3 Where in London is the Jerusalem Chamber?

4 In which country is the Drakensberg mountain range?

5 Which war began on June 25th, 1950?

6 Which British driver was World Motor Racing Champion in 1969, 1971 and 1973?

7 Under which stretch of water would you be if you were on Le Shuttle?

8 Sun, spectacled, brown and sloth are all species of what?

9 When was the National Trust founded?

10 Who, on TV, played Jack Ford in *When the Boat Comes In* and a teacher in *The Beiderbecke Affair*?

11 Of which two gases is Jupiter mainly composed?

12 Who played Dr Cameron in the TV series *Dr Finlay's Casebook*?

13 What was Clint Eastwood's character in *Rawhide* called?

14 On which river does the French city of Chartres stand?

15 What was the name of *David Copperfield*'s old nurse?

Things you didn't know...

Roy Rogers was so devoted to Trigger that when the horse died he had it stuffed and mounted.

Answers to page 249

1 Matt LeBlanc, 2 Mozart, 3 H E Bates, 4 Cape Canaveral, 5 The sousaphone, 6 Antonia, 7 Paper Lace, 8 Jonathon Swift, 9 Lipstick kiss on brow, 10 Monaco, 11 Stone anchor, 12 Mick Fitzgerald, 13 Aniseed, 14 John Barry, 15 La Marseillaise.

QUIZ 246

Answers on page 250

1 Which UK group had 1987 hits with *Heart and Soul and China in Your Hand*?

2 Who is the first female in the order of accession to the British throne?

3 Which Frenchman is credited with the creation of the European Economic community?

4 Which is the main trophy for eights won at Henley Royal Regatta?

5 To which group of dogs does the Irish Setter belong?

6 Which fish has a poisonous, serrated spine on it's tail?

7 In the RAF how many squadrons make up a wing?

8 What is the capital of Portugal?

9 What did Doctor Foster step in on his way to Gloucester?

10 Who played the title character in the TV series *My Wife Next Door*?

11 Which city is the setting for *Saturday Night Fever*?

12 What was the last battle of the Wars of the Roses?

13 Which singer's catchphrase was "You ain't heard nothing yet"?

14 Which Harrod's boss became Chairman of Fulham FC?

15 What name is given to ornamental gilded bronze, used to decorate furniture?

Things you didn't know...

North Dakota is known as the Flickertail State because of the large population of squirrels that live there.

Answers to page 250

1 Bob Hoskins, 2 Gipsy Moth IV, 3 Anne Archer, 4 Queen Victoria, 5 The Yang, 6 Eggs, 7 Corsica, 8 George Harrison, 9 Devon, 10 Bucephalus, 11 A sea battle, 12 Eighteen, 13 Kon-Tiki, 14 Teflon, 15 Shoulder Pork and ham.

QUIZ 247

Answers on page 247

1 Who played Joey in TV's *Friends*?

2 Which composer wrote the *Paris, Prague and Jupiter* symphonies?

3 Who wrote *The Darling Buds of May*?

4 Which NASA launch site was known as Cape Kennedy from 1963 to 1973?

5 What musical instrument was invented by John Philip Sousa?

6 From whom did Shylock wish to take his pound of flesh?

7 Who had a Number One hit in 1974 with *Billy Don't be a Hero*?

8 Who wrote *Gulliver's Travels*?

9 How did the killer mark his victims in *No Way To Treat a Lady*?

10 Of which sovereign state is Prince Rainier III ruler?

11 What is a killick?

12 Who said, after winning the Grand National: "Sex is an anti-climax after that"?

13 What do fennel leaves taste of?

14 Who performed the theme song for the James Bond film *Dr No*?

15 What is the French national anthem called?

Things you didn't know...

An Ohio law states that pets have to carry lights on their tails at night.

Answers to page 247

1 Cramp, 2 Switzerland, 3 Westminster Abbey, 4 South Africa, 5 Korean, 6 Jackie Stewart, 7 English Channel, 8 Bear, 9 1895, 10 James Bolam, 11 Hydrogen and helium, 12 Andrew Cruickshank, 13 Rowdy Yates, 14 River Eure, 15 Peggotty.

QUIZ 248

Answers on page 248

1 In the British Telecom adverts, which cockney actor said, "It's good to talk"?

2 Which yacht is preserved alongside the Cutty Sark at Greenwich?

3 Who played Michael Douglas's wife in *Fatal Attraction*?

4 Who was known as the Widow of Windsor?

5 In Chinese cosmology, what is the contrast and complement to the Yin?

6 Which ingredient, vital to choux pastry, is missing from puff pastry?

7 On which island was Napoleon Bonaparte born?

8 Which of the four Beatles was the youngest?

9 In which county is the resort of Budleigh Salterton?

10 What was Alexander the Great's famous warhorse called?

11 What does the Glorious First of June commemorate?

12 How many players are in an Australian Rules football side?

13 What was the name of the raft Thor Heyerdahl used to sail from Peru in 1947?

14 By what name is polytetrafluoroethylene better known?

15 What does the name Spam stand for?

Things you didn't know...

Swedish tennis maestro Bjorn Borg stopped shaving four days before each major championship.

Answers to page 248

1 T'pau, 2 Princess Beatrice, 3 Jean Monnet, 4 Grand Challenge Cup, 5 Gundogs, 6 Stingray, 7 Three, 8 Lisbon, 9 A puddle, 10 Hannah Gordon, 11 New York, 12 Battle of Bosworth Field, 13 Al Jolson's, 14 Mohamed Al Fayed, 15 Ormolu.

QUIZ 249

Answers on page 253

1 Which disease characterised by stiffness and spasms is popularly called lockjaw?

2 Who was British open golf champion in 1995?

3 Which locomotive holds the speed record for steam locomotives?

4 Which country invaded Kuwait in 1990?

5 Who was the original English clown?

6 Who had 1980s Top Ten Hits with *System Addict, Find the Time,* and *Rain or Shine*?

7 Who said: "The lion and the calf shall lie down together, but the calf won't get much sleep."?

8 Which Italian island was the first place of exile of Napoleon I of France?

9 Which Hampshire air show is held biennially in September?

10 Which American film producer produced the early Bond films as well as *Cockleshell Heroes* and *Chitty Chitty Bang Bang*?

11 Who was World Darts Champion 5 times between 1980 and 1986?

12 Edward de Vere, 17th Earl of Oxford, is claimed by some as the real author of what?

13 Where was the first land battle of the Falklands War?

14 By what other name is a Dublin Bay Prawn called?

15 In which film did Whoopi Goldberg play a character called Deloris?

Things you didn't know...

Tutankhamen's coffin weighs 2,450lb and is made of solid gold.

Answers to page 253

1 U-2, 2 Lichfield, 3 Miss Pears, 4 Pasta, 5 Billy Crystal, 6 Lead, 7 *Dallas,* 8 Fire, 9 Sebastian Coe, 10 Bernadette Devlin, 11 Beach Boys, 12 Hunter's moon, 13 Steve Cauthen, 14 15, 15 Robert Mugabe.

QUIZ 250

Answers on page 254

1 Which *Coronation Street* character was played by Warren Jackson before he was replaced by Adam Ricketts?

2 In which sport is the America's Cup contested?

3 What word describes the permanent disappearance of a species ?

4 Who wrote *The Magus, The French Lieutenant's Woman* and *Daniel Martin*?

5 Which actor plays Chief Supt Brownlow in *The Bill*?

6 In which US state are The Everglades?

7 With which trade is London's Hatton Garden associated?

8 What did Jack Horner eat in the corner?

9 Which group had *A Momentary Lapse of Reason* in 1987?

10 Who said: "Don't point that beard at me: it might go off"?

11 Which rock star died when the car he was travelling in crashed into a tree September 1977?

12 In George Orwell's *1984* what is Britain called?

13 Which character from a comic was known as The Pilot of the Future?

14 Which member of the Royal family married Marina of Greece?

15 Which county won the Cricket County Championship seven times in succession in the 1950s?

Things you didn't know...

Kapok, used for stuffing cushions and cuddly toy, grows on trees.

Answers to page 254

1 Shark, **2** 27, **3** Rainfall, **4** Robin Cook, **5** Dieting, **6** Gross Domestic Product, **7** Italian, **8** Yellow, **9** Greta Garbo, **10** Ron Davies, **11** Whoopi Goldberg, **12** Steptoe and Son, **13** Who Dares Wins, **14** Uruguay, **15** Wine.

QUIZ 251

Answers on page 251

1 Which aircraft, piloted by Gary powers, was shot down by Russia on 1st May.1960?

2 Which British cathedral has three spires?

3 What title was Emma Cox the last to hold?

4 What is the generic name for spaghetti, macaroni and lasagne, etc?

5 In the film *When Harry Met Sally*, who played Harry?

6 Galena is the chief source of which metal?

7 *Knots Landing* was a spin-off from which other soap opera?

8 What would you keep in a cresset?

9 Who became MP for Falmouth and Camborne in 1992?

10 Later to be Mrs McAliskey, who became MP for Mid Ulster in 1969?

11 Who had a 1966 hit with *Good Vibrations*?

12 What is the full moon following the harvest moon called?

13 Who was the first jockey to win the English Derby and the Kentucky Derby?

14 How many players are there in a hurling team?

15 Who was the leader of Zanu who became Zimbabwe's first president?

Things you didn't know...

The World's first drinking straw was patented in January 1888.

Answers to page 251

1 Tetanus, 2 John Daly, 3 The Mallard, 4 Iraq, 5 Grimaldi, 6 Five Star, 7 Woody Allen, 8 Elba, 9 Farnborough, 10 Cubby Broccoli, 11 Eric Bristow, 12 Shakespeare's works, 13 Goose Green, 14 Scampi, 15 *Sister Act*.

QUIZ 252

Answers on page 252

1 What kind of fish is a hammerhead?

2 What is the cube of 3?

3 What is measured using a pluviometer?

4 Who became Foreign Secretary in May 1997?

5 What would you be doing if you practised banting?

6 What does the abbreviation GDP stand for?

7 What is the official language of San Marino?

8 What colour is the Circle Line on a map of the London Underground?

9 Which actress is supposed to have said 'I want to be alone'?

10 Which Welsh Secretary resigned after a 'serious lapse of judgement' on Clapham Common in September 1998?

11 Which actress starred in *The Colour Purple, Jumpin Jack Flash* and *Ghost*?

12 Which Galton and Simpson T.V. comedy was set in Oil Drum Lane?

13 What is the motto of the Special Air Service?

14 Which South American country hosted the Copa America in 1995?

15 To what is the French word 'chambre' applied?

Things you didn't know...

Dallas/Fort Worth airport covers a larger area than the whole of Manhattan.

Answers to page 252

1 Nicky Tilsley, 2 Yachting, 3 Extinction, 4 John Fowles, 5 Peter Ellis, 6 Florida, 7 Diamonds, 8 Christmas Pie, 9 Pink Floyd, 10 Groucho Marx, 11 Marc Bolan, 12 Airstrip one, 13 Dan Dare, 14 Duke of Kent, 15 Surrey.

QUIZ 253

Answers on page 257

1 In which Dickens novel does Richard Carstone appear?

2 In the TV series *Telford's Change*, what was Telford's job?

3 In which country is the city of Kosice?

4 What is the boiling point of water on the Fahrenheit scale?

5 What finally stood in for Roy Hattersley when he couldn't appear on *Have I Got News For You* on TV?

6 Which fashion designer designs under the Emporio label?

7 In the USA, what does the John Birch Society oppose?

8 Who painted the ceiling of the Sistine Chapel?

9 With what is the organisation CER N concerned?

10 Which French phrase means an arrangement involving a married couple and the lover of one of them?

11 Who had Top Ten hits with *Red Light Spells Danger, Suddenly,* and *Caribbean Queen*?

12 Which actress played Alf Garnett's daughter in TV's *Till Death Us Do Part*?

13 The Colorado Beetle attacks what cultivated plant in particular?

14 Who wrote the tragic novel *Wuthering Heights*?

15 Which ex-England football star is the father of a television weather forecaster?

Things you didn't know...

Vexillology is the term for the study of flags.

Answers to page 257

1 Goat, 2 French, 3 Malcolm Bradbury, 4 Pale Blue, 5 Jack Brabham, 6 Doge, 7 New York, 8 Pontiac, 9 Cycling, 10 Pimento, 11 Dolphin, 12 John Monk, 13 The Koran, 14 Los Angeles, 15 Mel Gibson.

QUIZ 254

Answers on page 258

1 Which city produces the most cars in the world?

2 Who painted *The Persistence of Memory*?

3 Who was *Botanic Man* in the 1978 TV series?

4 Of which country is Christmas Island a territory?

5 Which Miss USA 1972 starred as *Wonder Woman*?

6 Which Harry presented TV's *Highway*?

7 What is America's smallest state?

8 Which country is Riyadh the capital of?

9 Who won his first Oscar for *One Flew Over the Cuckoo's Nest*?

10 In which year did John Glenn become the first American to orbit the earth?

11 Which UK singer's real name is Gordon Sumner?

12 Which film featured Elvis Presley's second screen appearance?

13 Which property comes befor Marylebone Station on a Monopoly board?

14 What was Fats Domino's only Top Ten hit called?

15 What is the name for a dislike of foreigners?

Things you didn't know...

The duckbilled platypus carries a poisonous sting.

Answers to page 258

1 Augusta, 2 Leicestershire, 3 Phoenix, 4 Chalk, 5 Womens 1500 metres, 6 Nottingham, 7 Lonnie Donegan, 8 Iva Majoli, 9 *Match of the Day*, 10 Coracle, 11 Limestone, 12 Alsatian, 13 Volkswagen, 14 Dry, 15 Philadelphia.

QUIZ 255

Answers on page 255

1 Which hoofed ruminant mammal belongs to the genus Capra?

2 What nationality was the painter Raoul Dufy?

3 Who wrote *The History Man*?

4 What colour beret is usually worn by United Nations peace-keeping troops?

5 Which Australian motor-racing driver was World Champion in 1959, 1960 and 1966?

6 What name was given to the elected leaders of Venice?

7 In which city is the Whitney art gallery?

8 Which American car manufacturer produces the Firebird?

9 In which sport are there madisons and pursuits?

10 What is another name for allspice?

11 On TV, what kind of creature was *Flipper*?

12 Who became General Secretary of the TUC in 1993 after 6 years of being it's deputy.

13 What is the most sacred book of muslims called?

14 Of which American city is Hollywood a suburb?

15 Who the voice of Captain John Smith in Walt Disney's *Pocahontas*?

Things you didn't know...

Sir Isaac Newton named the colours of the rainbow.

Answers to page 255

1 *Bleak House,* 2 Bank manager, 3 Slovakia, 4 212F, 5 A tub of lard, 6 Armani, 7 Communism, 8 Michelangelo, 9 Nuclear Research, 10 Menage A Trois, 11 Billy Ocean, 12 Una Stubbs, 13 Potato, 14 Emily Brönte, 15 Bobby Charlton.

QUIZ 256

Answers on page 256

1 What is the capital of US state Maine?

2 In which English county is Charnwood Forest?

3 Which city is served by Sky Harbour airport?

4 Which sort of rock forms most of the Chiltern Hills and the White Cliffs of Dover?

5 Algerian athlete Hassiba Boulmerka won an Olympic gold medal in 1992 in which event?

6 Whose dialling code was 0602 prior to April 16th 1995?

7 Who had a Number One hit with *My Old Man's A Dustman*?

8 Which Croatian tennis player beat Martina Hingis to win the 1997 French Open?

9 What is the name of the BBC long-running Saturday night soccer programme?

10 What name is given to the boat with an oval wickerwork frame covered with a leather skin?

11 Marble is formed by the metamorphosis of which rock?

12 How is a German shepherd dog otherwise known?

13 Which car manufacturer produced the Jetta?

14 What does the word brut signify on a French wine bottle?

15 In which city was the American Constitution signed?

Things you didn't know...

The Chinese were the first to use toilet paper.

Answers to page 256

1 Detroit, 2 Dali, 3 David Bellamy, 4 Australia, 5 Lynda Carter, 6 Secombe, 7 Rhode Island, 8 Saudi Arabia, 9 Jack Nicholson, 10 1962, 11 Sting's, 12 *Loving You*, 13 Northumberland Avenue, 14 *Blueberry Hill*, 15 Xenophobia.

QUIZ 257

Answers on page 261

1 Which English buccaneer and explorer sailed around the world in the Golden Hind?

2 Who played the title role in the 1980 film *Brubaker*?

3 Last Bus to Woodstock in 1975 was the first novel to feature which detective?

4 What was the name of Louis XV's mistress?

5 Whose biography did Clifford Irving fake?

6 On which horse did Fred Winter win the Grand National in 1957?

7 Who lived at 221b Baker Street?

8 Which country did Salvador Dali come from?

9 What name is given to the study of language sounds?

10 Who was the princess in *Sleeping Beauty*?

11 The face of *Aladdin* in the Disney film was based on that of which film actor?

12 Which French novelist defended Dreyfus in an open letter entitled J'Accuse?

13 Which footballer made a record with Lindisfarne?

14 Which European capital city shares its name with Rigsby's cat in *Rising Damp*?

15 In America, what is a cayuse?

Things you didn't know...

Boy Eskimos are taught to smoke a pipe, often when they are as young as three years old.

Answers to page 261

1 Lucille Ball, **2** Zinc, **3** An Air Raid Siren, **4** Knave of Hearts, **5** Bamboo, **6** 9, **7** Atlantic City's, **8** Gypsy, **9** Shirley MacLaine, **10** David Essex, **11** Michael, **12** Barry Foster, **13** Walk on the moon, **14** Will Carling, **15** Prince Harry.

QUIZ 258

Answers on page 262

1 What is the collective word for a group of foxes?

2 Who said "It's not the men in my life that counts - it's the life in my men"

3 Which Irish novelist and dramatist won the Nobel prize for Literature in 1969?

4 What was Dexy's Midnight Runners first Number One hit?

5 Which 20th century monarch married the eldest daughter of Denmark's Christian IX?

6 Which sport is Sabina Park famous for?

7 Which Bob hosted TV quiz show *Blockbusters*?

8 Which team did Sunderland play in their 1973 appearance in the FA Cup final?

9 With which sport would you associate Joe Montana?

10 In which city is the United Nations Building?

11 Who played Al Capone in the 1987 film *The Untouchables*?

12 The skyline of which Italian city has been dominated since 1488 by a cathedral dome designed by Filippo Brunelleschi?

13 What kind of plant is fescue?

14 Who, in 1907, was the first woman to receive the Order of Merit?

15 Which airline was originally called Dobrolet?

Things you didn't know...

*Red rain, caused by red dust from the Sahara, falls
frequently throughout Europe.*

Answers to page 262

1 Sweet William, **2** H G Wells, **3** Harrier, **4** Grasmere, **5** Paul Henreid,
6 Philippines, **7** *Mission Impossible*, **8** 1884, **9** *Close Encounters of
the Third Kind*, **10** Edinburgh, **11** Cassius Clay, **12** Vincent Price, **13**
Sir Thomas More, **14** France, **15** Tavares.

QUIZ 259

Answers on page 259

1 Who played the title role in *I Love Lucy*?

2 Which metal is extracted from sphalerite?

3 What was a Moaning Minnie during the Second World War?

4 In *Alice's Adventures in Wonderland* who stole the tarts that were made by the Queen of Hearts?

5 Which plant can grow up to three feet in 24 hours?

6 What is the maximum number on the Richter scale?

7 Upon which town's streets was Monopoly originally based?

8 *Everything is coming up roses* is from which musical?

9 Who won the Best Actress Oscar in 1983 for *Terms of Endearment*?

10 Whose first hit record was *Rock On* in 1973?

11 Who is Kirk Douglas's famous son?

12 Which actor was TV's *Van der Valk*?

13 What was Charles Conrad the third person to do, in 1969?

14 Which rugby player was Princess Diana linked with?

15 Which member of the Royal family abseiled down a dam without a safety helmet in August 1998?

Things you didn't know...

More than 500 songs and musical pieces have been written about or dedicated to Abraham Lincoln.

Answers to page 259

1 Sir Francis Drake, **2** Robert Redford, **3** *Inspector Morse*, **4** Madam de Pompadour, **5** Howard Hughes, **6** Sundew, **7** Sherlock Holmes, **8** Spain, **9** Phonetics, **10** Aurora, **11** Tom Cruise, **12** Emile Zola, **13** Paul Gascoigne, **14** Vienna, **15** A horse.

QUIZ 260

Answers on page 260

1 What is the common name for the garden flower Dianthus Barbatus?

2 Who wrote the novel *Kipps*?

3 Which VTOL fighter was nicknamed The Jump Jet?

4 Which village in the Lake District was the home of William Wordsworth and his sister Dorothy?

5 Who played Ingrid Bergman's husband in *Casablanca*?

6 In which country are the Tagalog a major ethnic group?

7 In which TV series did Leonard Nimoy work for the I.M.F.?

8 When was the first part of the Oxford English Dictionary published?

9 Devil's Tower in Wyoming played an important part in which 1977 film?

10 In which British city is Usher Hall?

11 Who was Olympic Boxing Light Heavyweight Gold medallist in 1960?

12 Whose early films included *The Song of Bernadette* and *Laura* before he made *House of Wax*?

13 Which former chancellor to Henry VIII was canonised in 1935?

14 What was the first country to use number plates on its road vehicles?

15 Who had Top Ten hists with *Heaven Must be Missing an Angel* and *Whodunnit*?

Things you didn't know...

The man who wrote 'I Left My Heart in San Francisco' died there.

Answers to page 260

1 Skulk, 2 Mae West, 3 Samuel Beckett, 4 Geno, 5 Edward VII, 6 Cricket, 7 Holness, 8 Leeds United, 9 American Football, 10 New York, 11 Robert De Niro, 12 Florence, 13 Grass, 14 Florence Nightingale, 15 Aeroflot.

QUIZ 261

Answers on page 265

1 Who is generally credited as being the inventor of the Television?

2 What was the occupation of Jack Ketch?

3 In which profession was Nelson Mandela qualified?

4 What is the setting for the opera *Billy Budd*?

5 Which Irish ghost is said to wail outside houses where a death is imminent?

6 Which animals collect in a crash?

7 Of which boat was Mark Litchfield skipper when it sank in 1995?

8 In which newspaper did the strip cartoon *Jane* appear?

9 What does the expression "The old woman is plucking her goose" mean?

10 How did the scientist Pierre Curie die?

11 With which war is Florence Nightingale chiefly associated?

12 Who presents the TV programme *You've Been Framed*?

13 Which sport is now believed to be the origin of the expression 'The Real McCoy'?

14 What is the name of the bass tuba that wraps around the player's body?

15 In which TV series did Richard Chamberlain play an Australian priest whose son also became a priest?

Things you didn't know...

The River Amazon has more than a thousand tributaries.

Answers to page 265

1 Guy Gibson, 2 William Tell, 3 *The Colbys,* 4 Cub, 5 Cosmetics, 6 Indianapolis 500, 7 Elaine Derbyshire, 8 Long-sightedness, 9 Eat it, 10 Whale, 11 Horse racing, 12 Parliament Square, 13 1894, 14 Simone de Beauvoir, 15 Silk.

QUIZ 262

Answers on page 266

1 Who directed and starred in the film *Citizen Kane*?

2 What are ossicles and osselets?

3 Which type of bullet was outlawed in 1899?

4 Which device allows a car's driving wheels to turn at different speeds when cornering?

5 In what year did the Falklands War take place?

6 Which bird is nicknamed Pharaoh's Chicken?

7 Which FA boss quit over a loans-for-votes row?

8 What was the actual practical purpose of a gargoyle?

9 What calendar did Britain adopt in 1752?

10 Which saint's cathedral is in Moscow's Red Square?

11 What term is used to measure the fineness of yarns?

12 Which singer had Top Ten hits in the 1980s with *Games Without Frontiers and Sledgehammer*?

13 On whose shoulders did the Old Man of the Sea hoist himself?

14 Which King of England's mother and son were both beheaded?

15 Which Nigel writes a column for the Daily Mail?

Things you didn't know...

Shirt buttonholes are vertical, but pyjama buttonholes are more often than not horizontal.

Answers to page 266

1 Heinz Harold Frentzen, 2 Coleslaw, 3 Dorset, 4 John Lennon, 5 Wordsworth, 6 Human form, 7 Pork, 8 Jack Hawkins, 9 Beer, 10 Aldeburgh, 11 Conductor, 12 W, 13 Antihistamine, 14 New Orleans, 15 England.

QUIZ 263

Answers on page 263

1 Who was the leader of The Dambusters?

2 What was Conrad Phillips most famous TV role?

3 Which soap was a spin-off from *Dynasty*?

4 What is the young of a shark called?

5 Which industry was launched by David McConnell in 1886 as a result of his selling volumes of Shakespeare door to door?

6 The trophy for winning which sporting event is made from eighty pounds of sterling silver?

7 Who plays the role of Emily Bishop in *Coronation Street*?

8 By what name is hypermetropia better known?

9 If you had a gigot what would you do with it?

10 From which creature is ambergris obtained?

11 With which sport do you associate Walter Swinburn?

12 In which London Square would you find statues of Abraham Lincoln, Winston Churchill and Jan Smuts?

13 In what year was the first ever Motor Show?

14 Which French writer had a life long morganitic marriage with Jean Paul Sartre?

15 Serigraphy is the art of printing onto which material?

Things you didn't know...

There are no turkeys in Turkey.

Answers to page 263

1 John Logie Baird, **2** Hangman, **3** Legal, **4** A warship, **5** Banshee, **6** Rhinoceroses, **7** The Maria Asumpta, **8** The Daily Mirror, **9** It's snowing, **10** Run over by a cart, **11** Crimean War, **12** Jeremy Beadle, **13** Boxing, **14** Sousaphone, **15** *The Thorn Birds*.

QUIZ 264

Answers on page 264

1 Who replaced Damon Hill in the Williams Grand Prix team in 1997?

2 Which popular dish means literally 'cabbage salad' in Dutch?

3 In which English county are Maiden Castle and Corfe Castle?

4 Which pop star once said 'we're more popular than Jesus now'?

5 Which English poet lived at Dove Cottage?

6 In *Gulliver's Travels* what form did the Yahoos take?

7 With which meat is apple sauce traditionally served?

8 Who led the bank robbers in the film *The League of Gentlemen*?

9 What alcoholic drink are hops used to flavour?

10 Which Suffolk town, famous for an annual music festival, was the first town in Britain to have a woman mayor?

11 What was the artistic profession of Wilhelm Furtwangler who died in 1954?

12 What is the chemical symbol for Tungsten?

13 Which type of drug is usually used to relieve allergies?

14 Which city is regarded as the home of jazz?

15 In which country is the TV News Agency Visnews based?

Things you didn't know...

Lord Nelson suffered from seasickness all his life.

Answers to page 264

1 Orson Welles, 2 Bones, 3 Dum Dum, 4 Differential, 5 1982, 6 Egyptian Vulture, 7 Graham Kelly, 8 Water spout, 9 Gregorian, 10 St Basil's, 11 Denier, 12 Peter Gabriel, 13 Sinbad the Sailor's, 14 James I's, 15 Dempster.

QUIZ 265

Answers on page 269

1 Of which American state is Columbus the capital?

2 Which natural feature has been nicknamed The Lamp of Phoebus?

3 Which skin condition is caused by overactivity and inflammation of the sebaceous glands?

4 Olympic airlines is the national airline of which country?

5 Which is the only Shakespeare play with an animal in the title?

6 Who was the first British Labour prime minister?

7 The island of Borholm in the Baltic Sea, belongs to which country?

8 What is the westernmost province of Canada?

9 Which comic was christened Arthur Jefferson?

10 Which city will host the 2000 AD Olympics?

11 Which golfer won the 1998 US Masters?

12 In which film did Kenneth More search for a German battleship?

13 Who sings the title song for the TV series *One Foot in the Grave*?

14 Who, in 1993, became the highest scoring Test batsman of all time?

15 Which is the largest lake in Wales?

Things you didn't know...

The second most frequently used vowel in the English language is A.

Answers to page 269

1 A snake, 2 Captain Sensible, 3 Loch Lomond, 4 Tin, 5 Joe Di Maggio, 6 Minorca, 7 Houdini, 8 Staffordshire, 9 Four, 10 Makepeace, 11 Value-added tax, 12 Tiffany, 13 Cats, 14 Amsterdam, 15 Patrick Moore (*The Sky at Night* since 1957).

QUIZ 266

Answers on page 270

1 What is the name of the professor in Cluedo?

2 Mary O'Brien is better known as who?

3 Which veteran actress played Hayley Mills' aunt in the film *Pollyanna*?

4 Which song, sung at the Last Night of the Proms, is Thomas Arne's most famous work?

5 What name is given to a mixture of mercury and any other metal?

6 The parliament of which island is called the Court of Tynwald?

7 Whose first solo Number One was *I'm Still Waiting*?

8 Who were the German husband and wife team who popularised underwater TV programmes in the 1950s and 1960s?

9 What sort of instrument is a flageolet?

10 Tarquin the Proud was the last king of where?

11 What is America's National Cemetery called?

12 Who was crop-dusted in the film *North By Northwest*?

13 On which river is Balmoral Castle?

14 What is the eleventh letter of the Greek alphabet?

15 Which British football club is known as The Bhoys?

Things you didn't know...

Camels are born without humps.

Answers to page 270

1 Frances Hodgson Burnett, **2** *Wuthering Heights,* **3** Tapioca, **4** John Cannon, **5** Kildare, **6** Gainsborough, **7** Mary, Queen of Scots, **8** Nitrogen, **9** Richard Adams, **10** *Dennis The Menace,* **11** Jerome Robbins, **12** Boer War, **13** Gottlieb Daimler, **14** *Lorna Doone,* **15** Milwaukee.

QUIZ 267

Answers on page 267

1 What sort of creature is a sidewinder?

2 Who had a Number One hit in 1982 with *Happy Talk*?

3 Which Scottish loch covers the largest area?

4 Which metallic element has the symbol Sn?

5 Who did Marilyn Monroe marry in 1954?

6 What is the second largest of the Balearic islands?

7 By what name did Erich Weiss become better known?

8 In which English county was willow-pattern china created?

9 How many pairs of legs do arachnids have?

10 What was William Thackeray's middle name?

11 What do the initials VAT stand for?

12 Which female vocalist had a Number One hit in 1988 with *I Think We're Alone Now*?

13 Which Lloyd-Webber musical does the song *Memory* come from?

14 In which city did Anne Frank write her diary?

15 Who is the longest serving presenter in television?

Things you didn't know...

Chess is the most widely played game in Russia.

Answers to page 267

1 Ohio, 2 Sun, 3 Acne, 4 Greece, 5 *The Taming of the Shrew*, 6 Ramsey MacDonald, 7 Denmark, 8 British Columbia, 9 Stan Laurel, 10 Sydney, 11 Mark O'Meara, 12 *Sink the Bismarck*, 13 Eric Idle, 14 Alan Border, 15 Lake Bala.

QUIZ 268

Answers on page 268

1 Who wrote the children's stories *Little Lord Fauntleroy and The Secret Garden*?

2 In which house did Catharine Earnshaw live?

3 Which pudding comes from the root of the cassava tree?

4 Who owned the High Chaparral ranch?

5 Which Irish county is Naas the county town of?

6 Who painted *The Blue Boy*?

7 Which Queen was the mother of James I of England?

8 Which colourless odourless gas is represented by the symbol N?

9 Who wrote *Watership Down*?

10 Which cartoon character has a dog called Gnasher?

11 Who choreographed *West Side Story*?

12 Which war was fought between 1899 and 1902?

13 Which German motor car manufacturer produced the first motorcycle by fixing an engine to a frame in 1885?

14 John Ridd is the male lead in which book with a girl's name as its title?

15 Which city provided the setting for television's *Happy Days* and *Laverne and Shirley* and is noted for its brewing industry?

Things you didn't know...

The average new-born baby spends 133 a minutes a day crying.

Answers to page 268

1 Plum, 2 Dusty Springfield, 3 Jane Wyman, 4 *Rule Britannia,* 5 Amalgam, 6 Isle of Man, 7 Diana Ross, 8 Hans and Lottie Hass, 9 A wind instrument, 10 Rome, 11 Arlington, 12 Cary Grant, 13 Dee, 14 Lambda, 15 (Glasgow) Celtic.

QUIZ 269

Answers on page 273

1 Which Sidney directed the film *Stir Crazy*?

2 Keith Holyoake was prime minister of which country during the 1960s?

3 Whose catchphrase was 'Shut That Door'?

4 Which famous battle took place in October 1805?

5 Which bone is between the femur and tibia?

6 Which Canadian city was originally called Ville-Marie?

7 What was the name of the eagle who escaped from the aviary at London Zoo in 1965?

8 Which is the oldest of the five English horse racing Classics?

9 In which state of the USA can Miami Beach and Palm Beach be found?

10 Who is the current Deputy prime minister?

11 Which country does Stilton cheese come from?

12 Which *EastEnders'* character gave birth on Christmas Day 1998?

13 What sort of creature is a hellbender?

14 What was Manfred Mann's first hit?

15 How many players did England use in the 1966 Football World Cup Finals?

Things you didn't know...

George Washington was the first American millionaire.

Answers to page 273

1 Tea, **2** Copenhagen, **3** Milk and Honey, **4** Seismograph, **5** Cinema, **6** Duck, **7** Piano, **8** Laurence Olivier, **9** Orleans, **10** Clarence House, **11** Recto, **12** F Scott Fitzgerald, **13** Max Bygraves, **14** Lacrosse, **15** Hard Times.

QUIZ 270

Answers on page 274

1 Which tree has the scientific name Aesculus?

2 What boy features in the *Winnie the Pooh* stories?

3 What name is given to the cultivation of plants without soil?

4 Which traditional vegetable dish from the Provence region of France is made with tomatoes, courgettes, aubergines, peppers and onions?

5 If you ordered pollo in an Italian restaurant what would you get?

6 What are Harley-Davidson famous for manufacturing?

7 What did Messrs Shockley, Bardeen and Brattain invent in 1947?

8 What is the minimum age at which a person can be elected to a seat in the House of Commons?

9 Who is generally credited as being the inventor of the Diesel engine?

10 Mustardseed is a character from which of Shakespeare's plays?

11 From what language do the words brandy, decoy and landscape come?

12 Which city is the county town of West Sussex?

13 How many compartments are there on a British roulette wheel?

14 In which country is the source of the Amazon

15 Who was responsible for the cartoon creation of *Girls of St Trinians*?

Things you didn't know...

Two million pigs are used to in the manufacture of Spam each year.

Answers to page 274

1 *Butterflies*, 2 Violin, 3 Earth, 4 Frank Bruno v. Mike Tyson, 5 Veterans Day, 6 Pyramid, 7 Hampshire, 8 *Greensleeves*, 9 Queen Victoria, 10 *Combine Harvester*, 11 Lerwick, 12 Oxfam, 13 Mayor of New York, 14 Peter Duncan, 15 Vanessa Paradis.

QUIZ 271

Answers on page 271

1 Assam, Darjeeling and Pekoe are all blends of what?

2 What is the capital of Denmark?

3 Which Israeli group won the Eurovision Song Contest in 1979?

4 Which instrument is used to measure the strength of earthquakes?

5 In which art form did German born Ernst Lubitsch gain fame?

6 If you ordered 'caneton' in a French restaurant what would you get?

7 With which musical instrument would you associate the jazz musicians Theolonius Monk and Art Tatum?

8 Who narrated the 26 part TV series *The World at War*?

9 Which French city was besieged by the English until the arrival of Joan of Arc?

10 What is the name of the Queen Mothers residence in London?

11 What is the right hand page of a book called?

12 Which writer described the 1920s as *The Jazz Age*?

13 Which singer hosted *Family Fortunes*?

14 Which team game has the positions first defence, in home and second attack?

15 In which Dickens novel does Thomas Gradgrind of Coketown appear?

Things you didn't know...

New York City has more rain in an average year than London.

Answers to page 271

1 Poitier, **2** New Zealand, **3** Larry Grayson, **4** Trafalgar, **5** Patella, **6** Montreal, **7** Goldie, **8** St. Leger, **9** Florida, **10** John Prescott, **11** England, **12** Bianca, **13** Salamander, **14** *5-4-3-2-1,* **15** 15.

QUIZ 272

Answers on page 272

1 Which sitcom starred Wendy Craig and Geoffrey Palmer has a married couple?

2 With which musical instrument was Jascha Heifetz associated?

3 Which is the third nearest planet to the Sun?

4 Which boxing match was the first major sporting event to be shown on a pay-per-view basis in the UK?

5 In the UK it is known as Armistice Day, what is the equivalent day in the USA known as?

6 The volume of what shape is equal to a third of the area of its' base times the height?

7 In which county is the naval base of Gosport?

8 Which song begins: "Alas my love, you do me wrong to cast me off discourteously"?

9 Who chose Ottawa to be the capital of Canada?

10 Which record by The Wurzels was a Number One hit in 1976?

11 Which is the most northerly town in Scotland?

12 What is the abbreviation of The Oxford Committee for Famine Relief?

13 What appointment did David Dinkins take up in the USA in 1989?

14 Which *Blue Peter* presenter went on to present his own daredevil programme?

15 Who had a Top Ten hit with *Jo le Taxi*?

Things you didn't know...

In the USA it is a criminal offence to alter the tune of the national anthem The Star Spangled Banner.

Answers to page 272

1 Horse Chestnut, 2 Christopher Robin, 3 Hydroponics, 4 Ratatouille, 5 Chicken, 6 Motorcycles, 7 The Transistor, 8 21, 9 Rudolf Diesel, 10 *A Midsummer Night's Dream*, 11 Dutch, 12 Chichester, 13 37, 14 Peru, 15 Ronald Searle.

QUIZ 273

Answers on page 277

1 Which two cartoon characters were used by the Ministry of Food during the Second World War to promote the benefits of vegetables?

2 Chania, Knossos and Sitia are towns on which Greek holiday island?

3 What is the name of Norman Beaton's barber shop?

4 What substance did Lister use to improve the hygiene of surgical operations?

5 Who played Louis Cyphere in the film *Angel Heart*?

6 What was the first name of the Marks who set up penny bazaars with Thomas Spencer in 1887?

7 Montego Bay is a tourist attraction on which Caribbean Island?

8 In which sport did Heather McKay remain unbeaten from 1962 to 1980, winning the British Open 16 times and the first two World Open Championships?

9 Which country lies between Zimbabwe and the sea?

10 What is John Le Carre's real name?

11 Which stretch of water separates Denmark from Sweden?

12 Which prosperous island country lies off the tip of Malaysia's mainland peninsula?

13 Who had Top Ten hits with *Don't Answer Me. Conversations* and *It's For You*?

14 Which Liverpool FC joint manager resigned in 1998?

15 Which group had the 1998 Christmas Number One?

Things you didn't know...

Chihuahua dogs were originally bred for their meat.

Answers to page 277

1 Danny Glover, 2 Wigan, 3 Chlorine, 4 Five, 5 Tom Jones, 6 Windmill, 7 Edinburgh, 8 Arkansas, 9 Madonna, 10 1957, 11 Sandwich Islands, 12 Lloyds of London, 13 Eight, 14 Judges, 15 Caerphilly.

QUIZ 274

Answers on page 278

1 Who was the star of the 1970 film *Little Big Man*?

2 What sort of creature is an oriole?

3 What is tansy?

4 Which was the first country to win the Football World Cup in its own country?

5 Of what was the Greek goddess Nyx the personification?

6 Which country is also known as Eire?

7 In which game are flattened iron rings thrown at a hob?

8 What was the nickname of the British 7th Armoured Division in the Second World War?

9 Wat Arun, The Temple of Dawn, is in which capital city?

10 With what art form was Donald McGill particularly associated?

11 Where is the most famous colony of Macaque Monkeys?

12 The pop duo Annie Lennox and Dave Stewart recorded under what name?

13 Which animal's milk is used to make Roquefort cheese?

14 Apart from a toothbrush, what else did the audience bring along in TV's *Don't Forget Your Toothbrush*?

15 In the bible who goes after Mark and before John?

Things you didn't know...

You use one calorie to read 650 words.

Answers to page 278

1 Hydrogen, 2 Alcoholics Anonymous, 3 Walt Disney, 4 Sharron Davies, 5 Gloucester, 6 Michael, 7 Epsilon, 8 Richard Llewellyn, 9 Emile Zola, 10 Ringway, 11 Hawaii, 12 Woodrow Wilson, 13 John Field, 14 River Derwent, 15 Orthodontics.

QUIZ 275

Answers on page 275

1 Who played Mel Gibson's partner in the *Lethal Weapon* films?

2 Which Rugby League team clinched their seventh successive championship in 1996?

3 Which poisonous halogen gas is represented by the symbol Cl?

4 How many piano concertos did Beethoven write?

5 Who had Top Ten hits in the 1960s with *Detroit City, I'm Coming Home* and *Love Me Tonight*?

6 Which London theatre boasted "We never closed."?

7 In which British city was the warning cry "Gardy Loo" used when people upstairs were emptying the slop out of the window?

8 In which US state is Little Rock, scene of race riots in 1957?

9 Who had a Number One hit with *La Isla Bonita*?

10 In what year was the first Sputnik satellite launched?

11 What was the former name of Hawaii?

12 Where does the Lutine Bell hang?

13 How many swimming legs does a lobster have?

14 In which book of the Bible is the story of Samson?

15 After Windsor, which is the largest castle in Britian?

Things you didn't know...

In Siena, Italy, a law forbids any woman christened Mary to ever work as a prostitute.

Answers to page 275

1 Dr Carrot and Potato Pete, 2 Crete, 3 *Desmonds,* 4 Carbolic Acid, 5 Robert De Niro, 6 Michael, 7 Jamaica, 8 Squash, 9 Mozambique, 10 David Cornwell, 11 The Kattegat, 12 Singapore, 13 Cilla Black, 14 Roy Evans, 15 Spice Girls.

QUIZ 276

Answers on page 276

1 Which is the lightest known substance

2 Which organisation, well known in Britain was founded by William Wilson in Ohio in 1935?

3 Who created *Mickey Mouse*?

4 Which British swimmer was the youngest contestant in the 1976 Montreal Olympics?

5 What town was the capital of Mercia?

6 Which King of Romania abdicated in 1947?

7 What is the fifth letter of the Greek alphabet?

8 Who wrote the best selling novel *How Green was my Valley* in 1939?

9 Which novelist defended Drefyus in an open letter in 1898?

10 What is Manchester's airport called?

11 In which US state is Pearl Harbor?

12 Who was US president throughout the First World War?

13 Which Irish-born composer created the piano nocturne?

14 On which river does the city of Derby stand?

15 Which branch of dentistry is concerned with the correction of badly positioned teeth?

Things you didn't know...

Lettuce is the only vegetable that is not sold frozen, bottled, processed or pre-cooked.

Answers to page 276

1 Dustin Hoffman, 2 A bird, 3 Herb, 4 Uruguay, 5 Night, 6 The Republic of Ireland, 7 Quoits, 8 Desert Rats, 9 Bangkok, 10 Seaside postcards, 11 Gibraltar, 12 Eurythmics, 13 Ewe, 14 Passport, 15 Luke.

QUIZ 277

Answers on page 281

1 In which London Borough is Poplar?

2 In which town was the first college of the University of Wales founded?

3 What is the name of the upper jaw-bone?

4 With which county cricket club did Ian Botham finish his playing career?

5 What did Grace Kelly's surname change to in 1956?

6 In which German City did the Nazi movement begin?

7 What English name is given to the great tower of a castle?

8 Who was the most famous sixteenth century English composer of church music?

9 Which singer had a Top Ten hit in 1962 with *Sun Arise*?

10 Who starred with John Voight in the film *Midnight Cowboy*?

11 Whose biography was called *Rich*?

12 According to Greek mythology the bravest Trojan was killed by Achilles. Who was he?

13 Which Roy was known as the Big 'O'?

14 What are the correct terms for the two main branches of Biology?

15 Which city, famous for its casinos, is in a desert?

Things you didn't know...

Elizabeth Taylor never throws away any of her clothes.

Answers to page 281

1 Forest, **2** Daniel Defoe, **3** Minim, **4** Gordon Brown, **5** Carousel, **6** Sonny, **7** John the Baptist, **8** Liquid Gold, **9** Greyfriars, **10** A marsupial, **11** 1972, **12** Alfred, **13** Robert, **14** The Laws Of Moses, **15** The kennel club.

QUIZ 278

Answers on page 282

1 Which group had a UK Number Two in 1972 with *Crazy Horses*?

2 Who was the first British sportswoman to earn a million pounds in a year?

3 Which animals' names translated into English means 'River Horse'?

4 Which UN agency was first convened in 1919, with the object of improving working conditions and living standards?

5 What was the title of Lonnie Donegan's first Number One hit?

6 With which meat is horseraddish sauce traditionally served?

7 *The Simspons* had a 1991 hit with which dance record?

8 What is a young goose called?

9 Who had a Number One hit with *The Lady in Red*?

10 Who was Chancellor of the Exchequer when Mrs. Thatcher resigned as Prime Minister in 1990?

11 In which month does the Queen celebrate her official birthday with the Trooping of the Colour ceremony?

12 Who has pop albums called *Picture Book and A New Flame?*

13 Which British company, famous for berets, takes its name from silk, angora & wool?

14 In which sport is the Stanley Cup contested?

15 In which London park is the Serpentine?

Things you didn't know...

In the fifteenth century Chinese scholars produced an encyclopaedia with 11,000 volumes.

Answers to page 282

1 *Great Expectations,* 2 20, 3 The Searchers, 4 Arsenal, 5 Wheat, 6 October, 7 Rob Lowe, 8 Flea, 9 Peter Sellers, 10 Bros, 11 Mariah Carey, 12 *Doctor in Distress,* 13 Sonny Liston, 14 Dracula, 15 Volga.

QUIZ 279

Answers on page 279

1 Which Nottingham club was managed by Brian Clough?

2 Who wrote *Robinson Crusoe*?

3 What word describes a musical note half the value of a semibreve?

4 Who was the Chancellor of the Exchequer in Tony Blair's first cabinet?

5 The song *You'll Never Walk Alone* comes from which musical?

6 What was the first name of heavyweight boxing champion Liston?

7 According to the Bible, who baptised Jesus?

8 Which group had a 1980 hit with *Dance Yourself Dizzy*?

9 At which school was Billy Bunter a pupil?

10 What sort of creature is a Tasmanian devil?

11 In which year did *Mastermind* begin on TV?

12 Who was the only English king to be nicknamed "The Great"?

13 Raymond Burr starred in the TV series *Ironside*. What is his christian name?

14 In the Bible, what did Joshua write on the stones at Mount Ebal?

15 What establishment for canine breeds and standards was founded in 1873?

Things you didn't know...

The average lead pencil will write 50,000 words before running out.

Answers to page 279

1 Tower Hamlets, 2 Aberystwyth, 3 Maxilla, 4 Durham, 5 Grimaldi, 6 Munich, 7 Keep, 8 Byrd, 9 Rolf Harris, 10 Dustin Hoffman, 11 Richard Burton, 12 Hector, 13 Orbison, 14 Botany and Zoology, 15 Las Vegas.

QUIZ 280

Answers on page 280

1 In which Dickens novel is Philip Pirrip a central character?

2 How many years of marriage are indicated by a china wedding anniversary?

3 Which pop group, who had three UK Number One's in the 1960s was named after a John Wayne film?

4 Which team won the FA Cup in 1993?

5 Which is the main crop of Australia, equal to all other crops combined?

6 In which month would you go to Munich for the beer festival?

7 Which 'brat pack' actor starred in *St Elmo's Fire* and *Wayne's World*?

8 Which insect belongs to the order Siphonaptera of which there are 1600 species?

9 Which British comic actor starred as a Viennese professor in the 1965 film *What's New Pussycat*?

10 Who had a Number One hit with *I Owe You Nothing*?

11 Who had a Number One hit with *Without You*?

12 Which was the last film in which Dirk Bogarde played Dr Simon Sparrow?

13 Who in 1964 did Cassius Clay defeat to become the heavyweight boxing champion orf the world?

14 Which vampire was created by Bram Stoker?

15 What is the name of the longest river in Europe?

Things you didn't know...

Oslo used to be known as Christiana.

Answers to page 280

1 The Osmonds, 2 Laura Davies, 3 Hippopotamus, 4 International Labour Organisation (ILO), 5 *Cumberland Gap,* 6 Beef, 7 *Do The Bartman,* 8 Gosling, 9 Chris de Burgh, 10 John Major, 11 June, 12 Simply Red, 13 Kangol, 14 Ice Hockey, 15 Hyde Park.

QUIZ 281

Answers on page 285

1 Which horse did Fred Winter train to win the Grand National in 1966?

2 Who gave £1 million to the labour party snubbing Chelsea supporter John Major?

3 Where do Glasgow Rangers play their home matches?

4 Which is the county town of Kerry?

5 Which British group had a Number One hit with *Karma Chameleon*?

6 Who was the star of the show *Lord of the Dance*?

7 Who was the only man to become Vice President and President of the USA without being elected to either post?

8 Who was the creator of "The Golden Calf" and the elder half brother of Moses?

9 Which multi-coloured diamond pattern, often seen on knitted socks, is named after a Scottish clan?

10 Ferencvaros play football in which country?

11 Androphobia is the fear of who or what?

12 Which Russian poet and novelist wrote *Dr Zhivago*?

13 What is the second largest city in sweden?

14 Which Aussie soap is set in Summer Bay?

15 Who was given ass's ears by Apollo for judging Pan to be a better musician than him?

Things you didn't know...

The only animal whose evidence is admissible in a court of law is a bloodhound.

Answers to page 285

1 A yearling, 2 Paul Gross (*Due South*), 3 Barbra Streisand, 4 Poliomyelitis, 5 Oscar Hammerstein, 6 Zephyr, 7 The Osmonds, 8 Hamilton, 9 Lincoln, 10 Cairo, 11 Orlando, 12 Ostrich, 13 Silicon, 14 Kiki Dee, 15 Canada.

QUIZ 282

Answers on page 286

1 Alfred, Farmingdale and Pixy are all types of what?

2 In which series did Detective Inspector Maggie Forbes appear?

3 During which war was the battle of Rourke's Drift?

4 Palma is the capital of which Balearic island?

5 What was Fleetwood Mac's 1997 album release?

6 The shipworm is not a worm. What is it?

7 Who sang with Elton John on *Act of War*?

8 Which is the longest river solely in England?

9 What was the title of Cliff Richard's 1968 Eurovision song?

10 Which chain of hills is called the backbone of England?

11 What sort of creature is a fritillary?

12 Which legendary Greek hero was sent by his uncle Pelias to fetch the Golden Fleece?

13 *Happy Birthday* by Stevie Wonder was a tribute to who?

14 The fabled bird, the griffin, has the head of which real bird?

15 Who is generally credited as being the inventor of the Thermometer?

Things you didn't know...

A hump-backed whale can travel more than 6,400 miles in its annual migrations.

Answers to page 286

1 Rita, 2 Will Smith, 3 Aluminium, 4 Spring onion, 5 An antelope, 6 German measles, 7 Jack Charlton, 8 The Toronto Blue Jays, 9 Woolworths, 10 Hungary, 11 Cars, 12 Paparazzi, 13 LOT, 14 Manchester, 15 Three.

QUIZ 283

Answers on page 283

1 What is a horse called, when it is 12 months old?

2 Who plays Benton Fraser in a BBC TV series?

3 Who has released duets with Donna Summer, Neil Diamond and Barry Gibb?

4 Which disease is prevented the the Sabin Vaccine?

5 Who collaborated with Jerome Kern to write the musical *Show Boat*?

6 Which model of car, produced by Ford in the 1960s, was named after the Greek word for the west wind?

7 Whose Top Ten hits included *Let Me In, The Proud One* and *Going Home*?

8 What is the capital of Bermuda?

9 Which is the main city of the Lindsey district of Lincolnshire?

10 Which is the largest city in Africa in population?

11 Which city is served by McCoy airport?

12 What is the largest living bird?

13 What is the principal chemical element found in sand?

14 Who joined Elton John on the Number One hit song *Don't Go Breaking My Heart*?

15 Which country is the leading producer of zinc in the world?

Things you didn't know...

James Garfield was the only ambidextrous US president.

Answers to page 283

1 Anglo, **2** Matthew Harding, **3** Ibrox Park, **4** Tralee, **5** Culture Club, **6** Michael Flatley, **7** Gerald Ford, **8** Aaron, **9** Argyle, **10** Hungary, **11** Men, **12** Boris Pasternak, **13** Gothenburg, **14** *Home and Away*, **15** Midas.

QUIZ 284

Answers on page 284

1 In *Coronation Street* which part is played by Barbara Knox?

2 Which rapper/actor had a Number One single in 1997 with the theme from his hit film, *Men in Black*?

3 Which is the most abundant metal in the earth's crust?

4 What popular salad food was originally an immature vegetable pulled early in the year?

5 Which long-legged bug is also known as a water strider?

6 How is the diease rubella commonly known?

7 Who played for England and managed the Republic of Ireland?

8 Which Canadian team became the first non-American team in 1992 to win baseball's World Series?

9 Barbara Hutton, who died in 1979, was the grand-daughter of the founder of which chain store?

10 In which country would you come from if your native tongue was Magyar?

11 What are Cowley, Dagenham and Luton famous for producing?

12 Which Italian word is used for freelance photographers who pursue celebrities?

13 What is the national airline of Poland?

14 In which British city was the 1819 Peterloo Massacre?

15 How many horns did the dinosaur triceratops have?

Things you didn't know...

Winston Churchill and Clement Attlee had the same nanny.

Answers to page 284

1 Apricot, 2 *The Gentle Touch,* 3 Zulu War, 4 Majorca, 5 The Dance, 6 A mollusc, 7 Millie Jackson, 8 The Thames, 9 *Congratulations,* 10 Pennines, 11 A butterfly, 12 Jason, 13 Martin Luther King, 14 Eagle, 15 Galileo Galilei.

QUIZ 285

Answers on page 289

1 What name was given to the open space or court of a stone built castle?

2 Which British city is served by Ringway airport?

3 Who had her jewels stolen at an airport in 1995?

4 Alex Graham created which cartoon strip character in 1963?

5 Which widespread medical disorder includes grand mal and petit mal forms?

6 What sort of creature is a Camberwell beauty?

7 What item of dress is a Sabot?

8 *Foot Tapper* was the last Number One hit record for which group?

9 Which country is Mexico's largest southern border neighbour?

10 Who had Top Ten hits in the 1980s with *I'm Still Standing, Passengers* and *Blue Eyes*?

11 In which town is the Wagner festival held in July?

12 Scotch and Drambuie make which cocktail?

13 What is the stage name of entertainer Robert Davies?

14 In which English county is Southend-on-Sea situated?

15 Who had a Number One hit in 1981 with *This Ole House*?

Things you didn't know...

An ant can lift fifty times its own body weight.

Answers to page 289

1 Oscar Wilde, 2 Puffin, 3 Uncle Tom, 4 L P Hartley, 5 Wat Tyler, 6 George Foreman, 7 Memphis, 8 Italy, 9 St John The Divine, 10 Mia Farrow, 11 Rowan Atkinson, 12 Courtney Pine, 13 Orthopaedics, 14 Human League, 15 Tom Cruise.

QUIZ 286

Answers on page 290

1 Who was the female star of the film *The African Queen*?

2 What is known as the Universal Solvent?

3 What is a durmast?

4 In which country is is Timbuktu?

5 Which group had albums called *Fireball* and *Machine Head*?

6 Which vegetable is said to have a taste similar to that of oysters?

7 By what name do we know Cherilyn Sarkasian LaPierre?

8 In which Commonwealth country is Waitangi Day the National Day?

9 What does the Dewey Decimal System classify?

10 How many games are there in a rubber of contract bridge?

11 What is a vessel equipped for catching fish by towing nets called?

12 With which sport do you associate Damon Hill?

13 Which club did George Graham leave to take over as manager at Tottenham Hotspur?

14 Which calendar did Britain adopt in 1752?

15 Which type of car do you most associate with T.Vs Nurse Gladys Emmanuel in *Open All Hours*?

Things you didn't know...

Northern Ireland suffers worse air pollution than any other part of the UK.

Answers to page 290

1 *Bergerac,* 2 Three, 3 Grenada, 4 Ferrets, 5 Baffin, 6 Dame Barbara Hepworth, 7 Lorry, 8 Douglas Fairbanks, 9 Fred Flintstone, 10 Malcolm MacDonald, 11 *Top Cat,* 12 A mushroom, 13 Oyster, 14 Battle of Balaclava, 15 Robin Wright.

QUIZ 287

Answers on page 287

1 Who wrote the plays *An Ideal Husband* and *Lady Windermere's Fan*?

2 Which division of penguin books was founded in 1941 to publish children's books?

3 What name was and is used by American Black Nationalist for negroes who are too subservient to white people?

4 Which British novelist wrote *The Go-Between*?

5 Who led the Peasant's Revolt of 1381?

6 Who had a 'rumble in the jungle' with Mohammad Ali?

7 In which Tennessee city was the American civil rights leader Martin Luther King assassinated in 1968?

8 In which country was Florence Nightingale born?

9 In the Bible, who are The Book of Revelations about?

10 Who starred as Hannah in the 1986 film *Hannah And Her Sisters*?

11 Which *Not the Nine O'Clock News* star was voted BBC Personality of the Year in 1981?

12 Which British jazzman released an album called *Underground*?

13 Which medical speciality is concerned with treating deformities caused by disease of and injury to the bones and joints?

14 Which band did Ian Craig Marsh and Martyn Ware break away from in order to form Heaven 17?

15 Who starred as Joseph in the 1992 film *Far And Away*?

Things you didn't know...

The suburbs of Russia are built on foundations of rubble and rubbish shipped from London in the nineteenth century.

Answers to page 287

1 Bailey, 2 Manchester, 3 Duchess of York, 4 Fred Basset, 5 Epilepsy, 6 A butterfly, 7 A Type of shoe, 8 The Shadows, 9 Guatemala, 10 Elton John, 11 Bayreuth, 12 A Rusty Nail, 13 Jasper Carrot, 14 Essex, 15 Shakin' Stevens.

QUIZ 288

Answers on page 288

1 Which TV detective was played by John Nettles?

2 In the story, how many men were in Jerome K. Jerome's boat?

3 Which island country in the West Indies was invaded by US troops in 1983?

4 A business is a collective noun describing which kind of animal?

5 Which William discovered the world's sixth largest island?

6 Which sculptor died in a fire that swept through their St. Ives' studio in 1975?

7 What type of vehicle is a juggernaut?

8 Which US actor starred in the films *The Prisoner of Zenda* and *Sinbad the Sailor*?

9 Which popular cartoon character was portrayed by John Goodman on film in the early 1990s?

10 Who scored 5 goals for England in an international in April 1975?

11 In which cartoon series did the characters try to avoid Officer Dibble?

12 What sort of plant is an ink cap?

13 A spat is the young of which mollusc?

14 During which battle did the infamous 'Charge of the Light Brigade' take place?

15 Who starred in the title role of Pen Densham's 1997 film version of *Moll Flanders*?

Things you didn't know...

The largest bird in the world, the ostrich, weighs 48,000 times as much as the smallest - the bee hummingbird.

Answers to page 288

1 Katherine Hepburn, 2 Water, 3 Tree, 4 Mali, 5 Deep Purple, 6 Salsify, 7 Cher, 8 New Zealand, 9 Books, 10 Three, 11 A trawler, 12 Motor racing, 13 Leeds United, 14 Gregorian, 15 Morris Minor.

QUIZ 289

Answers on page 293

1 Which sport only newspaper was launched in March 1998?

2 Who played veteran catcher Crash David in the 1988 film *Bull Durham*?

3 For which British contralto singer did Elgar write his *Sea Pictures*?

4 Who asked 'What do you want, if you don't want money'?

5 From whom did the animals seize the farm in *Animal Farm*?

6 Which body of water connects Europe with the Far East?

7 Paul McCartney and Stevie Wonder teamed up for which Number One song?

8 Which British cathedral has a clock with no face?

9 What does CD-Rom stand for?

10 Which U.S. president is famous for making the Gettysburg Address?

11 Who won the women's 400m hurdles at the 1992 Olympic Games?

12 How does a Japanese billiard table differ from others in the world?

13 What is the capital of Australia?

14 Of which chemical element is coal a form?

15 Which allergic condition is also called nettle rash and hives?

Things you didn't know...

Cary Grant was originally tipped to play James Bond.

Answers to page 293

1 Kinks, 2 Penelope, 3 An insect, 4 A fish, 5 Goitre, 6 *Brothers in Arms* by Dire Straits, 7 African elephant, 8 Ottawa, 9 *The Owl and the Pussycat,* 10 Suffolk Punch, 11 Needs, 12 Anne Bancroft, 13 Bette Davis, 14 The Goons, 15 St Peter Port.

QUIZ 290

Answers on page 294

1 Who recorded the album *Definitely, Maybe*?

2 Which British thriller writer created the characters Hercule Poirot and Miss Marple?

3 Near which European city was the Battle of Waterloo fought?

4 Which rock singer and guitarist had a hit with *Purple Haze*?

5 Which is the world's oldest stock exchange?

6 Which Italian city gives its name to a sausage and a sauce popular with spaghetti?

7 Who wrote *Puck of Pook's Hill*?

8 On a standard typewriter keyboard, which is the only vowel not on the top line?

9 Who was Chancellor of the Exchequer when Sir Winston Churchill was PM between 1951-55?

10 Of which state of the USA is Dover the capital?

11 In which modern country would you locate the birthplace of Mohammed?

12 Who painted *Sunflowers* which sold for almost £25,00,000 at Sotheby's in 1987?

13 What is the capital of New Zealand?

14 In which city could you climb the Spanish Steps?

15 From which country did the famous wartime traitor Vidkun Quisling come?

Things you didn't know...

Underwater hockey is known as octopush.

Answers to page 294

1 Mozarts, 2 Queensland, 3 Paul Verhoeven, 4 Winston Churchill, 5 Clark Gable and Lana Turner, 6 A tree, 7 22, 8 Peugeot 403 Cabriolet, 9 Garth Brooks, 10 *Little Lord Fauntleroy*, 11 *Bohemian Rhapsody*, 12 *Andy Pandy*, 13 Mae West, 14 Corgi, 15 St Paul.

QUIZ 291

Answers on page 291

1 Which group had a Top Ten hit with *Dedicated Follower of Fashion* in 1966?

2 Who was the faithful wife of Odysseus in Homer's *Odyssey*?

3 What sort of creature is a water boatman?

4 What sort of creature is a lemon sole?

5 What is the enlargement of the the thyroid gland called?

6 In 1986 which compact disc was the first to sell a million copies worldwide?

7 Which is larger, an Indian elephant or and African elephant?

8 What is the capital of Canada?

9 Who dined on mince and slices of quince?

10 Which breed of draught horse originates from East Anglia?

11 What must when the Devil drives?

12 Who played Dustin Hoffman's seducer in *The Graduate*?

13 Which actress played the English queen in the 1939 film, *The Private Lives of Elizabeth and Essex*?

14 Which comedy team had a 1956 Top Ten hit with *I'm Walking Backwards for Christmas*?

15 What is the name of the only town in Guernsey?

Things you didn't know...

The pigtail was banned in China in 1991 because it was a symbol of feudalism.

Answers to page 291

1 Sport First, 2 Kevin Costner, 3 Dame Clara Butt, 4 Adam Faith, 5 Mr Jones, 6 Jones, 7 Red Sea, 8 *Ebony and Ivory*, 9 Salisbury, 10 Compact Disc Read Only Memory, 11 Abraham Lincoln, 12 The legs are shorter, 13 Gospels, 14 Canberra, 15 Carbon.

QUIZ 292

Answers on page 292

1 Whose musical works were catalogued by kochel numbers?

2 Of which Australian state is Brisbane the capital?

3 Which director was responsible for *Starship Troopers* and *Robocop*?

4 During the Second World War, who did Norman Shelley imitate in radio broadcasts?

5 The 1948 film *Homecoming* starred which two Hollywood legends as an army surgeon and his nurse?

6 What is a honey locust?

7 How many letters are in the Hebrew alphabet?

8 Which type of car do you most associate with *Columbo*?

9 Which country artist released an album entitled *Sevens*?

10 In which book by Frances Hodgson Burnett is the title character the grandson of the Earl of Dorincourt?

11 The first pop video was used to promote which single that first topped the charts in 1975?

12 Which popular children's programme ran for only twenty-six episodes but was repeated frequently between 1953 and 1970?

13 Who said: I do all my writing in bed; everyone knows I do all my best work there'?

14 What is the Queen's favourite breed of dog?

15 Which saint and missionary wrote the epistles to the Corinthians and Galatians in the New Testament?

Things you didn't know...

Some parts of the Moon have been more carefully mapped than some parts of the Earth.

Answers to page 292

1 Oasis, 2 Dame Agatha Christie, 3 Brussels, 4 Jimi Hendrix, 5 Antwerp, 6 Bologna, 7 Rudyard Kipling, 8 A, 9 Rab Butler, 10 Delaware, 11 Saudi Arabia, 12 Van Gogh, 13 Wellington, 14 Rome, 15 Norway.

QUIZ 293

Answers on page 297

1 Which dish normally consists of rice, cooked flaked fish and hard boiled eggs?

2 Who presented Channel 4's *Whose Line is it Anyway*?

3 How much would you be paid if you held an honorary post?

4 What is the capital of Egypt?

5 Of which English city is Sutton Coldfield a suburb?

6 In which country is the Apennines mountain range?

7 In which 1939 film did Judy Garland sing *Over the Rainbow*?

8 In which city is the Vatican City?

9 What is the correct name for the bone commonly referred to as the thigh bone?

10 Which artificial transuranic element is represented by the symbol Fm?

11 Who wrote *Diana - Her True Story*?

12 Which *Brookside* character returned in 1997 after a long break from the Close?

13 Which US president was assassinated by John Wilkes Booth?

14 Which large deer is known as a moose in North America?

15 Which US attorney defended both OJ Simpson and Louise Woodward?

Things you didn't know...

The first Metropolitan policemen carried football rattles which they sounded to summon help.

Answers to page 297

1 George Bernard Shaw, 2 Rich, 3 Mexico, 4 Harold Macmillan, 5 Seth, 6 Lollipop, 7 Notre Dame, 8 Vincent Van Gogh's, 9 *King Lear*, 10 *Flamingo Road*, 11 *Dick Whittington*, 12 Nicholas Monsarrat, 13 Vulpine, 14 A tree, 15 Jacques Santer.

QUIZ 294

Answers on page 298

1 Which US actor starred in the films *The Public Enemy* and *The Roaring Twenties*?

2 Who plays Rachel in TV's *Friends*?

3 Which golfer was nicknamed the "Golden Bear"?

4 How many stomachs does a cow have?

5 Which singer dropped her surname for her album *Girl*?

6 With which British composer was the tenor Sir Peter Pears closely associated?

7 How is the fruit of the gourd Cucurbita pepo, associated with Hallowe'en, better known?

8 Who had a Top Ten hit single in 1985 with *Every Time You Go Away*?

9 In the castle of which West Yorkshire market town was Richard II murdered?

10 Which lanthanide element is represented by the symbol Lu?

11 Which was the first battle of the English Civil War?

12 What is the SI unit of work or energy, named after a British physicist?

13 What should be added to a car's water-cooling system in cold weather?

14 Which comic actor made his film debut as a pregnant man in *Rabbit Test*?

15 With which branch of the Germany armed forces was Alfred von Tirpitz associated?

Things you didn't know...

James Dean was driving a Porsche Spyder when he crashed and died in 1955.

Answers to page 298

1 Mary Anne Nichols, 2 Sagittarius, 3 Sir Joshua Reynolds, 4 Matt Dillon, 5 Charles Lindbergh, 6 Merlin, 7 Maureen Rees, 8 England and Australia, 9 Smallville, 10 Jack Shepherd, 11 Captain Sensible, 12 Red Hot Poker, 13 McKern, 14 Al Jolson, 15 Three.

QUIZ 295

Answers on page 295

1 Who wrote the plays *Major Barbara* and *Arms and the Man*?

2 What was Richard Burton's biography called?

3 With which Central American country are the Aztecs associated?

4 Which former prime minister was created Earl of Stockton in 1984?

5 Who was the younger brother of Cain and Abel?

6 *My Boy*, according to Millie, is called what?

7 Which French cathedral is built on an island in the River Seine?

8 *Red Vineyard at Arles* was which artist's only sale during his lifetime?

9 In which Shakespeare play does Cordelia appear?

10 Which American soap opera starred Morgan Fairchild, Mark Harmon and Stella Stevens?

11 Which pantomime character marries Alice Fitzwarren?

12 Which British novelist is best known for his 1951 book *The Cruel Sea*?

13 If dogs are canine and horses are equine, what are foxes?

14 What is a hornbeam?

15 Who was the president of the European Commission until 1998?

Things you didn't know...

In America it is fashionable to serve coloured vegetables, including red Brussel sprouts.

Answers to page 295

1 Kedgeree, **2** Clive Anderson, **3** Nothing, **4** Cairo, **5** Birmingham, **6** Italy, **7** *The Wizard of Oz*, **8** Rome, **9** Femur, **10** Fermium, **11** Andrew Morton, **12** Barry Grant, **13** Abraham Lincoln, **14** Elk, **15** Barry Scheck.

QUIZ 296

Answers on page 296

1 Who was the first victim of Jack the Ripper?

2 Which is the only sign of the zodiac to start and finish with the same letter?

3 To which English artist did James Boswell dedicate his famous *The Life of Samuel Johnson*?

4 Who starred as unrepentant drug fiend Bob Hughes in Drugstore Cowboy?

5 Which US aviator made the first solo non-stop flight across the Atlantic Ocean?

6 Which bird has the scientific name 'Falco columbarius'?

7 Who was the star of BBC's *Driving School* series?

8 Which two countries play cricket for the Ashes?

9 Where did *Superman* spend his childhood?

10 Who starred as Dectective Superintendent Charles Wycliffe in TV's *Wycliffe*?

11 Who had a Number One hit in 1982 with *Happy Talk*?

12 The plant Kniphofia is better known by what name?

13 Which Leo played *Rumpole of the Bailey*?

14 Which popular singer became famous for his blacked-up face and the song *Mammy*?

15 In the RAF, how many squadrons make up a wing?

Things you didn't know...

Franklin D. Roosevelt was once sent a telegram a quarter of a mile long.

Answers to page 296

1 James Cagney, 2 Jennifer Aniston, 3 Jack Nicklaus, 4 Four, 5 Dannii Minogue, 6 Benjamin Britten, 7 Pumpkin, 8 Paul Young, 9 Pontefract, 10 Lutetium, 11 Edgehill, 12 Joule, 13 Antifreeze, 14 Billy Crystal, 15 Navy.

QUIZ 297

Answers on page 301

1 In which film did Tom Cruise take Dustin Hoffman to Las Vegas?

2 Which actress starred in the films *Cabaret* and *Arthur*?

3 Which British artist painted a portrait of Winston Churchill that was destroyed on the instructions of Lady Churchill?

4 Which symbol denotes a battlefield on an Ordnance Survey map?

5 In Greek mythology who was God of the Underworld?

6 Which city is served by Queen Alia airport?

7 Who wrote *The Forsyte Saga*?

8 Which 1960s TV series featured Clarence the cross-eyed lion?

9 Which holy sounding character was created by Leslie Charteris?

10 Linonophobia is the fear of what?

11 Who was once reported to have bitten off a bat's head on stage?

12 What was the profession of Iain McCallum in the ITV drama series of the same name?

13 Which breed of cats are bred to have 'piggy' faces, with noses little more than stumps??

14 Which TV game show's original line-up featured Robert Robinson as compere, and Patrick Campbell and Frank Muir as team captains?

15 Who shot Marvin Gaye in 1984?

Things you didn't know...

John Lennon is thought to have written 'You've Got To Hide Your Love Away' for the Beatles gay manager Brian Epstein.

Answers to page 301

1 Kenny Dalglish, 2 Runner Bean, 3 Clock, 4 Severn Road Bridge, 5 The Great Barrier Reef, 6 Michael Jackson, 7 Pablo Picasso, 8 Chad, 9 *Poldark,* 10 Curly, 11 Crust, 12 Jean Boht, 13 Michael Jackson, 14 Blamire, 15 Portugal.

– 299 –

QUIZ 298

Answers on page 302

1 Which monkeys are known for their blue and red faces and buttocks?

2 Which *Coronation Street* character fell for a conman and ended up in prison?

3 If you ordered pamplemousse in a French restaurant, what woud you get?

4 Who is the current vice-president of the USA?

5 According to Greek Legend, which son of Priam was killed by Achilles?

6 What type of monkey is used as an organ grinder's monkey?

7 Which Scottish Formula One driver won the Australian Grand Prix in 1997?

8 Which British poet wrote the moral fable *Rasselas*?

9 What was Hilary Clinton's previously job?

10 Who was *The Lone Ranger*'s companion?

11 According to Arthurian legend, which wizard counselled and assisted Arthur and his father Uther Pendragon?

12 What was the title of the book about the Watergate scandal written by reporters Bernstein and Woodward?

13 A musket ball fired from the French ship Redoubtable killed which famous Englishman?

14 Which British national daily newspaper closed down in 1995?

15 Which infection of the large intestine can be bacterial or amoebic?

Things you didn't know...

David Essex was an extra in Carry On Henry but his performance ended up on the cutting room floor.

Answers to page 302

1 Charlotte, 2 Monitor, 3 Grant Fox, 4 Agadir, 5 A fish, 6 Charles I, 7 Elton John, 8 Black, 9 Nigeria, 10 Frigga, 11 Terry Venables, 12 1983, 13 Harold Wilson, 14 Baghdad, 15 A cereal grass.

QUIZ 299

Answers on page 299

1 Which former player tried to buy Celtic football club in 1998?

2 Which vegetable has varieties called Red Knight, Enorma and Red Emperor?

3 In cockney rhyming slang what is meant by 'dickory dock'?

4 Which bridge connects Haysgate to Almondsbury?

5 What is the largest coral reef in the world?

6 Who did Debbie Rowe marry in 1996?

7 Which artist was one of the pioneers of cubism and painted the Spanish Civil War-inspired painting Guernica?

8 Of which African country is N'djamena the capital?

9 Which popular period TV drama featured the adventures of a square in 18th-century Cornwall?

10 What is Norman Watts' nickname in *Coronation Street*?

11 What is the name of the earth's outer layer?

12 Who starred as Ma Boswell in *Bread*?

13 Which US singer released an album called *Blood On The Dancefloor* in 1997?

14 Which part did Michael Bates play in *Last of the Summer Wine* prior to his death?

15 TAP is the national airline of which country?

Things you didn't know...

The Russian postal service will not deliver letters containing chewing gum.

Answers to page 299

1 *Rain Man,* 2 Liza Minnelli, 3 Graham Sutherland, 4 Crossed swords, 5 Pluto, 6 Amman, 7 John Galsworthy, 8 Daktari, 9 *The Saint,* 10 String, 11 Ozzy Osbourne, 12 Police pathologist, 13 Persian, 14 *Call My Bluff,* 15 His father.

QUIZ 300

Answers on page 300

1 Which Brönte sister wrote Shirley?

2 Which famous BBC arts magazine, introduced by Huw Wheldon, was axed in 1965?

3 In Rugby Union which country amassed 126 points in one game in the 1987 World Cup?

4 Which city in Morocco was devasted by an earthquake in 1960?

5 What sort of creature is a dab?

6 Which English king was beheaded in 1649?

7 How is the British rock pianist and singer Reginald Dwight better known?

8 What is the traditional colour for a London taxi?

9 Of which African country is Lagos the former capital?

10 After which Norse goddess is Friday named?

11 Which former England football manager failed in his bid to lead Australia to the 1998 World Cup finals?

12 In which year of the 1980's was Shergar kidnapped?

13 Who became leader of the Labour Party on St. Valentine's Day 1963?

14 What is the capital of Iraq?

15 What is sorghum?

Things you didn't know...

*Muscular strength reaches a peak at the age of 25
– after that it goes into decline.*

Answers to page 300

1 Mandrills, 2 Dierdre, 3 Grapefruit, 4 Al Gore, 5 Hector, 6 Capuchin monkey, 7 David Coulthard, 8 Samuel Johnson, 9 Lawyer, 10 Tonto, 11 Merlin, 12 *All the President's Men,* 13 Lord Nelson, 14 Today, 15 Dysentery.

QUIZ 301

Answers on page 305

1 Which disease would you have if an Australian said you were suffering from 'dog's disease'?

2 In Cockney slang, which device is referred to as 'a dog'?

3 Which British monarch was known as the Virgin Queen?

4 To where did the Royal Observatory move in 1990?

5 What meat appears in a *Punch and Judy* show?

6 Knights in jousting competitions traditionally used what weapon?

7 Which gas is represented by the symbol Ne?

8 Which city is sometimes called the 'Paris of the East'?

9 What is the butler's name in *The Addams Family*?

10 At which Maryland presidential retreat did Anwar Sadat and Menachem Begin agree to a framework for peace in the Middle East?

11 In which American state is Salmon River?

12 Under what name did Loretta Lynn's sister have a Top Ten hit in 1977 with *Don't it Make My Brown Eyes Blue*?

13 Which conspirator was discovered in a cellar under the Houses of Parliament in November 1605?

14 In which English county are March and Godmanchester?

15 What was the very first product made by Philips, Eindhoven?

Things you didn't know...

Sweden was the first country to ban aerosol cans.

Answers to page 305

1 Mercury and Venus, 2 Horace Walpole, 3 May, 4 The Strand, 5 Pegasus, 6 Little Caesar, 7 Edwards, 8 St John's, 9 Skiing, 10 Jason Donovan, 11 George Bernard Shaw, 12 Eric Clapton, 13 Moses, 14 Dirk Bogarde, 15 Shirley MacLaine.

QUIZ 302

Answers on page 306

1 In London, what was the Tyburn?

2 Which famous dancing troupe was formed by Margaret Kelly?

3 Which duke commanded the British forces at Waterloo?

4 What was Marilyn Monroe's character name in *Some Like It Hot*?

5 Which planet is eighth from the sun?

6 Which Scottish explorer discovered the Victoria Falls?

7 Which soothing lotion consists of a pink powder of zinc oxide and iron oxide suspended in water?

8 In which city is the Walker Art Gallery?

9 Who wrote *The Tenant of Wildfell Hall*?

10 Which type of car do you most associate with *Mr. Bean*?

11 Which bandleader's first name, which was never used, was Alton?

12 After Pacific, Atlantic and Indian, which is the next largest ocean?

13 Which two apostles was Zebedee the father of?

14 Which boxer was known as the 'Louisville Lip'?

15 On which English moorland was R D Blackmore's novel *Lorna Doone* set?

Things you didn't know...

There are more than 17 miles of corridor in the Pentagon.

Answers to page 306

1 The Gambia, 2 Sir Noel Coward, 3 *Nobody's Perfect*, 4 Sumo wrestling, 5 Mel Gibson, 6 Moose, 7 Potato, 8 Ice cube, 9 Innerspace, 10 David Nixon, 11 Malaysia, 12 Potomac River, 13 Judaism, 14 Chan, 15 Bing Crosby.

QUIZ 303

Answers on page 303

1 Which two planets are nearer to the sun than the earth is?

2 Which British author wote the gothic novel *The Castle of Otranto*?

3 For which month is emerald the Birthstone?

4 In which London thoroughfare are the Law Courts?

5 What was the name of the winged horse in Greek mythology?

6 Which classic gangster movie featured a character called Enrico Bandello?

7 What was the maiden name of banned athlete Diane Modahl?

8 Which capital of a West Indian island share its name with the capital of a Canadian province?

9 With which sport do you associate Alberto Tomba?

10 Who had a Number One hit in 1991 with *Any Dream Will Do*?

11 Which writer said 'England and America are two countries divided by a common language!'?

12 Who had a Top Ten hit with *I Shot The Sheriff*?

13 Who led the Israelites out of Egypt to the Promised Land?

14 Which actor wrote the book *A Postillion Struck by Lightning*?

15 Who starred as Aurora Greenway in *The Evening Star*?

Things you didn't know...

Walt Disney is the only Hollywwod producer to be honoured with a postage stamp.

Answers to page 303

1 Influenza, 2 Telephone (dog and bone), 3 Elizabeth I, 4 Cambridge, 5 Sausages, 6 Lance, 7 Neon, 8 Shanghai, 9 Lurch, 10 Camp David, 11 Idaho, 12 Crystal Gayle, 13 Guy Fawkes, 14 Cambridgeshire, 15 Light bulbs.

QUIZ 304

Answers on page 304

1 Of which African country is Banjul the capital?

2 Which dramatist, composer and actor wrote the plays *Blithe Spirit* and *The Vortex*?

3 What is the last line in the 1959 film *Some Like it Hot*?

4 In which sport would you go to a basho?

5 Who played the lead role in the film *Mad Max*?

6 What is the largest member of the deer family?

7 If you were served 'aloo' in an Indian restaurant which vegetable would you have?

8 Which rapper starred alongside Elizabeth Hurley in the film *Dangerous Ground*?

9 Which 1987 film starred Dennis Quaid and Martin Short and won an Oscar for the Best Visual Effects?

10 Who was the first British magician to become a television star?

11 Of which Asian country is Kuala Lumpur the capital?

12 On which river does Washington DC stand?

13 What is the religion of the Jews called?

14 Which very common Chinese surname means 'old' in English?

15 Which singer won Best Actor award in *Going My Way* in 1945?

Things you didn't know...

Women in Iceland do not change their name when they marry.

Answers to page 304

1 A stream, 2 Bluebell girls, 3 The Duke of Wellington, 4 Sugar Kane, 5 Neptune, 6 Livingstone, 7 Calamine lotion, 8 Liverpool, 9 Anne Bronte, 10 Mini, 11 Glenn Miller, 12 Arctic, 13 James and John, 14 Muhammad Ali, 15 Exmoor.

QUIZ 305

Answers on page 309

1 By what name is Ilyich Ramirez Sanchez better known?

2 Which TV series features Mr Spock and Captain Kirk?

3 Which musical instrument has dampers, hammers and strings?

4 By what name is the lightning beetle better known?

5 The song *The Lady is a Tramp* comes from which musical?

6 On which river does the German spa city of Wiesbaden stand?

7 Which king of England married Isabella of France?

8 Who succeeded Neil Kinnock as Leader of the Labour Party?

9 Which part of the eye is responsible for its colour?

10 How is the great bell in the clock tower of the Palace of Westminster known?

11 How many episodes of *Fawlty Towers* were made?

12 On British coins does the Queen's head face to the left or the right?

13 Which animal are the Cornish rex and Devon rex varieties of?

14 Which large desert is situated in Chile?

15 In which month is Rememberance Sunday?

Things you didn't know...

The odds against a Royal Flush in poker are 649,739 to 1.

Answers to page 309

1 Mayfair, 2 Flamingo, 3 Rice, 4 A wild ass, 5 John Napier, 6 Specials, 7 Ounce, 8 *Oliver Twist,* 9 A fish, 10 Krone, 11 Spandau, 12 Seraphim, 13 Once (in 1951), 14 Spiders, 15 St Pauls.

QUIZ 307

Answers on page 310

1 Which song begins: "When you left me all alone, at the record hop; told me you were going out for a soda pop"?

2 Which Danish writer is best known for fairty tales such as *The Ugly Duckling* and *The Snow Queen*?

3 Which optical phenomenon consists of an arc of light across the sky composed of the colours of the spectrum?

4 What is the capital of Albania?

5 On which channel could *The Jack Docherty Show* be seen?

6 What colour is a ship's starboard light?

7 In *Coronation Street*, who owns The Kabin

8 Which is the oldest of the colleges at Cambridge founded in 1248?

9 What does the acronym UNESCO stand for?

10 What is another name for the German shepherd dog?

11 What sort of creature is an anaconda?

12 To which genus of trees does the maple belong?

13 Who wrote *Room at the Top* and *Life at the Top*?

14 To which continent is pampas grass native?

15 On TV, what are Martin Platt, Charlie Fairhead and Gladys Emmanuel?

Things you didn't know...

Racing greyhounds have their noseprints, which are as individual as human fingerprints, kept on record to prevent fraud.

Answers to page 310

1 Organisation of Petrleum Exporting Countries, **2** Mildew, **3** Sir Edwin Landseer, **4** William Faulkner, **5** Renoir, **6** Paul Gauguin, **7** Radio 3, **8** Julia Watson, **9** Austrian, **10** Monaco, **11** Black, **12** A water beetle, **13** Drury Lane Theatre, **14** France, **15** Manfred Mann.

QUIZ 307

Answers on page 307

1 On a British Monopoly board which is the last property you pass before reaching 'GO'?

2 Which long-legged, long-necked wading bird has white plumage tinged with pink?

3 Which food item is most consumed by humans throughout the world?

4 What sort of creature is a kiang?

5 Which Scottish mathematician invented logarithms?

6 Which British group had a 1981 Number One hit record with *Ghost Town*?

7 What is the alternative name for a snow leopard?

8 In which Dickens novel does the character Fagin appear?

9 What sort of creature is a John Dory?

10 What is the unit of currency in Norway?

11 Rudolf Hess was the last prisoner in which jail?

12 In the celestial hierarchy, what is the highest order of angels?

13 How many times did the Conservative Party win a general election whilst Winston Churchill was its leader?

14 What is arachnophobia the fear of?

15 Which cathedral is regarded as Wren's masterpiece?

Things you didn't know...

The Queen's Corgis dine on fresh rabbit, pork and chicken, very rarely are they fed canned food.

Answers to page 307

1 *Carlos The Jackal*, 2 *Star Trek*, 3 Piano, 4 Firefly, 5 Pal Joey, 6 The Rhine, 7 Edward II, 8 John Smith, 9 The iris, 10 Big Ben, 11 13 . Six in 1975 and seven in 1979, 12 To the right, 13 Cat, 14 Atacama, 15 November.

QUIZ 308

Answers on page 308

1 What does the acronym OPEC stand for?

2 What is the general name for a fungus that forms a thin white coating on plants?

3 Which painter and sculptor was responsible for the lions at London's Trafalgar Square?

4 Which US novelist wrote *Absalom, Absalom!*?

5 What was the surname of the French Impressionist painter whose son became a famous film director?

6 Which artist wrote the book *Noa Noa*?

7 Nick Kenyon was Controller of which Radio channel in 1996?

8 Who played Barbara 'Baz' Hayes in the TV series *Casualty*?

9 What nationality was the conductor Herbert von Karajan?

10 Which is the most densely populated state in Europe?

11 In heraldry, which colour is denoted by sable?

12 What sort of creature is a whirligig?

13 Which London theatre was managed by Colley Cibber, David Garrick and Richard Brinsley Sheridan?

14 Which country won the 1998 football World Cup?

15 Which UK group formed in 1962 and were originally called Mann-Hugg Blues Brothers?

Things you didn't know...

In America there is a magazine called 'Chocolate News' – It comes in a glossy brown cover and actually smells of chocolate.

Answers to page 308

1 *Lipstick On Your Collar,* **2** Hans Christian Anderson, **3** Rainbow, **4** Tirana, **5** Channel 5, **6** Green, **7** Rita, **8** Peterhouse, **9** United Nations Educational, Scientific and Cultural Organisation, **10** Alsatian, **11** A snake, **12** Acer, **13** John Braine, **14** South America, **15** Nurses.

QUIZ 309

Answers on page 313

1 Sir Alfred Munnings who died in 1959, is best remembered for what type of paintings?

2 Which cartoon character is Boo Boo's buddy?

3 In which country was actor and director Mel Gibson born?

4 Which Englishman was murdered outside the Dakota Building in New York in 1980

5 Which US duo asked you to *Walk Right Back* in 1961?

6 Which car manufacturer produced the Panda?

7 Who won an Oscar for his role in *Harry and Tonto*?

8 'Darbies' are a slang term for which items?

9 Which American five-a-side court game was invented by James Naismith?

10 In what year did the D-Day landings take place?

11 Which motorway runs south from Perth to the Firth of Forth bridge?

12 Who had a Number One hit in 1989 with *Especially For You*?

13 What did Derek Trotter name his son in *Only Fools and Horses*?

14 How many sides has a parallelogram?

15 From which Asian country did calico originally come?

Things you didn't know...

The table fork was introduced to England by Thomas Coryat in 1608.

Answers to page 313

1 Tonga, 2 Ernest Hemingway, 3 Mark James, 4 Schiedam, 5 An antelope, 6 Meknes, 7 Pete Goss, 8 A dog, 9 Champion, 10 J.D. Salinger, 11 Girl, 12 Sheridan Le Fanu, 13 Talus, 14 Nicaragua, 15 Mead.

QUIZ 310

Answers on page 314

1 In Greek mythology who was God of the Seas?

2 Which town in Kent is one of the Cinque Ports, and considered to be the landing place of Julius Caesar?

3 How is the Italian city of Napoli known in English?

4 Which is the most successful instrumental single of all time in the UK?

5 What is the world's longest river?

6 Which political party was led by Clement Attlee from 1935 to 1955?

7 Which scheme allows all or part of a person's legal costs to be paid from public funds?

8 What form of sentence was introduced to the UK by the 1972 Criminal Justice Act?

9 Who would use a trochee?

10 Which US inventor designed the Clermont, one of the earliest steamships?

11 Which Scottish novelist wrote *The Heart of Midlothian*?

12 What is a score of forty all in a game of tennis called?

13 The young of which snakelike fish are known as elvers?

14 In which year was the first and second class post system introduced in Britain?

15 How many states are there in the USA?

Things you didn't know...

Around nine hundred different chemicals are contained in cigarette smoke.

Answers to page 314

1 Eddie Cochran, **2** The Seatons, **3** *Wheel of Fortune,* **4** Ford, **5** Cliff Richard, **6** 40, **7** Wyatt Earp, **8** Istanbul, **9** Puffin, **10** Canada, **11** *Silence is Golden,* **12** The Rockies, **13** Romania, **14** Badger, **15** Ivan the Terrible.

QUIZ 311

Answers on page 311

1 Which country was formerly known as the Friendly Islands?

2 Which US novelist wrote *For Whom the Bell Tolls*?

3 Which British golfer beat Greg Norman at a 3rd extra play-off hole to win the 1997 Spanish Open?

4 Which town in South Holland province is famous for its gin distilleries?

5 What sort of creature is a nyala?

6 Which city was known as the Moroccan Versailles?

7 Which British round-the-world yachtsman turned back into a force-nine gale to rescue French competitor Raphael Dinelli in 1997?

8 What sort of creature is a Rhodesian ridgeback?

9 What was the name of Gene Autry's horse?

10 Which US novelist wrote *The Catcher in the Rye*?

11 According to the comedy, There's a what in my soup?

12 Which Irish novelist wrote *Uncle Silas*?

13 What is the correct name for the bone commonly referred to as the ankle?

14 Of which country is Managua the capital?

15 Which alcoholic drink consists of fermented honey and water?

Things you didn't know...

All polar bears are left-handed.

Answers to page 311

1 Horses, 2 Yogi Bear, 3 The USA, 4 John Lennon, 5 Everly Brothers, 6 Fiat, 7 Art Carney, 8 Handcuffs, 9 Basketball, 10 1944, 11 M90, 12 Jason Donovan, 13 Damien, 14 Four, 15 India.

QUIZ 312

Answers on page 312

1 Who had a Number One hit with *Three Steps to Heaven* in 1960?

2 What was the name of the north-eastern family coping with the Depression in the TV series *When the Boat Comes In*?

3 Which ITV game show was hosted by Bradley Walsh and Jenny Powell?

4 Which company made the first production-line car?

5 Who had Number One hits with *I Love You and The Minute You're Gone*?

6 How many squares are there on a Monopoly board?

7 Which American had brothers called Baxter, Jim, Morgan and Virgil?

8 Which Turkish city was once called Constantinople?

9 What is the children's division of Penguin books called?

10 In which country can the Great Slave Lake be found?

11 What was the title of the *Tremeloes'* 1967 Number One hit?

12 In which mountain system does the Colorado River rise?

13 Which country did the gymnast Nadia Comaneci represent at the 1976 Olympics?

14 Which animal lives in a sett?

15 Who was the first tsar of Russia?

Things you didn't know...

The Canary Islands are not named after birds but dogs. The original name was Insulae Canariae, meaning Island of the Dogs.

Answers to page 312

1 Poseiden, 2 Deal, 3 Naples, 4 Stranger On The Shore (Acker Bilk), 5 Nile, 6 Labour Party, 7 Legal aid, 8 Community Service, 9 A poet, 10 Robert Fulton, 11 Sir Walter Scott, 12 Deuce, 13 Eels, 14 1968, 15 50.

QUIZ 313

Answers on page 317

1 What is the capital of Western Australia?

2 How were the Poor Knights of Christ and of the Temple of Solomon better known?

3 What was the artistic profession of Emily Dickinson?

4 From which country does authentic maiolica pottery come?

5 Which film, a remake of a French comedy, starred Billy Crystal and Robin Williams?

6 Who is said to have described Lord Archer's books as 'trashy' in September 1996?

7 Which gas is represented by the symbol He?

8 Which country knocked England out of the 1998 World Cup Finals in France?

9 Which star of *The Mask* played Harvey Keitel's wife in *Head Above Water*?

10 Which actor played the father in the sitcom *How's your Father*?

11 Dipsophobia is the fear of what?

12 Which French novelist wrote *The Outsider* and *The Plague*?

13 Which word describes an organism living in or on another organism of a different species?

14 Of which country is the River Glomma the longest river?

15 Favourite, Figaro and Autumn King are varieties of which vegetable?

Things you didn't know...

The average tiger lives to the age of 12.

Answers to page 317

1 St Moritz, **2** Vic Reeves, **3** *Paint Your Wagon,* **4** Theodore Roosevelt, **5** Hang Seng Index, **6** Slade Prison (in *Porridge*), **7** Indian Ocean, **8** Paul Schofield, **9** Turkey, **10** Tim Allen, **11** Raven, **12** Chatsworth, **13** Widows, **14** Cycling, **15** The Name of the Rose.

QUIZ 314

Answers on page 318

1 Which county won the 1997 County Championship in cricket?

2 What sort of creature is a Samoyed?

3 Which US composer wrote 4' 33"?

4 What name is given to an explosive mixture of potassium nitrate, charcoal and sulphur?

5 Who wrote *The Old Curiosity Shop*?

6 Which group had a Number One hit in 1983 with *Is There Something I Should Know*?

7 In which university city can the Ashmolean Museum be found?

8 By what name is phenol also known?

9 How are Clarissa Dickson Wright and Jennifer Paterson better known?

10 Of which European country are the Magyars the largest ethnic group?

11 Which Welsh mountain system includes Snowdonia, Plynlimon, and the Black Mountains?

12 How many events are there in the decathlon in athletics?

13 What was the regiment in *Soldier, Soldier* called?

14 Which country's legislative assembly was known as the Reichstag?

15 Which martial arts actor died shortly after starring in the film *Enter The Dragon*?

Things you didn't know...

Lassie's human co-star Tommy Rettig was sentenced to five and a half years in prison in 1976 for smuggling cocaine from Peru.

Answers to page 318

1 *David Copperfield*, 2 Television, 3 Weasel, 4 Andy Green, 5 Neptune, 6 Cheshire, 7 Henry Williamson, 8 *Little Women*, 9 Privet, 10 Roy Lichtenstein, 11 Impatiens, 12 Lapwing, 13 Kenneth Branagh, 14 Kylie Minogue, 15 British Columbia.

QUIZ 315

Answers on page 315

1 Which Swiss resort is famous for its Cresta Run?

2 By what name is anarchic comic Jim Moir better known?

3 Which film musical starred Lee Marvin, Clint Eastwood and Jean Seberg?

4 Who was President of the USA from 1901 to 1909?

5 What is the Hong Kong equivalent of London's FTSE?

6 What was the name of the prison where Norman Stanley Fletcher served a five year sentence?

7 In which ocean are the Maldive Islands?

8 Who played Sir Thomas More in the 1966 film *A Man For All Seasons*?

9 Which meat is traditionally eaten in the USA on the fourth Thursday in November?

10 Which *Home Improvement* star played insensitive city type Michael Cromwell in the film *Jungle 2 Jungle*?

11 Which type of bird did Noah release first from the Ark?

12 Which country house is the seat of the Duke of Devonshire?

13 Which group of people are collectively known as an ambush?

14 In which sport might you encounter a 'peleton' and a 'maillot jaune'?

15 What was the title of the book by Umberto Eco which was made into a film in 1986 starring Sean Connery as a thirteenth century monk?

Things you didn't know...

Dudley Moore was born with a club foot.

Answers to page 315

1 Perth, 2 Templars, 3 Poet, 4 Italy, 5 Father's Day, 6 Norma Major, 7 Helium, 8 Argentina, 9 Cameron Diaz, 10 Harry Worth, 11 Drinking, 12 Albert Camus, 13 Parasite, 14 Norway, 15 Carrot.

QUIZ 316

Answers on page 316

1 Which Dickens' hero marries Dora Spenlow and, after her death, Agnes Wickfield?

2 *Marquee Moon* was the debut album of which New Wave group?

3 To which family of animals does the polecat belong?

4 Who drove the car Thrust SSC that first broke the land speed record in September 1997?

5 Which was the only planet to be discovered in the nineteenth century?

6 In which English county is Jodrell Bank situated?

7 Which author created *Tarka the Otter*?

8 What is the best known book written by Louisa May Alcott?

9 John Alderton played Bernard Hedges in the long running series, *Please Sir*, what was his nickname?

10 Which pioneer of Pop Art died in New york in 1997?

11 Which genus of plants includes busy lizzie and touch-me-not?

12 Which bird is also called the peewit or green plover?

13 Who directed and starred in the 1989 film *Henry V*?

14 Which vocalist had a Top Ten hit single in 1991 with *If You Were With Me Now*?

15 In which Canadian province is the city of Vancouver?

Things you didn't know...

Debbie Reynolds was such a virtuous child she earned 48 merit badges as a Girl Scout.

Answers to page 316

1 Glamorgan, 2 A dog, 3 John Cage, 4 Gunpowder, 5 Charles Dickens, 6 Duran Duran, 7 Oxford, 8 Carbolic acid, 9 *Two Fat Ladies,* 10 Hungary, 11 The Cambrian Mountains, 12 Ten, 13 The King's Own Fusiliers, 14 Germany's, 15 Bruce Lee.

QUIZ 317

Answers on page 321

1 In Arthurian legend, which knight of the Round Table was the lover of Guinevere?

2 Which unexplained phenomenon takes its name from the German for noisy ghost?

3 What was Romeo's surname in *Romeo and Juliet*?

4 Which fish-eating sea bird has a large triangular bill that is very brightly coloured in the breeding season?

5 Who starred alongside John Travolta as Castor Troy in the film, *Face Off*?

6 In what year was the hit film *Grease* released?

7 In which US state was the marine preserve that was home to *Flipper*?

8 Which action movie veteran starred in the film *Maximum Risk*?

9 Which Apache Indian chief surrendered to federal troops in 1886 and dictated his life story?

10 How many gold medals did Jesse Owens win at the 1936 Olympics in Berlin?

11 Which desert is the driest in the world?

12 Who won a Best Actor Oscar for his role in the film *True Grit*?

13 What sort of creature is a flycatcher?

14 What does the acronym NATO stand for?

15 Which cult TV series began its fourth season with an episode called *Herrenvolk*?

Things you didn't know...

It is illegal to catch whales in the US state of Oklahoma – which is an inland state!

Answers to page 321

1 1,000, **2** Tim Burton, **3** Latvia, **4** Vladimir Nabokov, **5** Napoleon Bonaparte, **6** Antonio de Oliveira Salazar, **7** Brittany, **8** Austria, **9** A fish, **10** France, **11** George Orwell, **12** The Bible, **13** A bird, **14** Gladiators, **15** Canadian.

QUIZ 318

Answers on page 322

1 Who played Julia Robert's gay friend in *My Best Friend's Wedding*?

2 Which two nations fought at the Battle of Agincourt?

3 In which discontinued events did Ray Ewry win his ten Olympic gold medals?

4 In which road did the Fire of London start in September 1666?

5 Which former Sex Pistols star released an album called *Psycho's Path*?

6 Which Rugby Union team defeated Sale 9-3 to win the 1997 Pilkington Cup Final?

7 What is a Pirani gauge used to measure?

8 How many horns does an Indian rhinoceros have?

9 From which tree does the chewing gum ingredient chicle come?

10 In which 1985 film did Michael J Fox star as a young man experiencing some unusual biological changes?

11 What is the largest continent in the world?

12 From which fruit is the spirit Kirsch made?

13 What sort of creature is a corncrake?

14 Which German general was known as the Desert Fox?

15 In which organ can grey matter and the cerebrum be found?

Things you didn't know...

Superglue was invented accidentally at the Kodak Eastman factory in the 1950s.

Answers to page 322

1 United Nations, 2 Kneecap, 3 Hector Berlioz, 4 Eternal, 5 Nirvana, 6 Mozart, 7 Mexico, 8 Merlin, 9 U2, 10 Aegean Sea, 11 Argentina, 12 Mongoose, 13 Queen Mary, 14 Chiropody, 15 Leicestershire.

Answers on page 319

1 How many American billions make up a British billion?

2 Who directed the 1994 Biopic *Ed Wood*?

3 Of which former Soviet republic is Riga the capital?

4 Which Russian-born novelist wrote *Lolita*?

5 Which French emperor was defeated at Waterloo?

6 Which dictator ruled Portugal from 1932 to 1968?

7 How is the French region of Bretagne known in English?

8 In which country was Adolf Hitler born?

9 What sort of creature is a flounder?

10 Which Rugby Union team won the 1997 Five Nations Championship?

11 Which British author wrote the novels *Animal Farm* and *Nineteen Eighty-Four*?

12 What was the Vulgate a version of?

13 What sort of creature is a tern?

14 In which series did rugby star Jeremy Guscott replace footballer John Fashanu as a presenter?

15 Along with the kayak, which other type of canoe is used in the Olympics?

Things you didn't know...

There was only one event in the very first Olympic Games in 776 BC. The astade which was a sprint over 20 yards (19.27m)

Answers to page 319

1 Lancelot, 2 Poltergeist, 3 Montague, 4 Puffin, 5 Nicolas Cage, 6 1978, 7 Florida, 8 Jean-Claude Van Damme, 9 Geronimo, 10 Four, 11 Atacama (Chile), 12 John Wayne, 13 A bird, 14 North Atlantic Treaty Organisation, 15 *The X Files*.

QUIZ 320

Answers on page 320

1 Which international organisation is represented by the initials UN?

2 How is the patella commonly known?

3 Which French composer wrote the *Symphonie Fantastique*?

4 Which all-girl group released an album called *Before The Rain*?

5 What is the supreme goal of Buddhists?

6 Who composed the tune to *Twinkle Twinkle Little Star*?

7 In which country could you visit the ruins of the Aztec civilisation?

8 What was the name of King Arthur's wizard?

9 Which Irish rock group had a 1983 Top Ten hit with *New Year's Day*?

10 In which sea are the Dodecanese Islands?

11 Aerolineas is the national airline of which country?

12 What kind of creature was *Rikki-Tikki-Tavi*?

13 What was the Queen Elizabeth's luxury sister ship?

14 Which paramedical speciality deals with the care of the feet?

15 Who lost to Essex in the 1998 final of cricket's Benson & Hedges cup?

Things you didn't know...

Seventeen year-old Sandy Lyle was the first golfer to represent his country at boy, youth and senior levels in the same year, 1975.

Answers to page 320

1 Rupert Everett, 2 England and France, 3 Standing jumps, 4 Pudding Lane, 5 John Lydon, 6 Leicester, 7 Low gas pressures, 8 One, 9 Sapodilla, 10 Teen Wolf, 11 Asia, 12 Cherries, 13 A bird, 14 Erwin Rommel, 15 Brain.

Answers on page 325

1 What is charlock?

2 On which farm did *Worzel Gummidge* live?

3 For what was Gerardus Mercator famous?

4 Which great Jazz violinist died in 1997 at the age of 89?

5 Which islet in the Firth of Forth is noted for its colonies of seabirds?

6 Which fruit has the Latin name prunus persica?

7 By what name was the popular wrestler Shirley Crabtree better known?

8 What college do officers of the British army attend?

9 Which group of people live in Greenland, Denmark, Alaska, Canada and Siberia?

10 What was the name of the country where Gulliver met the Little People?

11 What type of creature is a Black Widow?

12 Who married the Earl of Bothwell in 1567?

13 Which Tony played Ted Roach in *The Bill*?

14 In *Brookside*, who was buried under the patio?

15 Who wrote *Love Story*?

Things you didn't know...

Between 1974 and 1983 Bob Paisly won 20 trophies, including six League Championships, as manager of Liverpool FC.

Answers to page 325

1 Billy Connolly, **2** Ambridge, **3** Spencer, **4** Paper size, **5** Alfred, **6** The World Cup, **7** Abba, **8** Milan, **9** Saxophone, **10** *Bullseye*, **11** Blood Poisoning, **12** Samaritans, **13** Vince, **14** 1939, **15** Mecanized Infantry Combat Vehicle.

QUIZ 322

Answers on page 326

1 In 1993, which country ranked third in terms of world population?

2 Who had a Number One hit in 1981 with *Tainted Love*?

3 What was the theme tune to the film *Breakfast at Tiffany's*?

4 Quinsy affects which part of the body?

5 Which former Archers actor played Tom Kirby in TV's *Noah's Ark*?

6 What does the place name suffix 'BURN' signify?

7 Who hosted the radio quiz show *Have a Go*?

8 What is the capital of Paraguay?

9 In which Middle Eastern city is the Dome of the Rock?

10 Which swimming stroke is named after an insect?

11 Which US state is situated on the Southern border of Colorado?

12 What is the main difference between porcelain and pottery?

13 Which group recorded the original of *Light My Fire*?

14 Of which US state is Columbia the capital?

15 In Greek mythology, what did the gods eat?

Things you didn't know...

When Ayrton Senna was buried in Brazil, a million people lined the streets and the Brazilian Air Force drew a heart in the sky.

Answers to page 326

1 The hair, **2** Einstein, **3** Blackshirts, **4** Patrick Duffy, **5** China, **6** Khartoum, **7** Toto, **8** Seven, **9** Hammersmith or Barnes, **10** Blackheads, **11** A Wookey, **12** Lennie Godber, **13** Third, **14** Scarborough Fair, **15** Fidelity.

QUIZ 323

Answers on page 323

1 Which comedian played John Brown in the film *Mrs Brown*?

2 In which fictional village is *The Archers* set?

3 What was Frank's surname in *Some Mothers Do 'Ave 'Em*?

4 What is Pott?

5 Which king is said to have burnt the cakes?

6 Which international football trophy was stolen in 1966?

7 Which group had a Number One hit single in 1980 with *Super Trouper*?

8 In which city is La Scala opera house?

9 What instrument was played by Jazz musician John Coltrane?

10 On which TV game show would contestants always win a 'Bully'?

11 What is the popular name for toxaemia?

12 Which helpful organisation was founded by the Rev Chad Varah in 1953?

13 Who was Pennys's boyfriend in *Just Good Friends*?

14 In what year did the Second World War Begin?

15 What does MICV stand for?

Things you didn't know...

British athlete Roger Black was banned from competing as a schoolboy because of a heart defect.

Answers to page 323

1 A herb, 2 Scatterbrook, 3 Maps of the earth, 4 Stephane Grappelli, 5 Bass Rock, 6 Peach, 7 Big Daddy, 8 Sandhurst, 9 Eskimo, 10 Lilliput, 11 Spider, 12 Mary, Queen of Scots, 13 Scannel, 14 Trevor Jordache, 15 Erich Segal.

QUIZ 324

Answers on page 324

1 Which part of your body would suffer from trichosis?

2 Which German-born genius won the 1921 Nobel Prize for Physics?

3 By what other name were the SS also known internationally?

4 On TV, who played *The Man From Atlantis*?

5 With which country did Britain fight against in The Opium War?

6 What is the capital of Sudan?

7 What is the name of the dog in *The Wizard of Oz*?

8 What do the numbers add up to on the opposite sides of a dice?

9 Name one of the two bridges under which the crews pass in the University Boat Race?

10 If you suffer from comedones, what have you got?

11 What sort of creature was Chewbacca in *Star Wars*?

12 What was the name of Richard Beckinsale's character in *Porridge*?

13 Numerically which president of the USA was Thomas Jeffeson?

14 In which Simon and Garfunkel song will you hear the line 'parsley, sage, rosemary and thyme'?

15 In medieval art, what did a dog signify?

Things you didn't know...

The Silverstone racing circuit is built on abandoned RAF runways.

Answers to page 324

1 USA, 2 Soft Cell, 3 *Moonriver,* 4 Throat, 5 Peter Wingfield, 6 Stream, 7 Wilfred Pickles, 8 Asuncion, 9 Jerusalem, 10 Butterfly, 11 New Mexico, 12 Pottery does not transmit light, 13 The Doors, 14 South Carolina, 15 Ambrosia.

QUIZ 325

Answers on page 329

1 Which *Brookside* character took part in the grand final of the talent competition Sing Like A Star in 1997?

2 Which US explorer became the first to reach the North Pole in 1909?

3 Which 1979 film starring Marlon Brando and Martin Sheen was an adaptation of Joseph Conrad's story *Heart of Darkness*?

4 What was the Princess of Wales' maiden name?

5 In the Bible which king's doom was foretold by the writing on the wall?

6 What sort of fruit is a Laxton Superb?

7 Of which country was Achmed Sukarno President from 1945 to 1962?

8 In Morse Code, which letter is represented by a single dot?

9 Who became British Home Secretary in 1997?

10 What was Barbara Castle's parliamentary constituency?

11 What is the capital of Russia?

12 Over what distance is the Cesarewitch run?

13 What colour was The Beatles' Submarine?

14 Which historical event is said to be commemorated in the nursery rhyme 'ring-a ring o'roses'?

15 To which track did the British Greyhound Derby move in 1985?

Things you didn't know...

Oprah Winfrey should have been called Orpah after the Biblical figure but the midwife spelt the name wrong on the birth certificate.

Answers to page 329

1 Orange, 2 Mika Hakkinen, 3 Kenya, 4 Sir Carol Reed, 5 A crocodile is   man-eating, 6 Massachusetts, 7 Orion, 8 Dublin, 9 A parish, 10 All parts of cathedral or church, 11 Hereford and Worcester, 12 1997, 13 Union, 14 Cambridge University, 15 Val Doonican.

QUIZ 326

Answers on page 330

1 Which prime minister took Britain into the Second World War?

2 How is the Christian feast of the Annunciation of the Virgin Mary commonly known?

3 On which river does Marlborough stand?

4 Of which ocean is the North Sea a section?

5 Which famous South African game reserve is on the border with Mozambique?

6 Which well known writer's first book *Child Whispers* was published in1922?

7 What are the legless larvae of houseflies and blowflies called?

8 In which city is the Trevi fountain?

9 Which daughter of Judy Garland won an Oscar for *Cabaret*?

10 Who, in 1949, became the youngest cricketer to win an England cap?

11 Which ship sent the first SOS?

12 Who did Edward VIII marry?

13 Which is the largest city in China in population?

14 Which former Australian prime minister was dismssed by the governor general in 1975?

15 Who directed the horror film *Halloween*?

Things you didn't know...

A camel's feet are soft and silky.

Answers to page 330

1 Pluto, 2 *Antiques Roadshow,* 3 Kew Gardens, 4 John Carpenter, 5 Ivan Lendl, 6 Jack Klugman, 7 John Merrick, 8 Iraq, 9 Nine, 10 Bruce Lee, 11 Baron Reith, 12 Dogger, 13 The Appalachian Trail, 14 Baritone, 15 Jean-Luc Godard.

QUIZ 327

Answers on page 327

1 What is the usual colour of the flight recorder in a modern aircraft?

2 Who won the Formula One World Championship in 1998?

3 In which African country is the port of Mombasa?

4 Who directed the films *The Third Man* and *Oliver*?

5 What is the important difference between a crocodile and an alligator?

6 Where did the lights all go down according to the Bee Gees?

7 Of which constellation is Rigel the brightest star?

8 What is the capital of the Republic of Ireland?

9 What is the Church of England's smallest administrative unit?

10 What connects a chevet, a slype and a crossing?

11 In which county is the market town of Kidderminster?

12 In which year did Hong Kong revert to Chinese control?

13 Soyuz was the name of a Russian spacecraft, what does Soyuz mean?

14 At which university did Prince Charles study?

15 Who had a Top Ten hit in 1966 with *What Would I Be*?

Things you didn't know...

America had enjoyed a 132 year monopoly on the America's Cup before Australia won it in 1983.

Answers to page 327

1 Lindsey Corkhill, 2 Robert Peary, 3 *Apocalypse Now,* 4 Spencer, 5 Belshazzar, 6 Apple, 7 Indonesia, 8 E, 9 Jack Straw, 10 Blackburn, 11 Moscow, 12 2 miles 2 furlongs, 13 Yellow, 14 The Great Plague, 15 Wimbledon.

QUIZ 328

Answers on page 328

1 Which planet crosses the path of Neptune?

2 Which World Cup anthem was a big hit for Fat Les in 1988?

3 Which Royal Gardens near Richmond were established in the 18th century?

4 Who directed the 1988 sci-fi film *They Live*?

5 Which Czech-born tennis player won the men's singles at the US Open from 1985 to 1987?

6 Which actor played the title role in *Quincy*?

7 What was *The Elephant Man's* real name?

8 In which modern country would you locate The Hanging Gardens of Babylon?

9 How many players are there in a baseball team?

10 Which actor and kung fu expert starred in the film *Enter the Dragon*?

11 Who was the director general of the BBC from 1927 to 1938?

12 Which sea area is surrounded by Tyne, Forties, German Bight and Humber?

13 What is the longest continuous footpath in the world?

14 Which adult male singing voice is lower than tenor and higher than bass?

15 Which French filmmaker directed *Week-End* and *Je Vous Salue, Marie*?

Things you didn't know...

American gangster Al Capone had a bullet-proof office chair.

Answers to page 328

1 Neville Chamberlain, **2** Lady Day, **3** River Kennet, **4** The Atlantic Ocean, **5** Kruger National Park, **6** Enid Blyton, **7** Maggots, **8** Rome, **9** Liza Minnelli, **10** Brian Close, **11** Titanic, **12** Mrs. Simpson, **13** Shanghai, **14** Gough Whitlam, **15** John Carpenter.

QUIZ 329

Answers on page 333

1 Which famous fictional detective was created by Sir Arthur Conan Doyle?

2 In which state of the USA is the city of Detroit situated?

3 Which French composer wrote the opera *Carmen*?

4 What is the capital of Belize?

5 Where was Jesus born?

6 *The Muppets* were derived from puppets on *Sesame Street*. Who was their creator?

7 Which magazine editor once said 'the only thing I really mind about going to prison is the thought of Lord Longford coming to visit me'?

8 What is the nickname of *Symphony No 31 in D* by Mozart?

9 At which sport was Betty Calloway a coach?

10 Which horse did Willie Carson ride on his first Derby win?

11 Which of these plants produces most food per acre? Is it pineapple, banana or melon?

12 Which French fashion designer was famous for his New Look and the H-line?

13 What is the name of the Spanish soup, served cold?

14 Which pop group derived their name from an unemployment benefit form?

15 Which Sioux Indian chief was killed in 1877 after surrendering to American troops?

Things you didn't know...

On average, dogs in the city live longer than those in the country.

Answers to page 333

1 Douglas Fairbanks, 2 Elaine Paige, 3 *Oh, Doctor Beeching!*, 4 Dana Scully and Fox Mulder, 5 Parakeet, 6 Cat, 7 Alexander the Great, 8 Midas, 9 Nuclear Power Station, 10 Cornwall, 11 Athens, 12 Urdu, 13 Las Palmas, 14 A bird, 15 *Tootsie*.

QUIZ 330

Answers on page 334

1 Where are the BBC gardens?

2 Which horse was written about by Anna Sewell in 1877?

3 Robert De Niro, Nick Nolte, Jessica Lange and Juliette Lewis starred in which nineties remake of a 1962 thriller?

4 Who had Top Ten hits with *I can't Explain, Happy Jack* and *Pictures of Lily*?

5 In 1930, which country did Amy Johnson fly to from England?

6 What do the initials NSPCC stand for?

7 Whose only Number One hit was *Barbados* in 1975?

8 Which British dramatist wrote *Look Back in Anger* and *The Entertainer*?

9 Which country in the Indian Ocean has Moroni as its capital?

10 In which English county is the market town of St Austell?

11 Who scored England's first goal of the 1998 World Cup Finals?

12 Who had a No 1 hit with *School's Out*?

13 Which British composer wrote the opera *Troilus and Cressida*?

14 What does Susan Hampshire suffer from?

15 What is the alternative to *Stars and Stripes* as a nickname for the national flag of the USA?

Things you didn't know...

The average human brain uses as much electricity as a 10-watt electric light bulb.

Answers to page 334

1 Spanish Civil War, **2** Kensington Gardens, **3** Yankee, **4** Pip, **5** Hogmanay, **6** Edward VIII, **7** Jacques Villeneuve, **8** Soprano, **9** Andy Garcia, **10** Branwell, **11** Nasser Hussain, **12** Sculpture, **13** David Attenborough, **14** Nevil Shute, **15** Liverpool and Juventus.

QUIZ 331

Answers on page 331

1 Which swashbuckling star starred in the silent films *The Three Musketeers, Robin hood* and *The Black Pirate*?

2 Who first played the title role in *Evita* in London's West End?

3 Which sitcom was set in Hatley station?

4 What are the names of the two FBI agents in *The X-Files*?

5 What type of bird is a budgerigar?

6 Persian, Siamese and Abyssinian are breeds of what domestic creature?

7 Which pupil of Aristotle was King of Macedon from 336 to 323 BC?

8 In legend, which king turned everything he touched into gold?

9 What was first opened in 1956 at Calder Hall?

10 Prince Charles is Duke of which English county?

11 In which city were the 1896 Olympic Games held?

12 What is the official language of Pakistan?

13 What is the largest city in the Canary Islands?

14 What sort of creature is a greenshank?

15 In which film did Dustin Hoffman's character dress up as a woman to get a job?

Things you didn't know...

There are half a million John Smiths living in the USA.

Answers to page 331

1 Sherlock Holmes, **2** Michigan, **3** Georges Bizet, **4** Belmopan, **5** Bethlehem, **6** Jim Henson, **7** Richard Ingrams, **8** Paris symphony, **9** Ice skating, **10** Troy, **11** Banana, **12** Christian Dior, **13** Gazpacho, **14** UB40, **15** *Crazy Horse*.

QUIZ 332

Answers on page 332

1 In which war did the term 'fifth column' originate?

2 Where in London is there a famous statue of *Peter Pan*?

3 Which word is used in radio call signs for Y?

4 Who replaced Nigel le Vaillant as the police surgeon in *Dangerfield*?

5 What is New Year's Eve called in Scotland?

6 Which king abdicated in 1936 because of objections to his liaison with the twice-divorced Mrs Wallis Simpson?

7 Who won the European Grand Prix at Nurburgring in 1996?

8 What is the highest adult female singing voice?

9 Who played the newly-elected DA in Sidney Lumet's *Night falls on Manhattan*?

10 What was the name of Charlotte, Emily and Anne Bronte's brother?

11 Who scored a double century in England's Test match victory over Australia at Edgbaston in 1997?

12 With which art form is Jacob Epstein associated?

13 Who presented the natural history series *The Living Planet* and *Life in the Freezer*?

14 Who wrote the novels *Pied Piper*, *No Highway* and *A Town Like Alice*?

15 Which two football teams contested the 1985 European Cup Final at which 39 fans died?

Things you didn't know...

Pearls are produced by shellfish other than oysters.

Answers to page 332

1 Barnsdale, 2 *Black Beauty,* 3 Cape Fear, 4 The Who, 5 Australia, 6 National Society for the prevention of Cruelty to Children, 7 Typically Tropical, 8 John Osborne, 9 Comoros, 10 Cornwall, 11 Alan Shearer, 12 Alice Cooper, 13 Sir William Walton, 14 Dyslexia, 15 *Old Glory.*

QUIZ 333

Answers on page 337

1 Which area of Britain was known as Caledonia to the Romans?

2 Which part of the UK's police forces is represented by the initials CID?

3 Which city is known as The Granite City?

4 Which British comedian played the part of Raquel Welch's husband in the 1974 film *The Three Musketeers*?

5 Which country is named after an Italian city?

6 Which British yachtsman was the first to sail alone non-stop around the world?

7 What is the lowest-pitched musical instrument of the violin family?

8 Which sport might involve a schuss?

9 How is the trachea commonly known?

10 Which Chinese surname means 'Prince' in English?

11 Which island is Cagliari the capital of?

12 What have Barnet, Hexham, Northampton, St Albans and Wakefield got in common?

13 Which British institution was nationalised on St Valentine's Day 1946?

14 In Russia, what was a gulag?

15 By what name are Tinky Winky, Dipsy, Laa-Laa and Po better known?

Things you didn't know...

The first American badminton club limited play on its courts to men and good-looking single women only.

Answers to page 337

1 Sam Peckinpah, 2 Hereward the Wake, 3 Spanish Civil War, 4 The Checkmates, 5 M. Stoute, 6 Carol II, 7 Purple, 8 C S Lewis, 9 Fish, 10 New Delhi, 11 Zambia, 12 Mary II, 13 Potage, 14 Gold, 15 Vodka and tonic.

QUIZ 334

Answers on page 338

1 What is the official language of China?

2 What was Anna Carteret's character in *Juliet Bravo* called?

3 Which was Richard Burton's last film?

4 Who wrote *The Count of Monte Cristo*?

5 Who made history in 1997 by becoming the youngest-ever US masters golf champion?

6 Which real-life character has been portrayed on film by Robert Taylor, Paul Newman, Kris Kristofferson and Emilio Estevez?

7 Which German town is famous for its castle, used as a supposedly escape-proof prisoner-of-war camp in the Second World War II?

8 What can be a box or part of the body?

9 At which ground do Preston North End play their home games?

10 Which John is married to actress Pauline Collins?

11 Which American prison was located in San Francisco Bay?

12 What do the initials GMT stand for?

13 Which legendary Greek hero killed the Minotaur of Crete with the help of Ariadne?

14 Which material did Carl Andre use in his Equivalent VIII, exhibited at the Tate Gallery in 1976?

15 Which English monarchs preceded and succeeded Elizabeth I?

Things you didn't know...

More perfume is used in Russia than in any other country.

Answers to page 338

1 Four, 2 Farrow, 3 Five, 4 1,500m, 5 Al Capp, 6 Hawk, 7 Ireland, 8 Lennox Lewis, 9 South America, 10 Broadcasting House, 11 The Marx Brothers, 12 *Bullseye,* 13 South Island, 14 Harold Macmillan, 15 Charles Perrault.

QUIZ 335

Answers on page 335

1 Who directed the films *Straw Dogs* and *The Wild Bunch*?

2 Which Anglo-Saxon leader of a revolt against William the Conqueror took refuge on the Isle Of Ely?

3 Which war began on July 18th 1936?

4 What was the name of Emile Ford's backing group?

5 Who trained Shergar to win the Derby in 1981?

6 Who abdicated as king of Romania in 1940?

7 What colour is traditionally associated with Roman emperors?

8 Who wrote *The Lion, The Witch and the Wardrobe*?

9 Which animal is represented by the zodiac sign of Pisces?

10 What is the capital of India?

11 The Victoria Falls lie on the boundary between Zimbabwe and which other country?

12 Which English queen died of smallpox at the age of 32?

13 Which French word describes any very thick soup?

14 Which metal has the symbol Au?

15 In the TV series *Minder*, which drink did Arthur Daley refer to as a 'VAT'?

Things you didn't know...

The most common name in the world is Mohammed.

Answers to page 335

1 Scotland, 2 Criminal Investigation Department, 3 Aberdeen, 4 Spike Milligan, 5 Venezuela, 6 Robin Knox-Johnston, 7 Double bass, 8 Skiing, 9 Windpipe, 10 Wang, 11 Sardinia, 12, All were battles in the Wars of the Roses, 13 Bank of England, 14 Prison Camp, 15 *Teletubbies*.

QUIZ 336

Answers on page 336

1 In the Bible, how many Gospels were there?

2 What is the correct collective name for a litter of piglets?

3 How many cards of the same suit are needed for a flush in poker?

4 What is the final event in the decathlon?

5 Which American cartoonist created L'il Abner?

6 An eyas is the young of which bird?

7 Of which country was Eamon De Valera president from 1959 to 1973?

8 Which British boxer defeated Oliver McCall in 1997 to regain the world heavyweight championship?

9 From which continent does the vicuna come?

10 Outside which London building would you find Eric Gill's sculpture *Prospero and Ariel*?

11 How were film stars Chico, Harpo, Groucho and Zeppo other wise known?

12 Which darts-based quiz show was hosted by Jim Bowen?

13 Of New Zealand's two principal islands, which is the larger, North Island or South Island?

14 Which British prime minister became the 1st Earl of Stockton?

15 Which French writer published the collection of fairy tales known as *Mother Goose*?

Things you didn't know...

The Hershey Bar, made in Hershey, USA, is the world's best-selling chocolate bar.

Answers to page 336

1 Mandarin, 2 Inspector Kate Longton, 3 1984, 4 Alexandre Dumas, 5 Tiger Woods, 6 Billy the Kid, 7 Colditz, 8 Chest, 9 Deepdale, 10 Alderton, 11 Alcatraz, 12 Greenwich Mean Time, 13 Theseus, 14 Bricks, 15 Mary I and James I.

QUIZ 337

Answers on page 341

1 Who designed London's St Paul's Cathedral?

2 Which bird is the national emblem of New Zealand?

3 Which British conductor founded the London Philharmonic Orchestra and the Royal Philharmonic Orchestra?

4 Which stretch of water separates the Scottish mainland from the Orkneys?

5 Of which country is Kabul the capital?

6 Which word should be used to describe a group of wolves, weasels or dogs?

7 Who starred in the films *Dirty Harry* and *The Good The Bad and The Ugly*?

8 Who had a Top Ten hit single in 1969 with *Tracks Of My Tears*?

9 Which US actress starred in the films *Platinum Blonde* and *Bombshell*?

10 Which harmony group was formed in California by sisters Anita, Bonnie and June?

11 Who designed the Statue of Liberty?

12 Hearts and Hibs come from which Scottish city?

13 Which dance comes from *Orpheus In The Underworld*?

14 In Greek mythology who was God of the Heavens and Earth?

15 In which English county is the market town of Mildenhall?

Things you didn't know...

Frankie Howerd once accidentally walked on stage at the Palladium carrying the Union Jack upside down.

Answers to page 341

1 Land's End, **2** *Spender,* **3** Donatella, **4** Zebedee, **5** Bending the legs, **6** Poult, **7** Roald Dahl's, **8** Drums, **9** Winchester, **10** Niagara, **11** Medical students, **12** Sharpeville, **13** Battle of Sedgemoor, **14** Mrs Bridges, **15** Western Samoa.

QUIZ 338

Answers on page 342

1 In which city is the Obelisk of Luxor?

2 Which English classical architect designed the Queen's House, Greenwich and the Banqueting Hall, Whitehall?

3 Which type of wood did Noah use to build his Ark?

4 Which Czech author wrote *The Trial* and *The Castle*?

5 Who is the leading character of the story that has a fairy called Tinker Bell?

6 From the 14th century to 1830 the eldest sons of French kings were known by what title?

7 What nationality was Ulrich Zwingli?

8 What was found buried at Sutton Hoo in 1939?

9 Who definded the Four Freedoms in 1941?

10 Which political party's HQ is at 150 Walworth Road in London?

11 Who directed the films *Rebecca*, *Psycho* and *The Birds*?

12 Who wrote the song *A Whiter Shade of Pale*?

13 Where do bees carry the pollen they collect?

14 What product according to the advert 'could you eat between meals without ruining your appetite'?

15 Which is the longest Classic horse race?

Things you didn't know...

In Ibiza it is considered bad luck to allow a priest on a fishing boat.

Answers to page 342

1 Fred Perry, **2** Robert the Bruce, **3** China, **4** Chimney sweep, **5** Alligator, **6** Alexis, **7** Caesar, **8** Made a will, **9** Cooking apple, **10** Austin, **11** Luke Skywalker, **12** Oregon, **13** Fox, **14** Athens, **15** Sweden.

QUIZ 339

Answers on page 339

1 What is the westernmost point of England?

2 What was the name of the Geordie detective played by Jimmy Nail on television?

3 What is the name of Gianni Versace's sister who stepped into his shoes at his fashion house?

4 Who was the father of the disciples James and John?

5 In ballet, what does plié mean?

6 What is a young turkey called?

7 Upon whose book and screenplay was the film, *Willy Wonka & the Chocolate Factory* based?

8 What sort of instruments are timpani, tabla and the bodhran?

9 What is the administrative capital of Hampshire?

10 Which North American river, noted for its spectacular Falls, connects Lake Erie and Lake Ontario?

11 Which type of students take the Hippocratic Oath?

12 In which South African township were over 60 demonstrators killed by the police in 1960?

13 Which was the last battle to take place on English soil?

14 What was the name of the cook in TV's *Upstairs Downstairs*?

15 Of which country is Apia the capital?

Things you didn't know...

According to an old-wives tale, rubbing the grease off church bells into your body cures shingles.

Answers to page 339

1 Sir Christopher Wren, **2** Kiwi, **3** Sir Thomas Beecham, **4** Pentland Firth, **5** Afghanistan, **6** Pack, **7** Clint Eastwood, **8** Smokey Robinson, **9** Jean Harlow, **10** Pointer Sisters, **11** Bartholdi, **12** Edinburgh, **13** Cancan, **14** Zeus, **15** Suffolk.

QUIZ 340

Answers on page 340

1 Who was the last British tennis player to win the men's singles title at Wimbledon?

2 Who led the victorious armies at the Battle of Bannockburn in 1314?

3 In which Asian country were fireworks invented?

4 What was Tom's job in *The Water Babies*?

5 Which animal takes its name from the Spanish 'el largato', meaning 'the lizard'?

6 Which character did Joan Collins play in *Dynasty*?

7 Who was Cleopatra's lover before she married Mark Antony?

8 What has a testatrix done?

9 What type of fruit is a Grenadier?

10 What is the state capital of Texas?

11 Which character was played by Mark Hamill in the film *Star Wars*?

12 Of which state of the USA is Salem the capital?

13 Which animal was traditionally called 'Russell'?

14 In which city can the Parthenon be found?

15 Which nation did Russia, Denmark and Poland fight against in the Great Northern War?

Things you didn't know...

In Waterloo, Nebraska, barbers are prohibited from eating onions between the hours of 7am and 7pm.

Answers to page 340

1 Paris, 2 Inigo Jones, 3 Gopher, 4 Franz Kafka, 5 Peter Pan, 6 Dauphin, 7 Swiss, 8 A Saxon ship, 9 Franklin D Roosevelt, 10 Labour Party, 11 Alfred Hitchcock, 12 Keith Reid and Gary Brooker, 13 On their back legs, 14 Milky Way, 15 St Leger.

QUIZ 341

Answers on page 345

1 Which crustacean is known for its habit of occupying empty snail shells?

2 Which Hungarian composer wrote the operetta *The Merry Widow*?

3 Who had a Number One hit single in 1986 with *True Blue*?

4 Which city is said to have been created by Romulus and Remus?

5 In which sport are the terms 'silly mid off' and 'extra cover' used?

6 In Roman mythology who was the God of Love?

7 The language of gypsies is related to which classical Asian language?

8 Alum Bay, Godshill and Carisbrooke Castle are all in which county?

9 In which country is the city of Perpignan?

10 The sun's heat is derived from the fusion of hydrogen and which other element?

11 Which is the largest asteroid in the Solar System?

12 In which state of the USA is the city of Orlando situated?

13 Which war ended on July 27th 1953?

14 Which Australian state completely surrounds the Australian Capital Territory?

15 Which British dramatist wrote *The Lady's Not For Burning*?

Things you didn't know...

Campbelltown, near the Mull of Kintyre, used to have 33 whisky distilleries. Now there are just two.

Answers to page 345

1 Brush, 2 Johannes Brahms, 3 William Blake, 4 Columbia, 5 The Quest, 6 Greece, 7 Alfred Hitchcock, 8 Mira Sorvino, 9 Mother Teresa, 10 Scottish National Party, 11 Shepherd, 12 Splinter, 13 Guyana, 14 Southern Cross, 15 Caesium.

QUIZ 342

Answers on page 346

1 What was Mary Hopkin's entry in the Eurovision Song Contest in 1970?

2 At what weight did Cassius Clay win his 1960 Olympic boxing title?

3 Of which fruit are the honeydew and cantaloupe varieties?

4 Who won the 1996 Japanese Formula 1 Grand Prix?

5 Which lake is surrounded by Kenya, Uganda and Tanzania?

6 Which Italian racing motorcyclist won a record 15 World Championship titles throughout the 1960s and 1970s?

7 What is the last book of the Old Testament?

8 In which opera would you find the characters Pamina, Tamino and the Queen of the Night?

9 Which actor's real name was William Pratt?

10 Which rugby team scored a record 60 points against Wales in the Five Nations Championship in 1998?

11 Where is the 2,000 Guineas held?

12 Which product is particularly associated with the German town of Dresden?

13 What sort of creature is a gerenuk?

14 What is the traditional nickname of people with the surname Miller?

15 Which British scientist discovered benzene?

Things you didn't know...

The first comb dates back to Scandinavia around 8000 BC.

Answers to page 346

1 A horse, 2 Buster, 3 Saffron, 4 Michael Bentine, 5 Aeroflot, 6 Darwin, 7 Al Capone, 8 Michael Collins, 9 A whirlpool, 10 Stalin, 11 Tennis, 12 Midwifery, 13 Georges Feydeau, 14 Fool's gold, 15 Rudolf Hess.

QUIZ 343

Answers on page 343

1 What is a fox's tail called?

2 Which German composer wrote *A German Requiem* and the *Alto Rhapsody*?

3 Who wrote the poem *The Tiger*?

4 The USA launched its first space shuttle in 1981. What was it called?

5 Which film marked the directing debut of Jean-Claude Van Damme?

6 Of which European country is the island of Rhodes a part?

7 Who directed the 1940 film *Rebecca*, based upon Daphne du Maurier's novel?

8 Which Oscar-winning actress starred with Lisa Kudrow in *Romy and Michele's High School Reunion*?

9 By what name is Agnes Gonxha Bejaxhui better known?

10 Which British political party was founded in 1934?

11 Which Cybill starred in *Moonlighting*?

12 Which rat trained the *Teenage Mutant Ninja Turtles*?

13 Of which South American country is Georgetown the capital?

14 What is the popular name for the constellation Crux?

15 Which metal is represented by the symbol Cs?

Things you didn't know...

American golfer Jack Nicklaus always carries three pennies in his pocket at tournaments.

Answers to page 343

1 Hermit crab, **2** Franz Lehar, **3** Madonna, **4** Rome, **5** Cricket, **6** Cupid, **7** Sanskrit, **8** Isle of Wight, **9** France, **10** Helium, **11** Ceres, **12** Florida, **13** Korean War, **14** New South Wales, **15** Christopher Fry.

QUIZ 344

Answers on page 344

1 What sort of creature is a palomino?

2 By what first name is Joseph Francis Keaton better known?

3 What herb comes from the dried stigmas of crocus flowers?

4 Who presented *Potty Time* on television?

5 What is the national airline of Russia?

6 Which Australian city is capital of the Northern Territory?

7 Which Brooklyn-born racketeer was sentenced to ten years' imprisonment for tax evasion?

8 Which famous Irish nationalist was killed in 1922 by republicans opposed to the partition treaty he helped to negotiate?

9 In Greek mythology, what sort of feature was Charybdis?

10 Born in 1879, which Russian revolutionary adopted a name which meant 'man of steel'?

11 With which sport do you associate Bjorn Borg?

12 Which nursing speciality is concerned with the care of women during pregnancy and childbirth?

13 Which French playwright wrote *A Flea in Her Ear*?

14 How is pyrite commonly known?

15 Who was Winston Churchill talking about when he said "The maggot is in the apple"?

Things you didn't know...

Manchester United's Kevin Moran was the first player to be sent off in an FA Cup Final.

Answers to page 344

1 *Knock, Knock who's There,* 2 Light-heavyweight, 3 Melon, 4 Damon Hill, 5 Lake Victoria, 6 Giacomo Agostini, 7 The Book of Malachi, 8 *The Magic Flute,* 9 Boris Karloff, 10 England, 11 Newmarket, 12 China, 13 An antelope, 14 Dusty, 15 Michael Faraday.

QUIZ 345

Answers on page 349

1 What name is given to the wood of the mahogany gum tree?

2 Who preceded Ed Tudor-Pole as presenter of *The Crystal Maze*?

3 What sort of creature is a sanderling?

4 Which British Olympic gold ice skating medallist died in 1995?

5 What is the stretch of mown grass between the tee and the green on a golf course called?

6 With the exception of the book of Psalms, which is the longest book in the Bible?

7 Which fruit comes from the plant Ananas comosus?

8 In which year did the First World War start?

9 What is the capital of Colombia?

10 What nationality was the artist Edvard Munch?

11 David Lean's film was about a passage to which country?

12 Of which US state is Columbus the capital?

13 Who was the first presenter of *Sale Of The Century*?

14 Which US band had a Top Ten hit single in 1979 with *Lady Lynda*?

15 Which British Formula One driver allowed his team-mate Mika Hakkinen to win the 1998 Australian Grand Prix?

Things you didn't know...

Madonna was sacked from her job at the fast-food restaurant Dunkin' Donuts for squirting jam at a customer.

Answers to page 349

1 Kidney stones, 2 Pericardium, 3 Pelota, 4 Somalia, 5 Newman, 6 The Trojan War, 7 Ottawa, 8 Ivan Turgenev, 9 Mexico, 10 Combustion, 11 Seaweed, 12 Marie Curie, 13 Nil By Mouth, 14 Oscar Wilde, 15 Harold Wilson.

QUIZ 346

Answers on page 350

1 Which German physicist formulated the quantum theory?

2 Which seaside town was Sir Laurence Olivier Baron Olivier of?

3 Who had Number One hits with *Tired of Waiting For You* and *Sunny Afternoon*?

4 Who edited a famous Dictionary of Music and Musicians in the late 19th century?

5 Which Prussian statesman was known as the Iron Chancellor?

6 Which bird added to a Crest completes a soap series?

7 Leo McKern, Patrick Cargill and Roy Kinnear all appeared in which 1965 film that spawned two UK Number One hit songs?

8 Which rock guitarist was the first to be honoured with an English Heritage blue plaque?

9 Who were Richard Branson's co-pilots on his attempt to fly around the world in a balloon in December 1998?

10 Which St Etienne singer recently released a solo album called *Lipslide*?

11 Who played the female lead in the *Ghostbusters* films?

12 What is politician Jim Callaghan's middle name?

13 Who played a female undertaker in the TV series *In Loving Memory*?

14 What was the title of the Small Faces' 1966 Number One hit?

15 Who became world snooker champion for a record-equalling sixth time in 1996?

Things you didn't know...

Annie Lennox met Dave Stewart when she was a waitress and he was one of her customers.

Answers to page 350

1 Edward VI, 2 Kuwait, 3 Air Force One, 4 Cambridge, 5 Mercury, 6 Queens or Richmond, 7 *So You Win Again*, 8 *West Side Story*, 9 Rouen, 10 Kirkwall, 11 Aston Martin DB5, 12 *Private Benjamin*, 13 Kenya, 14 Seaman, 15 Anita Roddick.

QUIZ 347

Answers on page 347

1 By what name are renal calculi better known?

2 What is the membranous sac which holds the heart called?

3 What is the fastest ball game in the world?

4 Of which African country is Mogadishu the capital?

5 Which Paul married actress Joanne Woodward?

6 According to Greek legend, which war was precipitated when King Menelaus's wife Helen fled Sparta with Paris?

7 What is the capital of Canada?

8 Which Russian novelist wrote *Fathers and Sons*?

9 In which country is the Sierra Madre mountain range?

10 What is the chemical process by which a substance combines with oxygen to produce heat and light called?

11 What is kelp?

12 Who was the first scientist to be awarded two Nobel prizes?

13 Which film marked the directorial debut of actor Gary Oldman?

14 Who wrote the poem *The Ballad of Reading Gaol*?

15 Which British PM said 'A week is a long time in politics'?

Things you didn't know...

Florence Nightingale kept a small owl in her pocket, even while serving in the Crimean War.

Answers to page 347

1 Jarrah, 2 Richard O'Brien, 3 A bird, 4 John Curry, 5 Fairway, 6 Isaiah, 7 Pineapple, 8 1914, 9 Bogota, 10 Norwegian, 11 India, 12 Ohio, 13 Nicholas Parsons, 14 The Beach Boys, 15 David Coulthard.

QUIZ 348

Answers on page 348

1 Who succeeded Henry VIII as monarch?

2 Which country was invaded by Iraq in 1990?

3 Which film starred Harrison Ford as the American president?

4 Which team won the 1996 University Boat Race?

5 Which planet is nearest the sun?

6 New York comprises of five districts: Brooklyn, Manhattan, the Bronx and two others. Name one?

7 What was the first UK Number One hit for Hot Chocolate?

8 Which musical is based on the story of *Romeo and Juliet*?

9 In which town was Joan of Arc executed by being burnt at the stake?

10 What is the capital of the Orkneys?

11 Which type of car do you most associate with James Bond in the film *Goldfinger*?

12 In which film did Goldie Hawn join the army?

13 Nairobi is the capital of which African country?

14 Which David keeps goal for Arsenal and England?

15 Which woman founded The Body Shop?

Things you didn't know...

American actress Natalie Wood suffered from hydrophobia, a fear of water. She died by drowning.

Answers to page 348

1 Max Planck, 2 Brighton, 3 Kinks, 4 Sir George Grove, 5 Bismarck, 6 Falcon, 7 *Help!*, 8 Jimi Hendrix, 9 Per Lindstrand and Steve Fossett, 10 Sarah Cracknell, 11 Sigourney Weaver, 12 Leonard, 13 Thora Hird, 14 All or Nothing, 15 Stephen Hendry.

QUIZ 349

Answers on page 353

1 Who wrote the horror stories The Rats, Haunted and The Spear.

2 For which constructor did Johnny Herbert drive for in the 1996 British Grand Prix?

3 For what did Madame Helen Blavatsky achieve fame?

4 In which city is the Taj Mahal?

5 What is the national flower of New Zealand?

6 Who sailed away to die on HMS Bellerophon?

7 Who made the first cross-Channel flight in 1909?

8 Into which river did the Pied Piper lead the rats?

9 What name is sometimes given to the legislative assembly of a country that is derived from the Latin for old man?

10 Which method of fortune-telling uses 78 cards?

11 In which ocean are the Maldives situated?

12 Who plays the abused, pregnant wife in the film *Nil By Mouth*?

13 With which musical instrument was Artur Rubinstein associated?

14 Which contagious skin infection, associated with small children, is characterised by encrusted yellow sores?

15 Which male vocalist of the Sixties had Number One hits with *Yeh Yeh*, *Get Away* and *Ballad of Bonnie and Clyde*?

Things you didn't know...

Queen Christina of Sweden had a 10cm-long cannon which she used to fire cannonballs at fleas.

Answers to page 353

1 *Porridge*, 2 Nebraska, 3 England and France, 4 Heart, 5 Retsina, 6 *Darling*, 7 Rudolf Hess, 8 Turkey, 9 Toronto, 10 Acute, 11 Feast of the assumption, 12 Prince, 13 Moscow, 14 Las Vegas, 15 Jim Wicks.

QUIZ 350

Answers on page 354

1 In which English county is the village of Stilton situated?

2 What was an ironclad?

3 Which unit of power is represented by the symbol W?

4 Which branch of mathematics uses symbols to represent unknown quantities?

5 Which organ is inflamed when one is suffering from nephritis?

6 What is the capital of Majorca?

7 Which Old Testament figure was swallowed by a great fish?

8 Which English queen has the same name as a type of plum?

9 Which swimmer won seven gold medals at the 1972 Olympics Games?

10 In the Bible what was the name of the place where Jesus was crucified?

11 Which Devon based religious sect was founded in 1830?

12 What is the Christian festival of Pentecost otherwise known as?

13 Which British tennis player defeated the Australian Mark Philippoussis at the Wimbledon Championships in 1997?

14 What is a galvanometer used to measure?

15 In which film did Sylvester Stallone and Kurt Russell star as rival cops who reluctantly team up to bring Jack Palance to justice?

Things you didn't know...

Walt Disney used to wash his hands up to 30 times an hour.

Answers to page 354

1 Hard, **2** Galtieri, **3** Guido Reni, **4** Tokyo, **5** *Old Mother Riley,* **6** Ian Paisley, **7** Sedan chair, **8** Strauss, **9** Denzel Washington, **10** Atlanta, **11** Smallpox, **12** Patrick Stewart, **13** Utah, **14** 29$\frac{1}{2}$ days, **15** Ray Wilkins.

QUIZ 351

Answers on page 351

1 Which Ronnie Barker comedy was set inside a prison?

2 In which state of the USA can the city of Omaha be found?

3 Which two countries fought each other in the Hundred Years' War?

4 Which four-chambered muscular organ pumps blood around the body?

5 Which wine is flavoured with pine resin?

6 In which film did Julie Christie win an Oscar playing a model?

7 Who was the last prisoner to be held in the Tower of London?

8 In which country is the Taurus mountain range?

9 What is Canada's largest city?

10 In mathematics what name is given to an angle that is less than 90 degrees?

11 What is celebrated on August 15th?

12 What name does British boxer Naseem Hamed give himself?

13 The Trans-Siberian railway runs from Vladivostock to which city?

14 Which Nevada city is famous for a row of luxury hotel and gambling casinos called the Strip?

15 Who was boxer Henry Cooper's manager?

Things you didn't know...

Louis XIX was king of France from breakfast until tea-time on 2nd August 1830, and then he abdicated.

Answers to page 351

1 James Herbert, 2 Sauber, 3 Spiritualism, 4 Ágra, 5 Kowhai, 6 Napoleon, 7 Louis Blériot, 8 Weser, 9 Senate, 10 Tarot reading, 11 Indian ocean, 12 Kathy Burke, 13 Piano, 14 Impetigo, 15 Georgie Fame.

QUIZ 352

Answers on page 352

1 How does Saturday's child work for a living?

2 Who led the junta which seized the Falklands in 1982?

3 Which Italian painter is best known for his ceiling fresco of Aurora?

4 Which was the first Asian city to host the Olympics?

5 Which washerwoman did Arthur Lucan play in fourteen films and on stage?

6 Who founded the Free Presbyterian Church of Ulster in 1951?

7 Which type of enclosed single-seater chair is carried on poles by two or more men?

8 Which composer did Kerwin Matthews play in *The Waltz King*?

9 Who played Malcolm X in the 1992 film of that name?

10 Where were the 1996 Olympic Games held?

11 By what name is the infectious desease variola better know?

12 Who plays Jean-Luc Picard in *Star Trek - The Next Generation*?

13 Which US state is known as the Beehive state or the Mormon state?

14 Roughly how long does it take for the moon to revolve round the earth?

15 Which England Football captain was sent off in 1986?

Things you didn't know...

Novelist Anthony Trollope invented the post-box.

Answers to page 352

1 Cambridgeshire, 2 An armoured wooden warship, 3 Watt, 4 Algebra, 5 The kidney, 6 Palma, 7 Jonah, 8 Victoria, 9 Mark Spitz, 10 Golgotha, 11 Plymouth Brethren, 12 Whit Sunday, 13 Greg Rusedski, 14 Small electric currents, 15 *Tango and Cash*.

QUIZ 353

Answers on page 357

1 What, according to his song, was Lonnie Donegan's 'Old Man'?

2 Who had a Number One hit with *Reet Petite*?

3 Which film was based on Conrad's *Heart of Darkness*?

4 Which member of the Beatles went on to form the band Wings?

5 In which scale is the temperature of boiling water taken as 212 degrees?

6 Which PM took Britain into the EEC?

7 Which Greek philosopher was condemned to death for atheism and corrupting the young?

8 In which futuristic film did Tina Turner play Auntie Entity?

9 Which religion was founded by Nanak?

10 What was the former name of Ghana?

11 In which year was the Peterloo massacre?

12 In the UK what is the maximum number of years between General Elections?

13 What is the largest planet in our solar system?

14 Which organ of the human body is affected by Bright's disease?

15 Which highly successful 1970's UK group's last Number One hit was called *Oh Boy* in 1975?

Things you didn't know...

The most common surname in China is Chang.

Answers to page 357

1 Sarah Brightman, 2 Arundhati Roy, 3 Harry S. Truman, 4 Swan, 5 *Cabaret*, 6 The Dons, 7 Cape Finisterre, 8 Wembley, 9 Brisket, 10 The Rolling Stones, 11 The Domesday Book, 12 Noel Coward, 13 Chequers, 14 A bird, 15 *The Charlatans*.

QUIZ 354

Answers on page 358

1 Which literary character's main opponent was Von Stalhein?

2 In which sport are banderillas used?

3 Which global beauty competition started in 1951?

4 In which London thoroughfare are the headquarters of the Horse Guards?

5 Which flying insects belong to the order Lepidoptera?

6 Who was Smike's friend?

7 Of which African country is Niamey the capital?

8 What was the first permanent English colony in America?

9 The eruption of which volcano buried the ancient city of Pompeii?

10 How is the explosive trinitrotoluene commonly known?

11 What colour is traditionally associated with Roman emperors?

12 With which sort of dance is Dame Margot Fonteyn associated?

13 Which Irish missionary and abbot set up a monastery on Iona?

14 Which nutlike seeds are produced by the tree Prunus amygdalus?

15 In which city did Leon Trotsky die?

Things you didn't know...

Only male canaries can sing.

Answers to page 358

1 Lima, 2 Grandfather, 3 Egypt, 4 Salmanazar, 5 Unicorn, 6 Heidi, 7 False prophets, 8 Nigel Benn, 9 Raven, 10 Vertigo, 11 Argentina, 12 Caffeine, 13 Dusty Springfield, 14 The dinar, 15 Michael Foot.

QUIZ 355

Answers on page 355

1 Which lover of Andrew Lloyd Webber had a *Timeless* album?

2 Who won the 1997 Booker Prize for the novel *The God of Small Things*?

3 Which US president pursued a programme of social reform called the Fair Deal?

4 Which large aquatic bird belongs to the genus Cygnus?

5 Which film did Liza Minnelli win her Best Actress Oscar for?

6 What is the nickname of Aberdeen football club?

7 What is the westernmost point of the Spanish mainland, literally 'land's end'?

8 Which ground hosts the FA Cup Final?

9 What name is given to a joint of beef cut from the breast next to the ribs?

10 Which British band had a Number One hit single in 1969 with *Honky Tonk Women*?

11 Which survey of England was carried out by officials of William the Conqueror in 1086?

12 Who wrote the play *Still Life* from which the film *Brief Encounter* was adapted?

13 What do Americans call the game we know as draughts?

14 What sort of creature is a dipper?

15 Which group released an album entitled *Tellin' Stories* in 1997?

Things you didn't know...

There are 4,000 different types of knot.

Answers to page 355

1 Dustman, 2 Jackie Wilson, 3 *Apocalypse Now!*, 4 Paul McCartney, 5 Fahrenheit, 6 Edward Heath, 7 Socrates, 8 *Mad Max (Beyond Thunderdome)*, 9 Sikhism, 10 Gold Coast, 11 1819, 12 Five, 13 Jupiter, 14 Kidney, 15 Mud.

QUIZ 356

Answers on page 356

1 Callao is the main port for which South American capital city?

2 What relationship was William the Conqueror to King Stephen?

3 Of which Middle East country is Alexandria the second largest city?

4 What bottle size is equivalent to twelve standard bottles?

5 Which mythological creature has a horn projecting from its forehead?

6 Johanna Spyri created which little girl?

7 Who, In the Sermon on the Mount, did Jesus warn would appear as wolves in sheep's clothing?

8 Which boxer was known as the 'Dark Destroyer'?

9 Which bird has the scientific name 'Corvus corax'?

10 Which Hitchcock film starring James Stewart was re-released in 1997?

11 Which country did Juan Peron rule?

12 What is the name of the stimulant found in tea and coffee?

13 Which singer joined The Pet Shop Boys on the 1987 hit single *What Have I Done To Deserve This*?

14 What was the unit currency of Yugoslavia?

15 Who succeeded Aneurin Bevan as Labour MP for Ebbw Vale?

Things you didn't know...

William Wordsworth was, at one time, thought to be a French spy and was followed for a whole month by a detective.

Answers to page 356

1 *Biggles,* 2 Bullfighting, 3 Miss World, 4 Whitehall, 5 Butterflies and moths, 6 *Nicholas Nickleby,* 7 Niger, 8 Jamestown, 9 Mount Vesuvius, 10 TNT, 11 Purple, 12 Ballet, 13 St Columba, 14 Almonds, 15 Mexico City.

QUIZ 357

Answers on page 361

1 In Spain what is the word for an afternoon nap?

2 Which animal has the scientific name 'Meles meles'?

3 Which Hungarian composer is best known for his *Variations on a Nursery Theme*?

4 Which arm of the Indian Ocean is connected to the Mediterranean Sea by the Suez Canal?

5 On which river does Canterbury stand?

6 Who stars as the American president in the film *Air Force One*?

7 How long did *Mary Poppins* say she would stay with the children?

8 What name is given to the sealskin covered canoe used by eskimos?

9 Which school did Prince William start at in 1995?

10 In which country can Mount Ararat be found?

11 On TV, who presents *This Is your Life*?

12 In which sport did Irina Rodnina win 23 World, Olympic and European gold medals?

13 Who wrote *The Railway Children*?

14 Which Birmingham reggae band released an album called *Guns In The Ghetto*?

15 With which musical instrument would you most associate Dame Myra Hess?

Things you didn't know...

Over 72,000 pairs of nylon stockings were sold in New York on the very first day they were put on sale.

Answers to page 361

1 Westminster Abbey, 2 Insect, 3 Mallard, 4 Capricorn, 5 Bengali, 6 A type of bread, 7 Danzig, 8 Algeria, 9 Jenny Lind, 10 Trotter, 11 Northern Ireland, 12 Marlon Brando, 13 Edward VIII (Duke of Windsor), 14 Peak District, 15 Tenerife.

QUIZ 358

Answers on page 362

1 In the Bible who was the elder sister of Moses?

2 Which 1968 film musical with Mark Lester in the title role won six Oscars?

3 Which 1980's UK group's last Number One hit was *Beat Surrender*?

4 Which Spanish city is the capital of Catalonia?

5 Which English king married Mary of Teck?

6 Which Canadian state extends the furthest east?

7 Where is Lord Montagu's National Motor Museum?

8 Which animal has the scientific name 'Oryctolagus cuniculus'?

9 Which canal links the Atlantic and Pacific oceans?

10 'Yenisey' and 'Irtysh' are both major examples of which kind of geographical feature?

11 Who succeeded Jack Charlton as manager of the Republic of Ireland's football team?

12 Of which country was Ferdinand Marcos President from 1965 to 1986?

13 Which Jewish state was founded in 1948?

14 Who was the famous daughter of James V of Scotland and Mary of Guise?

15 Which city is served by Capodichino airport?

Things you didn't know...

Georges Simenon, the man who created the French detective Maigret, claimed to have slept with 10,000 women.

Answers to page 362

1 Lord Byron, 2 Psalms, 3 *The Game,* 4 Snooker, 5 Woody Allen, 6 Toy Town, 7 Tennis, 8 *Tom, Dick & Harry,* 9 Backbone, 10 Ramadan, 11 Jimmy Connors, 12 Hydrogen, 13 George Stephenson, 14 60, 15 Adam Ant.

QUIZ 359

Answers on page 359

1 In which historic London church can The Coronation Chair be found?

2 What sort of creature is a treehopper?

3 Which bird has the scientific name 'Anas platyrhynchos'?

4 The goat represents which star sign?

5 Which language is predominantly spoken in Calcutta?

6 What is a pumpernickel?

7 What do the Germans call the Polish city of Gdansk?

8 What is the second largest country in Africa?

9 Which soprano was known as The Swedish Nightingale?

10 What was the surname of *Only Fools and Horses* characters Del Boy and Rodney?

11 Where are the Sperrin mountains?

12 Who played mobster Carmine Sabatini in the 1990 film *The Freshman*?

13 Who was the third husband of Bessie Wallis Warfield?

14 Which was the first British National Park?

15 Which is the largest of the Canary Islands?

Things you didn't know...

Cats cannot taste sweet things.

Answers to page 359

1 Siesta, 2 Badger, 3 Erno Dohnanyi, 4 The Red Sea, 5 Great Stour, 6 Harrison Ford, 7 Until the wind changed, 8 Kayak, 9 Eton, 10 Turkey, 11 Michael Aspel, 12 Ice Skating, 13 Edith Nesbit, 14 UB40, 15 Piano.

QUIZ 360

Answers on page 360

1 Which British poet wrote the verse satire *Don Juan*?

2 Which is the longest book of the Old Testament?

3 Which film from the director of *Seven* starred Michael Douglas and Sean Penn?

4 What game is played by Ronnie O'Sullivan?

5 Who directed the film musical *Everyone Says I Love You*?

6 Where did Larry the Lamb live?

7 In which sport did McNamara and McNamee compete?

8 In the film *The Great Escape*, what were the names of the three principle tunnels dug?

9 What does an invertebrate not have?

10 What name is given to the ninth month of the Muslim year?

11 Which tennis player has been sued by his own fan club?

12 Which element is found in all acids?

13 Which engineer constructed the Stockton and Darlington railway and provided its first locomotives?

14 How many litres are there in 13.20 gallons?

15 Who had a hit with *Goody Two Shoes*?

Things you didn't know...

Kangaroos cannot jump if their tails are lifted off the ground.

Answers to page 360

1 Miriam, **2** *Oliver!*, **3** Jam, **4** Barcelona, **5** George V, **6** Newfoundland, **7** Beaulieu, **8** Rabbit, **9** Panama, **10** Rivers, **11** Mick McCarthy, **12** Philippines, **13** Israel, **14** Mary Queen of Scots, **15** Naples.

QUIZ 361

Answers on page 365

1 Which religious sect was founded by Joseph Smith in 1830?

2 In which year was the Iranian Embassy in London seized?

3 Roger Daltry played the title role in which Ken Russell film?

4 What is the day before Ash Wednesday called?

5 Who wrote *The Agony and the Ecstasy*?

6 Which British actor starred in the film *Saturday Night and Sunday Morning*?

7 Which planet in our solar system was discovered by William Herschel in 1781?

8 Who replaced Roy Hodgson as manager of Blackburn Rovers?

9 In which US city did the 'St Valentine's Day Massacre' take place in 1929?

10 Which car manufacturer produced the Tipo?

11 Which Kent bowler finished with figures of 6-60 when England beat Australia in a Test Match in December 1998?

12 Who wrote *The Call of the Wild* and *White Fang*?

13 In the Old Testament, who was the father of David's friend Jonathan?

14 Which seven-a-side ball game is played in a swimming pool?

15 Which *EastEnders'* character had a baby on Christmas Day in 1998?

Things you didn't know...

There are around 3 million species of animal on Earth.

Answers to page 365

1 HMS Bounty, 2 Claudius, 3 John the Baptist, 4 Django Reinhardt, 5 Edith Nesbit, 6 Jackson Pollock, 7 Dartmoor, 8 Libya, 9 One hundred degrees, 10 Norwich, 11 Odysseus, 12 Henry Moore, 13 The Spice Girls, 14 Capital Gains Tax, 15 Pigs.

QUIZ 362

Answers on page 366

1 In which TV series does Bill Maynard play a character called Claude?

2 What sort of creature is a hake?

3 In which country is the Yellow River?

4 What nickname was given to *Star Trek's* Dr Leonard McCoy

5 Who was prime minister of Japan from 1941 to 1944?

6 Who does 'The Beast' fall in love with?

7 Which Italian-born US gangster was imprisoned for tax evasion in 1931?

8 What does an anemometer measure?

9 What is the unit of currency in Lebanon?

10 Doha is the capital of which Arab state?

11 Which blonde film star sang about her *Secret Love*?

12 Which country was previously called Kampuchea?

13 Which British composer wrote the operas *Billy Budd* and *Death in Venice*?

14 Who was the first US president to resign office?

15 The islands of Sumatra, Java and Bali are part of which country?

Things you didn't know...

*The British eat more sweets and confectionary
than any other nation does.*

Answers to page 366

1 Pampas, 2 Danny Blanchflower, 3 Greece, 4 Florida Keys, 5 Tulip,
6 The Drifters, 7 Catterick, 8 Horse racing, 9 Uranus, 10 Ankara, 11
Germany and Japan, 12 The Trent, 13 Closed shop, 14 Mata Hari,
15 Bronze.

QUIZ 363

Answers on page 363

1 On which ship was William Bligh the victim of a famous mutiny?

2 Which Roman Emperor succeeded Caligula?

3 According to the New Testament, who baptised Christ?

4 Which Belgian jazz guitarist led the quintet of the Hot Club de France with Stephane Grappelli from 1934 to 1939?

5 Which British author wrote *The Story of The Treasure Seekers*?

6 Which American artist became the first exponent of tachism or action painting?

7 Which Devon moorland is the site of a high-security prison?

8 Of which country is Tripoli the capital?

9 What is the boiling point of water in degrees Celsius?

10 Which cathedral city is the administrative centre of Norfolk?

11 According to Greek legend, who was the father of Telemachus?

12 Which famous Yorkshire-born sculptor died in 1986?

13 Which group became the first to reach Number One with their first five singles?

14 Which tax on the profits from disposal of an asset was introduced in 1965?

15 Which creatures are also called hogs or swine?

Things you didn't know...

Bob Hoskins sampled many varied occupations, such as circus fire-eater and steeplejack, before becoming an actor.

Answers to page 363

1 The Mormons, 2 1980, 3 *Tommy*, 4 Shrove Tuesday, 5 Irving Stone, 6 Albert Finney, 7 Uranus, 8 Brian Kidd, 9 Chicago, 10 Fiat, 11 Dean Headley, 12 Jack London, 13 Saul, 14 Water polo, 15 Bianca.

QUIZ 364

Answers on page 364

1 What are the flat, treeless plains of Argentina called?

2 Who captained Spurs when they did the double in 1961?

3 The Pindus Mountains are primarily in which country?

4 By what name are the small islands off the southern tip of Florida known?

5 Which flower derives its name from the Persian word for 'turban'?

6 Who had a Top Ten hit single in 1975 with *There Goes My First Love*?

7 Which North Yorkshire village is famous for its barracks and racecourse?

8 With which sport is Lester Piggott associated?

9 Which giant planet orbits the sun every 84 years, between Saturn and Neptune?

10 What is the capital of Turkey?

11 Which two countries signed the Anit-Comintern pact in 1936?

12 On which river does the city of Nottingham stand?

13 What is the name for a place of work in which all employees are required to belong to a union?

14 Which Dutch courtesan and secret agent was executed by the French in 1917?

15 Gunmetal is a type of which alloy?

Things you didn't know...

James Watt was arrested twice for flashing.

Answers to page 364

1 *Heartbeat,* 2 A fish, 3 China, 4 Bones, 5 Hideki Tojo, 6 Beauty, 7 Al Capone, 8 Wind, 9 Pound, 10 Qatar, 11 Doris Day, 12 Cambodia, 13 Benjamin Britten, 14 Richard Nixon, 15 Indonesia.

QUIZ 365

Answers on page 369

1 Which British novelist wrote *Bulldog Drummond*?

2 Which author created Gunga Din?

3 Which English cartoonist was best known for his illustrations for Lewis Carroll's *Alice* books?

4 Who played Nora Batty in TV's *Last Of The Summer Wine*?

5 In which states of the USA can Kansas City be found?

6 Who was Germany's leader throughout the Second World War?

7 What is the religious practice of driving out evil spirits called?

8 What is the highest peak in the Alps?

9 Under what pseudonym did Sir William Connor write in *The Daily Mirror*?

10 Who was the Greek equivalent to the Roman goddess of love, Venus?

11 Which horse won three Cheltenham Gold Cups in the 1960s?

12 Of which African country is Nouakchott the capital?

13 In which Italian city were the 1960 Olympic games held?

14 What is the capital of New Zealand?

15 What sort of creature is a chow chow?

Things you didn't know...

Your right lung takes in more air than the left lung.

Answers to page 369

1 America, 2 Rolf Harris, 3 Amman, 4 Lord Salisbury, 5 Homogenic, 6 Sudan, 7 Makepeace, 8 *Kojak*, 9 Hornblower, 10 Africa, 11 Wandsworth, 12 Idaho, 13 Women, 14 Mauritius, 15 Aardvark.

QUIZ 366

Answers on page 370

1 What sort of creature is a parakeet?

2 Which British-born silent film star was best known for playing a bowler-hatted tramp?

3 Who starred in the lead role of the Jane Campion film *The Portrait Of A Lady*?

4 Who played the title role in the TV series *Sharpe*?

5 What is the name of the comedian behind the irresponsible Alan Partridge?

6 If you are playing Southern Cross you are playing a form of which game?

7 Who succeeded Neil Kinnock as leader of the British Labour Party?

8 Which *EastEnders* character was played by Paul Nicholls?

9 How many muscles has an elephant's trunk got?

10 Which famous British secret agent was created by Ian Fleming?

11 Which city, now in West China, is the capital of Tibet?

12 In which country can Mount Everest be found?

13 Who composed *Rhapsodie Espanole*?

14 Who starred as boxer James J Corbett in the 1942 film *Gentleman Jim*?

15 Which bird has the scientific name 'Hirundo rustica'?

Things you didn't know...

The Roman Emperor Claudius choked to death on a feather that his doctor put down his throat to make him vomit.

Answers to page 370

1 Sri Lanka, **2** *Mary Poppins*, **3** Western Australia, **4** Birmingham, **5** *One Day In Your Life,* **6** John Steinbeck, **7** Upsilon, **8** Lawrence Dallagio, **9** Keith Harris, **10** Seventeen, **11** Chemical elements, **12** Leto, **13** Soup, **14** David Livingstone, **15** April.

QUIZ 367

Answers on page 367

1 What was the name of the first yacht to win the America's Cup?

2 Which Australian entertainer released the 1997 album *Can You Tell What It Is Yet*?

3 What is the capital of Jordan?

4 Who was the last person to sit in the House of Lords whilst serving as prime minister?

5 What was Bjork's 1997 album release?

6 What is the largest country in Africa?

7 What was the middle name of the writer William Thackeray?

8 Which bald detective was played by Telly Savalas?

9 Which fictional hero first appeared as a midshipman in the 1937 novel *The Happy Return*?

10 In which continent is the Cape of Good Hope?

11 In which town is the Brewing company of Young and Co based?

12 In which American state are the towns of Anaconda and Moscow?

13 What does a philogynist like?

14 Which island country in the Indian Ocean has Port Louis as its capital?

15 Which animal's name comes first in the dictionary?

Things you didn't know...

Samantha Janus, Babes in the Wood star, came 10th in the 1991 Eurovision Song Contest with A Message to Your Heart.

Answers to page 367

1 Sapper, **2** Rudyard Kipling, **3** Sir John Tenniel, **4** Kathy Staff, **5** Kansas and Missouri, **6** Hitler, **7** Exorcism, **8** Mont Blanc, **9** Cassandra, **10** Aphrodite, **11** Arkle, **12** Mauritania, **13** Rome, **14** Wellington, **15** A dog.

QUIZ 368

Answers on page 368

1 Which island country has two official languages, Sinhalese and Tamil?

2 Which PL Travers' book was made into a film in 1964, for which the actor playing the title character won an Oscar?

3 What is the largest state of Australia?

4 Near which English city is Bournville, the site of a garden village founded by George Cadbury?

5 What was Michael Jackson's first solo UK Number One hit?

6 Who wrote *Of Mice and Men*?

7 Which letter of the Greek alphabet is the equivalent to 'U'?

8 Which Rugby Union international was captain of Wasps in 1996/97 season?

9 Which ventriloquist was famous for Orville the duck and Cuddles the monkey?

10 How old was Pele when he first played in the football World Cup Finals?

11 What are listed in a periodic table?

12 In Greek mythology, who was the mother of Apollo and Artemis?

13 Bouillabaisse is what kind of fish dish?

14 Who published the book *Missionary Travels* in South Africa in 1857?

15 Which is the first month of the year to have exactly thirty days?

Things you didn't know...

There are more chickens than people in England.

Answers to page 368

1 A bird, 2 Charlie Chaplin, 3 Nicole Kidman, 4 Sean Bean, 5 Steve Coogan, 6 Poker, 7 John Smith, 8 Joe Wicks, 9 40,000, 10 James Bond, 11 Lhasa, 12 Nepal, 13 Maurice Ravel, 14 Errol Flynn, 15 Swallow.

QUIZ 369

Answers on page 373

1 Which surgeon performed the first human heart transplant?

2 In the film *Four Weddings and a Funeral* which actor played the part whose death led to the funeral?

3 The song *Take My Breath Away* performed by Berlin was used in which 1986 film?

4 What is the nickname of Wimbledon football club?

5 Who owned the High Chaparral ranch?

6 Who played Mandy Wilkin in the sitcom *Game On*?

7 Which Roman emperor murdered his wife Octavia in order to marry Poppaea?

8 On which Radio 1 DJ's show did The Faces, Led Zeppelin and David Bowie, among others, make their debut?

9 Who directed the films *On The Waterfront* and *East of Eden*?

10 Scenes from which battle were the first to appear on a British commemorative postage stamp?

11 Which band fronted by Louise Wener were *Pleased to Meet You* in 1997?

12 Who did Neil Kinnock replace as leader of the Labour Party?

13 Which Rugby Union player became the youngest-ever All Black when he made his debut against France in 1994 at the age of 19?

14 Which German chess player was World Champion from 1894 to 1921?

15 Mogadiscio is the capital of which African country?

Things you didn't know...

Eddie Cochran's last recording before he was killed in a car crash was Three Steps to Heaven.

Answers to page 373

1 Engelbert Humperdinck, 2 Escudo, 3 *Volcano*, 4 UB40, 5 India, 6 George Harrison, 7 Amy Johnson, 8 Damascus, 9 *All Creatures Great and Small,* 10 Bowls, 11 Boy George, 12 Franklin D. Roosevelt, 13 Sean Connery, 14 North Yorkshire, 15 1988.

QUIZ 370

Answers on page 374

1 Which famous Irish horror novelist was business manager to the actor Henry Irving?

2 Who replaced David Coleman as host of BBC 1's *A Question of Sport*?

3 What sort of creature is a rail?

4 Which character did David Jason play in *Porridge*?

5 What was the full title of the seventh film in the *Star Trek* series which starred Patrick Stewart and William Shatner?

6 Which US rock group released an album in 1997 called *The Colour And The Shape*?

7 What is a Howgate Wonder?

8 Which writer was portrayed by Vanessa Redgrave in a 1979 film which also starred Dustin Hoffman and Timothy Dalton?

9 Which 1969 film musical starred Barbra Streisand, Walter Matthau and Michael Crawford?

10 Which police series is based at Sun Hill police station?

11 How many legs has a spider got?

12 Which planet takes approximately 165 years to orbit the sun?

13 How many tricks must a bridge pair win to obtain a grand slam?

14 Nobles, unites, bezants and angels were all what?

15 Which William, who died in 1984, was a famous band leader and pianist?

Things you didn't know...

Thirteen-year-old Belgian schoolgirl Sandra Kim won the 1986 Eurovision Song Contest to become the youngest winner ever.

Answers to page 374

1 In the blood, **2** Java, **3** Swim the Channel, **4** Spanish, **5** Robert Mitchum, **6** Ascot, **7** Adam, **8** Malawi, **9** Friesian, **10** Dorchester, **11** Italy, **12** Nepal, **13** Jonas Salk, **14** Henry James, **15** Jellystone Park.

QUIZ 371

Answers on page 371

1 Which international singer was born Arnold Dorsey, in Madras?

2 What is the main unit of currency on the island of Madeira?

3 Which 1997 disaster movie starred Tommy Lee Jones and Anne Heche?

4 Which British group had a 1983 Number One hit record with *Red Red Wine*?

5 In which country did gymkhanas originate?

6 Which member of the Beatles released a solo album called *Extra Texture*?

7 Which British aviator established several long-distance records with her flights to Australia and Tokyo during the 1930s?

8 Which city is reputed to be the oldest in the world?

9 Which TV series was based upon the autobiographical books of James Herriot?

10 With which sport do you associate Tony Allcock?

11 Who is the lead singer of Culture Club?

12 Who was president of the USA from 1933 to 1945?

13 Which film star's biography was called *Neither Shaken Nor Stirred*?

14 In which English county is the Fylingdales early-warning radar station situated?

15 In what year was the Lockerbie bombing?

Things you didn't know...

Demi Moore was born cross-eyed.

Answers to page 371

1 Dr. Christiaan Barnard, 2 Simon Callow, 3 *Top Gun,* 4 The Dons, 5 John Cannon, 6 Samantha Janus, 7 Nero, 8 John Peel's, 9 Elia Kazan, 10 Battle of Britain, 11 Sleeper, 12 Michael Foot, 13 Jonah Lomu, 14 Emanuel Lasker, 15 Somalia.

QUIZ 372

Answers on page 372

1 Where exactly in your body is fibrin found?

2 What is the smallest of the Greater Sunda Islands?

3 What did Gertrude Ederle become the first woman to do in 1926 which later led to a tickertape parade attended by two million people?

4 What was the nationality of the artist Goya?

5 Which American played a teacher in the film *Ryan's Daughter*?

6 At which course are the Coventry Stakes run?

7 In the Bible, who was the father of Cain and Abel?

8 Of which African country is Lilongwe the capital?

9 Which breed of cattle produces most of Britain's milk?

10 Which Dorset town was known as Casterbridge in Thomas Hardy's novels?

11 Which country does Parmesan cheese come from?

12 In which country is Katmandu?

13 Who developed the first vaccine against polio?

14 Whose novel was the film *The Wings of the Dove*, starring Helena Bonham Carter, based upon?

15 Which Park was home to Yogi Bear and Boo-Boo?

Things you didn't know...

Arthur Negus dropped and smashed a viewer's prized clock on The Antiques Roadshow. The owner was not upset.

Answers to page 372

1 Bram Stoker, **2** Sue Barker, **3** A bird, **4** Blanco, **5** *Star Trek: Generations,* **6** Foo Fighters, **7** An apple, **8** Agatha Christie, **9** *Hello. Dolly!,* **10** *The Bill,* **11** Eight, **12** Neptune, **13** Thirteen, **14** Coins, **15** Basie.

QUIZ 373

Answers on page 377

1 What is the capital of Bosnia and Hercegovina?

2 Which star is also called the Dog Star?

3 Which instrument measures a plane's height above sea level?

4 Which bird has the scientific name 'Fratercula arctica'?

5 Who played the Southern belle in the 1938 film *Jezebel*?

6 Which country issued a 12d black stamp in 1851?

7 Of which country was Achmed Sukarno President from 1945 to 1962?

8 Which Italian architectural style was introduced into England by Inigo Jones?

9 Which semi-aquatic carnivorous mammals belong to the genus Lutra?

10 Which large island became an integral part of Denmark in 1953, and gained self-government under Danish sovereignty in 1979?

11 Which British novelist wrote *Brideshead Revisited*?

12 What is the largest lake in the British Isles?

13 Which actress was tagged the 'Teenage Meryl Streep'?

14 Which American golfer who did much to popularise the sport won the Open Championship in 1961 and 1962?

15 There are 78 cards in which type of pack?

Things you didn't know...

In Holland people with red hair are considered to bring bad luck.

Answers to page 377

1 Dublin, 2 Steve Smith, 3 Tennessee, 4 Brasilia, 5 Bath, 6 Fig, 7 Royal National Lifeboat Institution, 8 Michael Bentine, 9 Vitamin C, 10 Israel, 11 Des Barnes, 12 Glasgow Rangers, 13 Edward Heath, 14 Wrinkled, 15 Japan.

QUIZ 374

Answers on page 378

1 Which instrument of the violin family is larger than a violin but smaller than a cello?

2 Ken Dodd had a Number One hit in 1965, what was it called?

3 By what name is the Gulf of Gascony now known?

4 Who played the Devil to Keanu Reeves' advocate in the film *Devil's Advocate*?

5 Which is the ancestral home of the Dukes of Bedford?

6 Which British doctor and middle-distance runner was the first man to run a mile in under 4 minutes?

7 Of which Caribbean country is Castries the capital?

8 Which Cornish village is said to have been the birthplace of King Arthur?

9 Which city is served by Mirabel airport?

10 Of which city was English merchant Dick Whittington Lord Mayor three times?

11 By what name is a camel with two humps called?

12 Which university was established in Birmingham in 1966?

13 Of which state of the USA is Raleigh the capital?

14 What form of rapid writing is associated with Sir Isaac Pitman?

15 Of which country is Tegucigalpa the capital of?

Things you didn't know...

Anyone caught detonating a nuclear device in the city of Chico, California could face a fine of up to $500.

Answers to page 378

1 *The Funeral,* 2 *Buck Rogers in the 25th Century,* 3 Jean-Philippe Rameau, 4 Tom Hanks, 5 Monopoly, 6 Titanium, 7 Female demon, 8 Hinny, 9 Guadalcanal, 10 Three minutes, 11 Daily Express, 12 John Wayne, 13 Arthur Rackham, 14 Paul Scott's, 15 Paris.

QUIZ 375

Answers on page 375

1 In which city was the 1994 Eurovision Song Contest held?

2 Who became the first Briton to win an Olympic high jump medal for 88 years in 1996?

3 Of which US state is Nashville the capital?

4 What is the capital of Brazil?

5 Which English city was known as Aquae Sulis to the Romans?

6 Which fruit from the tree Ficus carica is known for its laxative properties?

7 What does the initials RNLI stand for?

8 Which member of *The Goons* presented *Potty Time*?

9 Which vitamin is also known as ascorbic acid?

10 In which country would one be likely to find a kibbutz?

11 Which *Coronation Street* character was played by Philip Middlemiss?

12 Which Scottish football team won the League Championship for the ninth sucessive year in 1997?

13 Which British Conservative prime minister took the UK into the EEC in 1973?

14 If your face was rugose, what would it be?

15 In which country were the 1998 Winter Olympic Games held?

Things you didn't know...

Everton FC used to be known as St Domingo's FC.

Answers to page 375

1 Sarajevo, 2 Sirius, 3 Altimeter, 4 Puffin, 5 Bette Davis, 6 Canada, 7 Indonesia, 8 Palladianism, 9 Otters, 10 Greenland, 11 Evelyn Waugh, 12 Lough Neagh, 13 Laura Dern, 14 Arnold Palmer, 15 Tarot.

QUIZ 376

Answers on page 376

1 Which 1997 film starred Christopher Walken, Christopher Penn and Vincent Gallo as three Italian American brothers?

2 Which US TV series co-starred Twiki the helpful robot?

3 Which French composer wrote the opera *Castor et Pollux*?

4 Who won the Oscar for Best Actor in both 1993 and 1994?

5 What board game was invented by Charles Darrow?

6 Which lightweight metal has the symbol Ti?

7 In ancient mythology, what was a lamia?

8 What is the name for the sterile offspring of a female ass and a male horse?

9 What is the largest of the Solomon Islands?

10 In professional boxing, how long does each round last?

11 In which daily newspaper does *Rupert the Bear* appear?

12 Who did Marion Morrison became better known as?

13 Which illustrator and watercolourist is best known for his children's book illustrations such as 1906's *Peter Pan*?

14 On which author's novels was *The Jewel in The Crown* based?

15 In which city can the Arc de Triomphe be found?

Things you didn't know...

Mary Queen of Scots was a keen golfer.

Answers to page 376

1 Viola, 2 *Tears*, 3 Bay of Biscay, 4 Al Pacino, 5 Woburn Abbey, 6 Sir Roger Bannister, 7 St Lucia, 8 Tintagel, 9 Montreal, 10 London, 11 Bactrian, 12 Aston, 13 North Carolina, 14 Shorthand, 15 Honduras.

QUIZ 377

Answers on page 381

1 Which athlete won his fourth successive Olympic long jump title in Atlanta in 1996?

2 What is Puck otherwise called in *A Midsummer Night's Dream*?

3 Who were the twin sons of Zeus and Leda?

4 Whose four wives included Ann Howe and Miranda Quarry?

5 In Greek mythology, which band of sailors accompanied Jason on the quest for the Golden Fleece?

6 What is the second largest island in the Mediterranean Sea?

7 What is the best selling single of all time?

8 Which day of the week is named after the Norse god Thor?

9 Who wrote the *Prisoner of Zenda*?

10 What is a glockenspiel?

11 Which Boulevard is the title of a musical?

12 In which European capital city is the Spanish Riding School based?

13 Which *Pride and Prejudice* character was played by Jennifer Ehle in the BBC drama?

14 According to the nursery rhyme, who pulled pussy out of the well?

15 Which cook has a book out called *Winter Collection*?

Things you didn't know...

New Zealand was the first country to give women the vote.

Answers to page 381

1 Prince Naseem Hamed, 2 Chris Boardman, 3 Patricia Highsmith, 4 *Independence Day,* 5 Gopher, 6 Germaine Greer, 7 Darts, 8 Andrew Johnson, 9 Suede, 10 Lonnie Donegan, 11 Mortgage Interest Relief At Source, 12 Avocet, 13 Blondie, 14 Anne Bancroft, 15 Gulf of Taranto.

QUIZ 378

Answers on page 382

1 Which French Riviera resort is the site of an annual film festival?

2 Which cartoon character did Jim Davis create?

3 Born in 1452, who recorded his scientific notes in mirror writing?

4 In *Last of the Summer Wine* who is married to Nora?

5 Which market town in Suffolk is the centre of British horse racing?

6 Who was King of England from 1199 to 1216?

7 What is the innermost and most sacred chamber of the ancient Jewish Temple in Jerusalem called?

8 Which is the second highest mountain in the world?

9 Near which Bavarian city did the Nazis hold huge rallies in the 1930s?

10 Which British actor starred in the films *The Ipcress File and Alfie*?

11 Who became US president after Lincoln's assassination?

12 Lisbon is the capital of which country?

13 On which day of the week are British elections always held?

14 Who was elected Ireland's eighth president in 1997?

15 What was the name of the Captain in *The Onedin Line*?

Things you didn't know...

An Aussie bowler conceded 62 runs off one eight-ball over. The batsman hit 9 sixes and 2 fours off the over which included four no-balls.

Answers to page 382

1 Formic, 2 Australia, 3 Ice Hockey, 4 *Maverick*, 5 Sharpe, 6 Alpha, 7 Guys, 8 None, 9 Ian Wright, 10 Victoria, 11 Robert Burns, 12 Beatrix Potter, 13 Titian, 14 Kent, 15 Lambda.

QUIZ 379

Answers on page 379

1 Which British featherweight boxer was awarded an MBE in 1998?

2 Which British cyclist shattered his own world record to win the 1996 world 4,000 metres pursuit title in Manchester?

3 Which US crime novelist wrote *Strangers on a Train*?

4 In the USA, which national holiday falls on 4th July?

5 What kind of animal was Phillip Schofield's puppet Gordon?

6 Who wrote *The Female Eunuch*?

7 The World Professional Championships of which sport moved to the Lakeside Country Club, Surrey in 1986?

8 Which US president was impeached in 1867?

9 What name is given to leather with a velvet-like nap?

10 Who was known as 'The King of Skiffle'?

11 What does MIRAS stand for?

12 Which wading bird is distinguished by its long, upturned bill?

13 Who had a UK Number One hit in 1979 with *Heart of Glass*?

14 Who played Mrs Robinson in the film *The Graduate*?

15 Bearing the same name as a town in Italy, what is the name of the large gulf on the south coast of Italy?

Things you didn't know...

Some Persian carpets have more than 300 knots per square inch.

Answers to page 379

1 Carl Lewis, 2 Robin Goodfellow, 3 Castor & Pollux, 4 Peter Sellers, 5 The Argonauts, 6 Sardinia, 7 Elton John's *Candle in the Wind* '97', 8 Thursday, 9 Anthony Hope, 10 A percussion instrument, 11 Sunset, 12 Vienna, 13 Elizabeth Bennet, 14 Little Tommy Stout, 15 Delia Smith.

QUIZ 380

Answers on page 380

1 Which acid is found in bee stings?

2 Around which country will you find all the Indian Ocean, the Coral Sea and the Bass Strait?

3 With which sport is Wayne Gretzky associated?

4 In which 1994 film did James Garner play the father of the character he played in a TV series of the same name?

5 Which Tom wrote the novel *Wilt*?

6 Which letter of the Greek alphabet is the equivalent to 'A'?

7 Who are with the dolls in the musical about gangsters?

8 How many kings of England have been called Philip?

9 Which striker beat Cliff Bastin's Arsenal goal-scoring record in 1997?

10 Who was the last queen of England by succession before Elizabeth II?

11 Which Scottish poet wrote *Poems, Chiefly in the Scottish Dialect*?

12 Who wrote *The Tale of Peter Rabbit* and *The Tailor of Gloucester*?

13 Which Venetian painter of the renaissance gave his name to a shade of red?

14 The Isle of Sheppey is situated off the coast of which English county?

15 Which letter of the Greek alphabet is the equivalent to 'L'?

Things you didn't know...

The first American bank robbery occurred in 1883.

Answers to page 380

1 Cannes, 2 Garfield, 3 Leonardo da Vinci, 4 Wally, 5 Newmarket, 6 John, 7 The Holy of Holies, 8 K2, 9 Nuremberg, 10 Michael Caine, 11 Andrew Johnson, 12 Portugal, 13 Thursday, 14 Mary McAleese, 15 James.

QUIZ 381

Answers on page 385

1 Who became British prime minister in 1945?

2 Which amber globe was named after a 1930s' Minister of Transport?

3 Which legendary creature is a beautiful woman above the waist and a fish below?

4 In which city is the Louvre?

5 Which English-born US actor starred in the Hitchcock films *To Catch A Thief* and *North By Northwest*?

6 Which bird has the scientific name 'Apus apus'?

7 What is the medical name for inflammation of the lining of the nose?

8 According to the Old Testament, who succeeded Moses as leader of the Israelites?

9 In which ocean are the Seychelles?

10 In the Bible, which two birds did Noah send out from the Ark?

11 Who owns Dartmoor Prison?

12 Which snooker player was runner-up in six World Championships in the 80s and 90s?

13 Which prophet was taken into heaven in a fiery chariot?

14 Which sometimes fatal infection is caused by the bacterium Legionella pneumophila?

15 Who wrote *The Last of The Mohicans*?

Things you didn't know...

There are 52 independent countries on the African continent.

Answers to page 385

1 *3 Times A Lady*, **2** Daniel Defoe, **3** Stuart Pearce, **4** Rosie, **5** Richard Harris, **6** Parmesan, **7** Waterman, **8** Thelma Barlow, **9** Wigan Athletic, **10** Cymbals, **11** David Niven, **12** Dog, **13** William Shakespeare, **14** River Ebro, **15** Sicily.

QUIZ 382

Answers on page 386

1 Of which Canadian province is Halifax the capital?

2 What is New York's largest concert hall?

3 Of which country was Peter the Great emperor?

4 Which Turkish city was formerly known as Byzantium and Constantinople?

5 Which British actress won an Oscar for her role in *The Prime of Miss Jean Brodie*?

6 Which playing card is often reffered to as 'The Black lady'?

7 In which game would you use the expression 'J'adoube'?

8 Which 1997 film focused on the relationship between Queen Victoria and he Scottish gillie?

9 What is the common name for the psychological Rorschasch Test?

10 *Thanks For The Memory* is the theme song of which veteran comedian?

11 Who was the PFA's Young Player Of The Year for 1992-1993?

12 Which brand of lager used the advertising slogan 'Follow the Bear'?

13 Who plays Tracey in the sitcom *Birds of a Feather*?

14 Which of the Bronte sisters wrote *Jane Eyre*?

15 Which comedy series starred David Jason, Gwen Taylor and Nicola Pagett?

Things you didn't know...

Fish can suffer from seasickness.

Answers to page 386

1 Mounties, 2 Yachting, 3 Rwanda, 4 Violin, 5 Lockhart, 6 Stet, 7 Joe Cocker, 8 Jaguar, 9 Spain, 10 An antelope, 11 Byron, 12 Anode, 13 Africa, 14 Neptune, 15 Mexico.

QUIZ 383

Answers on page 383

1 What was The Commodores 1978 Number One hit?

2 Who was sometimes referred to as the first true English novelist?

3 Which former England skipper was lucky to escape alive after his car was involved in a collision with a lorry in August 1998?

4 In the book title, who did writer Laurie Lee have cider with?

5 Who starred in the title role of the 1970 film *A Man Called Horse*?

6 Which cheese is usually grated over pasta dishes and soup?

7 Which Dennis starred in *Minder* and *On The Up*?

8 Who played Mavis Wilton in *Coronation Street*?

9 Which Football league club plays at Springfield Park?

10 Which percussion instruments can be clashed together, struck or put together in a hi-hat?

11 Which British film actor wrote the autobiography *The Moon's a Balloon*?

12 What is a talbot, often seen in heraldic designs?

13 Which British writer died on his fifty-second birthday on St George's Day 1616?

14 What is the second largest river in Spain?

15 Of which Mediterranean island is Palermo the capital?

Things you didn't know...

Homework in Spanish primary and secondary schools was banned in September 1984.

Answers to page 383

1 Clement Attlee, **2** Belisha Beacon, **3** Mermaid, **4** Paris, **5** Cary Grant, **6** Swift, **7** Rhinitis, **8** Joshua, **9** Indian Ocean, **10** A dove and a raven, **11** Prince Charles, **12** Jimmy White, **13** Elijah, **14** Legionnaires' disease, **15** James Fenimore Cooper.

QUIZ 384

Answers on page 384

1 By what name are the RCMP more commonly known?

2 Soling, Star and Finn are all categories in which sport?

3 Of which African country is Kigali the capital?

4 What instrument does Stephane Grappelli play?

5 What was the name of the Detective Inspector in *No Hiding Place*?

6 Which word, used in proof reading, means 'Leave as printed' or 'Let it stand'?

7 Who had a little help from his friends in 1968?

8 Which type of car is also the name of a big cat?

9 Which country does the holiday island of Ibiza belong to?

10 What sort of creature is a saiga?

11 Which British poet is revered as a hero in Greece?

12 What is the term for a positive electrode?

13 In which continent is the world's longest river?

14 Which Roman sea god is identified with the Greek Poseidon?

15 In which modern country would you locate The world's largest pyramid?

Things you didn't know...

Julie Andrews disliked her 'nice-girl' image so much that she once wore a badge saying "Mary Poppins is a Junkie".

Answers to page 384

1 Nova Scotia, 2 Carnegie Hall, 3 Russia, 4 Istanbul, 5 Maggie Smith, 6 The Queen of Spades, 7 Chess, 8 Mrs Brown, 9 Ink blot test, 10 Bob Hope, 11 Ryan Giggs, 12 Hofmeister, 13 Linda Robson, 14 Charlotte, 15 *A Bit of a Do*.

QUIZ 385

Answers on page 389

1 Which former mistress of Earl Spencer teamed up with his estranged wife in a pre-divorce court hearing?

2 Diplopia is the technical name for which medical disorder?

3 In which county is Dartmoor?

4 What is a nematode?

5 In which sport did Phil Read win many World Championships?

6 What was the title of the Bruce Willis film in which he played a chameleon-like assassin?

7 Who played J.R. Ewing in *Dallas*?

8 Which infection of a membrane around the eye is sometimes known as pinkeye?

9 Where was Shakespeare's *Romeo and Juliet* set?

10 Which group of islands are known as Islas Malvinas to the Argentinians?

11 In which month does the grouse shooting season start in Britain?

12 What is the traditional nickname of people with the surname Murphy?

13 Which author created *Thomas the Tank Engine*?

14 In what year was the first crossword published in Great Britain?

15 What is the name of Prospero's daughter in *The Tempest*?

Things you didn't know...

The people of Liechtenstein once held a referendum to decide where to place a public toilet.

Answers to page 389

1 Fallow, 2 Cats, 3 Berkshire, 4 Quinine, 5 Charles Lamb, 6 Skegness, 7 Internation Monetary Fund, 8 Clement Attlee, 9 Anne Boleyn, 10 Juliana, 11 Treacher, 12 Canberra, 13 Yellow, 14 A dog, 15 *Grand Hotel*.

QUIZ 386

Answers on page 390

1 Which is the largest city in China?

2 In the Bible, who replaced Judas Iscariot as one of the 12 Apostles?

3 In which American city was Al Capone based?

4 For which constructor did Martin Brundle drive for in the 1996 British Grand Prix?

5 In which English city was the first Salvation Army brass band formed?

6 In which organ can the pineal gland be found?

7 What name is given to a female horse under four years old?

8 What is the common name for the scapula?

9 In which British city can the Clifton Suspension Bridge be found?

10 In 1949, which country became the first to leave the Commonwealth?

11 Of which South American country is La Paz the administrative capital?

12 What is the capital of Japan?

13 Which is the only place in Europe where monkeys live in the wild?

14 Where on a ship would you find the lubber's hole?

15 What is the difference between meteors and meteorites?

Things you didn't know...

Hunting dogs which were not owned by William the Conqueror had three toes removed to slow them down when trying to catch game.

Answers to page 390

1 Gross National Product, 2 Peru, 3 Cherry, 4 Cyprus, 5 Mountain ranges, 6 Stamps, 7 Willem Dafoe, 8 The Tower of London, 9 Lenny Henry, 10 Boy George, 11 Blasphemy, 12 Pigbag, 13 James Cagney, 14 Minguel Indurain, 15 The leg.

QUIZ 387

Answers on page 387

1 What is the term for arable land left unseeded for one season?

2 Which creatures collect in a clowder?

3 Newbury is in which English county?

4 Which drug is obtained from the Yellow Cinchona plant?

5 Which British essayist and critic is best remembered for his *Essays of Elia*?

6 At which resort did Billy Butlin open his first holiday camp?

7 Which specialised agency of the united nations is known by the initials IMF?

8 Who was the first Labour pm after the Second World War?

9 Who was the mother of Elizabeth I?

10 Who was the Queen of the Netherlands from 1948 to 1980?

11 Which Bill played Arthur Fowler on television?

12 What is the capital of Australia?

13 What colour was Bobby Shafto's hair?

14 What sort of creature is a mastiff?

15 Which film, set in Berlin and based on a novel by Vicki Baum, starred Greta Garbo and Joan Crawford?

Things you didn't know...

It takes 492 seconds for sunlight to reach the Earth.

Answers to page 387

1 Chantal Collopy, 2 Double vision, 3 Devon, 4 Type of worm, 5 Motor Cycling, 6 *The Jackal,* 7 Larry Hagman, 8 Conjunctivitis, 9 Verona, 10 Falkland Islands, 11 August, 12 Spud, 13 Rev. Awdry, 14 1913, 15 Miranda.

QUIZ 388

Answers on page 388

1 What does GNP stand for?

2 *Paddington Bear* comes from which country?

3 Of what fruit is the morello a variety?

4 On which island in the Mediterranean Sea is the port of Famagusta?

5 What are the Ghats?

6 What does a philatelist collect?

7 Who played the hi-jacking villain of *Speed 2*?

8 In which royal fortress on the Thames were Lady Jane Grey and Anne Boleyn imprisoned?

9 Which *Comic Relief* stalwart was awarded a CBE in 1998?

10 Which former Culture Club singer mixed half the tracks on the Ministry of Sound album, *The Annual III*?

11 What is the legal name for a spoken or written insult against religious belief or sacred objects?

12 Which band had a Top Ten hit single in 1982 with *Papa's Got A Brand New Pigbag*?

13 Who starred as the paranoid gang leader in the 1949 film *White Heat*?

14 Who won the Tour de France for the third successive year in 1993?

15 In which part of the body can the tibia be found?

Things you didn't know...

Ronald Reagan once said "The thought of being President frightens me and I do not think I want the job".

Answers to page 388

1 Shanghai, **2** Matthias, **3** Chicago, **4** Jordan, **5** Salisbury, **6** The brain, **7** Filly, **8** Shoulder blade, **9** Bristol, **10** Republic of Ireland, **11** Bolivia, **12** Tokyo, **13** Gibraltar, **14** On the mast, **15** A meteorite is a meteor that has landed.

QUIZ 389

Answers on page 393

1 Of which inland sea is the Sea of Azov an arm?

2 Thursday is named after which god?

3 According to legend, which King of Wessex burnt a peasant housewife's cakes?

4 On which Chinese dialect is the official language of China based?

5 Which Italian city is known as Firenze in Italian?

6 Which hereditary disease causes the blood not to clot properly?

7 Bill Travers and Virginia Mckenna followed *Born Free* with which 1969 film about an otter?

8 Who was Sherlock Holmes' companion?

9 Who hosts the sports quiz *They Think It's All Over*, alongside team captains Gary Lineker and David Gower?

10 Which king led the English forces at the Battle of Bannockburn?

11 What is the study of the behaviour and flow of air around objects?

12 By what name are Mick, Bill,, Charlie and Brian better known?

13 Which instrument usually has 47 strings?

14 Which county's motif is a standing bear next to a ragged staff?

15 Of which country is Belmopan the capital?

Things you didn't know...

Lord Byron resorted to curlers to give him wavy hair.

Answers to page 393

1 Anniversary of the Queen's accession, **2** Derek, **3** South, **4** Coventry, **5** Acetic, **6** *Wuthering Heights,* **7** Madonna, **8** 40, **9** Wins, **10** Toad, **11** 2, **12** *Men in Black,* **13** Salem, **14** The River Mersey, **15** Calcutta.

QUIZ 390

Answers on page 394

1 Who became King of the Scots after killing Macbeth in 1040?

2 With which sport do you associate Laura Davies?

3 What is the capital of India?

4 What is the name given to a young horse?

5 Which bell hangs in the underwriting room at Lloyd's and is rung when news arrives of a missing ship?

6 Which word means a dollar, a male rabbit and a back-arching jump?

7 Which King of England was the youngest son of William the Conqueror?

8 Which Elvis film was based on the play *A Stone For Danny Fisher*?

9 Who was the subject of the Mel Brooks' film subtitled *Men in Tights*?

10 Which British city contains the Jew's House, the Usher Gallery and the National Cycle Museum?

11 Which band had a Top Ten hit single in 1980 with *Too Nice To Talk To*?

12 Venetian blinds originated in which country?

13 What item of clothing took Britain by storm in 1955?

14 Which letter of the Greek alphabet is the equivalent to 'K'?

15 Which Sunderland rock group released an album called *At The Club*?

Things you didn't know...

When you stroke a dog or cat your blood pressure drops – and so does the animal's.

Answers to page 394

1 Rock, 2 Lunar, 3 Barry Hearn, 4 The Sahara, 5 Meg Ryan, 6 Andean Condor, 7 Ceres, 8 Robert Hardy, 9 Funchal, 10 Kris Kristofferson, 11 St Albans, 12 1900-1909 (1909), 13 1916, 14 San Diego, 15 Liverpool.

QUIZ 391

Answers on page 391

1 Why should flags be flown on Government buildings on February 6th?

2 On TV what was the name of Mavis Wilton's husband?

3 Which part of the pacific is the setting for a musical?

4 Through which British city did Lady Godiva ride naked?

5 Which acid is found in vinegar?

6 Which nineteenth century novel was the title of a UK Number One hit in 1978?

7 Which singer starred in the comic film *Body of Evidence*?

8 How old is a quadragenarian?

9 According to a Nick Berry song title every loser does what?

10 Which amphibian has the scientific name 'Bufo bufo'?

11 How many goals did Scotland score in the 1998 World Cup Finals?

12 Which Sci-fi blockbuster starred Will Smith and Tommy Lee Jones?

13 In which American city were 19 witches executed in 1692?

14 Which river enters the Irish Sea via Liverpool and Birkenhead?

15 Which city is served by Dum Dum airport?

Things you didn't know...

Modern pencils do not contain lead.

Answers to page 391

1 Black Sea, 2 Thor, 3 Alfred the Great, 4 Mandarin, 5 Florence, 6 Haemophilia, 7 *Ring of Bright Water,* 8 Dr Watson, 9 Nick Hancock, 10 Edward II, 11 Aerodynamics, 12 The Rolling Stones, 13 Harp, 14 Warwickshire, 15 Belize.

QUIZ 392

Answers on page 392

1 What can be classified as igneous, sedimentary or metamorphic?

2 Which term means related to the moon?

3 Who was snooker player Steve Davis' manager in the 1980's?

4 What is the world's largest desert?

5 Which actress is married to actor Dennis Quaid?

6 Which is the worlds largest bird of prey?

7 Who was the ancient Italian goddess of corn?

8 Who starred in the title role of the classic TV series *Winston Churchill - The Wilderness Years*?

9 What is the capital of Madeira islands?

10 Which singer and actor wrote the Janis Hoplin hit *Me and Bobby McGee*?

11 How is the Roman city of Verulamium known today?

12 In which decade were old age pensions first introduced?

13 In what year did the Easter Rising take place in Dublin?

14 Which city is served by Lindbergh airport?

15 Near which English city would you find the Wirral?

Things you didn't know...

The comma was introduced to the English language in about 1520.

Answers to page 392

1 Malcolm III, **2** Golf, **3** New Delhi, **4** Foal, **5** Lutine Bell, **6** Buck, **7** Henry I, **8** *King Creole*, **9** *Robin Hood*, **10** Lincoln, **11** *The Beat*, **12** Japan, **13** Jeans, **14** Kappa, **15** Kenickie.

QUIZ 393

Answers on page 397

1 By what name is the clavicle commonly known?

2 Who was president of Nicaragua from 1981 to 1990?

3 After which Roman general was the Fabian Society named?

4 Which rugby club did Richard Branson buy a 15% shareholding in early in 1997?

5 Which Christian name derives from the Gaelic for 'handsome'?

6 In which county is Ragley Hall situated?

7 Of which African country is Matabeleland an area?

8 Which gas is manufactured by the Haber Process?

9 Which former Royal husband is now married to Sandy Pflueger?

10 Who starred as Harry Angel in the film *Angel Heart*?

11 Which fishing port is situated 9 miles south of Great Yarmouth?

12 James Hutton is generally regarded as the founder of which scientific discipline?

13 In which country is the Roman Catholic shrine and pilgrimage centre of Fatima?

14 Which important figure in the history of nursing was the first woman to receive the Order of Merit?

15 Who wrote The Ambassadors?

Things you didn't know...

Field Marshal Viscount Montgomery was a vegetarian.

Answers to page 397

1 Cutty Sark, **2** Kate Bush, **3** Glenn Miller, **4** Hong Kong, **5** Architect, **6** Lewis Carroll, **7** Poland, **8** Oliver Hardy, **9** Austria, **10** German, **11** John Knox, **12** The Tower of London, **13** Jurgen Klinsmann, **14** Thrombosis, **15** Isle of Wight.

QUIZ 394

Answers on page 398

1 How many players are in a Rugby League team?

2 Which British novelist wrote *Animal Farm*?

3 Who was the first professional cricketer to be knighted?

4 What was the sequel to Lewis Carroll's *Alice's Adventures in Wonderland* called?

5 Who was the little boy brought up by wolves in *The Jungle Book*?

6 What sort of creature is a pug?

7 Which Basketball team won the Classic Cola Cup in 1996?

8 Who did Lyndon B Johnson succeed as US president in 1963?

9 Who was prime minister of the Soviet Union from 1964 to 1980?

10 Apart from Cairo, which other capital stands on the river Nile?

11 In which English county is the district of Torbay located?

12 In which county is High Wycombe situated?

13 What was the theatrical profession of Joseph Grimaldi?

14 What is the capital and chief port of Tasmania?

15 Which US rock group had a Top Ten hit single in 1989 with *Patience*?

Things you didn't know...

Harpo Mark liked to greet visitors to his house in the nude.

Answers to page 398

1 Lacrosse, 2 Saint Andrew, 3 John Smith, 4 Lambeth Walk, 5 Michael Bond, 6 Horace, 7 Hebrides, 8 Richie Woodhall, 9 Proxima Centauri, 10 Heifer, 11 Odin, 12 Venus, 13 Mordred, 14 Poland, 15 Monarchies.

QUIZ 395

Answers on page 395

1 Which sailing ship, named after the witch in Burns's poem *Tam O'Shanter*, is preserved in dry dock at Greenwich?

2 Who had a Number One hit with *Wuthering Heights*?

3 Which band leader was on a plane which went missing on a flight across the Channel to Paris in 1944?

4 Where would you be if you were standing on Victoria Peak?

5 What was the profession of Ludwig Mies van der Rohe?

6 Who wrote *The Hunting of the Snark*?

7 Of which European country was General Jaruzelski prime minister from 1981 to 1985?

8 Who was Stan Laurel's comedy partner?

9 In which country does the small rould cheese Quargel originate?

10 What is the official language of Liechtenstein?

11 Which Scottish Protestant reformer met John Calvin in Geneva?

12 In which royal fortress can the British Crown Jewels be found?

13 Which German footballer scored the first goal in the 1994 World Cup finals?

14 What is the formation of a blood clot inside a blood vessel called?

15 On which island is Queen Victoria's country residence Osborne House situated?

Things you didn't know...

Che Guevara suffered from asthma.

Answers to page 395

1 Collar bone, 2 Daniel Ortega, 3 Fabius Maximus, 4 London Broncos, 5 Kenneth, 6 Warwickshire, 7 Zimbabwe, 8 Ammonia, 9 Captain Mark Phillips, 10 Mickey Rourke, 11 Lowestoft, 12 Geology, 13 Portugal, 14 Florence Nightingale, 15 Henry James.

QUIZ 396

Answers on page 396

1 Which ball game of North American Indian origin is 10-a-side for men and 12-a-side for women?

2 Which of the apostles was the brother of Saint Peter?

3 Who was Labour leader before Tony Blair?

4 Which popular dance of the 1930s comes from the musical *Me and My Girl*?

5 Who created *Paddington Bear*?

6 What was the first name of Rumpole of the Bailey?

7 Which group of islands include Skye and Mull?

8 Which Telford based boxer failed to win the WBC middleweight title in October 1996?

9 Which is the nearest star to the Earth, after the Sun?

10 What name is given to a cow that has not has a calf?

11 Who was the supreme god in Norse mythology?

12 Which Roman goddess has appeared in the title of UK Top Twenty hits by Frankie Avalon, Mark Wynter and Bananarama?

13 Who was the treacherous nephew of King Arthur against whom he was mortally wounded fighting?

14 Which country's international car registration letters are PL?

15 What have Norway, Sweden, Denmark, Belgium, Netherlands, Spain and the United Kingdom all got that Germany, France and Italy have not?

Things you didn't know...

Mozart was only 35 years old when he died.

Answers to page 396

1 Thirteen, 2 George Orwell, 3 Jack Hobbs, 4 *Through the Looking-Glass,* 5 Mowgli, 6 A dog, 7 The London Towers, 8 John F Kennedy, 9 Aleksei Kosygin, 10 Khartoum, 11 Devon, 12 Buckinghamshire, 13 Clown, 14 Hobart, 15 Guns n' Roses.

QUIZ 397

Answers on page 401

1 Which element has the lowest boiling point?

2 What is a bullace?

3 Who married Bianca de Macias on 12th May 1971?

4 What is the outer layer of skin called?

5 In which soap opera do the Sugdens and Windsors appear?

6 Which *EastEnders'* character was knocked down and killed by Frank Butcher on New Year's Eve 1998?

7 Who described Newcastle's women as dogs, Alan Shearer as Mary Poppins and football fans mugs?

8 What age was Mozart when he completed his first symphony?

9 Near which British seaside resort are the Great and Little Ormes?

10 In which smash hit British film did Robert Carlyle play Gaz?

11 Which animal caused the death of William III?

12 Who starred as King George III in the hit movie *The Madness of King George*?

13 Which is the world's largest computer manufacturer?

14 Who wrote *All Quiet On the Western Front*?

15 In which film is this the last line: "Tomorrow is another day."?

Things you didn't know...

The sleeping pill was invented in the first century BC.
It was made from mandrake and henbane.

Answers to page 401

1 Brigitte Bardot, 2 *Goldfinger,* 3 River Lune, 4 Six, 5 Gerry and the Pacemakers, 6 Zugspitze, 7 Seven, 8 Trueman, 9 Madagascar, 10 An amphibian, 11 Navigation and botany, 12 Denise Lewis, 13 Portugal, 14 Henry I, 15 Antonia Salieri.

QUIZ 398

Answers on page 402

1 What is the capital of Oman?

2 What bottle size is equivalent to two standard bottles?

3 Who hosts the BBC1 sports chat show *On Side*?

4 On TV, whose stooges have included Rodney Bewes, Derek Fowlds and Roy North?

5 Whose verse autobiography was called *Summoned by Bells*?

6 Which number is represented by MDLV in Roman numerals?

7 Who replaced Jeremy Paxman as presenter of TV's *You Decide*?

8 Which ex-sportsman wrote the novel *Hot Money*?

9 How long does it take the Earth to travel one and a half million miles?

10 What is the capital of Greece?

11 In which country is the Atacama Desert?

12 What nationality was Goliath, the giant killed by David?

13 Which character has been played on film by Sean Connery and by his son Jason Connery?

14 Which actor was originally due to play the lead role in *Beverly Hills Cop*?

15 Which item of clothing was named after the British cavalry officer James Thomas Brudenell?

Things you didn't know...

The first sets of dentures were in use around the 16th century.

Answers to page 402

1 Hormones, **2** George I, **3** Wilson, **4** Gaby Roslin, **5** Leander, **6** Ukraine, **7** A wild cat, **8** Axes, **9** Clink, **10** Michelle Gayle, **11** Abseiling, **12** Vermont, **13** Bernard Hepton, **14** Derbyshire, **15** Whoopi Goldberg.

QUIZ 399

Answers on page 399

1 Which famous actress was born Camille Javal?

2 Which James Bond villain had a Rolls Royce with the registration number AU 1?

3 On which river does Lancaster stand?

4 How many named people went to Widdicombe Fair with Uncle Tom Cobbleigh and the singer?

5 Which was the first group to have all their first three singles reach Number One in the UK charts?

6 What is the highest mountain in Germany?

7 How many people play in a netball side?

8 What is the surname of cricketer Fiery Fred who retired in 1968?

9 Which is the only island where you will find lemurs in the wild?

10 What sort of creature is a salamander?

11 Captain Bligh was elected a fellow of the Royal Society for services to what?

12 Which British athlete came second in the 1998 Sports Personality of the Year competition organised by the BBC?

13 If you flew due east from New York, which European country would you cross first?

14 Who became King of England in 1100?

15 Mozart was allegedly poisoned by which Italian composer?

Things you didn't know...

Actress Maureen Lipman is married to writer Jack Rosenthal.

Answers to page 399

1 Helium, **2** Fruit, **3** Mick Jagger, **4** Epidermis, **5** *Emmerdale,* **6** Tiffany, **7** Newcastle United directors Freddie Shepherd and Douglas Hall, **8** 8, **9** Llandudno, **10** *The Full Monty,* **11** Mole, **12** Nigel Hawthorne, **13** IBM, **14** Erich Remarque, **15** *Gone With The Wind.*

QUIZ 400

Answers on page 400

1 What sort of substances are adrenaline, cortisone, insulin and oestrogens?

2 Who was the first divorced monarch after Henry VIII?

3 What is Ronald Reagan's middle name?

4 Who presented *The Real Holiday Show* on TV?

5 According to Greek legend, who was Hero's lover?

6 Of which former Soviet republic is Kiev the capital?

7 What sort of creature is a cougar?

8 What is the plural of axis?

9 Which slang word for prison came into use from the name of a famous prison in Southwark in London?

10 Which former *EastEnders* star released an album entitled Sensational?

11 What word is used to describe descending a sheer face by sliding down a doubled rope?

12 In which US state are the Green Mountains?

13 Who played the camp commandant in the TV series *Colditz*?

14 Matlock is the administrative centre of which county?

15 Which comedienne starred in the title role of the basketball film *Eddie*?

Things you didn't know...

Former US President Gerald Ford and Secretary of State Henry Kissinger both guested on the TV soap Dynasty.

Answers to page 400

1 Muscat, **2** Magnum, **3** John Inverdale, **4** *Basil Brush*, **5** Betjeman, **6** 1555, **7** John Humphrys, **8** Dick Francis, **9** A day, **10** Athens, **11** Chile, **12** Philistine, **13** *Robin Hood*, **14** Sylvester Stallone, **15** Cardigan.

QUIZ 401

Answers on page 405

1 Which country is Muscat the capital of?

2 In ten-pin bowling, what term is used when all ten pins are knocked down with a single ball?

3 In which year were the British Railways nationalised?

4 With which sport do you associate brothers Leon and Michael Spinks?

5 A hart is the male of which kind of animal?

6 Which type of car to you most associate with Arthur Daley in TV's *Minder*?

7 Which musical won Best Film Oscar in 1969?

8 What is the only insect that can turn its head to look directly behind it?

9 Who partnered Eric Morecambe on television?

10 Who was Wimbledon Women's Singles Champion in 1994?

11 Of which Caribbean country is Saint John's the capital?

12 Which group's Top Ten hits of the Seventies included *Coz I Luv You, Look Wot You Dun* and *Take Me Bak 'Ome*?

13 Of which African country is Freetown the capital?

14 Who is the British director of the film *One Night Stand*?

15 In which sport is the Alfred Dunhill Cup contested?

Things you didn't know...

John Cleese played an art gallery visitor in a 1979 episode of Dr Who.

Answers to page 405

1 Vietnam, 2 Fructose, 3 Louis Armstrong, 4 C.S. Lewis, 5 Hitler, 6 The Beatles, 7 Henry Fonda, 8 Philip, 9 *Triangle,* 10 The Dallas Cowboys, 11 April, 12 Jimmy Clitheroe's, 13 *Biggles,* 14 TV John, 15 Atlanta.

QUIZ 402

Answers on page 406

1 Who was Prime Minister when old age pensions were first introduced in the UK?

2 Which British architect is famous for his design of the Crystal Palace for the Great Exhibition of 1851?

3 Which animal volunteered to dig Cock Robin's grave?

4 What was banned in the USA by the 18th Amendment?

5 What sort of creature is a guppy?

6 Which English screen legend played Jack Nicholson's accomplice in the 1997 film *Blood and Wine*?

7 Which British novelist wrote *Precious Bane*?

8 In which US city can the Lincoln Memorial be found?

9 What is the capital of Barbados?

10 What is the highest mountain entirely in Italy?

11 Of which Asian republic is Manila the capital?

12 Which Norwegian explorer led the first expedition to reach the South Pole?

13 What is inflamed if one is suffering from phlebitis?

14 In which 1988 film did Arnold Schwarzenegger play the top enforcer of the Red Army?

15 Which American actress made the news in 1993 by not appearing in the film *Boxing Helena*?

Things you didn't know...

A hotel at Jukkasjarvi, Swedish Lapland is made entirely of ice. It melts every April and has to be rebuilt the following winter.

Answers to page 406

1 Oedipus, 2 Margaret Thatcher, 3 *Peanuts,* 4 Crocodile, 5 Katmandu, 6 One, 7 Hypnos, 8 The Dead Sea, 9 Wolf, 10 White Horse Inn, 11 Four, 12 Richard Attenborough, 13 Herman Melville, 14 The New Forest, 15 1471.

QUIZ 403

Answers on page 403

1 In which country is the port of Haiphong located?

2 Which sugar occurs naturally in honey, fruits and green leaves?

3 Which US jazz trumpeter was nicknamed "Satchmo"?

4 Which British author wrote the children's books chronicling the land of Narnia?

5 Who had a mountain retreat at Berchtesgaden?

6 Which pop group comprised John Lennon, Paul McCartney, George Harrison and Ringo Starr?

7 Which US actor starred in the films *Twelve Angry Men* and *On Golden Pond*?

8 In *Rising Damp* which character was the son of an African tribal chief?

9 Which TV series, set on a North Sea ferry starred Kate O'Mara?

10 Which team won American football's Super Bowl in 1996?

11 In which month of 1996 were Prince Andrew and Sarah Ferguson divorced?

12 "Some mothers do 'ave' em" was a catchphrase on whose comedy radio programme?

13 Which hero featured in books by Captain W.E. Johns?

14 Which Hamish Macbeth character was played by on TV by Ralph Riach?

15 Which city is served by William B Hartsfield airport?

Things you didn't know...

Bicycle Polo was an Olympic demonstration sport in 1908.

Answers to page 403

1 Oman, 2 Strike, 3 1948, 4 Boxing, 5 Deer, 6 Jaguar XJ6, 7 *Oliver,* 8 The praying mantis, 9 Ernie Wise, 10 Conchita Martinez, 11 Antigua and Barbuda, 12 Slade's, 13 Sierra Leone, 14 Mike Figgis, 15 Golf.

QUIZ 404

Answers on page 404

1 In Greek mythology who solved the riddle of the Sphinx?

2 The first volume of whose memoirs, published in October 1993, were called *The Downing Street Years*?

3 US President Jimmy Carter made his fortune from which food crop?

4 To which order of animals does the gavial belong?

5 Which city is the starting point for most attempts on Mount Everest?

6 In speedway, what is the maximum number of gears allowed on a motorcycle?

7 Who was the Greek equivalent of Morpheus, the Roman god of sheep?

8 In which sea does the River Jordan flow?

9 Which animal has the scientific name 'Canis lupus'?

10 From which musical does the song *Goodbye* come?

11 How many standard bottles are there in a Jeroboam?

12 Who driected the 1982 film *Gandhi*?

13 Who wrote the novel *Moby-Dick*?

14 Which woodland area of Hampshire is noted for its ponies?

15 Which BT. Number do you ring to find out who phoned you last?

Things you didn't know...

When Gary Player opens a box of golf balls, he discards all the odd-numbered balls and plays only with the even-numbered ones.

Answers to page 404

1 Herbert Henry Asquith, **2** Sir Joseph Paxton, **3** Owl, **4** Alcohol, **5** A fish, **6** Michael Caine, **7** Mary Webb, **8** Washington DC, **9** Bridgetown, **10** Gran Paradiso, **11** The Philippines, **12** Roald Amundsen, **13** A vein, **14** *Red Heat,* **15** Kim Basinger.

QUIZ 405

Answers on page 409

1 Who is the only prime minister to have been buried in St Paul's Cathedral?

2 In which country did the 'Thuggee' - from which we derive the word thug - operate?

3 Who stars as Inspector Wexford in *The Ruth Rendell Mysteries*?

4 In which novel by John Buchan did the character Richard Hannay make his first appearance?

5 Who is generally credited as being the inventor of the rocking chair?

6 Which once common disease was also known as The White Death?

7 Which golfer secured the half point that ensured that Europe won the 1997 Ryder Cup?

8 Who played the title role in the 1994 film *Forrest Gump*?

9 Which *Dr Who* actor also starred in *Campion*?

10 Which British author wrote *Charlie and the Chocolate Factory*?

11 In which continent is the Gobi Desert situated?

12 Ardbeg and Port Askaig are towns on which Scottish island?

13 Which 1972 film starring Barbra Streisand and Ryan O'Neal was named after a cartoon character's catchphrase?

14 Which traditional Scottish dish may be boiled in a sheep's stomach?

15 Are the Channel Islands part of the UK?

Things you didn't know...

Sir Alec Douglas-Home, the former British prime minister, played first-class cricket for Middlesex.

Answers to page 409

1 John McEnroe, **2** Ken Hom, **3** Ray Stevens, **4** Led Zeppelin, **5** A shark, **6** Tommy Dorsey, **7** Edward VIII, **8** Rosarian, **9** Jules Rimet, **10** Calorie, **11** Joan Jett and the Blackhearts, **12** William Pitt, **13** Bing Crosby, **14** Pluto, **15** Swansea.

Answers on page 410

1 According to the Christian calendar, what is the first day of Lent?

2 What sort of creature is a chameleon?

3 What is the capital of Iran?

4 Who played the title role in the 1997 film version of *The Saint*?

5 On which river does Durham stand?

6 What was banned under the USA's Prohibition from 1919 to 1933?

7 What is the capital of Romania?

8 Which country has the largest Muslim population?

9 What was King Arthur's magical sword called?

10 The song *Who wants to be a Millionaire* comes from which musical?

11 Who had a Top Ten hit single in 1979 with *If I Said You have A Beautiful Body Would You Hold It Against Me*?

12 A pandemonium is the collective noun describing which kind of bird?

13 Which author created *Phineas Finn*?

14 In which film did George Lazenby play the part of James Bond?

15 Which country on the mainland of Europe is closest to the the island of Corfu?

Things you didn't know...

Rudolph Hess was a great fan of the soap opera Dynasty.

Answers to page 410

1 *Happy Days*, 2 Juan Manuel Fangio, 3 Harry Webb, 4 Antonio, 5 Lord's, 6 British Grand Prix, 7 Hope Lange, 8 Mark Ramprakash, 9 TASS, 10 Twelve, 11 The Drifters, 12 Sir Barnes Wallis, 13 Jason, 14 Kidneys, 15 Muscles.

QUIZ 407

Answers on page 407

1 Which US tennis player won the Wimbledon men's singles title in 1981, 1983 and 1984?

2 Which chef wrote a book called *Hot Wok*?

3 Who had a 1974 Number One with *The Streak*?

4 Which heavy metal band started out as the New Yardbirds?

5 What sort of creature is a tope?

6 Which big band's theme song was *I'm getting sentimental over you*?

7 Who 'found it impossible to carry the heavy burden of responsibility ... without the help of the woman I love' in 1952?

8 What name is given to a professional rose grower?

9 Who was football's World Cup originally named after?

10 Which unit is defined as the heat required to raise the temperature of one gram of water by one degree Centigrade?

11 Who had a Top Ten hit single in 1982 with *I love Rock 'n' Roll*?

12 Who became British prime minister at the age of 24?

13 Who had a top ten hit with *White Christmas*?

14 Apart from the planet Earth, which other planet was not included in Gustav Holst's suite *The Planets*?

15 In which British city was the film *Twin Town* set?

Things you didn't know...

The British navy lost its rum ration in 1973.

Answers to page 407

1 Duke of Wellington, **2** India, **3** George Baker, **4** *The Thirty-Nine Steps,* **5** Benjamin Franklin, **6** Tuberculosis, **7** Colin Montgomerie, **8** Tom Hanks, **9** Peter Davison, **10** Roald Dahl, **11** Asia, **12** Islay, **13** *What's Up, Doc?*, **14** Haggis, **15** No.

QUIZ 408

Answers on page 408

1 *Mork and Mindy* and *Laverne and Shirley* were spin-offs from which long-running series?

2 Which Argentinian motor-racing driver was World Champion a record five times during the 1950s?

3 What is Cliff Richard's real name?

4 What is the name of the *Merchant of Venice*?

5 At which cricket ground did Harold "Dickie" Bird umpire his last Test match?

6 In 1962, which race at Aintree had the fastest average speed?

7 Who played Selena Cross in the film *Peyton Place*?

8 Which England cricketer scored his maiden Test Century in the Bridgetown Test against the West Indies in 1998?

9 What is the acronym of the Russian news agency?

10 In mythology, how many labours did Hercules perform to atone for killing his own family?

11 Who had a Top Ten hit in 1974 with *Kissin' In The Back Row Of The Movies*?

12 Which British aeronautical engineer is best known for his invention of the bouncing bomb?

13 Who led the Argonauts in search of the Golden Fleece?

14 Which bodily organs are supplied with blood by the renal artery?

15 What does a myologist study?

Things you didn't know...

John F Kennedy was buried without his brain after it was lost during the autopsy which followed his assassination.

Answers to page 408

1 Ash Wednesday, 2 A lizard, 3 Tehran, 4 Val Kilmer, 5 Wear, 6 Alcohol, 7 Bucharest, 8 Indonesia, 9 Excalibur, 10 *High Society,* 11 The Bellamy Brothers, 12 Parrots, 13 Anthony Trollope, 14 *On Her Majesty's Secret Service,* 15 Albania.

QUIZ 409

Answers on page 413

1 Which 1997 erotic thriller starred Rebecca De Mornay as a psychologist?

2 What is the real name of the ITN journalist played by Stephen Dillane in the film *Welcome to Sarajevo*?

3 What sort of creature is a spaniel?

4 Which British rock group released an album called *Some Things Never Change* in 1997?

5 What is the world's longest-running TV science fiction serial?

6 Who hosted the Radio 4 programme *Start the Week* until 1987?

7 Who wrote *To The Lighthouse* and *Mrs Dalloway*?

8 Which unit of power, devised by the engineer James Watt, is abbreviated to hp?

9 Of what is petrology the study?

10 What sort of creature is a Clydesdale?

11 Which former member of The Smiths released the album *Maladjusted*?

12 Who wrote the book *Schindler's Ark*?

13 Which political party was led by Harold Wilson from 1963 to 1976?

14 From where does Cathay Pacific Airways come?

15 Who wrote the lyrics to the musical *Starlight Express*?

Things you didn't know...

Around one in ten autistic children possess extraordinary talent for music or mathematics.

Answers to page 413

1 Fog, 2 *The Fugitive,* 3 Brenda Emmanus, 4 Robert Menzies, 5 Guernsey, 6 Saturn, 7 Whitehall, 8 Methane, 9 Somerset House, 10 A bird, 11 Sri Lanka, 12 Thursday, 13 Oscar Wilde, 14 Clive Sinclair, 15 M5.

QUIZ 410

Answers on page 414

1 What is the world's largest and deepest ocean?

2 Which soap opera enjoyed an Italian break during a special five-episode week in 1997?

3 Which two countries are connected by the Khyber Pass?

4 Which artificial element is represented by the symbol Es?

5 Which British novelist wrote *The Alexandria Quartet*?

6 Which fictional police station provides the setting for *The Bill*?

7 On which date is the Christian feast of Epiphany celebrated?

8 On what date did the Euro become currency for eleven European countries?

9 Who was the oldest woman to sit in the House of Commons?

10 Which British novelist wrote *Hurry on Down* and *The Contenders*?

11 How is a harmonica commonly known?

12 Which woodwind instrument is also called the octave flute?

13 Of which Asian country is Karachi the largest city?

14 What is a young kangaroo called?

15 Which plant's leaves are the traditional antidote to nettle stings?

Things you didn't know...

The Statue Of Liberty's torch was originally lit with a bonfire.

Answers to page 414

1 Pluto, 2 Oasis, 3 Liverpool, 4 Kit Carson, 5 Andres Escobar, 6 Athena, 7 Rugby, 8 James Michener, 9 Queen Victoria, 10 Four, 11 Orchids, 12 Sir Frank Whittle, 13 Rambo, 14 David Bellamy, 15 Bogota.

QUIZ 411

Answers on page 411

1 What is a collection of cloud near the ground surface reducing visibility to less than 1km called?

2 In which film did Harrison Ford play the role of Dr. Richard Kimble?

3 Which presenter of *The Clothes Show* was also be seen on TV's *Open University*?

4 Who was prime minister of Australia from 1949 to 1966?

5 On which island did Victor Hugo write *Les Miserables*?

6 With which planet would you associate the Cassini Division?

7 In which London thoroughfare was Charles I beheaded?

8 Which gas, known as marsh gas, has the chemical formula CH4?

9 To which London building did the Courtauld Institute of Art move in 1989-90?

10 What sort of creature is a honeycreeper?

11 Who won the cricket World Cup in 1996?

12 According to the nursery rhyme, a child born on which day of the week has 'far to go'?

13 Who wrote *The Ballad of Reading Gaol* under the name of C.3.3.?

14 Who invented the ZX80 computer?

15 Which motorway connects Birmingham to Exeter?

Things you didn't know...

In the original version of Gone With The Wind the glamorous Scarlett O'Hara was called Pansy.

Answers to page 411

1 *Never Talk To Strangers*, **2** Michael Nicholson, **3** A dog, **4** Supertramp, **5** *Dr Who*, **6** Richard Baker, **7** Virginia Woolf, **8** Horsepower, **9** Rocks, **10** A horse, **11** Morrissey, **12** Thomas Kenneally, **13** The Labour Party, **14** Hong Kong, **15** Richard Stilgoe.

QUIZ 412

Answers on page 412

1 Which is the furthest planet from the sun?

2 Which group had a hit in 1997 with the single *Stand By Me*?

3 Which team did Newcastle play against in the 1974 FA Cup final?

4 After which US frontiersman was Carson City named?

5 Which Colombian footballer was murdered after scoring an own goal against the USA in the 1994 World Cup?

6 Who was the Greek equivalent to Minerva, the Roman goddess of wisdom?

7 Thomas Arnold was headmaster of which public school?

8 Which novelist wrote the book on which the musical *South Pacific* was based?

9 Which British monarch died in 1901?

10 How many characters were at the Mad Hatter's Tea Party in *Alice's Adventures in Wonderland*?

11 From which type of flower are vanilla pods obtained?

12 Who is generally credited as being the inventor of the Jet engine?

13 Which fictional hero first appeared in the 1982 film *First Blood*?

14 Which popular botanist presented the TV programmes *Up a Gum Tree*, *Backyard Safari* and *Moa's Ark*?

15 What is the capital of Colombia?

Things you didn't know...

Tennis was originally known as sphairistike.

Answers to page 412

1 The Pacific, **2** *EastEnders,* **3** Afghanistan and Pakistan, **4** Einsteinium, **5** Lawrence Durrell, **6** Sun Hill, **7** January 6th, **8** 1st January 1999, **9** Irene Ward, **10** John Wain, **11** Mouth organ, **12** Piccolo, **13** Pakistan, **14** A Joey, **15** Dock.

QUIZ 413

Answers on page 417

1 Norman Dagley was a World Champion in which sport?

2 In which country is the island of Mindanao?

3 Which ancient forest of Nottinghamshire is famous for its associations with Robin Hood?

4 What sort of mammal is a drill?

5 Which German composer wrote the oratorio *Carmina Burana*?

6 Where was the planned destination of the borrowed London bus in the UK film *Summer Holiday*?

7 Which Great Lake is linked with Lake Ontario via the Welland Ship Canal?

8 Which German-born US diplomat was jointly awarded the Nobel Peace Prize for helping to negotiate an end to the Vietnam War?

9 Which band had a Top Ten hit single in 1988 with *Left To My Own Devices*?

10 Which country has its seat of government at The Hague?

11 Which pedal is depressed when changing gears in a manual car?

12 Who became Nelson's mistress and bore him a child in 1801?

13 Who had a Top Ten hit single in 1983 with *It's Raining Men*?

14 Which British novelist wrote *The Scarlet Pimpernel*?

15 In which team game do you try to move backwards all the time?

Things you didn't know...

Redwood trees, which can grow higher than 300 feet, are the tallest living things on earth.

Answers to page 417

1 Micky Spillane, **2** Jeffrey Archer, **3** Eight, **4** 12, **5** Canada, **6** *Candle in the Wind*, **7** Linda Blair, **8** Dutch, **9** Shaun Pollock, **10** India and Sri Lanka, **11** Venezuela, **12** Goat, **13** A bird, **14** Peter Phillips, **15** Boris Pasternak.

QUIZ 414

Answers on page 418

1 Djakarta is the capital of which country?

2 In which city is the opera house Gran Teatre del Liceu?

3 Who had Top Ten hits in the 1980s with *Run To the Hills, Can I Play With Madness* and *The Evil That Men Do*?

4 Which US actress co-founded United Artists and married Douglas Fairbanks?

5 Which West Indian island is the world's main source of natural asphalt?

6 What was Helen Shapiro *Walking Back to* in 1961?

7 If a woman is nubile, what does that mean ?

8 Which scientist cousin of Charles Darwin coined the term "eugenics"?

9 At what time does the Queen give her Christmas Day speech?

10 How is the constellation Ursa Minor known in English?

11 Who had a Top Ten hit single in 1979 with *In the Navy*?

12 Which future British prime minister was present at the Battle of Omdurman?

13 What was the popular name for the scandal that forced the resignation of Richard Nixon in 1974?

14 Which director's last film was *Family Plot* in 1976?

15 Which two trees are mentioned most often in the Bible?

Things you didn't know...

Corrugated paper was originally invented for making hatbands.

Answers to page 418

1 125, **2** Buckland, **3** *Have I Got News For You,* **4** Basil, **5** Edmonton, **6** Graham Greene, **7** Tiger-cat, **8** North Yorkshire, **9** Bathsheba, **10** King Camp Gillette, **11** Pakistan, **12** A.S. Byatt, **13** It was the first time in the tournaments history that all the defending champions retained their titles, **14** Sistine Chapel, **15** Hook.

QUIZ 415

Answers on page 415

1 Detective Mike Hammer was created by which author?

2 Who wrote the book *First Among Equals*?

3 How many legs does a scorpion have?

4 How many people usually sit on a jury?

5 Of which country was Brian Mulroney prime minister?

6 Which Elton John song was rewritten for Princess Diana's funeral?

7 Who played the possessed girl Regan in *The Exorcist*?

8 What nationality was the painter Vincent Van Gogh?

9 Which cricketer took four wickets in four balls in his debut match for Warwickshire?

10 Which two countries are separated by the Palk Straits?

11 Trinidad lies off the coast of which South American country?

12 With which animal would you associate 'hircine'?

13 What sort of creature is an oystercatcher?

14 What is the name of the Queen's first grandchild?

15 In 1958, which Russian writer declined a Nobel Prize?

Things you didn't know...

Iceland has no railway system or army.

Answers to page 415

1 Billiards, 2 The Philippines, 3 Sherwood Forest, 4 A monkey, 5 Carl Orff, 6 Athens, 7 Lake Erie, 8 Henry Kissinger, 9 The Pet Shop Boys, 10 The Netherlands, 11 Clutch, 12 Lady Hamilton, 13 The Weather Girls, 14 Baroness Orczy, 15 Tug of war.

QUIZ 416

Answers on page 416

1 If all the tiles are used in a game of Scrabble, how many squares on the board would remain uncovered?

2 In which former abbey in Devon can you see Drakes's Drum?

3 Which topical TV news quiz is chaired by Angus Deayton?

4 Which herb is used to make the Italian Pesto?

5 What is the capital of the Canadian province of Alberta?

6 Which British novelist wrote The Power and the Glory and The Third Man?

7 What is a margay?

8 In which English county is the town of Harrogate?

9 Who was the mother of King Solomon?

10 Who is generally credited as being the inventor of the Safety razor?

11 In which country is the city of Rawalpindi?

12 Who is the Booker Prize-winning sister of Margaret Drabble?

13 What was unique about the Wimbledon winners of 1984?

14 What is the principal chapel of the Vatican, whose ceiling was painted by Michelangelo?

15 Which Steven Spielberg film starring Robin Williams and Dustin Hoffman, was based on characters created by J.M. Barrie?

Things you didn't know...

Until 1984 Belgians had to choose their children's names from a list of 1,500 officially approved ones drawn up in the Napoleonic era

Answers to page 416

1 Indonesia, **2** Barcelona, **3** Iron Maiden, **4** Mary Pickford, **5** Trinidad, **6** Happiness, **7** Marrigeable, **8** Sir Frances Galton, **9** 3pm, **10** Little Bear, **11** The Village People, **12** Winston Churchill, **13** Watergate, **14** Alfred Hitchcock, **15** Fig and cedar.

QUIZ 417

Answers on page 421

1 What is the state capital of Connecticut?

2 What hard dark wood is traditionally used for the black keys on a piano?

3 Which royal residence contains St George's Chapel and the Albert Memorial Chapel?

4 Which actor played *Sinbad the Sailor* in the 1947 film?

5 Which famous public school was described in Thomas Hughes's novel *Tom Brown's Schooldays*?

6 Who won the men's 100m at the Barcelona Olympics in 1992?

7 Which US rock band released an album called *Nine Lives* in 1997?

8 Which musical term means gradually becoming softer?

9 By what name is Jerusalem known in the Old Testament?

10 Which capital is nearest to the Equator?

11 Which member of the McDonald family left *Coronation Street* in late 1997?

12 In which country is the drachma a unit of currency?

13 Which city is the administrative centrel of Suffolk?

14 Which pop group named itself after a 1956 John Wayne film?

15 Who had a Top Ten hit single in 1975 with *Please Mr. Postman*?

Things you didn't know...

The city of Houston, Texas, is built on a swamp and is slowly sinking.

Answers to page 421

1 New York City, 2 Geranium, 3 William Shakespeare, 4 Sabena, 5 Captain Frederick Marryat, 6 Rowing, 7 Rommel, 8 Suffolk, 9 Phoenix, 10 Broadstairs, 11 Quarter-mile, 12 A fish, 13 The Aegean, 14 The Canary Islands, 15 Frank Williams.

QUIZ 418

Answers on page 422

1 Who won four gold medals at the 1936 Olympics?

2 What is the world's best-selling book?

3 What is the first name of James Bond villain *Goldfinger*?

4 What is the traditonal number of witches in a coven?

5 Which Japanese pottery is glazed and biscuit fired?

6 What name is given to small immature fruits of the cucumber used for pickling?

7 To which genus of plants do sweet williams and carnations belong?

8 Which Miss is a musical set in Vietnam?

9 Who was the first singer to record fifty singles that entered the UK Top Ten?

10 Which US agency was set up by John F Kennedy in 1961 to provide skilled volunteer workers for developing countries?

11 Which US actor starred in the films *The Graduate* and *Kramer vs Kramer*?

12 Whom did Zeus seduce whilst assuming the guise of a swan?

13 Which bird can be bald or golden?

14 In 1986 which body within the Solar System was explored by the European Giotto space probe?

15 Who was the first woman to fly solo across the Atlantic Ocean?

Things you didn't know...

The harp is the only stringed instrument in an orchestra which isn't played with a bow.

Answers to page 422

1 West Germany, 2 St Peter, 3 Guadeloupe, 4 Sapporo, 5 Jeff Goldblum, 6 Greece, 7 Surrey, 8 A bird, 9 *Return Of The Jedi*, 10 Santo Domingo, 11 Carl Lewis, 12 Arizona, 13 Pete Townshend, 14 Acting, 15 Chris Evans and Danny Baker.

QUIZ 419

Answers on page 419

1 In which US city is Greenwich Village?

2 What is the usual name for a pelargonium cultivated as a garden plant?

3 Which writer left his wife his 'second best bed' in his will in 1616?

4 What is the national airline of Belgium?

5 Who wrote *Mr Midshipman Easy* and *Children of the New Forest*?

6 With which sport do you associate Steven Redgrave?

7 Which army commander was known as 'The Desert Fox'?

8 In which English county is Bury St Edmunds?

9 Which legendary bird was supposedly able to rise from the ashes?

10 Where did Charles Dickens write *David Copperfield*?

11 What is the distance of a drag race?

12 What sort of creature is an orfe?

13 In which sea can the island group known as the Sporades be found?

14 Lanzarote and Tenerife are part of which island group?

15 Which Formula One motor-racing boss was awarded a knighthood in 1998?

Things you didn't know...

Chop Suey was invented in New York, not China.

Answers to page 419

1 Hartford, **2** Ebony, **3** Windsor Castle, **4** Douglas Fairbanks, **5** Rugby, **6** Linford Christie, **7** Aerosmith, **8** Diminuendo, **9** Salem, **10** Quito (Ecuador), **11** Andy, **12** Greece, **13** Ipswich, **14** The Searchers, **15** The Carpenters.

QUIZ 420

Answers on page 420

1 Which nation have been the football World Cup's runners-up the most times?

2 To which saint is Westminster Abbey dedicated?

3 Basse-Terre is the capital of which Caribbean island?

4 Which Japanese city was the site of the 1972 winter Olympics?

5 Who stars as Dr. Ian Malcolm in the film *The Lost World*?

6 Of which European country is Piraeus the main port?

7 In which English county is the town of Guildford situated?

8 What sort of creature is a kookaburra?

9 In which sci-film, re-released in 1997, does the fearsome Jabba the Hut kidnap Princess Leia?

10 What is the capital of the Dominican Republic?

11 Which US athlete won four gold medals at the 1984 Olympics?

12 In which state of the USA is the Grand Canyon situated?

13 Which British guitarist composed the rock opera *Tommy*?

14 With which branch of the arts would you associate Sarah Siddons?

15 Which two television and radio celebrities took 'Gazza on the Razza' before the World Cup Finals in 1998?

Things you didn't know...

The waiting rooms at one of Peking's railway stations can hold around 14,000 people.

Answers to page 420

1 Jesse Owens, 2 The Bible, 3 Auric, 4 Thirteen, 5 Raku, 6 Gherkins, 7 Dianthus, 8 Saigon, 9 Elvis Presley, 10 Peace Corps, 11 Dustin Hoffman, 12 Leda, 13 Eagle, 14 Halley's Comet, 15 Amelia Earhart.

QUIZ 421

Answers on page 425

1 What sort of creature is a devil's coach horse?

2 Which self-deluding knight was created by the Spanish author Cervantes?

3 Who played the Emperor's English tutor in the 1987 film *The Last Emperor*?

4 Who was the third husband of Mary, Queen of Scots?

5 Which comedy double act worked as welders before forming a singing duo called The Harper Brothers?

6 Which painter was born Domenikos Theotokopoulos?

7 Who starred as Sam Malone in TV's *Cheers*?

8 Between which lakes is the Swiss resort of Interlaken?

9 Who played Lucy in *Dallas*?

10 In which country is the industrial city of Kawasaki?

11 In which state of the USA is the city of Memphis situated?

12 What do the initials CND stand for?

13 In mathematics, what does rms stand for?

14 Who commanded the English Army at Crecy in 1346?

15 How was Ho Chi Minh City known until 1976?

Things you didn't know...

Tooth decay is the most common disease in the world.

Answers to page 425

1 Benjamin Disraeli, 2 Italy, 3 The River Trent, 4 Lethe, 5 Ligature, 6 Francis Chichester, 7 Mount Kosciusko, 8 Rome, 9 Eighteen, 10 Rhode Island, 11 Jack Warner's, 12 Pacific, 13 Glenn Close, 14 Nectar, 15 Trivial Pursuit.

QUIZ 422

Answers on page 426

1 La Guaira is the main port for which South American capital city?

2 Which language is predominantly spoken in Madras?

3 Under what name did singer Don Van Vliet find fame?

4 What was the name of Hopalong Cassidy's horse?

5 The leaves of the mulberry tree are the favourite food of which creature?

6 Which spirit is distilled from molasses derived from sugar cane?

7 In which country is the 7,316 feet Mount Kosciusko mountain?

8 In Kung-Fu what name do Buddhist priests give to Kwai Chang Caine?

9 Who directed and starred in the 1990 film *The Two Jakes*?

10 Which coloured flag warns of oil in motor racing?

11 What is the chemical symbol for Sodium?

12 On which river does Leicester stand?

13 Which organ is at the opposite end of the pulmonary artery from the heart?

14 What sort of creature is a Sealyham?

15 What does the Chemical symbol 'AS' stand for?

Things you didn't know...

It takes 43 muscles to frown but only 17 to smile.

Answers to page 426

1 Argentinian, 2 The House of Commons, 3 A leap year, 4 Argentina, 5 Nick Tilsley and Leanne Battersby, 6 Jason Donovan, 7 Windsor, 8 Ray Kroc, 9 Mike Oldfield, 10 Babbitt Metal, 11 Shirley Maclaine, 12 40, 13 Transuranic, 14 Adriatic, 15 England and France.

QUIZ 423

Answers on page 423

1 Who was prime minister when Queen Victoria was given the additional title of 'Empress of India'?

2 In which country was the operatic tenor Enrico Caruso born?

3 Which English river flows through Nottingham?

4 Which mythological river caused those who drank from it to forget their former lives?

5 What name is given to something used to tie a blood vessel to stop it bleeding?

6 Who sailed around the world in the Gipsy Moth IV?

7 What is the highest mountain in Australia?

8 In which city are the Spanish Steps?

9 In the UK, what is the minimum age at which you can be summoned for jury service?

10 What is the smallest state of the USA?

11 Whose catchphrase was "Mind my bike"?

12 Of which ocean is the Bering Sea a section?

13 Which actress plays the vice president in *Air Force One*?

14 Which sugary solution produced by flowers attracts insects and encourages pollination?

15 Which board game was invented by Canadians Scott Abbott and Chris and John Haney?

Things you didn't know...

Cleopatra's real name was Auletes.

Answers to page 423

1 A beetle, 2 Don Quixote, 3 Peter O'Toole, 4 James Hepburn, 5 Cannon and Ball, 6 El Greco, 7 Ted Danson, 8 Brienz and Thun, 9 Charlene Tilton, 10 Japan, 11 Tennessee, 12 Campaign for Nuclear Disarmament, 13 Root-mean-square, 14 Edward III, 15 Saigon.

QUIZ 424

Answers on page 424

1 What nationality was the five-times formula one World Champion, Juan Fangio?

2 What is the usual name given to the lower house of the British Parliament?

3 What is a bissextile year?

4 The Uruguay River forms the majority of the boundary between Brazil and which other country?

5 Which *Coronation Street* teenage couple took a trip to Scotland to get married in 1998?

6 Who had a Number One hit in 1989 with *Sealed With a Kiss*?

7 Which castle was badly damaged by fire in 1992?

8 Who founded the McDonalds hamburger chain?

9 Who recorded the album *Tubular Bells*?

10 What soft alloy of tin, antimony and copper is named after its inventor?

11 Who is Warren Beatty's famous sister?

12 At the start of a game of draughts, how many squares are not covered by pieces?

13 Which adjective describes elements with a higher atomic number than uranium?

14 Which sea would you be in if you swam off the east coast of Italy?

15 Which two countries fought the Hundred Years' War?

Things you didn't know...

In the original version of Cinderella the slipper that she loses was made of fur, not glass.

Answers to page 424

1 Caracas, 2 Tamil, 3 Captain Beefheart, 4 Topper, 5 Silkworm, 6 Rum, 7 Australia's, 8 Grasshopper, 9 Jack Nicholson, 10 Yellow and Red striped, 11 Na, 12 River Soar, 13 Lungs, 14 A dog, 15 Arsenic.

QUIZ 425

Answers on page 429

1 According to Greek legend a centaur was a cross between a human and which other animal?

2 Of which state of the USA is Sacramento the capital?

3 What breed of dog is Pluto?

4 Which artist was the subject of Brian and Michael's 1978 Number One *Matchstalk Men and Matchstick Cats and Dogs*?

5 Who was British prime minister at the outbreak of the First World War?

6 Who served in the RAF during the Second World War despite having lost his legs in a flying accident?

7 Which country completely surrounds the Sea of Marmara?

8 Whom did Virginia Wade beat in the final to win the 1977 Wimbledon Singles tournament?

9 Who did Bruce Willis play in the TV series *Moonlighting*?

10 Which British three-day-event horse rider won gold medals in the 1968 and 1972 Olympic Games?

11 What are the international vehicle registration letters for Gibraltar?

12 Which lady golfer won the 1997 Standard Register Tournament for the fourth year running?

13 What was the occupation of *Our Man in Havana* by Graham Greene?

14 In which war was the Battle of Marston Moor fought?

15 In which English county is the town of Basildon situated?

Things you didn't know...

Windscreen wipers were first introduced in 1921.

Answers to page 429

1 *Tommy*, **2** Copper, **3** Washington, **4** Apollo, **5** *Bull Durham*, **6** Tamagotchi, **7** Still Waters, **8** A bird, **9** The Atlantic Ocean, **10** Chicago, **11** Copenhagen, **12** Yellow fever, **13** Neil Diamond, **14** The Lighthouse Family, **15** Adolf Eichmann.

QUIZ 426

Answers on page 430

1 Which flamboyant American runner won three gold medals at the 1988 Olympics, while her sister-in-law won two?

2 Portuguese athlete Rosa Mota won an Olympic gold medal in 1988 in which event?

3 What distinction is shared by the rivers Thames, Shannon, Forth, Tyne and Humber?

4 Who starred as Lt.John Dunbar in *Dances With Wolves*?

5 In which country was the singer and actress Marlene Dietrich born?

6 Which chemical element has the symbol Hg?

7 Who said of Linford Christie: "He's a well balanced athlete. He's got a chip on each shoulder."?

8 What was first tested by Brian Trubshaw?

9 Which stimulant is found in coffee and tea?

10 Which US folksinger wrote the songs *Where Have All the Flowers Gone* and *Kisses Sweeter than Wine*?

11 Of which country was Norman Kirk prime minister from 1972 to 1974?

12 What is a didgeridoo?

13 Which former presenter of TV's *Hospital Watch* is Britain's longest-serving radio phone-in host?

14 Which 'period' followed Pablo Picasso's Blue period?

15 At which English racecourse is the Grand National Steeplechase run?

Things you didn't know...

Al Capone was killed by syphilis - despite being the first sufferer to be treated with antibiotics.

Answers to page 430

1 American, 2 C or F, 3 Fair Isle, 4 Caves, 5 Cinque Ports, 6 New Zealand, 7 One hundred, 8 Tottenham Hotspur, 9 The Kinks, 10 Bournemouth, 11 Thomas Fairfax, 12 *Shooting Fish*, 13 Janet Jackson, 14 Bakerloo, 15 Bryan Robson.

QUIZ 427

Answers on page 427

1 Which 1975 film musical included the singing talents of Oliver Reed, Jack Nicholson and Tina Turner?

2 Which metallic element has the symbol Cu?

3 Of which state of the USA is Olympia the capital?

4 Who was the twin brother of Artemis?

5 In which film did Kevin Costner play a baseball player?

6 What is the name of the Japanese electronic pet which became popular in 1997?

7 What was the title of the album released by the Bee Gees in 1997?

8 What sort of creature is a grebe?

9 Of which ocean is the Sargasso Sea a section?

10 Which American city was almost totally destroyed by fire in 1871?

11 What is the capital of Denmark?

12 Which acute tropical viral disease transmitted by mosquitoes takes its name from the jaundice it causes?

13 Which singer-songwriter made a *Beautiful Noise* in 1976?

14 Which group sent *Postcards from Heaven* in 1997?

15 Which German nazi leader was abducted by Israeli agents in Argentina in 1960?

Things you didn't know...

When the QE2 set sail for the South Atlantic during the Falklands War she carried on board three million Mars bars.

Answers to page 427

1 Horse, 2 California, 3 Bloodhound, 4 L.S. Lowry, 5 Asquith, 6 Sir Douglas Bader, 7 Turkey, 8 Betty Stove, 9 David Addison, 10 Richard Meade, 11 GBZ, 12 Laura Davies, 13 Vacuum cleaner salesman, 14 English Civil War, 15 Essex.

QUIZ 428

Answers on page 428

1 What nationality was the poet Robert Frost?

2 Which two musical notes have no actual flats?

3 Which of the Shetland Islands gives its name to a style of knitting?

4 Speleology is the study and exploration of which natural phenomena?

5 By what collective name are Sandwich, Dover, Hythe, Romney and Hastings known?

6 In which country was Dame Kiri Te Kanawa born?

7 How many cents are in a US dollar?

8 Which football team's home ground is White Hart Lane?

9 Which popular British band of the 1960s released an album called *To The Bone* in 1997?

10 Which British resort did Thomas Hardy refer to as Sandbourne in Wessex novels?

11 Which English general led the New Model Army to victory over Charles I at Naseby?

12 Which 1997 British film starred Kate Beckinsale and Stuart Townsend?

13 Which member of the Jackson family released the album *The Velvet Rope*?

14 Which tube line runs from Baker St. to Waterloo?

15 Which England midfielder scored after 27 seconds against France in the 1982 football World Cup Finals?

Things you didn't know...

Around 10 per cent of the world's surface is covered with ice.

Answers to page 428

1 Florence Griffith-Joyner, 2 Marathon, 3 All have areas of sea named after them, 4 Kevin Costner, 5 Germany, 6 Mercury, 7 Derek Redmond, 8 Concorde, 9 Caffeine, 10 Pete Seeger, 11 New Zealand, 12 A musical intrument, 13 Robbie Vincent, 14 Rose period, 15 Aintree.

QUIZ 429

Answers on page 433

1 Which golfer has won a fifth successive European Order of Merit title in 1997?

2 What is a sheepshank?

3 Which animals live in a drey?

4 In which month does Hilary term normally begin at Oxford University?

5 Which scale is used to measure the hardness of minerals?

6 How many tentacles does an octopus have?

7 How many grams are in a kilogram?

8 Which comedian and author wrote the autobiography *Moab is My Washpot*?

9 Who killed Achilles by shooting him in the heel with an arrow?

10 In which language did Samuel Beckett originally write *Waiting for Godot*?

11 In the zodiac, which animal is linked with Capricorn?

12 Which author created *Uncle Remus*?

13 Which author created *Samuel Whiskers*?

14 Which British economist wrote the *General Theory of Employment, Interest and Money*?

15 Which Scottish group released an album called *10* in 1997?

Things you didn't know...

Cheetahs were raced at Romford greyhound stadium in 1937.

Answers to page 433

1 A dog, 2 Pharos of Alexandria, 3 Cross of Lorraine, 4 Pisa (Italy), 5 Whitney Houston, 6 Worcestershire, 7 Ian Broudie, 8 *Steel Magnolias,* 9 Jack, 10 Alice Springs, 11 Botswana, 12 Pennyweight, 13 Black taxis, 14 In secret, 15 The Battle of New Orleans.

QUIZ 430

Answers on page 434

1 Which 11-a-side field game starts with a bully-off?

2 What latitude is shared by all points on the equator?

3 Who played the title role in the 1967 film *Cool Hand Luke*?

4 Which East London borough was created in 1965 from the former metropolitan boroughs of Bethnal Green, Stepney, and Poplar?

5 Which British filmmaker directed *Strangers on a Train, Psycho* and *The Birds*?

6 Who are Tinky Winky, Dipsy, Laa Laa and Po?

7 In which country is the port of Casablanca located?

8 Which Saint's feast day falls on 11th November?

9 In botany, what name is given to the process whereby the embryonic plant in a seed starts to produce roots and shoots?

10 For which film did John Wayne win his only Oscar?

11 Which English composer wrote a *Sea Symphony* and a *London Symphony*?

12 How was the French fashion designer Gabrielle Chanel popularly known?

13 Which song took Lena Martell to Number One in 1979?

14 What sort of creature is a ray?

15 Which alkali metal is represented by the symbol Rb?

Things you didn't know...

The phrase 'Hip, hip, hooray' was first used as a battle cry by knights at the Crusades.

Answers to page 434

1 A butterfly, 2 *Brief Encounter,* 3 New Zealand, 4 Michael , 5 *Goodnight Sweetheart,* 6 37 degrees, 7 Suet, 8 Alf Roberts, 9 Electromotive force, 10 Russia, 11 Cambodia, 12 Boxing, 13 Reliant Regal Robin, 14 *Perfect Scoundrels,* 15 Fluorine.

QUIZ 431

Answers on page 431

1 What sort of creature is a setter?

2 Which ancient lighthouse was one of the Seven Wonders of the World?

3 Which symbol originally regarded as Joan of Arc's, did French resistance fighters adopt during the Second World War?

4 Which city is served by Galileo Galilei airport?

5 Whose Top Ten hits include *How Will I Know*, *Greatest Love of All* and *So Emotional*?

6 In which English county is the Wyre Forest?

7 Who is the Lightning Seeds' singer?

8 Which film centred around a beauty parlour and starred Sally Field, Dolly Parton, Daryl Hannah and Julia Roberts?

9 Who is older, Bobby or Jack Charlton?

10 Geographically, which well known town is situated almost in the centre of Australia?

11 Of which African country is Gaborone the capital?

12 Dwt. was an abbreviation for what?

13 Manganese Bronze Holdings are the makers of which famous vehicle?

14 What does 'sub rosa' mean?

15 Which battle was the title of a UK hit record by Lonnie Donegan in 1959?

Things you didn't know...

Human beings shed and replace their outer layer of skin every 28 days.

Answers to page 431

1 Colin Montgomerie, 2 A knot, 3 Squirrels, 4 January, 5 Mohs' scale, 6 Eight, 7 One thousand, 8 Stephen Fry, 9 Paris, 10 French, 11 Goat, 12 Joel Chandler Harris, 13 Beatrix Potter, 14 John Maynard Keynes, 15 Wet Wet Wet.

QUIZ 432

Answers on page 432

1 What sort of creature is a swallowtail?

2 Which film involves a long meeting between Laura Jesson and Dr. Alec Harvey?

3 To which country does the coral island of Niue belong?

4 Jackie, Tito, Jermaine and Marlon were all members of The Jacksons. Who is missing?

5 What is the title of the 1990s comedy in which Nicholas Lyndhurst travels back in time to the Second World War?

6 To the nearest whole number, how many degrees Centigrade should a human's blood temperature be?

7 What is the hard waxy fat around the kidneys and loins of cattle and sheep called?

8 Which *Coronation Street* character died at a New Year's Eve party in 1998?

9 What do the initials emf stand for?

10 Which country is Aeroflot from?

11 Phnom penh is capital of which country?

12 With which sport was Henry Cooper associated?

13 Which type of car do you most associate with Derek Trotter in *Only Fools and Horses*?

14 Which comedy series set in Ireland starred Peter Bowles & Bryan Murray?

15 Which halogen gas is represented by the symbol F?

Things you didn't know...

London's Science Museum is built over a maze designed by Prince Albert.

Answers to page 432

1 Hockey, 2 O degrees, 3 Paul Newman, 4 Tower Hamlets, 5 Alfred Hitchcock, 6 *Teletubbies*, 7 Morocco, 8 St. Martin, 9 Germination, 10 *True Grit*, 11 Ralph Vaughan Williams, 12 Coco Chanel, 13 *One Day at a Time*, 14 A fish, 15 Rubidium.

QUIZ 433

Answers on page 437

1 Which US novelist wrote *One Flew Over the Cuckoo's Nest*?

2 At which city in NW France is a famous 24-hour motor race held annually?

3 Which South African actor played Inspector Barlow in *Z Cars*?

4 Which fashion designer created the Space Age Collection in 1964?

5 In which American city was JF Kennedy assassinated in?

6 Gynophobia is the fear of who or what?

7 Which film first featured the song *White Christmas*?

8 Which animal represents the constellation Capricornus?

9 Which former middle-distance runner was appointed chief executive of the British Athletic Federation in 1997?

10 Who had a Number One hit single in 1979 with *I Don't like Mondays*?

11 Who had a Number One hit single in 1985 with *Into the Groove*?

12 Which *Dynasty* actress starred in the film *The Bitch*?

13 What sort of creature is a basilisk?

14 Which New Zealand prime minister, first elected in 1984, refused to allow nuclear armed ships to dock in New Zealand?

15 Who directed the 1981 film *An American Werewolf in London*?

Things you didn't know...

Harrods' water is supplied from its three private wells.

Answers to page 437

1 Diana, 2 Robert Shaw, 3 Greg Rusedski, 4 Clef, 5 David Bowie, 6 Bill Maynard, 7 Heather Small, 8 Opera, 9 Leo Tolstoy, 10 Jennifer Ehle, 11 Nitrogen, 12 Romans, 13 *The Jewel in the Crown*, 14 *The Scarlet Pimpernel*, 15 Michael Schumacher.

QUIZ 434

Answers on page 438

1 Which country plays some of its home cricket test matches at the Kensington Oval?

2 In which European country can the majority of Basque people be found?

3 In which fictional village is *Noel's House Party* set?

4 Which king of the Huns was known as the Scourge of God?

5 Which group had a Number One hit in 1960 with *Shakin 'All Over*?

6 Phobos and Deimos are moons of which planet?

7 What was first built by Henry Winstanley in 1698 and has been rebuilt three times since, having been successively destroyed by storm, fire and erosion?

8 What is used to cover the lean parts of meat in the method of cooking known as 'barding'?

9 George I was the first British monarch of which Royal House?

10 Who was England's manager for the 1990 World Cup in Italy?

11 Which Italian composer wrote the opera *Lucia di Lammermoor*?

12 What sort of bird is a picus viridis?

13 What was Larry Grayson's catchphrase?

14 If two equals ten, four equals a hundred, and eight equals a thousand, what does five equal?

15 Which nocturnal bird of prey has barn, snowy and tawny varieties?

Things you didn't know...

Only one in five babies is born on the day predicted by doctors.

Answers to page 438

1 Gabriel Faure, **2** Neil Armstrong, **3** Seaweed, **4** The Mayflower, **5** Jack Dempsey, **6** Illinois, **7** Oslo, **8** Boris Becker, **9** Geoff Hurst, **10** Armenia, **11** Farne Islands, **12** California, **13** The heart, **14** Menai Strait, **15** An elephant.

QUIZ 435

Answers on page 435

1 Which of the Mitford sisters married the British Fascist leader Sir Oswald Mosley?

2 Which actor was stung in the film *The Sting*?

3 Which British tennis player beat Michael Chang and Andre Agassi to reach the final of the 1997 Sybase Open?

4 What is the French word for 'key' and the name for a symbol used in music notation?

5 Which pop legend released the single *Seven Years In Tibet*?

6 Which TV actor starred in *Heartbeat*, *The Gaffer* and *Oh No, It's Selwyn Froggitt*?

7 Who is the lead singer of M People?

8 What art form is the Glyndebourne Festival famous for?

9 Which Russian author wrote *War and Peace*?

10 Which star of the adaptation of *Pride and Prejudice* played Constance in the film *Wilde*?

11 Which common gas was once called azote?

12 Which is the first epistle in the New Testament?

13 Which book is missing from this sequence: *The Day of the Scorpion*, *The Towers of Silence* and *A Division of the Spoils*?

14 Which novel by Baroness Orczy is about an English nobleman who smuggles aristocrats out of France?

15 Which racing driver went out of the 1997 European Grand prix after driving into Jacques Villeneuve?

Things you didn't know...

Thomas Edison constructed the world's first electric typewriter.

Answers to page 435

1 Ken Kesey, 2 Le Mans, 3 Stratford Johns, 4 Pierre Cardin, 5 *Dallas*, 6 Women, 7 Holiday Inn, 8 The goat, 9 David Moorcroft, 10 Boomtown Rats, 11 Madonna, 12 Joan Collins, 13 A lizard, 14 David Lange, 15 John Landis.

QUIZ 436

Answers on page 436

1 Which French composer and pupil of Sain-Saens is best known for his requiem?

2 Who was the first man to walk on the moon?

3 What are kelp and wrack examples of?

4 What was the name of the ship in which the Pilgrim Fathers sailed from England to New Plymouth, Massachusetts in 1620?

5 Who lost his world heavyweight boxing title to Gene Tunney in 1926?

6 In which US state is the city of Chicago situated?

7 Which city is served by Fornebu airport?

8 Who won the men's final at the 1996 Australian Open tennis tournament?

9 Who is the only footballer to have scored a hat-trick in the World Cup Final?

10 Of which former Soviet republic is Yerevan the capital?

11 Which rocky island group off Northumberland is associated with St Cuthbert and Grace Darling?

12 Which US state includes the cities of San Francisco and Los Angeles?

13 Which organ of the body contains a tricuspid valve?

14 Which channel separates the island of Anglesey from the mainland of NW Wales?

15 What sort of creature was the star of the film *Larger Than Life*?

Things you didn't know...

Bombay has more video libraries than any other city in the world – around 15,000 at the last count.

Answers to page 436

1 West Indies, 2 Spain, 3 Crinkley Bottom, 4 Attila, 5 Johnny Kidd and the Pirates, 6 Mars, 7 Eddystone Lighthouse, 8 Bacon, 9 Hanover, 10 Bobby Robson, 11 Gaetano Donisetti, 12 Woodpecker, 13 Shut That Door, 14 101, 15 Owl.

QUIZ 437

Answers on page 441

1 What sort of creature is a Hungarian puli?

2 Who directed the films *Tootsie* and *Out of Africa*?

3 On which great river does the German city of Cologne stand?

4 Which innovation was first introduced in Britain in 1932 with the slogan 'The Gift is Mine, The Choice is Thine?

5 Which actor starred in the sitcoms *It Ain't Half Hot Mum* and *Never the Twain*?

6 In the Old Testament, who were the parents of Cain?

7 Which slang term for a person from a particular British city is derived from the name of a meat stew popular in the area?

8 Which liqueur is said to be made to Bonnie Prince Charlie's secret recipe, left behind when he fled to Skye?

9 Which prison formerly stood on the present site of the Old Bailey?

10 Of which ocean is the White Sea a gulf?

11 In which war did the Battle of Sedan take place?

12 Who headed the committee investigating 'sleaze' in public life in 1995?

13 Which Oscar-winning actor starred in the TV series *Smiley's People* and *Tinker, Tailor, Soldier, Spy*?

14 From which country does the dish chilli con carne originate?

15 Who co-starred as Count Vronsky in the 1997 film version of Tolstoy's *Anna Karenina*?

Things you didn't know...

Baby whales can grow at the rate of 10lb per hour.

Answers to page 441

1 American football, **2** Sidney Poitier, **3** Albert, **4** Beaver, **5** Thomas Hardy, **6** Gilbert and Sullivan, **7** London Borough of Brent, **8** Puissance, **9** Rice, **10** Tony Hatch, **11** Saudi Arabia, **12** Pangolin, **13** Shane Richie, **14** Cadmium, **15** Mali.

QUIZ 438

Answers on page 442

1 How many legs do insects have?

2 Which actor has played the parts of Charles I, Disraeli, Hitler, the Pope, a Suffragette and a Jedi?

3 Which female singer/songwriter released an album called *Nine Objects Of Desire*?

4 Papillon is the French word for what?

5 Of which country is Port Moresby the capital?

6 Schnauzer is a breed of which animal?

7 Of which African country is Nouakchott the capital?

8 What was the title of the last album released by the Australian rock band INXS before the death of their lead singer Michael Hutchence?

9 What is the capital of Cuba?

10 Which British explorer was first to bring back the potato and tobacco plant from America?

11 Which US prosecutor led the probe into Bill Clinton's fling with Monica?

12 Which actress had five husbands including Orson Welles, Prince Aly Khan, the singer Dick Haymes and the producer James Hill?

13 Which English novelist wrote *The Rachel Papers* and *Money*?

14 Who wrote the best-selling books *Fever Pitch* and *High Fidelity*?

15 Which system of taxation is represented by the initials PAYE?

Things you didn't know...

The first book on plastic surgery was written in 1597.

Answers to page 442

1 Elkie Brooks, 2 Isle of Man, 3 Pastern, 4 Orienteering, 5 George III, 6 0, 7 France, Morocco and Spain, 8 Marsupials, 9 *Gandhi*, 10 Magnum, 11 Bonaparte, 12 Solder, 13 Michigan, 14 Margaret Thatcher, 15 Sir Lancelot.

QUIZ 439

Answers on page 439

1 In which sport are the officials called zebras?

2 In the 1967 film *Guess Who's Coming to Dinner*, which actor did 'come to dinner'?

3 What is the name of Prince Rainier of Monaco's son?

4 Which large aquatic rodent builds lodges and dams?

5 Which British novelist and poet wrote *Jude the Obscure*?

6 Which partnership produced operattas such as *The Mikado* and *The Pirates of Penzance*?

7 In which London borough is Wembley Stadium?

8 What is the correct name for the high jump event in showjumping?

9 Which staple foodstuff is the main ingredient of the Japanese drink saké?

10 Who wrote the theme music to *Neighbours*?

11 In which Middle East country is the city of Riyadh situated?

12 Which armoured mammal is also known as the scaly anteater?

13 Who was the host of TV's *Lucky Numbers*?

14 Which metal is represented by the symbol Cd?

15 Of which African country is Bamako the capital?

Things you didn't know...

Author Raymond Chandler's wife Cissy did the housework in the nude.

Answers to page 439

1 A sheepdog, 2 Sydney Pollack, 3 Rhine, 4 Book Tokens, 5 Windsor Davies, 6 Adam and Eve, 7 Scouse, 8 Drambuie, 9 Newgate, 10 Arctic, 11 Franco-Prussian War, 12 Lord Nolan, 13 Sir Alec Guinness, 14 USA, 15 Sean Bean.

QUIZ 440

Answers on page 440

1 Who had a Top Ten hit single in 1977 with *Pearl's A Singer*?

2 On which island would you find the Laxey Wheel?

3 What part of a horse's leg extends from the fetlock to the hoof?

4 In which navigational sport do competitors run round a series of control points using a map and compass?

5 Who was king of Great Britain and Ireland when the American colonies were lost?

6 Which is the only number that cannot be represented by Roman numberals?

7 Name the three countries which have both a Mediterranean and an Atlantic coastline?

8 Which name is applied to the order of mammals which includes bandicoots, kangaroos, koalas and wombats?

9 Which 1982 film included a scene involving over 250,000 extras?

10 What name is given to a wine bottle that holds the equivalent of two normal bottles?

11 What was the surname of the French emperor Napoleon I?

12 Which alloy is melted to form a joint between other metals?

13 Of which U.S.state is Lansing the capital?

14 Which British prime minister began privatising nationalised industries in the 1980s?

15 In Arthurian legend, who was Sir Galahad's father?

Things you didn't know...

You can have your car blessed by a Buddhist monk in Tokyo.

Answers to page 440

1 Six, **2** Alec Guinness, **3** Suzanne Vega, **4** Butterfly, **5** Papua New Guinea, **6** Dog, **7** Mauritania, **8** *Elegantly Wasted*, **9** Havana, **10** Sir Walter Raleigh, **11** Kenneth Starr, **12** Rita Hayworth, **13** Martin Amis, **14** Nick Hornby, **15** Pay As You Earn.

QUIZ 441

Answers on page 445

1 Which actor starred in the title role of the sitcom *Chance In a Million*?

2 Which heavy metal has the chemical symbol Mo?

3 Of which sea is the Gulf of Finland an arm?

4 Which British city developed out of the Roman fort of mancunium?

5 Which butterfly gets its name from the large purple eyespots on its wings?

6 What nationality is the playwright Athol Fugard?

7 How is deoxyribonucleic acid commonly known?

8 Which 1997 film starred Pierce Brosnan as a volcanologist?

9 To which genus of plants do azaleas belong?

10 Which American popular novelist died in October 1997 at the age of 81?

11 Which carbohydrate is also known as milk sugar?

12 In which country are the Catskill Mountains found?

13 Whose ear did Mike Tyson bite in a 1997 boxing match?

14 Who won the 1997 Formula One world drivers' championship?

15 In which country did the dish 'chop-suey' originate?

Things you didn't know...

A Chinese priest let his fingernails grow for 27 years.

Answers to page 445

1 A musical instrument, 2 *Thief Takers,* 3 The Queen Elizabeth, 4 Boris Godunov, 5 A deer, 6 Comets, 7 Tangent, 8 Chess, 9 Ralph Fiennes, 10 Giraffes, 11 Georges Bizet, 12 *Going Straight,* 13 Charles II, 14 The Mediterranean Sea, 15 Leviticus.

QUIZ 442

Answers on page 446

1 A skulk is a collective noun describing a group of which carnivorous animals found in Britain?

2 Which great Italian tenor died in 1957?

3 What is the technical name for abnormally high blood pressure?

4 Who wrote the book on which the 1970 film *The Godfather* was based?

5 On how many properties can you build houses or hotels in a game of Monopoly?

6 Of which country is Harare the capital?

7 By what name was the Russian city of St Petersburg known from 1924 to 1991?

8 By what name is deuterium oxide commonly known?

9 In what year were the first Olympics held in Britain?

10 What impressions may be made up of loops, whorls and arches?

11 A giant figure of Christ is one of the landmarks of which former capital of Brazil?

12 How many players are on the court at one time in a basketball game?

13 Which king of England was the eldest son of John of Gaunt?

14 In which English county is the country house Dorneywood?

15 What name is given to the cleansing of fabrics and garments using solvents other than water?

Things you didn't know...

Pigeons in Venice were fed grain mixed with contraceptives to stop them breeding.

Answers to page 446

1 Pisa, 2 Rubens, 3 Marmite, 4 Mont Blanc, 5 *Boogie Nights,* 6 Keith Chegwin, 7 Suva, 8 Peru, 9 The Luftwaffe, 10 Alan Turner, 11 River Cher, 12 US Navy SEALS, 13 Steve McQueen, 14 Picabo Street, 15 Edinburgh.

QUIZ 443

Answers on page 443

1 What is a mandolin?

2 Which ITV drama series about the Flying Squad returned for a third series in 1997?

3 Destroyed by fire in 1972, by what name was the Seawise University known when it was built in 1938?

4 Which Russian tsar was the subject of a play by Pushkin, on which Mussorgsky based an opera?

5 What sort of creature is a wapiti?

6 Kohoutek, Tempel-Tuttle and Halley's are all what?

7 What is the name for a straight line that touches a curve at only one point?

8 Which game originated in India under the name Caturanga?

9 Which *Schindler's List* star played a hideously scarred man in *The English Patient*?

10 To which family of animals does the okapi belong?

11 Which French composer wrote the opera *Carmen*?

12 What was the title of the sequel to BBC's *Porridge*, in which Fletcher got out of jail?

13 Which king of England, Scotland and Ireland had Nell Gwyn as his mistress?

14 In which sea can the Strait of Messina be found?

15 What is the third book of the Old Testament?

Things you didn't know...

Earl Christopherson of Seattle patented a device to enable people to look inside their own ears.

Answers to page 443

1 Simon Callow, 2 Molybdenum, 3 The Baltic Sea, 4 Manchester, 5 Peacock butterfly, 6 South African, 7 DNA, 8 *Dante's Peak*, 9 Rhododendron, 10 Harold Robbins, 11 Lactose, 12 USA, 13 Evander Holyfield, 14 Jacques Villeneuve, 15 USA.

QUIZ 444

Answers on page 444

1 Which Italian city is famous for its Leaning Tower?

2 Whose Antwerp house now contains some of El Greco's finest paintings?

3 Which tangy spread is named after a French earthenware cooking pot?

4 What is the highest mountain in Italy?

5 Which 1998 film saw Burt Reynolds' return to the big screen as Jack Horner, a pimp and pornographer?

6 Who presented the TV series *Cheggars Plays Pop*?

7 What is the capital of Fiji?

8 In which country could you visit the ruins of the Inca civilisation?

9 What is the German air force called?

10 What part does Richard Thorpe play in *Emmerdale*?

11 On which French river does the magnificent chateau of Chenonceaux, stand?

12 What is the elite force that Demi Moore's character strives to join in the film *GI Jane*?

13 Which American actor starred in the films *Bullitt, Papillon* and *The Great Escape*?

14 Which female skier became the first American to win the downhill at the Alpine World Championships in 1996?

15 In which British city would you find Salisbury Crags?

Things you didn't know...

Eric Sykes was once sacked from his job for singing Bing Crosby's 'In the Blue of the Night' with a bucket on his head.

Answers to page 444

1 Foxes, **2** Beniamino Gigli, **3** Hypertension, **4** Mario Puzo, **5** 22, **6** Zimbabwe, **7** Leningrad, **8** Heavy water, **9** 1908, **10** Cuckoo, **11** Rio de Janeiro, **12** Ten, **13** Henry IV, **14** Buckinghamshire, **15** Dry cleaning.

QUIZ 445

Answers on page 449

1 Which band of light crossing the night sky is composed of innumerable stars that are too faint to be seen individually?

2 Which butterfly has the same name as a bird?

3 Whitehorse is the capital of which Canadian province?

4 Which Dublin-born painter is famous for his *Study after Velazquez*?

5 Which aromatic plant used as a seasoning is also known as origanum?

6 Which successful plot of 1820 was led by Arthur Thistlewood?

7 What was a pennyfarthing?

8 What was the name of the shortsighted character whose voice was supplied by Jim Backus?

9 Which planet was discovered by Clyde Tombaugh in 1930?

10 What is the Sunday before Easter called?

11 Who was the longest serving prime minister in the twentieth century?

12 Who donated £50,000,000 to the National Gallery in 1985?

13 In which year of the 1980's was Rainbow Warrior blown up in Auckland harbour?

14 Which British novelist wrote *Bleak House*?

15 Water, Pygmy and Common are all types of which animal living in Britain?

Things you didn't know...

Lord Byron kept a pet bear at Cambridge University.

Answers to page 449

1 A horse, 2 *Stake Out*, 3 *I'll Be There*, 4 *Jerry Maguire*, 5 European Free Trade Association, 6 Jacques Villeneuve, 7 Nebraska, 8 John Wayne, 9 Manaus, 10 Portugal, 11 Gwen Taylor, 12 Ewan McGregor, 13 A bird, 14 Tudor House, 15 *The Wizard of Oz*.

QUIZ 446

Answers on page 450

1 Who, in the 1980s, became the first cricketer since W.G. Grace to have his portrait commissioned by the National Portrait Gallery?

2 Who was Britain's prime minister from 1905 to 1908?

3 With whom did Diana Ross have a 1974 Top Ten UK hit called *You are Everything*?

4 From which plant does the drug digitalis come?

5 Who played Andy Warhol in the film *Basquiat*?

6 What was the name of Marmalade's only Number One hit in the UK?

7 In the Old Testament, who was the father of Rehoboam?

8 What is the capital of Mongolia?

9 What sort of creature is a red mullet?

10 By what term is the clothing business better known?

11 Which vegetable has varieties called 'Regal Minerve' and 'Connover's Colossal'?

12 Which country does Pavarotti come from?

13 Who was Home Secretary in the Heath government from 1970 but resigned in 1972?

14 In which sea is the Isle of Man situated?

15 Which book of the Old Testament is also known as the Psalter?

Things you didn't know...

Richie Valens suffered from aerophobia.
He died in a plane crash.

Answers to page 450

1 Oxford and Cambridge, 2 Le Ann Rimes, 3 Swarm, 4 Jarrow, 5 Radius, 6 Larry Grayson, 7 *Twelfth Night*, 8 Nemesis, 9 Prince Philip, Duke of Edinburgh, 10 John Milton, 11 A rope, 12 Binary digit, 13 0, 14 Bill Gates, 15 Cedar.

QUIZ 447

Answers on page 447

1 What sort of creature is a pinto?

2 Which film co-starred Richard Dreyfuss and Emilio Estevez as a pair of Seattle cops?

3 Which song provided Top Ten hits for The Jacksons and Mariah Carey?

4 Which 1997 film starred Tom Cruise as a top sports agent?

5 What does the acronym EFTA stand for?

6 Which Formula One driver won the 1997 Brazilian Grand Prix?

7 Of which state of the USA is Lincoln the capital?

8 Which US film actor starred in the classic westerns *Red River, and Rio Bravo*?

9 Which large city stands on the Rio Negro and is the Amazon's state capital?

10 Of which country is the Algarve the most southerly province?

11 Which *Duty Free* star played a Deputy Mayor in TV's *A Perfect State*?

12 Which *Trainspotting* star made a guest appearance on the medical drama show *ER*?

13 What sort of creature is a gallinule?

14 In the game of Cluedo in which house do all the events happen?

15 Which classic film starring Judy Garland was based on a novel by L Frank Baum?

Things you didn't know...

*'Sharon' is Elton John's nickname from Rod Stewart.
Elton calls Rod 'Phyllis'.*

Answers to page 447

1 The Milky Way, 2 Cardinal or peacock, but not the swallowtail, 3 Yukon, 4 Francis Bacon, 5 Marjoram, 6 The Cato Street Conspiracy, 7 A bicycle, 8 *Mr. Magoo,* 9 Pluto, 10 Palm Sunday, 11 Margaret Thatcher, 12 J. Paul Getty Jr., 13 1985, 14 Charles Dickens, 15 Shrew.

QUIZ 448

Answers on page 448

1 Which British universities compete in an annual Boat Race on the River Thames?

2 Which 14-year-old country singer won two awards at the 1997 Grammy awards ceremony in New York?

3 Which word should be used to describe a group of bees, flies or locusts?

4 Which town in Tyne and Wear is associated with the Venerable Bede and Hunger Marches?

5 What is a straight line from the centre of a circle to the circumference called?

6 Who presented the TV show *Sweethearts* in 1987?

7 Which play starts with the line 'If music be the food of love, play on'?

8 In Greek mythology, who was the goddess of divine retribution?

9 Who was made a Field Marshal, a Marshal of the Royal Air Force and an Admiral of the Fleet on January 15th 1953?

10 Which English poet wrote *Paradise Lost* and *Regained*?

11 To a sailor especially, what is a hawser?

12 In computing, of what is 'bit' an abbreviation?

13 What is four cubed minus eight squared?

14 Who is the co-founder and chief executive of Microsoft?

15 What is the national tree of Lebanon?

Things you didn't know...

George V kept all the clocks at Sandringham thirty minutes fast so that he would never be late for an appointment.

Answers to page 448

1 Ian Botham, **2** Sir Henry Campbell-Bannerman, **3** Marvin Gaye, **4** Foxglove, **5** David Bowie, **6** *OB-LA-DI-OB-LA-DA*, **7** Solomon, **8** Ulan Bator, **9** A fish, **10** The rag trade, **11** Asparagus, **12** Italy, **13** Reginald Maudling, **14** The Irish Sea, **15** Psalms.

QUIZ 449

Answers on page 453

1 What is the body's largest artery?

2 Which 1971 film directed by Stanley Kubrick was based on a novel by Anthony Burgess?

3 To what sort of animal does the adjective ovine relate?

4 Which architect designed the Guggenheim Museum in New York?

5 Which fish can be alevins, parr, smolts and grilse at various stages in their life cycle?

6 What was the title of the 1997 album from the Rolling Stones?

7 What name is given to the great epidemic of plague that ravaged medieval Europe?

8 In which children's programme did the Why Bird appear?

9 Which single word connects the US State Department, Noel Edmonds and a Shakespearian weaver?

10 What is the capital of the Republic of Congo?

11 Which English Benedictine monk and missionary is known as the Apostle of Germany?

12 Grandfather, cuckoo and carriage are types of what?

13 Which Irish singer's largely retrospective album *Paint the Sky* featured her memorable hit *Orinoco Flow*?

14 What bottle size is equivalent to twenty standard bottles?

15 In which English county is the town of Watford situated?

Things you didn't know...

Bruce Willis stammered as a child.

Answers to page 453

1 California, 2 Three, 3 Poseidon, 4 The Czech Republic, 5 Uma Thurman, 6 Canals, 7 Michael Douglas, 8 Loch Ness, 9 Challenger, 10 14, 11 Madrid, 12 Meerkat, 13 Piano, 14 *It's Not Unusual,* 15 Beagle.

QUIZ 450

Answers on page 454

1 Which city providing the setting for Kay Mellor's TV drama *Band of Gold*?

2 Which country does Gorgonzola cheese come from?

3 Who found Lucy Locket's pocket?

4 Which artist painted *Harvest in Provence*, which was sold at Sotheby's for £8.8 million in 1997?

5 What was Capability Brown's first name?

6 Who has presented *Give Us a Clue* and *Child's Play*?

7 Which form of carbon is most likely to be found in a lead pencil?

8 Which star of TV's *The Brothers* was the sixth Doctor in *Dr Who*?

9 From which country does Capodimonte porcelain come?

10 Who was the first musical performer to have five Top Ten singles from one album?

11 How many of the planets in the solar system are bigger than Earth?

12 What is added to whisky to make a Whisky Mac?

13 Which letter of the Greek alphabet is the equivalent to 'O'?

14 Which composer did Dirk Bogarde play in *Song Without End*?

15 What is the unit of currency in Denmark?

Things you didn't know...

Charles VI of France was so mad he was convinced he was made of glass.

Answers to page 454

1 Piccadilly, 2 Sir Frank Whittle, 3 General Custer, 4 St Nicholas, 5 *The Dukes of Hazzard,* 6 Gromyko, 7 Lac Leman, 8 Julienne, 9 River Medway, 10 Charlatans, 11 Irene, 12 Maud Grimes, 13 Atlantic Ocean, 14 *Space Jam*, 15 Betamax.

QUIZ 451

Answers on page 451

1 Through which state of the USA does the San Andreas Fault run?

2 How many level teaspoons would it take to fill a level tablespoon?

3 In Greek mythology, who was the chief god of the sea, identified with the Roman Neptune?

4 Of which country is Prague the capital?

5 Who plays Poison Ivy in the film *Batman and Robin*?

6 What did the Italian astronomer Giovanni Schiaparelli call the strange markings he observed on the planet Mars?

7 Who starred as the unfaithful New York attorney in the 1987 film *Fatal Attraction*?

8 At which Scottish loch has a monster been frequently reported?

9 What was the name of the U.S. Space Shuttle which crashed during take-off in 1986?

10 How many pictures make up the Stations of the Cross?

11 What is the capital of Spain?

12 Which South African mammal is also called a suricate?

13 What instrument did Liberace play?

14 What was the title of Tom Jones' Number One debut single which entered the chart in 1965?

15 What breed of dog is Snoopy?

Things you didn't know...

The wolf became extinct in England in the early 16th century but survived in Scotland until 1743 and Ireland until around 1770.

Answers to page 451

1 The aorta, 2 *A Clockwork Orange,* 3 Sheep, 4 Frank Lloyd Wright, 5 Salmon, 6 *Bridges to Babylon,* 7 The Black Death, 8 *Playdays,* 9 Bottom (Foggy Bottom, Crinkley Bottom and *Bottom*), 10 Brazzaville, 11 St Boniface, 12 Clock, 13 Enya's, 14 Nebuchadnezzar, 15 Hertfordshire.

QUIZ 452

Answers on page 452

1 On which London thoroughfare is Fortnum and Masons?

2 Who designed and flew the first British jet aircraft?

3 Which American general's 'last stand' was at the Battle of Little Bighorn?

4 Who is the patron saint of children?

5 In which TV series did Sorrell Booke play Boss Hogg?

6 Who was Russian Foreign Minister from 1957 to 1985?

7 What do the French call Lake Geneva?

8 What culinary word describes vegetables cut into very thin pieces?

9 Which river passes through Tonbridge, Maidstone, Rochester, Chatham and Gillingham?

10 Who had a 1996 Top Ten hit with *One to Another*?

11 What is the Greek equivalent of the Roman deity Pax?

12 Who was Reg Holdsworth's mother-in-law in *Coronation Street*?

13 Of which ocean is the Bay of Fundy an inlet?

14 Which 1997 film starred Bill Murray, basketball player Michael Jordan and Bugs Bunny?

15 Which video-cassette system, introduced in the 1970s, couldn't compete with VHS and disappeared?

Things you didn't know...

The American black widow spider is 15 times more venomous than a rattlesnake.

Answers to page 452

1 Bradford, 2 Italy, 3 Kitty Fisher, 4 Vincent Van Gogh, 5 Lancelot, 6 Michael Aspel, 7 Graphite, 8 Colin Baker, 9 Italy, 10 Michael Jackson (from the album *Thriller*), 11 Four (Jupiter, Saturn, Uranus and Neptune), 12 Ginger wine, 13 Omega, 14 Liszt, 15 Krone.

QUIZ 453

Answers on page 457

1 What name is given to an athletics event such as running or hurdling?

2 What is the clown in *The Simpsons* called?

3 The Chinese call it the Huang Ho. What do we call it?

4 Which member of the Royal Family was formerly called Lady Elizabeth Bowes-Lyon?

5 Which seaside resort is famous for its Tower and its Golden Mile?

6 Which pop group derived their name from a John Wayne film of the same name?

7 Who wrote the novels *A Passage to India* and *A Room with a View*?

8 To which modern mammal is the mammoth related?

9 What is a more common name for a marmot?

10 Which town in Northern Belgium is famous for its lace making?

11 How many degrees are there in a semi-circle?

12 Ellen Douglas is the heroine of which Sir Walter Scott poem?

13 Which US vice president killed his political rival Alexander Hamilton in a duel?

14 Of which metal is malachite an ore?

15 Which kingdom was ruled by Herod the Great?

Things you didn't know...

A cod can produce eight million eggs at a time.

Answers to page 457

1 W.C.Fields, 2 Sir Richard Steele, 3 Kama, 4 James Woods, 5 Alfred, 6 Biff Fowler, 7 Salmonella, 8 26 days, 9 Blue Whale, 10 The West Country, 11 Roy, 12 Norman Beaton, 13 Bradford City, 14 Beryl Reid, 15 John Cleese.

QUIZ 454

Answers on page 458

1 What was the name of the ship that carried the Pilgrim Fathers to America?

2 Which is the only one of the Great Lakes completely within the US?

3 To what is hay fever an allergic reaction?

4 By what name was the British pirate Edward Teach known?

5 What colour is the natural dye cochineal?

6 Which is the largest city in Africa?

7 On which mountain did Moses receive the Ten Commandments?

8 What name is shared by ranges of mountains in Scotland and Australia?

9 Which female vocalist had a Top Ten hit single in 1981 with *Kids in America*?

10 What is the capital of the Swiss canton of Valais?

11 Which city is served by Hanedi airport?

12 Postage stamps from Switzerland bear the inscription 'Helvetia'. In which language does Helvetia mean Switzerland?

13 Which was the first country to place a man-made object on the surface of the moon?

14 Which letter of the Greek alphabet is the equivalent to 'Z'?

15 What name is given to a device for finding the direction of magnetic north?

Things you didn't know...

The Chinese Crested Dog is completely hairless.

Answers to page 458

1 Three, 2 Cairo, 3 Leicestershire, 4 Tanzania, 5 Tim Henman, 6 Tirol, 7 Mohandas, 8 Brigadier, 9 Scorpio, 10 Over 20mm, 11 General Galtieri, 12 John and Edward I, 13 Buckingham Palace, 14 George Formby, 15 James Agee.

QUIZ 455

Answers on page 455

1 By what name was comic actor William Claude Dukenfield better known?

2 Which essayist and dramatist , founder of The Tatler and The Spectator, wrote the play *The Funeral*?

3 Who is the god of love in Hindu mythology?

4 Which actor was the voice of Hades in Disney's *Hercules*?

5 Which of the Harmsworth brothers became the first Viscount Northcliffe?

6 Which *Emmerdale* character married Linda Glover?

7 Which bacteria can cause typhoid fever and food poisoning?

8 How many days is the Tour De France scheduled to last?

9 What is the world's largest living mammal?

10 Which part of Britain, because of local pronunciation, is some times called Zedland?

11 What is John Major's middle name?

12 Which actor played the title role in *Desmond's*?

13 Which football league side plays home matches at Valley Parade?

14 Which actress called her autobiography *So Much Love*?

15 Which *Monty Python* star played *Robin Hood* in the 1981 film *Time Bandits*?

Things you didn't know...

Blue Peter pet, Petra the mongrel puppy, died two days after being introduced. A replacement was found and the viewers were never told.

Answers to page 455

1 Track, 2 Krusty, 3 Yellow River, 4 The Queen Mother, 5 Blackpool, 6 The Searchers, 7 E M Forster, 8 Elephant, 9 Groundhog, 10 Mechelen, 11 180, 12 *Lady of the Lake*, 13 Aaron Burr, 14 Copper, 15 Judaea.

QUIZ 456

Answers on page 456

1 In the Bible how many people were thrown into the fiery furnace?

2 Apart from Khartoum, which other capital stands on the river Nile?

3 In which English county is the market town of Melton Mowbray?

4 Of which African country is Dodoma the capital?

5 Which British tennis player knocked number five seed Yevgeni Kafelnikov out of the Wimbledon Championships in 1996?

6 Of which Austrian province is Innsbruck the capital?

7 What was Mahatma Gandhi's first name?

8 What rank is above a Colonel in the Army?

9 Which zodiac sign is between Libra and Sagittarius?

10 What calibre should a firearm be to be classed as artillery?

11 Who was the president of Argentina when they invaded the Falkland Islands?

12 Which English Monarchs preceded and succeeded Henry III?

13 For which London building was the Marble Arch originally designed as a gateway?

14 Which famous English comedy star was born blind but gained his sight after a fit of coughing?

15 Which American author wrote the Pulitzer Prize-winner *A Death in the Family*?

Things you didn't know...

Mediaeval monks used to call the toilet the necessarium.

Answers to page 456

1 The Mayflower, 2 Michigan, 3 Pollen, 4 Blackbeard, 5 Red, 6 Cairo, 7 Mount Sinai, 8 Grampians, 9 Kim Wilde, 10 Sion, 11 Tokyo, 12 Latin, 13 USSR, 14 Zeta, 15 Compass.

QUIZ 457

Answers on page 461

1 What is the currency of Argentina?

2 Which word should be used to describe a group of monkeys or kangaroos?

3 Which animal gives us nutria fur?

4 Where are Mary Queen of Scots and Queen Elizabeth I both buried?

5 In which country do the Walloons live?

6 Who invented the Kodak camera?

7 In which English county can the Forest of Dean be found?

8 Which group comprises Gaz Coombes, Mickey Quinn and Danny Goffey?

9 Which British writer created the character *Noddy* in 1949?

10 Who wrote *Dr Zhivago*?

11 What is the capital of Brazil?

12 Which sport is believed to have originated on Pentecost Island as an initiation ceremony?

13 What sort of creature is a yellowhammer?

14 The island of Sicily is at the toe of which country?

15 Which US golfer won the 1997 British Open?

Things you didn't know...

*The Honourable Company of Edinburgh Golfers,
founded in 1744, is the world's oldest golf club*

Answers to page 461

1 John Spencer, 2 Wild mustard, 3 Julie Christie, 4 Cassius Clay, 5 QANTAS, 6 Lee Westwood, 7 Morocco and Swaziland, 8 Weightlifting, 9 Foula, 10 Green, 11 Bertrand Russell, 12 Melbourne, 13 Crete, 14 Tom Cruise, 15 Tokyo.

QUIZ 458

Answers on page 462

1 Who wrote Mrs Dalloway and To the Lighthouse?

2 How many times did Scarlett O'Hara marry in Margaret Mitchell's novel *Gone With the Wind*?

3 In which US city is the famous Times Square?

4 How old was Eddie Cochrane when he was killed in a car crash?

5 In which village was the Royal Airforce College founded?

6 Which king led the Huns from 445 to 450 AD?

7 What were the names of the characters that John Thaw and Dennis Waterman played in *The Sweeney*?

8 Which countries of Africa does the Equator pass through?

9 Of which two elements is water composed?

10 Who rode naked through the streets of Coventry?

11 What was the original name of Drake's ship 'The Golden Hind'?

12 In which programme does Dawn French play Geraldine Grainger?

13 Which actor played a bank manager in the television series Telford's Change?

14 Sofia is the capital of which European country?

15 What is the name of the miniature breed of horse bred in Argentina?

Things you didn't know...

Divina Galica, a British lady skier, tried unsuccessfully to enter into Formula One motor racing but never qualified for a race.

Answers to page 462

1 Vistula, **2** Madrid, **3** One million, **4** Gold Coast, **5** Dennis Bergkamp, **6** Coup de Grace, **7** David Essex, **8** Pentonville Road, **9** Roger Daltrey, **10** Mrs Beeton, **11** Cochineal, **12** Pericles, **13** Limpopo, **14** El Alamein, **15** Agatha Christie.

QUIZ 459

Answers on page 459

1 Who was the first man to win the World Professional Snooker title at the Crucible Theatre in Sheffield?

2 By what name is the annual herb charlock also known?

3 Who was the female star of the film *Dr Zhivago*?

4 Under what name did boxer Muhammad Ali first win the world heavyweight championship?

5 What is the national airline of Australia?

6 Which British golfer won the 1998 Freeport McDermott Classic?

7 What are the only two kingdoms in Africa?

8 With which sport do you associate Precious McKenzie?

9 Which of the Shetland Isles is regarded as Britain's most remote island?

10 The first London post boxes were not red - what colour were they?

11 Which Briton won a Nobel Prize for in 1950?

12 Which city hosted the summer Olympics in 1956?

13 On which Greek island was the painter El Greco born?

14 Which *Top Gun* star married Nicole Kidman?

15 Which city has the largest population in the world?

Things you didn't know...

Two days before the Second World War started, the BBC stopped broadcasting midway through a Mickey Mouse cartoon.

Answers to page 459

1 Peso, 2 Troop, 3 Coypu, 4 Westminster Abbey, 5 Belgium, 6 George Eastman, 7 Gloucestershire, 8 Supergrass, 9 Enid Blyton, 10 Boris Pasternak, 11 Brasilia, 12 Bungee jumping, 13 A bird, 14 Italy, 15 Justin Leonard.

QUIZ 460

Answers on page 460

1 What is the longest river in Poland?

2 What is the highest capital in Europe?

3 How many millimetres are there in a kilometre?

4 What was the former name for Ghana?

5 Which Arsenal player was named 1997/8 Footballer of the Year by the Football Writers Association?

6 What is the French for 'Blow of Mercy'?

7 Who had a Number One hit single in 1975 with *Hold Me Close*?

8 In Monopoly, which property completes the group containing The Angel, Islington and Euston Road?

9 Which pop singer played the title role in the film *Tommy*?

10 Who wrote the 'Book of Household Management'?

11 Which red food colouring is made from the crushed bodies of insects?

12 According to A Shakespeare play, who was Prince of Tyre?

13 Which river forms the boundary between Zimbabwe and South Africa?

14 Which Egyptian village was the scene of a decisive Allied victory in 1942?

15 Who created the Belgian detective Hercule Poirot?

Things you didn't know...

Rudolph Valentino's wife, minor actress Jean Acker, left him on their wedding night.

Answers to page 460

1 Virginia Woolf, 2 Three, 3 New York City, 4 21, 5 Cranwell, 6 Attila, 7 Jack Regan and George Carter, 8 Gabon, Congo, Zaire, Uganda, Kenya and Somalia, 9 Hydrogen and Oxygen, 10 Lady Godiva, 11 *The Pelican*, 12 *Vicar Of Dibley*, 13 Peter Barkworth, 14 Bulgaria, 15 Falabella.

QUIZ 461

Answers on page 465

1 In which decade of the 19th Century did the Alamo fall to the Mexican Army?

2 The common medical condition emesis is better known as?

3 Who invented the motorcycle?

4 Who led the Israelites to the promised land after the death of Moses?

5 Which is the brightest star in the constellation Aries?

6 Who won the 1996 Melbourne Cup?

7 Which hit film featured six unemployed steelworkers who turn to stripping?

8 Which *Brookside* character was played by Ryan Jones?

9 Which Italian won the Mens Olympic marathon in 1988?

10 Which island in the Barents Sea is the title of a novel by Alistair McLean?

11 Which group had a 1973 Number One with *Rubber Bullets*?

12 In which year was footballer Bobby Moore accused of stealing a bracelet from a hotel shop?

13 Which woman was known as The Green Goddess?

14 In which book of the Old Testament would you find the story of the writing on the wall?

15 Who wrote the plays *The Glass Menagerie* and *Cat On a Hot Tin Roof*?

Things you didn't know...

Prince Albert Victor, grandson of Queen Victoria was suspected of the Jack the Ripper murders.

Answers to page 465

1 Flax, 2 Hectare, 3 Shakespears Sister, 4 Martin Bormann, 5 The Beach Boys, 6 Cruet, 7 Rome, 8 Daley Thompson, 9 The homeless, 10 *Cracker*, 11 Stephanie Cole, 12 Salvation Army, 13 Aircraft, 14 On a coin, 15 Egypt.

QUIZ 462

Answers on page 466

1 What was the name of George Harrison's only Number One hit?

2 How did Michael Fagan achieve notoriety in 1982?

3 Which science teacher was tried for teaching Darwin's theory of evolution in Tennessee in 1925?

4 Who had a Number One hit single in 1974 with *Tiger Feet*?

5 Who starred in the title role of the 1991 film *Bugsy*?

6 Who starred in the title role of the 1965 film *Cat Ballou*?

7 How often are elections to the European Parliament held?

8 Which city is the most heavily populated in Africa?

9 Who wrote the 1997 Number One song *A Perfect Day*?

10 Which British charity was founded in 1895 to preserve land and buildings of historic interest or beauty?

11 What is the stretch of mainly hexagonal basalt columns on the north coast of Antrim called?

12 Which city hosted the summer Olympics in 1964?

13 What is the most extensively-grown foodstuff in the world?

14 Which England bowler took a hat-trick of wickets against Australia in January 1999, the first bowler to do so against the Australians for over a hundred years?

15 Which British city is associated with the Roman city of Verulamium?

Things you didn't know...

The glow from six large fireflies provides enough light to read a book.

Answers to page 466

1 Thalia, 2 The Lake District, 3 Roy Castle, 4 South, 5 An arachnid, 6 Pall Mall, 7 Pear, 8 The emperor penguin, 9 Paul Newman, 10 Dodo, 11 Volkswagen Beetle, 12 Corfu, 13 Ravens, 14 Samuel, 15 Gravity.

QUIZ 463

Answers on page 463

1 From which plant is linseed oil derived?

2 Which metric unit of area is equal to 10,000 square metres?

3 Which duo had a 1992 Number One hit with *Stay*?

4 Who was Hitler's personal secretary who was sentenced to death at the Nuremberg Trails?

5 Which legendary group released the four-disc audio documentary *The Pet Sounds Sessions*?

6 What is a condiment container called?

7 What is the capital of Italy?

8 Which British decathlete won gold medals at the 1980 and 1984 Olympics?

9 For which section of society does the charity Shelter campaign?

10 Which programme won the Bafta Award for Best Drama series in 1996?

11 Who starred as elderly mother Peggy in the sitcom *Keeping Mum*?

12 What name was adopted by the Christian Mission in 1878?

13 What was Sir Geoffrey De Havilland famous for designing and manufacturing?

14 Where would you find two sides called the reverse and the obverse?

15 In which country is the Aswan High Dam?

Things you didn't know...

The eyes of the woodcock bird are set so far back in its head that it has a 360-degree field of vision.

Answers to page 463

1 1830's, 2 Vomiting, 3 Daimler, 4 Joshua, 5 Hamal, 6 Saintly, 7 *The Full Monty,* 8 Matthew Farnham, 9 Gelindo Bordin, 10 Bear Island, 11 10 CC, 12 1970, 13 Diane Moran, 14 Daniel, 15 Tennessee Williams.

QUIZ 464

Answers on page 464

1 In Greek mythology, which Muse was the patron of comedy?

2 Which Cumbrian region became a National Park in 1951?

3 Which presenter of *Record Breakers* was a stooge for Jimmy James and Jimmy Clitheroe in the 1950s?

4 What nationality is the playwright Athol Fugard?

5 What sort of creature is a harvestman?

6 In which London thoroughfare would you find The Atheneum, Army and Navy and Royal Automobile Club?

7 What type of fruit is a Concorde?

8 What is the largest seabird?

9 Which American actor appeared in the films *Hud, The Sting* and *The Color of Money*?

10 Which large flightless bird of Mauritius was extinct by the end of the 17th century?

11 What sort of car was the star of the films *The Love Bug,* and *Herbie Rides Again*?

12 Where was *My Family and Other Animals* set?

13 An unkindness is a collection of what?

14 Who anointed Saul as the first king of Israel?

15 Which fundamental force of nature controls the tides?

Things you didn't know...

The national flower of South Africa, the sugarbush, depends on forest fires for survival.

Answers to page 464

1 *My Sweet Lord,* **2** Broke into Buckingham Palace and sat on the Queen's bed, **3** John Scopes, **4** Mud, **5** Warren Beatty, **6** Jane Fonda, **7** Every 5 years, **8** Cairo, **9** Lou Reed, **10** The National Trust, **11** Giant's Causeway, **12** Tokyo, **13** Wheat, **14** Darren Gough, **15** St Albans.

QUIZ 465

Answers on page 469

1 What type of animal was Baloo in Kipling's *The Jungle Book*?

2 Which word for a violent criminal is derived from a Hindu sect who murdered travellers?

3 What surname are you most likely to have if your nickname was Chalky?

4 What percentage of the votes must a candidate poll in an election to avoid losing his or her deposit?

5 Which horse won the 1996 Cheltenham Gold Cup?

6 Which rugby team won the Five Nations title in 1996?

7 Which British athlete broke the world indoor triple jump record in 1998?

8 How many faults are incurred for a refusal in showjumping?

9 Which food should be stirred with a spurtle?

10 In which country is the city of Wagga Wagga?

11 What is the capital of Turkey?

12 In which city did Sigmund Freud die?

13 Who has fronted the Happy Mondays and Black Grape?

14 In which continent is the Kalahari Desert situated?

15 Which famous prizes for literature and journalism were established by the will of a US newspaper publisher?

Things you didn't know...

Lassie, the canine TV star, brought 152 villains to justice, rescued 73 animals, leapt through 47 windows and jumped off 13 cliffs,

---

Answers to page 469

1 Yosemite, 2 *Scarecrow and Mrs King,* 3 The Humber, 4 Marseille, 5 Woodpecker, 6 Andrew, Duke of York, 7 Traitor's Gate, 8 Pat Butcher, 9 Pink Floyd, 10 Yaks, 11 A snail, 12 Antwerp, 13 George Michael, 14 3 Degrees, 15 Fidelio.

QUIZ 466

Answers on page 470

1 On which island is the Indonesian capital Jakarta situated?

2 On which river does the town of Chatham stand?

3 Who won the 1997 World Cup Sevens rugby competition in Hong Kong?

4 Which flower was the symbol of the House of Lancaster?

5 What is the unit of currency in Ecuador?

6 What was supposed to flow in the veins of the Greek gods?

7 Hallowe'en is the eve of which Christian festival?

8 Who owns Lundy Island?

9 Which British golfer won the 1997 Volvo PGA Championship at Wentworth?

10 Which London theatre was the temporary home of the National Theatre Company from 1963 to 1976?

11 In which religion is Purim a festival?

12 Which British naval explorer was killed on Hawaii on St. Valentine's Day 1779?

13 Which cave on the island of Staffa inspired an overture by Mendelssohn?

14 Which warship was destroyed by an Exocet on 4th May 1982?

15 Which titled actress is married to actor Michael Williams?

Things you didn't know...

In Japan it is considered bad luck to pick up a comb with its teeth facing your body.

Answers to page 470

1 Baker Street, 2 An oil rig, 3 Badgers, 4 Tom Selleck, 5 David Mellor, 6 Highgate cemetary, 7 Great Train Robbery, 8 Chelsea, 9 Teeth, 10 Sir Christopher Wren, 11 Claire Danes, 12 Portsmouth, 13 Bill Grundy, 14 Cher, 15 Bonsai.

QUIZ 467

Answers on page 467

1 Which is the highest waterfall in the USA?

2 Which American series starred Kate Jackson and Bruce Boxleitner?

3 Spurn Head lies at the estuary to which river?

4 Near which French city is the HQ of the Foreign Legion?

5 Which bird has the scientific name 'Picus viridis'?

6 Who was the last member of the Royal Family to be given a Peerage in 1986?

7 Which water gate lies under St Thomas's Tower in the Tower of London?

8 What part does Pam St. Clement play in *Eastenders*?

9 Who had a UK Number One hit in 1979 with *Another Brick in the Wall*?

10 What kind of wild cattle with shaggy coats and upturned horns live in the mountains of Tibet?

11 Which small creature can have up to 25,000 teeth?

12 Where did the 1920 summer Olympics take place?

13 Who got to Number One with Elton John in 1991?

14 *When will I see you again*, was which female group's only Number One hit?

15 What is the name of the only opera that Beethoven wrote?

Things you didn't know...

According to an age-old custom, carrying a dead shrew in your pocket wards off rheumatism.

Answers to page 467

1 Bear, 2 Thug, 3 White, 4 5%, 5 Imperial Call, 6 England, 7 Ashia Hansen, 8 Three, 9 Porridge, 10 Australia, 11 Ankara, 12 London, 13 Shaun Ryder, 14 Africa, 15 Pulitzer Prizes.

QUIZ 468

Answers on page 468

1 In which thoroughfare did Sherlock Holmes live?

2 What was the Alexander Keilland?

3 Which animals were dachshunds originally bred to hunt?

4 Which actor played the title role in *Magnum P.I.*?

5 Which former politician hosts the radio phone in *Six-O-Six*?

6 Where are George Eliot and Herbert Spencer buried?

7 What happened near Cheddington in Buckinghamshire on 7th August, 1963?

8 What is Bill and Hillary Clinton's daughter called?

9 Odontophobia is the fear of what?

10 Who designed St Paul's Cathedral, London?

11 Who starred opposite Leonardo DiCaprio in *Romeo & Juliet*?

12 Which First Division club knocked Premier Division Nottingham Forest out of the 1998/99 FA Cup?

13 Who did the BBC suspend after appearing to goad the Sex Pistols into swearing on television?

14 Who had a 1998 Number One with *I Believe*?

15 What name is given to the art of dwarfing trees and shrubs?

Things you didn't know...

Wisconsin is nicknamed the Badger State because miners are believed to have made their homes underground.

Answers to page 468

1 Java, 2 River Medway, 3 Fiji, 4 Red Rose, 5 Sucre, 6 Ichor, 7 All Saints' Day, 8 National Trust, 9 Ian Woosnam, 10 Old Vic, 11 Judaism, 12 Captain James Cook, 13 Fingal's Cave, 14 HMS Sheffield, 15 Dame Judi Dench.

● TIE BREAK QUESTIONS ●

1 In Mozart's opera, how many lovers did Don Giovani have in Spain?

1,003

2 In what year was the leap day last omitted in the Gregorian calendar?

1900

3 How many bones are there in the human skull?

22

4 Great Britain has produced only one 'charity' stamp. In which year was it issued?

1975

5 When did ITV start broadcasting?

1955

6 How much was Larry Hagman said to be paid per episode of *Dallas*?

$100,000

7 How much recording tape moves past the heads of a cassette recorder each second?

1 7/8 inches

8 What is Doyle's number in The Professionals?

45

9 In which year did Sadler's Wells hold it's first Gilbert and Sullivan festival?

1984

10 What, to the nearest half million, was the population of England at the beginning of Elizabeth I reign?

4,000,000

11 How long is a newly born crocodile?

8 inches approx

12 How many years after Waterloo did Napoleon die?

6

13 How many feathers are on a standard badminton shuttlecock?

16

14 How many quires make a ream?

20

15 How much did a colour TV license cost in 1974?

£12

16 When did Radio 1 start?

1967

17 What is the average number of hairs per square inch of scalp?

1,200

18 Which year does the Union Jack date from?

1801

19 How long did Queen Victoria reign?

64 years

20 When were the last wild boars seen in England?

1683

21 How many pints of milk are needed to make 1lb of cheddar cheese?

8

22 In which year were family allowances introduced?

1945

23 In 1971, how many inhabitants did the Pitcairn Islands have?

92

24 When was the Court of Criminal Appeal set up?

1907

25 How many runners are there in an Olympic biathlon relay team?

4

26 How many teams played in the Minor Counties cricket championship?

21

27 What is the Farenheit equivalent of gas mark 7?

425 F

28 The average European uses how much domestic water a day?

40 gallons

29 How many feet high is a tennis court net in the centre?

3 feet

30 In men's fencing competitions, how many hits are needed to win?

5

31 A horse is measured in hands. How many hands is a pony at most?

14.2

32 How many lines are there in a Spenserian stanza?

9

33 How many incisors should a human adult have?

8

34 What percentage of French wines are labelled Appellation Controlee?

15%

35 When did the last British troops leave Suez?

1956

36 How many times was Bobby Charlton capped by England?

106

37 How many hours ahead of GMT is Moscow?

3

38 How many records are castaways allowed on *Desert Island Discs*?

8

39 When did Charles Dickens die?

1870

40 How many numbers are on a British roulette wheel?

37

41 In which year did the Jack the Ripper murders occur?

1888

42 In which year did the Thames dry up for 9 miles from it's source?

1976

43 For how long has the cockroach, in it's modern form, existed on earth?

250,000,000 years

44 For how long was Mary Queen of Scots a prisoner in England?

19 years

45 How many Spanish Steps are there in Rome?

138

46 How many dots are there on a standard set of dominoes?

168

47 How many legal opening chess moves for white are there?

20

48 For how long can a bed-bug exist without eating?

1 year

49 What is the area of the Isle of Wight in square miles?

147

50 How deep was the first oil well?

70 feet

51 When were the first Winter Olympics held?

1924

52 When was the last Frost Fair held on the frozen Thames?

1914

53 How long do duck eggs take to hatch?

27 days

54 For how long did the longest-serving parliament of the 20th century sit?

9 years, 6 months

55 When was the first version of *Gentlemen Prefer Blondes* filmed?

1928

56 In which year were all 3 Apollo 11 astronauts born?

1930

• TIE BREAK QUESTIONS •

57 How many orbits did John Glen complete in his 1st space flight?

3

58 What are the two Olympic ski-jumping distances?

70 and 90 metres

59 When did Jim Morrison of The Doors die?

1971

60 How old was the Queen when she married?

21

61 In tennis, how far are the service lines from the net?

21 feet

62 How many Shillings did Sherlock Holmes' Stradivariud violin cost him?

55

63 How high is a soccer goal?

8 feet

64 How many semitones are there in an octave?

12

65 What percentage of an egg's weight is its shell?

12%

66 How many people were convicted for the murder of Aldo Moro?

63

67 How many teeth does a mature male horse have?

40

68 At what age does a Jewish boy celebrate his Bar Mitzvah?

13

69 What is the area telephone code for New York City?

212

70 At what age does a filly become a mare?

5

71 How many crocus stamens are needed to make 1 ounce of saffron dye?

4,500

72 How many dots are on a regular 6-sided die?

21

73 How many points wins a game of cribbage?

121

74 How many brain cells does an average 30 year old lose per day?

100,000

75 How many people attended the Last Supper?

13

76 In which year was Shakespeare was born?

1564

77 How many fences in the Grand National are jumped twice?

14

78 How many times per second does a housefly beat its wings?

190

79 In showjumping, how many faults are incurred if the rider falls off?

8

80 How long did King Edward VIII's abdication broadcast last?

1 minute

81 How many prisoners were held in the Black hole of Calcutta?

146

82 How many people died as a direct result of the Great Fire of London?

6

83 Which is the longest psalm in the Bible?

119

85 How many letters are there in the Greek alphabet?

24